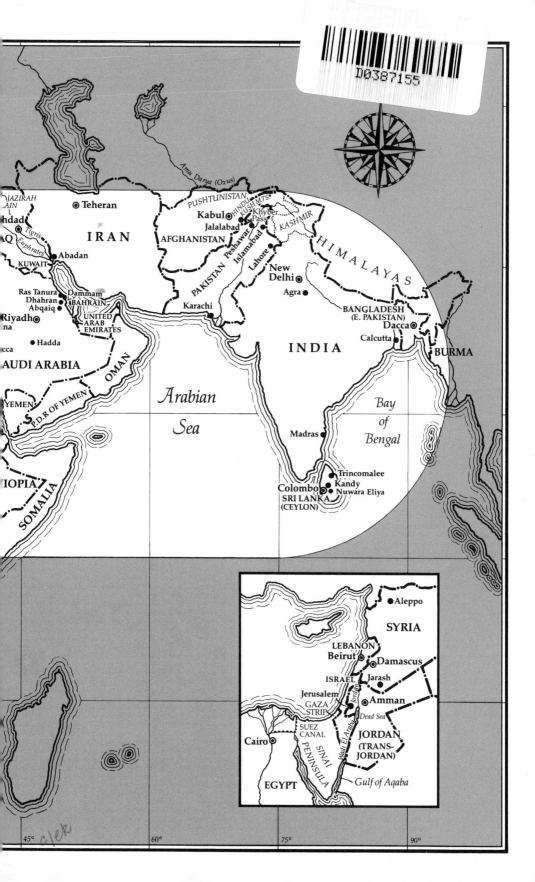

ENVOY TO THE MIDDLE WORLD

Envoy to the Middle World

ADVENTURES IN DIPLOMACY

Ambassador George McGhee

Foreword by Dean Rusk

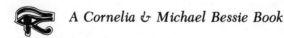 *A Cornelia & Michael Bessie Book*

HARPER & ROW, PUBLISHERS, New York
Cambridge, Philadelphia, San Francisco, London
Mexico City, São Paulo, Sydney

To Cecilia, full partner in these diplomatic ventures,
for her constant support and great spirit

Grateful acknowledgment is made for permission to reprint:

Excerpts from *Present at the Creation: My Years in the State Department* by Dean Acheson.
Copyright © 1969 by Dean Acheson. By permission of W. W. Norton & Company, Inc. and
Hamish Hamilton, Ltd.

FIRST EDITION
Designer: Sidney Feinberg

Library of Congress Cataloging in Publication Data

McGhee, George Crews, 1912–
    Envoy to the Middle World.

    "A Cornelia & Michael Bessie book."
    Includes index.
    1. McGhee, George Crews, 1912–   .   2. United States
—Foreign relations—1945–1953.   3. United States—
Foreign relations—Underdeveloped areas.   4. Under-
developed areas—Foreign relations—United States.
5. Diplomats—United States—Biography.   I. Title.
E748.M47A34   1983   327.73   82–49007
ISBN 0-06-039025-5

83 84 85 86 87 10 9 8 7 6 5 4 3 2 1

Contents

Acknowledgments

I have received valuable assistance in the writing of this volume, for which I am grateful. There was much more material available in the archives and publications of the Department of State on the period under review than could be utilized, and this posed the problem of selection. There was also the question of the focus of the book, what points it would make. For the initial formulation of the concept of the book and the selection and organization of material, I am particularly indebted to Ambassador Martin F. Herz of the Institute for the Study of Diplomacy, Georgetown University, and to Betty Sarah Wouk.

Valuable initial overall advice leading to improvement of the manuscript was received from Ambassador Martin J. Hillenbrand, then Director General of the Atlantic Institute; Dr. George R. Packard, Dean of the School of Advanced International Studies, The Johns Hopkins University; Dr. Peter F. Krogh, Dean, School of Foreign Service, Georgetown University; and Colonel William Evans-Smith, Director, Foreign Area Studies, The American University.

Fleming Fraker provided thorough basic research of the Department of State archives for material for the book. Excellent research and editorial assistance was contributed at a later stage by Robert Rinehart and Alison Raphael of Foreign Area Studies, The American University. Sallie Coolidge was most helpful in providing overall editing of the final manuscript, with suggestions for excision and addition of material. Kristin Pfoutz provided a thorough final editing.

Many members of the Historical Office, Bureau of Public Affairs, Department of State, provided valuable assistance in obtaining access to material and in providing an overall evaluation of my manuscript.

I am particularly indebted to Dr. David Trask, Dr. Paul Claussen, Dr. Nina J. Noring, and Dr. Stanley Shaloff. Members of the Classification Center, Bureau of Administration, and Jessie Williams in Foreign Affairs Information Management, Department of State, were most generous in helping me obtain access to particular materials.

Several of my former colleagues during the period under review were kind enough to read portions of the manuscript and offer helpful comments: Ambassador Loy W. Henderson on the chapters on India and Ambassadors Raymond A. Hare, Parker T. Hart, and J. Rives Childs on the chapter on Saudi Arabia. Harold D. Nelson and Richard F. Nyrop of Foreign Area Studies, The American University, gave helpful criticism on the summary in the final chapter, as did A. W. Clausen, president of the World Bank, and his colleagues.

I am deeply indebted to my wife, Cecilia, for her indispensable contributions covering people, conversations, impressions, and happenings on those occasions described in the book when she accompanied me. Much of the personal side of our visits would otherwise have been lost.

Dr. Athelstan Spilhaus, distinguished oceanographer and cartographer, kindly made the necessary calculations for a map of the Middle World based on its approximate geographical center, which is by chance the city of Mecca in Saudi Arabia.

Dr. Daniel J. Boorstin, Librarian of Congress, gave useful advice as to conclusions the volume might make. Ambassador Bernard Burrows, a high official of the British Foreign Service during the period under review, with whom I had a most pleasant association, was kind enough to read my manuscript and make helpful comments from a British viewpoint.

I am particularly indebted to former Secretary of State Dean Rusk, for being willing to write the Preface for the book.

To Peggy Smedley, Rhonda Rose, and Joyce Griffith of Middleburg, Virginia, who were most helpful in typing and correcting the manuscript, I also want to express sincere thanks. To my valued assistant Odette Goodsite I wish to express appreciation for excellent editorial assistance.

I accept full responsibility, of course, for all opinions expressed in the book.

GEORGE C. McGHEE

Foreword

During World War II and the years immediately following that great struggle, the United States was forced to find and to give heavy responsibilities to a large number of young people. One of the ablest of these was George McGhee, a young oil geologist out of Texas whose scientific education had been broadened and deepened at Oxford University. Although not a member of the career Foreign Service, his long and distinguished career in the conduct of our foreign relations earned him the accolade of a true professional in diplomacy. He has now given us this account of his rich experience in what he has called the Middle World—that vast area reaching from the Strait of Gibraltar to the Bay of Bengal and from the Caspian Sea to the Cape of Good Hope.

Most Americans have long since forgotten the national surge, immediately after V-J Day, to put the war behind us and to "return to normalcy"—to borrow the phrase so prevalent after World War I. Lend Lease was suddenly cancelled; it was taken for granted that the new United Nations would somehow deal with world affairs; we were preoccupied in shifting our powerful economy from war to peace and in absorbing into civilian pursuits the millions of servicemen returning home. We demobilized almost completely and almost overnight; by the summer of 1946 we did not have a single division nor a single group in our Air Force which could be called ready for combat; the ships of our Navy were being put into mothballs as rapidly as possible and those that remained afloat were being manned by skeleton crews; our defense budget for three fiscal years came down to a little over $11 billion.

It took the West a few years to discover that its sweeping demobilization had apparently subjected Joseph Stalin to intolerable temptations. Instead of a period of repose which might have produced a disarmed and isolationist America, Stalin's actions and attitudes alerted the West to the reality of dangers which the war itself had not put to rest. Stalin tried to keep Azerbaijan, the first case before the U.N. Security Council; he rejected the invitation to participate in the Marshall Plan and declined to negotiate seriously on the Baruch Plan to eliminate all nuclear weapons. He demanded two eastern provinces of Turkey, supported the guerrillas in Greece, had a hand in the communist coup d'etat in Czechoslovakia, blockaded Berlin and supported the assault of the North Koreans against South Korea. The Cold War was on.

When the British informed Washington in February 1947 that they could no longer play a significant role in Greece, it became necessary for the United States to decide whether it should shake off its post-war lethargy and assume responsibilities which it had hoped to avoid. In making his decision to provide substantial aid to Greece and Turkey, President Truman knew that a great deal of persuasion would be necessary to get the support of the Congress and of the American people. What came to be known as the Truman Doctrine derived from this persuasive effort; although the language seemed to point to world-wide commitments, its purpose at the time was to win support for aid to Greece and Turkey.

George McGhee was called upon to coordinate this aid to Greece and Turkey. He brought to his task an ebullience of spirit, an understanding of the legislative process, and a down-to-earth sense of management. It was his first sub-cabinet responsibility and his demonstrated abilities led him on to the tortured problems of the Palestine refugees, appointment as Assistant Secretary of State for the Near East, South Asia, and Africa, and Ambassador to Turkey during the Truman years.

It is worth noting that during the period when George McGhee carried official responsibility for our relations with the "Middle World," President Truman and Secretary Dean Acheson were heavily preoccupied with other pressing matters—the Marshall Plan, the construction of NATO, Stalin's blockade of Berlin, the occupation of Japan, the attack on South Korea. One result was that George McGhee had substantial delegated authority and ample room for initiative, imagination, and the exercise of personal responsibility. The vast area that was his concern was and is of crucial importance to the course of world events, to relations among the so-called Great Powers, and to the prospects for a stable peace. It was and is an area in which we have discovered some of the limits of power and have come to understand that a share of disappointment and frustration is inescapable in a world which does not take orders from Washington or Moscow. George McGhee's reflections on this experience deserve careful study by the historian and will be of lively interest to the general reader. He records events as he lived through them and combines facts with his own assessments of Middle World leaders, problems, and policies. Some of the leaders he vividly portrays are no longer here but the problems and policies he shows from the inside are still very much with us, and will be for some time to come. In the final chapter of this book, George McGhee reflects upon the present scene and the tasks which lie ahead.

There is much wisdom here, rooted in a service and an experience that leave us all in his debt for a book which adds much to our understanding of that mysterious, troubled, very important Middle World.

—DEAN RUSK

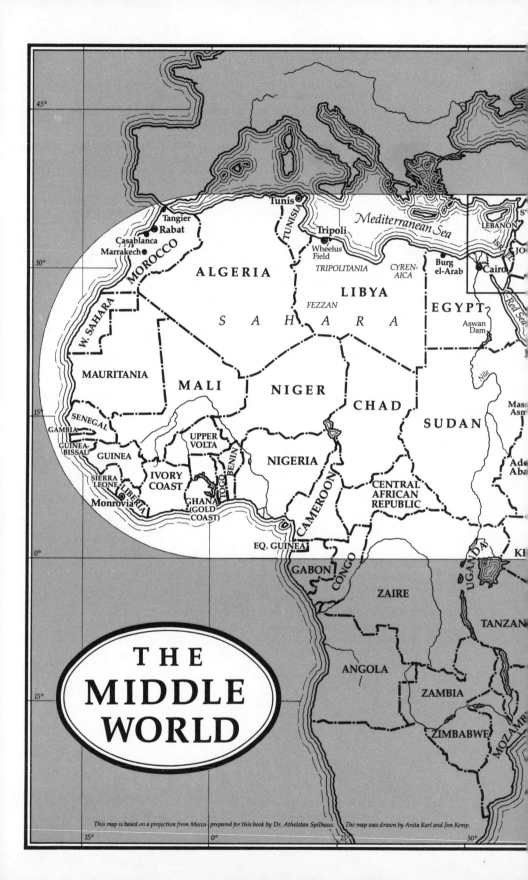

THE
MIDDLE
WORLD

This map is based on a projection from Mecca prepared for this book by Dr. Athelstan Spilhaus. The map was drawn by Anita Karl and Jim Kemp.

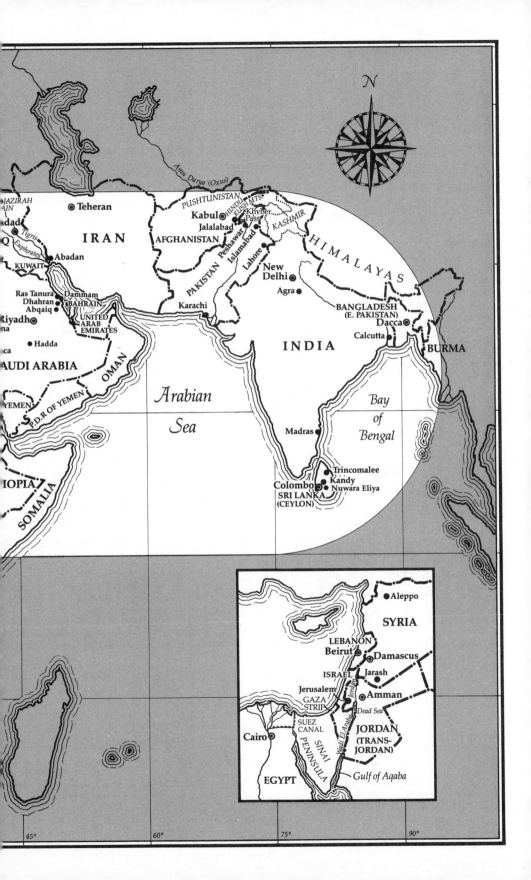

Introduction

This volume covers the period 1949 through 1951, with a review bringing it up to date in 1983. It concerns a vast area stretching from Morocco through India comprising most of the states which emerged from colonialism into independence after the Second World War. I should perhaps, at the outset, explain how I happened to be the Assistant Secretary of State for the area which I choose to call the Middle World, and describe my background and attitude toward my task.

I was born in Waco, Texas, of Old-South English stock and was raised in Dallas, where my father had settled as a banker. As a boy, I combed the fields for fossils and rocks, which have always intrigued me, and which led to my early selection of geology as a profession. Later, my interests also encompassed the science of geophysics and were directed, as would be natural for a Texan, toward prospecting for oil. After receiving my undergraduate degree at Oklahoma University in geology and physics, I won a Rhodes scholarship and took my doctor of philosophy degree in the physical sciences at Oxford University. The three years I spent in Oxford and England had a profound influence on my later life, and would lead me far afield from my original profession.

Oxford offered valuable friendship with other Rhodes scholars studying a variety of subjects, as well as with many English and Commonwealth students. My interests gradually expanded to include history, social sciences, politics, and the arts—subjects I had paid little attention to in undergraduate years. Oxford, which had trained countless Englishmen for Parliament and government service, gave me a new sense of values. I decided that I would stick to geology for the time being, but as soon as fortune permitted I would transfer my activities to some form of public life, perhaps politics. I also acquired a very high regard for the British as a people, and Britain as a world power.

After graduation from Oxford, I joined a group who were forming a company to make seismic surveys for oil companies. Later I became an independent producer or "wildcatter." An early success in discovering an oilfield, and the war, provided me in 1941 the opportunity I had hoped for. I joined the War Production Board before Pearl Harbor, and later entered the British-American Combined Raw Materials Board which had been set up to allocate scarce materials among the allies.

I subsequently served three years as a naval lieutenant, including duty for the last year of the war as naval liaison officer for Major General Curtis LeMay, commander of the 21st Bomber Command—the B-29's—in the air war against Japan from the Marianas Islands. And, upon my release from the Navy after the surrender of Japan, I applied for entry into the State Department as special assistant to a distinguished fellow Texan, William S. Clayton, who had left his well-known cotton firm to become Assistant Secretary (later Under Secretary) of State for Economic Affairs. As far as status in the Department was concerned, I started at the bottom, but I was very happy to be able to begin a career in foreign affairs.

Both what I learned from working with Clayton, a man I greatly admired, and chance, led to my appointment as Washington coordinator for Public Law 75, the Greek-Turkish Assistance Act of 1948. Under Clayton, I had served as chairman of the interdepartmental committee which set this program in motion. Its goal was to carry out the Truman Doctrine, to save Greece and Turkey from Communist takeover. The Greek army, with our help, was successful in defeating the leftist Greek guerrillas, with an assist from Tito's break with the Soviet Union. Turkey was strengthened. My own role in directing the program made me a likely candidate for the new position of Assistant Secretary for Near East, South Asian and African Affairs (NEA), following President Harry Truman's surprise reelection in 1948.

My outlook in this new position was strongly influenced by both my war and postwar experiences. American leadership, manpower, and resources had been crucial to Allied victory over the Axis powers. Our aid to Greece and Turkey had shown how desperately our support was needed and how effective we could be. I had developed confidence in our country's ability to help other nations recover from the ravages of war, overcome their inherited problems and protect themselves from what we perceived to be the threat of aggressive Soviet Communism. This cause seemed to be a good one, and working for it gave me a strong sense of personal satisfaction, as a form of public service I had learned to value at Oxford. As a young man of thirty-seven, I also wanted to learn more about the world, and to make my mark. My approach was idealistic and, undoubtedly, somewhat naïve. All of this was running through my mind when, on a June day in 1949, with my burgeoning family present, I was sworn in as Assistant Secretary of State by Secretary Dean Acheson.

My government service during this period was made much more challenging by Secretary Acheson and Under Secretary James E. Webb, two men I admired greatly. Both stimulated me and gave me freedom to carry out my task. Dean Acheson possessed, in my judgment, one of the most brilliant minds that has been applied to American foreign policy. He became Secretary in 1949 at a time when we desperately needed to recreate the Western alliance and develop an overall strategy for overcoming the ravages of war and standing up to the Soviets. Acheson provided the leadership through this period which resulted in the enormous success of the Marshall Plan and NATO. Under Secretary Webb was Acheson's loyal and effective deputy and administrator. He instilled confidence in the Department on the part of Congress. We were all lucky to serve under Harry Truman, a great President.

My twenty years in the State Department gave me a great respect for our Foreign Service, particularly those stationed in our diplomatic outposts. Duty in the far reaches of the Middle World inspires, I believe, a more dedicated approach from that in the more comfortable capitals. There were in our area no "political" appointees in the sense usually employed, except in the case of our Ambassador to Israel. Because of his close association with the Zionist movement, James G. McDonald was considered by the career officers an outsider, to be treated with reserve. The remaining officers were in general rugged individualists who came from all sections of the country. Few were Ivy League. They were as a group honest in their views and reporting. They called the shots as they saw them—without fear of reprisal, even when dealing with the highly sensitive Arab-Israeli issue.

The NEA Bureau as a whole, moreover, was characterized by a group loyalty and esprit de corps that was unique in the Department. It felt in a sense cut off from the rest of the Department, as the

Middle World seemed cut off from the rest of the world. NEA officers realized that the peoples of their area were not so sophisticated as those of the Western world, that they were survivors of a different era. Members of the bureau felt themselves the protector of defenseless peoples, and this attitude included defending them from those colonial powers who appeared to be unnecessarily delaying their departure. This brought occasional conflicts with the European Affairs bureau. Officers dealing with French affairs who had served in the Embassy in Paris often could not understand why we stood up for people who did not seem capable of governing themselves. In the end, of course, decisions were reached on the basis of the U.S. interest, but there was often a little tension.

As deputies I was privileged to have Raymond A. Hare and later Burton Y. Berry, who had served previously as director of the office of African and Near Eastern Affairs. Able, loyal, both went on to important ambassadorships. Berry was succeeded in his Near Eastern responsibilities by the astute and effective G. Lewis Jones, Jr., director of the new office of Near Eastern Affairs. As director of the office of Greek, Turkish and Iranian Affairs, William M. Rountree, later to be Assistant Secretary and Ambassador, was a tower of strength. Elmer H. Bourgerie served with distinction as director of the office of African Affairs after its creation in 1950. Elbert G. Matthews, director of the Office of South Asian Affairs, dealt skillfully with the difficult problems of Kashmir and Indian neutralism.

NEA had outstanding career ambassadors in Loy W. Henderson, Joseph C. Satterthwaite, Henry F. Grady, Parker T. Hart, John C. Wiley, Jefferson Caffery, J. Rives Childs and many others. I wish to pay tribute to other devoted and untiring officers: Arthur Z. Gardiner, who served as my special assistant, Stephen P. Dorsey, Economic Adviser; William J. Handley, Labor Adviser; Mary E. Hope, Public Relations Adviser; Harry N. Howard, U.N. Adviser; and John B. Howard, Legal and Planning Adviser. Although I was not technically a career officer, I believe that I was, over my twenty years of service, accepted as being the equivalent of one. But my later roles in the State Department are different stories.

Modern Italy, Greece, Turkey, and Israel, although once the seats of Middle World empires, are not included in this narrative. Although Greece, Israel, and Turkey were part of my Departmental responsibilities and I visited them often, I feel that they require separate treatment. Greece is an integral part of the West; indeed, it is a prime source of Western civilization. It has been independent for over a century and is a member of NATO and the Common Market. Turkey, although of Asiatic origins, has been a member of the European state-system since the Treaty of Karlowitz in 1699, is a member of NATO, and has over several centuries developed strong ties with Europe and the United States. Present-day Israel is a modern state founded in 1948 mainly by Jewish people of European origin. It lives in but is not really a part of the Middle World.

This account undoubtedly appears to magnify my own role. I have, of course, concentrated on those events in which I played a direct part and of which I can give a first-hand account. We had in the countries concerned able ambassadors who were in daily contact with the governments. The President, the Secretary of State, and other high Washington officials were often involved in the affairs of the Middle World. In retrospect I am amazed at our confidence, at the time, in our country's ability to help these people solve their enormous problems. Our role in defeating Germany and Japan, and in saving Greece and Turkey from Soviet takeover, undoubtedly gave us an exaggerated view of our capacity to help other peoples with quite different backgrounds.

My narrative is chronological and includes official visits to Middle World countries, consultations in London and Paris, Washington policy formulation, and regional conferences of U.S. officials abroad over which I presided. These different episodes are not in all cases linked and often wide gaps are left, particularly in the daily pulling and hauling that goes on in the vast Department bureaucracy in the formulation and implementation of policy. Together, however, I hope these accounts will provide some insight into the Middle World of that day and how U.S. policies toward this area evolved. In the final chapter I attempt an evaluation of how well we succeeded and where we failed.

Much of the material included in this volume is in the published *Foreign Relations of the United States*, Chapter VI, for 1949, and Chapter V for 1950 and 1951. I have drawn heavily on my own published material in these volumes: memoranda of conversations, interdepartmental memoranda, telegrams, miscellaneous letters and reports of regional meetings held overseas, some drafted by myself and some by others who are credited in *Foreign Relations*. Material available has in general been paraphrased in reinforcing my own memory.

Of particular value has been the opportunity to study and publish certain documents from the British Foreign Office, which have been released through 1951 and are available to researchers in the very efficient British Public Records Office in Kew, London. What an opportunity it is to be able to read an independent interpretation of events in which you participated, and to have access to the candid views of skilled officers of another service, many old friends, including their evaluation of yourself. I have tried to be even-handed in reporting both the favorable and adverse aspects of what they said. As can be seen I appear on occasion to have given them trouble, for which I hope they have after so many years forgiven me. For my part, I have no grievances to forgive them.

1

The Middle World, 1949

The Middle World is not a term in general usage. It is my hope to make it so. I use it in this book because I believe it provides a helpful basis for thinking about an important area of the world whose many countries, while differing greatly, have much in common. The concept of the Middle World includes lands stretching on a west-east axis from Morocco and the Pillars of Hercules, at the western end of the Mediterranean, to the Indian subcontinent and the Bay of Bengal on the east. To the north, the Middle World is bounded by the lands of the Europeans, the Slavs, the Central Asian nomadic peoples, and the Chinese. To the south, it extends through the waist of Africa and to the Indian Ocean. To the east, it is bounded by almost impenetrable mountains, although the Middle World peoples have throughout history had continuous contacts with Southeast Asia.

Although such a grouping of peoples and states is relatively arbitrary, the concept of the Middle World not only provides a useful focus for these memoirs, but has a compelling basis in history, anthropology, geography, the arts, and literature. Geographically, the area encompassed by the Middle World is characterized by major mountain ranges, great rivers, vast deserts, fertile valleys, and proximity to navigable waters. Most of it lies between north latitudes 20 and 40 degrees and has a temperate climate. It does not, except in Central Africa, possess great mineral wealth but has more of the planet's oil than any other area.

The peoples of the Middle World, moreover, have certain attributes which distinguish them from those in other regions. Although of many ethnic origins, they all come from old and deeply rooted races. Many have within their homelands strong nomadic tendencies. They are deeply religious; all of the five leading world religions—

Christianity, Judaism, Hinduism, Buddhism, and Islam—originated in the Middle World. Today the area is predominately Muslim. The peoples of the Middle World also have great artistic talents, which have been given coherence by and have in turn contributed to their religions. Islam provides an example in the harmony of the many arts that were involved in the building of the great mosques.

Although the Middle World contains neither the geographical nor population center of the world, much of world history has taken place there. Starting in the fifth millennium B.C., it was the cradle of the earliest civilizations, the seat of the first empires, and the center of conflicts. The lands lying to the north in Europe and Asia were for the most part seemingly too cold, too forested, or too drab to bring out the best of the creative instinct in early man. Inhabitants of these regions faced too great a struggle merely to survive. The flowering of Chinese civilization came later, in the second millennium B.C., and the great civilizations of the Western Europeans did not blossom until the second millennium A.D.

For centuries access to and within the Middle World was provided mainly by sailing vessels, through the Mediterranean in the west and the Red Sea and Indian Ocean in the east. The great Sahara desert—whose name means "sea of sand"—constituted a barrier to the south, but provided a link by caravan to ancient African kingdoms, which are considered a part of the Middle World. Starting in the seventh century A.D., empires were established in the broad savannah belt below the desert in what is now the Sudan. Later there emerged the Yoruba forest states farther south. During the pre-colonial era these empires were linked with the rest of the Middle World by a network of trade routes that led from the "inland ports" of Marrakech in Morocco and Ghadames in Libya.

The changing balance in the Middle World between the peoples of the settled areas and the nomads brought invasions and retaliations. In the absence of modern defensive weaponry, the advantage usually lay with the aggressor. Religion was less a restraint to war than a weapon of conquest. Power based on force was the order of the day. The individual existed to do the ruler's bidding.

Civilization as we know it began in the watered areas in the heart of the Middle World, in the basins of the Tigris and Euphrates rivers and the Nile. Recorded history started here some five thousand years ago. The Middle World saw the beginnings of literature, the arts, science, and the law. The record which began with the discovery of writing in the third millennium B.C., chronicles a series of conquering races, the Sumerians, Babylonians, Assyrians, and Persians, who created empires spreading east and west from their Mesopotamian heartland. The Phoenicians of the Levant coast established colonies all around the Mediterranean and extended their seaborne commercial ventures to Britain, West Africa, and India. Carthage, the most important Phoenician outpost, created a hegemony over the Western Mediterranean that was later to be contested by the Greeks and Romans. In the second millennium B.C. the Minoan civilization flourished in Crete.

Greece was a center of city-states with a distinctive political life by the eighth century B.C. By colonizing the eastern Mediterranean and extending its Hellenic culture, Greece made an enormous contribution to the emerging civilization of the Middle World. The Persians later had their day, controlling the Fertile Crescent and all of Asia Minor, until Xerxes' fleet faltered in 479 B.C. at Salamis after nearly conquering Greece. In return, Alexander of Macedon invaded Asia Minor in 334 B.C. and went on to conquer the available eastern world, as far as the Indus River and the mountains of South Central Asia, subduing Egypt and Persia on the way. The three great empires created by Alexander's chieftains after his death, in Syria, Greece, and Egypt, were to dominate the Middle World for centuries, diffusing Hellenic culture.

Later the Romans, who had started on the road to conquest from central Italy in the sixth century B.C., had by the end of the first century B.C. extended their rule over the Middle World from the Atlantic to the gates of Persia. Carthage was destroyed by Rome in 146 B.C., Jerusalem was taken in A.D. 70. The Romans gave the West a valuable synthesis of Greek and oriental values derived from the Middle World. In A.D. 330, the Roman emperor Constantine—beset by new hordes emerging from barbarism in northern Europe and Central Asia, and by a revived Persian empire to the east—transferred his seat of power from Milan to the ancient Greek city of Byzantium, renamed Constantinople. Here, protected by almost impregnable walls and by the Golden Horn, an inlet of the Bosphorus, the Byzantine Empire also controlled the wealth and manpower of Asia Minor, which put it in a better position to survive.

The Byzantine Empire ruled from the very heart of the Middle World for over eleven hundred years, its power declining after the seventh century and finally coming to an end with the conquest of Constantinople by the Turks in A.D. 1453. The Byzantine Empire, which was a Christian continuation of the Roman Empire in the

Greek-speaking East, with its emphasis on religious doctrine and law and philosophy, had a deep influence on the character of the Middle World. The Empire also made its own artistic contribution to the Middle World, an important example being Hagia Sophia church built in Constantinople in the sixth century A.D.

Meanwhile the Arabs, aroused by their zeal for their new and powerful religion, burst out of their desert heartland in the Arabian peninsula in the seventh century, conquering the Middle World and converting its peoples to Islam from Spain to the Punjab in India. Islamic science, law, and culture made an important contribution to Middle World civilizations. Islam remains today one of the most powerful influences in the Middle World as a religion, a basis for government, a way of life, and the inspiration for literature and the arts.

The Turks, from their homeland in Turkestan in the heart of Central Asia, came into the Middle World relatively late in history. The Seljuq Turks forced their entry into Asia Minor in 1071 by defeating the Byzantine Emperor at Mansikert in present eastern Turkey. The Ottoman Turks, starting in the thirteenth century from the seat they had established around Bursa (the ancient Prusa) in northwest Anatolia, became over several centuries the rulers of most of the Middle World, conquering what remained of the Byzantine Empire and the older Arab kingdoms. At its height in the sixteenth century, the Ottoman Empire stretched from Morocco in the west to Persia in the east, from the Danube in the north to the Sahara desert in the south, and completely surrounded the Black Sea. Although in establishing their empire the Ottomans took advantage of the weakness of their Muslim brothers, they provided the Muslim world political unity and, through the Caliphate of the Sultans, a focal point for their religion.

The Turks were stern rulers, but they held together in their empire peoples normally at war with each other, resulting in long periods of peace and progress. The Turks in general respected the rights of the minorities they conquered and preserved and disseminated the indigenous cultures of their empire, particularly that of Persia. By the time of the final collapse of the Ottoman Empire at the end of the First World War, the Turks, who created the last of the great Middle World empires, had made an indelible impact.

There were other centers of civilization in the Middle World. Ethiopia was an isolated Coptic Christian empire in the south dating back to A.D. 300. After the seventh century A.D., Morocco was a focal point for Islam in the west. India had formerly been an independent empire, but starting in A.D. 1000 it became the pawn of the more vigorous Muslim Mongols and Turks from the north and Persians from the west. Afghanistan was often the seat of powerful Islamic rulers following its creation as a state in the eighteenth century.

And finally, beginning with the Portuguese conquests in Africa and India in the late fifteenth century, the ultimate subjugation of the Middle World came in the form of modern European colonialism. In the nineteenth century, the Europeans, particularly the British, made colonies of most of the Middle World. With the help of modern firearms and sophisticated administration, the Europeans retained their control until the Second World War. It is not to be assumed, of course, that the colonial powers were motivated in their conquests only by selfish motives. Both Britain and France saw in their roles a great civilizing mission. Britain, in particular, attempted to plant in its colonies the seeds of parliamentary democracy and fair administration. The fact that India is today a practicing democracy attests to the sincerity of the British intent.

The European conquest of the Middle World and the beginnings of its decline took place before the Americans had established much of a presence there. Prior to the Second World War, only our most venturesome scholars, missionaries, and traders had penetrated the curtain created by the Middle World's European rulers. When the Europeans were finally forced to withdraw, a power vacuum was created. To those of us in the U.S. government responsible for this area at that time, there appeared to be a clear threat that the Soviet Union, which had been probing for weaknesses in Western Europe, China, Greece, Turkey, and Iran, would also attempt to penetrate the weak new states of the Middle World. I will, in the chapters that follow, attempt to explain from my own experiences how we tried to help fill the vacuum there and assist these states to withstand the Soviet threat.

By the end of the Second World War, the strains of that protracted conflict, plus widespread condemnation of colonialism as an institution, had made it inevitable that the Middle World states would proceed toward independence. The U.S. exerted a very considerable influence to that end. Pressure did not result so much through government action—although the role of President Roosevelt is well known—as from our history and public attitudes. Our own successful revolution spoke more loudly than our words.

The period of colonial withdrawal following World War II constitutes a fascinating epoch in world history. It was carried out by the colonial powers with varying degrees of reluctance—and mixed success. Progress by the newly emerging nations of the region in establishing stable regimes was spotty. Starting in 1947, the U.S. found itself in direct contact for the first time with the leaders of scores of new nations. And the fact that our ambassadors and other officials were entering these new countries just as the colonial powers were retiring, created tensions. There was suspicion that we were accelerating the turnover unduly and for our own benefit. There were accusations that we were attempting to influence peoples we ourselves did not fully understand. In many cases this was undoubtedly true.

Americans were, of course, already involved in the Middle World. We raised money to help the starving. Our ships called at Middle World ports. We traded with Middle World merchants. We had fought the Barbary pirates. These encounters did not, however, provide relationships of great depth. Indeed, the American public tended to have greater interest in the ancient empires of Alexander and the pharaohs than in the modern states of the same region. Much of what we had learned of the Middle World had been interpreted by the colonial powers in a self-serving way. Despite our Judaeo-Christian roots, our thinking was distorted by religious prejudices and by our ignorance of the great cultures of the area.

Having never been an important colonial power, America was suspect in this regard only because of our European associations. While our economy had been strengthened by the Second World War, the economies of most of the rest of the world had been devastated. As a result, after the departure of the Europeans, we were the only country capable of providing aid to the new nations that emerged. Only we had the needed capital and production goods. The Middle World was desperately in need of help, and America responded. Flushed with the confidence of having led the coalition that defeated Germany and Japan, Americans were willing to make the additional effort which we thought was required to save the new countries of the Middle World from Communism.

In general I believe the people of the Middle World received us gladly despite what they considered to be our obsessive preoccupation with Communism, ranking the threat we perceived from the Soviet Union above their own needs. As a result we were, within a very few years, drawn irresistibly into the affairs of these unfamiliar regions. The departing colonial powers, disappointed at having to give up property and advantage, often resented what even they knew to be inevitable. In general, however, I believe they also accepted our entry with good grace, particularly the British who needed us. We were alternately encouraged by success in our efforts to assist the new states and dismayed by rebuffs.

It fell to my lot to be the first American Assistant Secretary of State for the broad area I have elected to call the Middle World. It included all of Africa except the Union of South Africa; the Middle East, including Greece and Turkey; and South Asia through Burma, including Afghanistan. The area comprised then around 600 million people in some 90 different political entities, most at the time still colonies or dependencies of the European powers. Although an assistant secretary of state was not at the time, nor today, an official of great importance in our governmental hierarchy, my powers exceeded considerably those of my predecessors. My area of jurisdiction was also disproportionately large in comparison with that of other bureaus.

I felt quite humble in undertaking my new duties in 1949. I had had first-hand experience in Greece and Turkey, where I had been involved as coordinator of the Greek-Turkish Aid Program, and in Morocco, where I had worked as a geologist for a French firm. I had also had an introduction to the Arab refugee problem. Despite this preparation, however, my assignment seemed an awesome one. I was solaced by the undeniable fact that no one could be an expert in all of such a vast area, at best only in parts of it.

The Middle World countries that had been colonies had previously made little direct impact on America or the world scene. Their external relations had been handled largely in London and Paris and Lisbon. Indeed, it would have been inappropriate at that time for us to seek direct political contacts with these countries or for high American officials to visit there. Moreover, our President, Secretary of State, and other cabinet officials were preoccupied with critical postwar domestic problems, the recovery of Europe, and the containment of Communism. No one had time for these strange new countries, which had been the outposts of other empires.

As a consequence, I was to be the first official from Washington of my rank or higher to visit most of the countries. A Middle World setting had occasionally been used for wartime meetings, such as Roosevelt's Casablanca Conference with Churchill in 1942, at which he met on the side with Mohammed V of Morocco. Roosevelt had met with King Ibn Saud onboard a destroyer in 1945. Prime Minister

Nehru of India and the Shah of Iran paid their first official visits to the U.S. in 1949 shortly after I assumed office. Although they were received by the President and Secretary of State, I was responsible for the arrangements for their visits and can provide an account of what happened. In the case of most Middle World leaders I visited who had not yet come to our country, I was the highest Washington official they had met.

Colonialism is not an issue today except in a historical sense. The world has passed it by with few regrets. Perhaps it would, however, be appropriate for me to give at this point as accurate a description as I can of my attitude toward the concept and institution of colonialism during the period under review. Having been raised in Texas, I had been exposed to the racial and discriminatory attitudes held at that time by the white majority there, to both the black and Mexican minorities. This was, in effect, a colonial attitude, even though Texans had themselves won freedom from Mexican domination and strongly opposed colonialism as such.

At Oxford I concentrated my studies on science, as I had before, and had in the beginning little interest in political issues. As my awareness of these questions grew, however, I went through a conservative reaction in my thinking at the time many of my fellow Rhodes scholars were undergoing a liberal—even a socialist—phase. I was greatly influenced by reading of the life of my benefactor, Cecil Rhodes, and his success in expanding the British Empire in Africa. Rhodes, along with Robert Clive and Warren Hastings, who had spearheaded British imperial interests in India, became my heroes. Colonialism appeared to me not an instrument of oppression but the bearing of the "white man's burden." I regretted being too late to be a part of the colonial era.

By 1949, I had come to see both racism and colonialism, which were under widespread attack, in quite a different perspective. I could not, however, fault the British attitude toward colonialism, since they had in my judgment adapted their colonial rule to changing circumstances and deserved credit for their accomplishments. Also, they appeared quite willing to withdraw once their colonies had been prepared for self-government. The Dutch also seemed willing to retire, in their way. The French, the Portuguese, the Italians, and the Belgians, however, gave the clear impression that they wanted to stay, and continue to derive what benefits they could from their colonial territories until they were forced out. To me this seemed not only impractical and out of date but immoral. My experience in

Morocco, where the French at the very end of the colonial era had forced themselves on a people who had achieved high intellectual and cultural standards under a stable hereditary regime in the eighth century, while Western Europe was still populated by relatively uncivilized warring factions, reinforced this view. This conviction undoubtedly influenced my attitude toward my responsibilities during the twilight of the colonial era. To say more would be beating a dead horse.

Upon undertaking my new duties as Assistant Secretary, I gave careful thought to the vast area under my jurisdiction. I tried to analyze the problems there and formulate a broad strategy for our government in dealing with them. As Coordinator for Aid to Greece and Turkey, the first of our postwar policies aimed at stopping Soviet advancement, I had clearly developed the point of view of a "cold warrior." In the Soviet press and in their Middle East broadcasts I was constantly denounced as such. I was not displeased with this. However, with my new responsibilities I could see that there were a great many problems in the Middle World, a region five times the size of the U.S., which were not related to the threat of Communism.

Upon undertaking my new duties I tried to devise the best strategy I could for the successful carrying-out of our foreign policy in the Middle World, which would enable us to use the limited instruments of policy we had available so they would reinforce each other, and thereby be more effective. Naturally I started out with the threat we perceived to be posed by the Soviets to the new Middle World states. The Free World's confrontation with the Soviets has often been described as an ideological conflict between Communism and capitalism; however, Marxist economic doctrine had been revealed not only as a threat in itself but as a front for Soviet imperialism.

The Middle World had had ample experience over its long past with conquerors and would-be conquerors. The Soviet threat was something new to the Middle World only in its technique, not in its objectives. I was confident, however, that the non-Communist states of this area would develop a realistic awareness of the threat and join us in resisting it.

In Europe the forces of Communism no longer had the initiative, as they had had only two years before. To the west of the area conquered by the Soviet army, the European nations had successfully withstood the inroads of Communist subversion. Under the Marshall Plan they had made progress toward economic recovery and the restoration of public confidence in their future. In Eastern Europe, the Soviets had recently suffered a major reversal in Yugoslavia and were fully occupied in holding the remainder of their bloc.

In China, the expansion of militant Communism was a great setback for the West. It would be impossible to gauge the full effects until their new leaders had had a chance to come to grips with the difficult practical problems they faced. At the same time, the rapid Communist takeover in China posed grave problems for the Soviet Union. The Soviets could be expected to attempt to maximize their influence over the Chinese Communists, and then to consolidate this vast area within their orbit.

I considered the Middle East to be vulnerable, particularly along its northern borders adjacent to the Soviet Union and the satellite states. However, with our help progress was being made in strengthening these exposed states. Greece was successfully liquidating the remnants of the guerrilla movement, based in Yugoslavia and Bulgaria, which had been organized and supported by the Soviets since 1946. In 1949, less than 2,000 guerrillas were fighting in Greece, compared with a maximum of 28,000 two years earlier. Turkey, with its traditional national unity and determination to resist Soviet encroachment, had successfully withstood demands for territory and military bases, renunciation by the U.S.S.R. of the Turko-Soviet Treaty of Friendship, and an intensive propaganda campaign. Having survived thirteen wars with Russia in modern history, Turkey was not likely to capitulate now.

Among the other nations threatened by the Soviets, it seemed to me that Iran deserved special credit for having, with our support, expelled in late 1946 a Soviet-sponsored puppet government in Azerbaijan, a province of Iran bordering the Soviet Union. For the past five years, Iran had firmly stood its ground against intimidation manifested by troop movements along its frontiers, Soviet-inspired incursions into Iranian territory, repeated demands for a Soviet oil concession as a front for penetration, and the full force of Soviet propaganda.

Despite the progress achieved, I felt we should not underestimate the seriousness of the Soviet threat, just as we should not overestimate the progress we had made in stemming the Communist tide. The conflict was drawing heavily upon our resources and upon the strength of other threatened nations. There was no cause for complacency and there could be no relaxation of vigilance. However, it was clear to me that the Soviet threat was by no means the only problem facing the world, and I feared that if we acted as though we thought it was, we would be according the Soviets undue credit and would fail to meet other challenges. There were many other world problems which I felt we should tackle with equal determination. Countries only recently freed from colonial rule were struggling for political and economic viability and self-respect among the family of nations. Their feeling of insecurity made it all the more difficult for them to work out compromises over long-standing conflicts with their neighbors. Looking to the future, I felt that these problems would constitute a threat to the Middle World even in the absence of the Soviet menace. Their diversity and complexity precluded any simple formula for their solution. Certainly, the mere extension of material aid, even if it were available in adequate amounts, would not in itself assure a solution.

In the Middle East, Iraq, Egypt, Saudi Arabia, and the Yemen had achieved independence only since the 1920s. Lebanon and Syria had followed as a result of the Second World War, and Jordan in 1946. Those states were still struggling to overcome the effects of long foreign influence. They were only beginning to seek opportunities for economic development and social reform. The basic political structure of the Middle East had been drastically changed by the emergence in 1948 of the new state of Israel, by the resulting large-scale Jewish immigration to Israel which must be assimilated, and by the 700,000 refugees from Palestine resulting from the hostilities. It was obvious that these problems were not the result of Communism and could not be solved by military force. Indeed, it was reassuring that Communist ideology had gained such little influence in the Middle East.

The continent of Africa at that time contained only four independent states: Egypt, Liberia, Ethiopia, and the Union of South Africa. However, a recent resolution of the Political and Security Committee of the UN General Assembly called for independence for Libya by 1952, and for Somaliland after ten years. These states would be confronted with problems similar to those faced in the Middle East. With Libya as an example, other African states could be expected to press for an acceleration of their time schedules for independence. The limitations on technical skills and investment capital in Africa made that continent a prime candidate for our Point Four Program of technical assistance. We had for some time been cooperating with the Liberian government in such a program, which showed what might be done in other African countries.

In South Asia, the threat of Chinese Communism was creating growing apprehension. However, Communist ideology appeared to have gained little influence. The more pressing problems were largely internal. India, Pakistan, Burma, and Ceylon had achieved independence within the last few years, all except Burma within the framework of the British Commonwealth. They faced the difficult task of creating new administrative structures. India and Pakistan had also to integrate their diverse ethnic groups, religious sects, and social classes, as well as the former princely states. They had to settle ten million refugees resulting from their separation.

South Asia's long domination by foreign powers had left a legacy of suspicion toward the West which would be overcome only slowly. This had been aggravated by our concentration on helping Europe first, which was interpreted in South Asia as indifference to their plight, even as Western solidarity "against the East." We recognized the desire of these states to be neutral in the struggle between the Soviet Union and the Western powers and had no desire to pressure them to abandon their position. We hoped that they would, however, associate themselves increasingly with the free world on important issues, on the basis of equality and partnership.

I felt that we must continue to help free nations resist Soviet expansion, seeking at all times to minimize the conflict and keep it from becoming military. But such a goal was only a minimum. It alone would not rally the people of the world to a common purpose. We needed to meet the challenge of the dynamic forces at play in the world, which had appeal for the new developing nations, if we hoped to attain their voluntary association with us.

In retrospect this all sounds dated and passé. It is obvious that we were preoccupied with the Cold War. I, myself, was overly optimistic that we could rally the weak new nations of the Middle World in the common defense with us and the Western World against a threat which they did not understand. All they could see were the overwhelming domestic problems surrounding them. I was far too optimistic, also, in my expectations for their economic development, and the abatement of deep rivalries. We now realize how appallingly little we knew then about these peoples. We were dealing with them directly for the first time, and our contacts were still with local officials trained in the colonial pattern, many at Oxford, Cambridge, or the Sorbonne.

I am also sure, in retrospect, that we underestimated the overriding preoccupation of the new states of the Middle World with the conflicts they had inherited from their past: such as those between India and Pakistan, Arabs and Jews, Ethiopia and Somalia, Morocco and Algeria, Iran and Iraq. These seemingly intractable problems, of which the Middle World appears to have a disproportionate share, are deeply rooted in ancient religious and dynastic struggles. So far they have proven impossible to resolve, and continue as overriding barriers to progress. It is with this background in mind that I thought it might be of interest, even for the general reader, to recall our first official contacts with the Middle World leaders based on my own experiences. These contacts constitute an important part of the historical record of our early relations with these countries. They may help us interpret subsequent developments in the Middle World, and prospects for the future.

2

The State Department and the World Scene, 1949–1951

Important U.S. foreign-policy decisions during the years 1949 through 1951 were made, of course, by President Harry S. Truman, based largely on the recommendations of his Secretary of State, Dean Acheson. Apart from his intellectual capacities and varied experiences as a leading international lawyer and high Treasury and State Department official, Acheson had the self-assurance that came from knowing he had the full confidence of the President. Although from quite different backgrounds, they worked together in complete harmony. Acheson was under all circumstances loyal to Truman. Truman was in turn quick to defend Acheson from the many attacks that were directed at him from Congress and the conservative private sector.

I was with the two on many occasions when the President, often with no White House adviser present, would listen to Acheson's description of some new policy on which he proposed to embark. Acheson and his staff would, of course, have done all the necessary preparation, including the sounding out of key congressmen. Truman would listen carefully, ask a few pertinent questions, and usually say: "That sounds right to me, Dean. I believe Congress will back us. Go ahead." Truman seldom showed concern about domestic political reactions. He paid close attention, however, to the attitude of key congressional leaders.

As Secretary of State, Acheson naturally had to focus his personal attention on the major decisions affecting global strategy and relations with our key allies. His Under Secretary, James Webb, relieved him as much as possible of day-to-day departmental matters. Although relatively new to foreign affairs, Webb had come to the Department with high-level experience both in business and government. He moved quickly to decentralize responsibility. He said to me once, "George, I want you to feel that you are the Secretary of State for your area. Any decision you feel comfortable in making, you make. If you don't feel easy about it, bring it to me. I will make it or help you get it made." With that he would send me back into the fray with a pat on the back, like a coach sending a football player back into the game.

For Acheson, it was as he described it in his memoirs, *Present at the Creation*,[1] a bad time to have assumed the helm of the State Department. He said that he saw that the world's "surrounding gloom had deepened, or remained impenetrable, in most areas." It seemed that the only bright spots were the early successes of the Marshall Plan, which had been launched June 5, 1947, with the announced aim of providing $14 billion to help the Western European democracies to restore their economies, devastated by the war. According to Acheson the Soviet Union was trying everywhere to spread chaos, for example through the guerrilla movement they supported in Greece as a prelude to the introduction of Communism. Chiang Kai-shek's rule on the Chinese mainland was in the last stages of collapse. Our occupation of Japan was a diminishing asset. The British were in trouble in Iran and Egypt, and the French in Indochina and North Africa. In the Middle East the impasse remained between Israel and the Arab states, following the 1948 Arab-Israeli War. All of this Acheson had to deal with as Secretary of State.

Much of Acheson's time during his term of office (1949–53) would be taken up with efforts to achieve an Arab-Israeli settlement, first through a negotiation already underway, by Dr. Ralph J. Bunche, United Nations Acting Mediator in Palestine.[2] None of these efforts, however, was to be successful. Progress was being made in European defense under the Brussels Defense Pact, signed on March 17, 1949, but this was marred by the Soviet blockade of Berlin, initiated on June 11 and fully imposed June 14, 1948, and the withdrawal of the Soviets from the four-power Berlin Kommandatura on June 16.[3] This was countered, however, by the successful Allied airlift. The ending of the blockade and the development of a long-range policy toward Germany were the principal questions Acheson would face as Secretary.

Apart from these problems, the highlights in our international relations which Acheson cited in his memoirs and which would absorb his attention during the period covered in these pages were: negotiation of the North Atlantic Treaty, which was signed on April 4, 1949; the Foreign Ministers' meeting in Paris in May 1949, which centered on the Berlin problem and the Austrian Treaty; the China White Paper of July 1949, and the intense attack on the government's China policy and Acheson personally; the North Atlantic Council meeting of May 1950, and the launching of the Schuman Plan, which was to lead to the creation of the Common Market; the outbreak of war in Korea on June 24, 1950, and the subsequent prosecution of the war; the Japanese Peace Treaty signed September 8, 1951; the crisis of the British position in Egypt and the proposed Middle East Command; and the NATO Council meeting in Ottawa of September 15-20, 1951, which resulted in the admission of Greece and Turkey to NATO.

Because of the pressure on Acheson created by so many critical world problems, the conduct of normal relations with the Middle World was largely left to my bureau. I did not make all of the policy decisions toward that vast array of countries. In the case of major issues it fell to me to recommend policies to the Secretary, which after departmental coordination could be evaluated in light of the impact on other areas and our overall relationship with our allies and the Soviet Bloc. It was always recognized, of course, that the final policy decision on matters he wished to concern himself with was that of the President.

During this period Acheson participated in many affairs affecting the Middle World, usually on a spot basis. He received as official visitors Prime Minister Jawaharlal Nehru of India, the Shah of Iran, Prime Minister Liaquat Ali Khan of Pakistan, and President William Tubman of Liberia. By and large, however, most matters affecting our area were the bureau's responsibility. We were expected to coordinate policy, on our own initiative, with our major allies. Since there were then no independent African states except Egypt, Liberia, Ethiopia, and the Union of South Africa, our involvement with the African continent was largely through discussions with the British, French, Belgians, and Portuguese. Although we knew that independence of the French North African colonies was coming, we still had only limited access to the emerging leaders of the new states there.

As for our relationship with the independent countries of South Asia, the independent Arab countries, Ethiopia, and Liberia, our bureau had a relatively free hand in attempting to establish good relations and build for the future. These countries seldom involved policy of great interest in the upper levels of our government. Our bureau had ample scope for managing the day-to-day conduct of our relations. All in all, we did not feel severely restricted as we pursued our daily tasks.

Looking back on that period today, I find, as historians have found before me, that our vision of the world was perhaps too confined to a narrow perspective. We were, we thought of necessity, greatly influenced by the exigencies of the Cold War. Even so, it seems to me that Truman and Acheson's broad policies were basically realistic, and inspired by a desire to further democratic institutions and human rights and better the condition of the common man throughout the free world. At the same time, the administration looked to our defenses, and those of our friends and allies, against the growing Soviet threat. I have no regrets in having participated in this effort.

In his memoirs, Acheson gives a summary of the world scene at the close of the year 1951, the time of my departure from the Department to become ambassador to Turkey.[4] It provides an interesting backdrop. Acheson says that he was happy that the NATO headquarters was finally a reality and that American troops had reinforced Europe. He thought progress was being made in restoring sovereignty to Germany, toward the organization of a European Defense Community, and the fulfillment of the Coal and Steel Plan. In the Middle East, however, Acheson says he thought we were losing ground. Progress in rebuilding Greece and Turkey and getting them into NATO was overshadowed by troubles threatening Iran and Egypt. He said he could, however, see progress toward peace and stability in Korea and the Philippines, and in Southeast Asia generally.

In my own area of responsibility I shared these concerns. My real regret in leaving the department when I did in December 1951, was that I had not been able to solve the Iranian oil crisis. I was also troubled over the growing impasse between Egypt and the United Kingdom. I was disappointed at the lack of progress in the Arab refugee problem, and toward an Arab-Israeli peace treaty.

3

Middle East Defense, 1949–1951

The Middle East, which is a British term normally including the Arab states west through Egypt, as well as Israel, Cyprus, Turkey, and Iran, will be used in this account where possible, rather than the designation Near East. The term Near East, which is more common in our usage, usually refers only to Israel and the adjacent Arab states, and is both restrictive and ambiguous. The Middle East has historically been of great strategic importance as a land bridge between the three continents—a traditional route of empire. To this was added transit by ship through the strategic Suez Canal and in recent times air landing and transit rights required for intercontinental flights. The Middle East is also the one greatest repository of oil in the world, with sixty per cent of world proven reserves and thirty-four per cent of production. It is because of the importance of Middle East defense which results from these strategic considerations that I have chosen to discuss it first.

Since the beginning of the nineteenth century, the Middle East has been of particular interest to the British because of its importance in keeping open the sea route to India, Britain's most prized possession. Even before the demise of the Ottoman Empire, the British had developed a network of defense treaties with Transjordan, Iraq, and Egypt, which granted them the right to maintain military bases and station troops in these countries. The British also administered Palestine as a mandate from the League of Nations.

The military key to the British position in the Middle East was Egypt, particularly the great Suez base, Fayad, with its supply depots, workshops, power stations, and its access both to the sea and Cairo. Also of importance were the Habbaniya and Shu'aiba bases in Iraq. During World War II, the British exercised command of Allied

Forces in the Middle East theater using their own, Commonwealth, and indigenous troops. And the U.S. supported British operations through the joint Middle East Supply Center in Cairo, bringing in supplies by sea through the Indian Ocean. After the Second World War, France gave up its mandates over Syria and Lebanon, leaving the British, as the only remaining European power, dominant in the area.

The U.S. was forced to take an increased interest in Middle East defense after the war, particularly in Turkey and Greece. In 1945, the Soviets terminated their twenty-year treaty with Turkey and demanded territory on Turkey's eastern border and participation in the defense of the Turkish straits. In 1945, the Soviets also sought to create a "democratic national autonomous government" in Azerbaijan in northwest Iran. These moves were checked by a strong reaction from President Truman, who saw the Soviet move as a possible prelude to conquest of the Middle East. In March 1946, the President sent the U.S.S. *Missouri* to Istanbul for the ostensible reason of carrying home the body of the Turkish ambassador, who had died in Washington in 1944.

However, the first direct U.S. involvement in Middle East defense was precipitated on February 24, 1947, when the British ambassador in Washington, Sir Oliver Franks, formally advised the Secretary of State that the U.K., because of financial limitations, could not continue to support the Greek army in its bitter struggle with the Communist-led guerrilla forces. The U.K. also advised us that it could no longer extend military assistance to Turkey. The American response on March 6, which came to be known as the Truman Doctrine, pledged support for free nations struggling against internal armed minorities supported from without, and nations subjected to external threats and pressures. That doctrine led to Public Law 75, which was signed by the President on May 22. As a result of it, we furnished $750 million worth of military and economic assistance to Greece and Turkey over the following two years.

Large military and economic missions were established in Athens, and smaller ones in Ankara, both under our ambassadors. I administered the program in Washington. Both of our missions, particularly that in Greece, became deeply involved in the internal affairs of those countries. We helped them build up, train, and supply their military forces. We took the lead in the reconstruction of Greece. It was our basic policy, however, that no American was to be exposed to combat. With our help, the Greek army was eventually successful in suppressing the guerrilla movement, and the Soviet threat against Turkey was checked. When they were established in 1947, the Marshall Plan and the Mutual Security Program became the sources of economic and military aid to both Greece and Turkey. We had gotten militarily involved in the Middle East and the Truman Doctrine remained in force.

The U.S. Joint Chiefs of Staff (JCS) had, in 1947, recognized officially that the security of the Eastern Mediterranean and Middle East was vital to our security.[1] It also became U.S. policy that we should be prepared to make full use of our political, economic, and, if necessary, military power to defend this area. The Joint Chiefs felt, too, that "it would be unrealistic for the U.S. to undertake to carry out such a policy unless the British maintained their strong strategic, political, and economic position in the Middle East and Eastern Mediterranean, and unless they and ourselves followed parallel policies in that area." Our air force had rights to use the Dhahran air base in Saudi Arabia and Wheelus Field in Tripoli, Libya. However, we had no assurances of permanent rights at these bases or anywhere else.

And yet the Mutual Defense Assistance Act of October 6, 1949, did not include in its authority the extension of military assistance, even on a reimbursable basis, for the Middle East and South Asian countries. Soon after assuming the position of Assistant Secretary, I directed a memorandum to the Coordinator for Military Assistance Programs asking that certain states in these areas—particularly India, Pakistan, Afghanistan, and Saudi Arabia—be added in any extension of the Act.[2]

In the U.S.-U.K. Middle East talks held in Washington on November 14, 1949, there was no specific discussion of increased U.S. military responsibility in the Middle East.[3] Michael Wright, head of the British delegation, in commenting on the devastating economic effect the loss of the Middle East would have on the British economy, said that it was to our common advantage that the U.S. government should concern itself increasingly with the Middle East. It would be our decision, but he assured us that his country would welcome it.

The conclusions of our Near Eastern Chiefs of Mission Conference held in Istanbul in late November of 1949 did not suggest any drastic changes in U.S. military policy toward the Middle East.[4] Military preparedness for countries not contiguous to the Soviet bloc, except for internal security, was not considered a Cold War factor. We saw no need for security pacts between the U.S. and Middle Eastern states. The only exception we anticipated was that it might become desirable to sell arms on a reimbursable basis to Saudi Arabia, with which we felt we should seek special ties.

In the meantime, the Cold War and the apparent Soviet threat to the Middle East became more intense. In my periodic discussions with the Joint Chiefs of Staff, however, I had been advised that U.S. military strategic interests in the Middle East were viewed as being almost negligible in light of interests in other areas.[5] This trend in thinking was confirmed in February 1950 by General Lyman Lemnitzer, the Director of the Office of Military Assistance.[6] This was obviously contrary to previously stated policy, but was explained as being entirely a question of priority. I argued that if military aid to the Middle East could not be justified on strategic grounds, it should be based, for political and psychological reasons, on the necessity for meeting minimum requirements of the countries of the area for perceived internal security and self-defense needs. Otherwise we could not hope to gain their cooperation.

In my testimony of March 1950 before the House Foreign Affairs Committee in behalf of the Foreign Assistance Act of 1950, HR7797, I said that against the background of a Cold War, the central geographic position of the Middle East, the convergence there of international surface and air routes, and its great cultural and natural resources, the Middle East assumed even greater importance. The political loss of the area in time of peace would be a major disaster comparable to its loss during war. The Soviet Union would be immeasurably strengthened and the Cold War prolonged. The Supplemental Report following the hearings said that in the committee's view our strategic interest in the area warranted the proposed expenditure.[7]

The Department admitted, when queried by the British Embassy, that my statement had gone further than anything we had said previously.[8] I have learned from the British archives that in September 1950, as background for a visit I was scheduled to make shortly to London, the British Embassy analyzed the basic differences in U.S.-U.K. views toward Middle East defense.[9] U.S. thinking, according to the embassy, gave priority to the defense of the outer ring of Greece, Turkey, and Iran, as countries already threatened, which would be the first to be attacked by the Soviets. We had successfully extended large-scale aid to Greece and Turkey for this reason. The British concept, on the other hand, started from Cairo and radiated outward. The U.S. was also thought by the embassy to be influenced by a perhaps subconscious reluctance to make commitments in the Arab world, because of pressures by American Jewish groups and misgivings about social and economic conditions in the Arab states.

On May 5, 1950, I held a meeting in my office with State and Defense officials, including General Lemnitzer, to discuss the use of existing legislation as a basis for providing arms to certain Middle Eastern countries, and the modification of the existing Mutual Defense Assistance Act for this purpose.[10] The Tripartite Declaration of May 1950 was motivated in large part by our desire to assure increased shipments of arms to the Arab states and Israel under controlled conditions. The Declaration was of such importance from the standpoint of Middle East defense that it will be dealt with separately in Chapter 17.

U.S.-U.K. military and political talks were held in Washington in July.[11] We were represented by Ambassador Philip Jessup and General Omar Bradley, and the British by Ambassador Sir Oliver Franks and Marshal of the Royal Air Force Lord Tedder. It was decided that we needed "an examination of the whole Middle East problem covering both political and military aspects, without prejudice as to what nations should provide the forces required in the various eventualities." This would appear to have pushed the door a little further ajar for U.S. entry into Middle East defense.

In an informal U.S.-U.K. discussion held in London on September 18, 1950, in which Michael Wright represented the U.K. and I represented the U.S., there was a review of the papers which had been prepared by the British Foreign Office and British Chiefs of Staff on the politico-military situation in the Middle East.[12] These papers were to be used for further Bradley-Tedder talks to be held in Washington in October. The new element contained in the British papers was the suggestion of a small U.S. ground force in Dhahran, Saudi Arabia, to which Wright added Tripolitania. There was also the suggestion for a joint U.S.-U.K. arms policy in the area. In response, I said that we considered the supply of military equipment to be largely a British responsibility, and that apart from Saudi Arabia our arms priorities would preclude our playing such a provider role.

In a memorandum to Jessup upon my return I pointed out the implications of the key paragraph of the British review he would be considering in October, which stated that "to retain the countries of the Middle East within the Western orbit is a vital Cold War objective, and the Allies must be prepared to make military sacrifices to that end."[13] I noted that this was contrary to JCS opposition to any measures which would commit U.S. forces to the Middle East in the event of war. I also stated my own view, for the first time, that the U.S. should give consideration to stationing forces at the Dhahran Air Base if this was acceptable to the Saudis. I believed that such forces, even if limited, would increase the confidence of the Middle East countries, particularly Saudi Arabia; would reassure U.S. oil company representatives in the Persian Gulf area; and would assist in oil denial to the enemy in the event of war.

In the October 1950 U.S.-U.K. political-military meeting, Ambassador Jessup and General Joseph Collins, Chief of Staff, United States Army, agreed to consider the possibility of U.S. participation with the U.K. and Egypt in an Egyptian base, and in arms supply to Egypt.[14] The U.S. side emphasized, however, that the U.K. could not count on American forces in the Middle East for at least the first two years of a general war.

In *Present at the Creation*, Acheson relates that in January 1951 he wrote a letter to General Marshall, then Secretary of Defense, asking for a study of American interests and policies in the entire area extending from the Mediterranean to India.[15] Our power had waxed and British power had waned. No power had, however, been substituted for that of the British in dealing with nationalist movements in Iran and Egypt, Acheson said, and differences between states such as India and Pakistan offered increasing opportunity for Soviet intrusion.

Acheson said that he did not propose relieving the U.K. and the Commonwealth of the primary responsibility for providing troops for the defense of the Middle East. Their own efforts and the assistance we were already giving in the area should, however, be coordinated in a plan for the defense of the area as a whole. We could perhaps offer small military training missions, places for Middle East military personnel in U.S. military schools, and limited equipment for training. Consideration might be given to a U.S.-U.K. military agency to stimulate and coordinate the efforts of all countries involved. The State Department hoped that the organization of such an agency would help solve the British impasse with the Wafd government in Egypt and the problem of British reluctance to accept an American as Mediterranean NATO commander, even though our Sixth Fleet constituted the principal force in the area. General Marshall agreed to the study on the condition that Greece and Turkey be excluded and left to NATO.

Our bureau was, of course, heavily involved in all of this. On September 8, 1951, I finally secured agreement between the Pentagon and a British working group on the terms for a Middle East Command.[16] This was an idea which had been kicked back and forth across the Atlantic for many months. Its purpose was to substitute a British Middle East Command for their fading treaty structure. It would provide the British with continued troop and base rights in the region. In the form now agreed to, there would be a British Supreme Allied Command, Middle East, with headquarters in Cairo, which would be directed by a Middle East Chief of Staff Committee that included Egyptian officers. The British Suez base would be turned over to the Egyptians, who would place it under the new command. British troops, beyond those which had been agreed to by Egypt, would be withdrawn.

On September 25, President Celal Bayer of Turkey told our Ambassador in Ankara, George Wadsworth, that Turkey would welcome a visit to Ankara by General Bradley, Field Marshal Sir William Slim, and General Charles Lecheres, representing the U.S., the U.K. and France, to discuss the Middle East Command. He promised to help the three governments in attempting to persuade Egypt to join. When the Egyptian government received word of what was coming, its opposition was so intense that it sent to the Egyptian Parliament legislation to abrogate the 1936 treaty with the British and the Sudan Condominium Agreement of 1899. The three generals arrived in Ankara on October 13 and the decision was made to present the proposal anyway, in the vain hope that the Egyptians would be influenced by such solidarity.[17] The Egyptian Prime Minister, Mustafa el-Nahas Pasha, rejected the proposal without reading it. Two days later the Egyptian Parliament abrogated the two treaties.

Although there followed some inconclusive discussions with the British over forming a Middle East Defense Organization without Egypt, an era in Middle East defense efforts had ended with that Ankara meeting. Later, in 1953, Secretary of State John Foster Dulles attempted to revive the basic command idea, without Egypt, through the Baghdad Pact, linking the "Northern Tier" of Turkey, Pakistan, Iraq, and Iran with Britain, in the Central Treaty Organization. Yielding to public opinion, King Hussein of Jordan declined entry. This military alliance fell apart after the overthrow in 1958 of the regency in Iraq under the pro-British Prime Minister Nuri al-Said. Nuri, who was murdered in the coup, had not been sufficiently attuned to the rising nationalist sentiment in Iraq, which made any defense arrangement in the old colonial mold unacceptable. The Baghdad Pact, which he had played an important role in forming, had resulted in a rallying of the Arab states around Nasser against Nuri.

The necessity for a Middle East defense structure was, of course, considerably diminished by the admission of Greece and Turkey to NATO on February 15, 1952. The two most powerful military forces of the area had now been incorporated in the overall NATO defense plans. They provided a shield protecting the softer, less defensible Arab states to the south. There was, however, still an eastern end to the shield, which the allies continued to try to protect through the ill-fated Middle East Defense Organization and the later, somewhat more successful Central Treaty Organization. The question of stationing U.S. troops in the Middle East, which I first raised in September 1949 in connection with Saudi Arabia, has never been resolved.

Renewed attention has, though, been given to this question since President Carter's warning to the Soviets on January 23, 1980, of our intention to defend the Persian Gulf area against outside aggression. The President said:

> Let our position be absolutely clear: An attempt by any outside force to gain control of the Persian Gulf region will be regarded as an assault on the vital interests of the United States of America, and such an assault will be repelled by any means necessary, including military force.

Possible sites for stationing U.S. military forces in the area still being considered no longer include Saudi Arabia, but center instead on the Sinai Peninsula and Egypt. Base rights for U.S. use in the event of hostilities in the Persian Gulf area are being sought with Oman, Somalia, and Kenya. The U.S. has also proceeded to develop a naval base on the island of Diego Garcia in the Indian Ocean, under rights obtained from the British.

Beginning in the Carter administration and continuing under President Reagan, the U.S. has developed mobile forces to deploy to these bases in the event of hostilities. In addition to naval support forces, this Ready Force, part of which is being trained at Fort Bragg, will in the event of emergency be transported by air to forward areas in Egypt and, one hopes, Saudi Arabia, where they can be deployed, if necessary, by parachute. Other forces can be landed by air in forward air bases in Egypt, Oman, or perhaps Saudi Arabia, with back-up forces arriving by sea. In July 1982, official U.S. sources listed about 25 U.S. naval vessels and one marine unit in the Indian Ocean and 5 vessels in the Persian Gulf. The Soviets were credited with about 30 vessels and 500 naval infantry in the Indian Ocean, with base rights in Aden and Socotra Island in South Yemen.

The evolution of U.S. policy toward Middle East defense begins and ends on an inconclusive note. The Middle East has always been a secondary theater. The military threat, whether from internal Communist subversion or a direct Soviet thrust to the Persian Gulf, has never been clearly defined. The building blocks of weak, resentful Arab states continue to defy incorporation in our defense concepts, as they once defied the British.

4

Early Days of the Arab Refugee Problem

February-June 1949.

The events described in this chapter, which occurred before my appointment as Assistant Secretary, explain how I happen to have become so deeply involved in the Middle East. They also deal with one of the area's most difficult problems and one which would occupy much of my time during the period under review. On November 29, 1947, the United Nations General Assembly had approved the partition of Palestine into an Arab and a Jewish State. Britain, who had held the territory under a League of Nations Mandate since 1920, withdrew its forces and Israel was declared an independent state on May 14, 1948. Egypt, Transjordan, Syria, Lebanon, Iraq, and Saudi Arabia rejected the partition and invaded on May 15. A truce was arranged under UN auspices by Count Folke Bernadotte on July 11 but hostilities did not cease until December, after Israeli forces invaded Egypt.

In the aftermath of the war, hundreds of thousands of Palestinian refugees, fleeing from the territory which had once been a part of the Palestine Mandate, found themselves trapped behind ceasefire lines and were prevented from returning to their homes by the new state of Israel. On November 19, 1948, the UN General Assembly had voted a $32 million fund to take care of the refugees. On December 11, 1948, the assembly passed a resolution, the famous Article II, which said that the refugees should, if they wished, be permitted to return to their homes and that, if they could not, they should be compensated. The Palestine Conciliation Commission (PCC) was established to help the Jews and Arabs reach an overall agreement on Palestine.

The PCC, the UN officials involved, and representatives of the interested nations fully recognized the importance of a solution to the refugee problem if there was to be a lasting peace in the Middle East. On January 28, 1949, a report from the U.S. Embassy in Cairo estimated that there were some 8,000 refugees in Egypt and 250,000 in Egyptian-occupied Palestine (the Gaza Strip); Amman reported 302,000 in Arab Palestine (the West Bank) and 89,000 in Transjordan; Beirut reported 90,000 in Arab Lebanon; Damascus reported up to 100,000 in Syria; and 5,000 were reported in Iraq. These estimates totalled 844,000.[1]

In late February 1949, Dean Rusk, newly appointed Deputy Under Secretary of State, called me into his office. He was a friend of long standing and later we were to become fellow Assistant Secretaries of State. During the years he was Secretary of State in the Kennedy administration, I served under him in a number of key positions. Dean is a man for whom I have the greatest respect and admiration.

At that meeting, Dean asked me what I thought about the Arab refugee problem, which was still in a state of flux and being dealt with on an ad hoc basis. I replied candidly that I had been concentrating on my work with Greece and Turkey and had paid little attention to it. He told me I had better find out about it, since it was the key to peace or war in the Middle East. He said that the refugees were being taken care of by the UN, but only on a temporary basis. He asked me whether I would like to go to the Middle East and see what could be done about the refugees under a long-term plan. He could offer me the title of Special Assistant to the Secretary with the rank of minister, which I had never been.

I demurred, pointing out that I was still busy winding up affairs under Greek-Turkish Aid. I had had a very difficult time dealing with Greeks and Turks for two years and didn't want to get into Arab-Israeli affairs. In a kindly but firm way, Dean suggested that my Greek-Turkish program was about over, having been succeeded by the Marshall Plan. He made it plain that if I wanted to stay on in the Department at my level I ought to accept his offer. Upon reflection, I did. My entry into the Middle East—which was to take me to the position of Assistant Secretary for the Near East, South Asia and Africa, and Ambassador to Turkey—was ordained.

On March 3, Rusk directed the following memorandum to Under Secretary of State Webb:[2]

> Subject: Assignment of Mr. George McGhee as U.S. Coordinator on Palestine Refugee Matters.
>
> 1. It is becoming increasingly clear that a final settlement of the

Palestine question will turn upon our ability to obtain some solution to the complicated question of Palestine refugees. There are now about 700,000 such refugees in Arab-held Palestine and in neighboring Arab states. Only an insignificant fraction of these can be absorbed by communities where they are now located. It is roughly estimated not more than a fourth might be returned to their former homes in Israel, in connection with a final peace settlement. The present United Nations program is a straight relief program which will terminate in September, and it is not expected that the United Nations will undertake any long range responsibility for these refugees.

2. The bulk of these refugees must be resettled in Arab-Palestine and in the neighboring Arab states. To do this, specific projects for settlement must be worked out and supported by means of Ex-Im Bank loans, International Bank loans, private capital, or other sources not now committed. Such projects would include irrigation and drainage projects which will make new lands available for settlement. Construction work on such projects would itself absorb a considerable number of refugee laborers.

The national interest of the United States is so heavily involved in the solution of this problem that we should detail immediately an American of high rank, diplomatic ability and sound judgment, as Special Assistant to the Secretary of State with personal rank of Minister, to mobilize the public and private resources of the United States which might be brought to bear on this problem.

It is strongly recommended that Mr. George McGhee be named to this post. Mr. McGhee's experience and performance with regard to Greek Assistance, his knowledge of the Department and of the agencies concerned, and his broad political and business experience would make him admirably suited for this assignment. I hope that you will agree and will put this assignment to Mr. McGhee in the strongest terms.

On March 11, the department advised Mark Ethridge, U.S. representative on the Palestine Conciliation Commission, that it was contemplating concentrating Palestine refugee activities in Washington under me as Special Assistant to the Secretary of State.[3] It was suggested that I participate anonymously in the upcoming PCC Beirut conference. Later I would call on Dr. Ralph J. Bunche, UN Acting Mediator on Palestine then in Rhodes, and would, after other visits in the area, return via London, where I could have consultations on the refugee problem with the British.

Soon after my appointment as Coordinator for Palestine Refugee Affairs, I directed a memorandum to Secretary Acheson, dated March 15, to obtain approval for the proposed terms of reference of my assignment.[4] My memorandum was based on an excellent policy statement, "Palestine Refugees," prepared jointly by the Office of Near Eastern, South Asian and African Affairs, and the Office of United Nations Affairs. My own knowledge of the problem was still very limited. The memorandum said:

It is recommended that:

(1) It be recognized as in the national interest of the United States that an early and effective solution be found to the problem of the Palestine refugees. Such solution should make possible their repatriation or resettlement in such a manner as to minimize present and potential political and economic tensions prejudicial to United States interests in the area affected.

(2) The United States be prepared to contribute such technical and financial assistance to the solution of this problem as it considers necessary, while at the same time refusing to accept sole responsibility for solution of the problem and seeking to confine US financial assistance there to within limits consistent with its national interests.

(3) A plan be developed as a matter of urgency for the implementation of this policy, including proposals for relief, rehabilitation, and long-range resettlement projects, estimated costs, expected source of funds and operational procedures, including the part to be played by the US, the governments in the affected area, other interested governments, and the UN.

I was filled with apprehension and foreboding. The Arab-Israeli War was only the latest round of a bitter historical conflict. It had aroused deep feelings on the part of the protagonists and their co-religionists and friends around the world. On March 17, I visited the UN headquarters to obtain background information from officials who had been struggling with the refugee problem. This was valuable, but I realized that I would learn more from Bunche, whom I was scheduled to see in Rhodes.

Ambassador Warren R. Austin arranged for me to visit with Israeli Foreign Minister Moshe Sharett, who was in New York. Keen and highly articulate, Sharett said he believed the PCC meeting in Beirut which I was to join would result in the Arabs uniting in forcing Israel to take back Arab refugees, thus relieving them of the problem and ruining Israel. As for the long-range solution, Sharett admitted the possibility of some repatriation of refugees in Israel. This would, however, depend on the state of the peace. It would also require land, money, and technical assistance on a large scale. Since the Arab homes of Palestine had largely been destroyed, the refugees must for the most part be absorbed in Transjordan, Iraq, and Syria. The money for this must come in part from Israel in the form of compensation, and from the international agencies. It was unlikely that the Arabs would be willing to accept technical assistance from Israel. Sharett was later to prove quite intractable on the refugee issue.

I flew from New York to Beirut, arriving on March 20. As we circled for landing, the city and its natural setting of tree-clad snow-capped mountains coming down to the sea under the brilliant Mediterranean sun presented a magnificent spectacle. Long known as the "playground of the Near East," it was difficult to realize that Lebanon had so recently been a part of a bitter conflict that would leave permanent scars. The charming way of life that the cultivated Lebanese, European expatriates, and Arab sheikhs had created here over the years would never be quite the same. It was hard for me to reconcile the bitter discussions I knew were in progress here with this tranquil scene.

Taken to the splendid St. George Hotel on the shore of St. George harbor, I established contact with Mark Ethridge and became a part of his and his wife Willie Snow's court. Mark, distinguished writer and editor, on leave from his post of publisher of the *Louisville Courier-Journal*, was a past master at leading and provoking discussion. He could with great skill prod and chide and stimulate those in meetings he chaired. Willie Snow, witty, clever, provocative, held sway over the informal PCC groups that would gather between meetings, at drinks and dinner time, on the terrace at the St. George overlooking the sea. Willie Snow was later to publish a book on her observations over this period that would raise many eyebrows.

I plunged immediately into discussions with Ethridge, and the PCC meetings, where I sat quietly in the back and listened to the seemingly futile debate going on. Much was said but there were few areas of agreement. Tempers were close to the edge as discussions ranged over the no man's land of refugees, compensation, borders, armistice agreements, and the elusive hope for a peace treaty. It soon became apparent that Ethridge and I held similar views on how to get started on doing something to help the refugees. On March 23, I joined him in a telegram to the Department seeking approval for our preliminary recommendations. We assumed that the UN relief program would be short-lived. The key to our long-range solution to the refugee problem was economic development. In order to carry this out the PCC must appoint a technical commission to develop plans, and provide technical and financial assistance.[5] My task was to spell out just how this could be done.

It had been agreed that I would, in the meantime, join Bunche at Rhodes for a few days and then proceed to Damascus, Baghdad, and Amman. Lebanon already had too many refugees and neither Saudi Arabia nor Egypt were likely prospects for any considerable number. Since the PCC was seized with discussions between Israel and the Arab states over refugees I saw no advantage in visiting Tel Aviv. That would come later. On the way home I would stop in London for a few days for discussions with the Foreign Office. No matter what course we pursued the British would play a key role, because of their former position in Palestine and their treaties with Iraq, Transjordan, and Egypt.

Mark and I were fully aware of the completely negative attitude toward refugees held by both the Arabs and Israelis. The Arabs stood by the UN Resolution of 1948 which affirmed the right of refugees so desiring to return to their homes. The Arab states didn't want to relieve Israel of its responsibility by settling refugees in their countries. They were glad to be able to use the refugees as a political weapon against Israel. They thought we should pressure Israel to take the refugees back. In fact, however, we had little leverage with Israel.

I arrived in Rhodes during the final days of the difficult negotiation over the Israel-Transjordan ceasefire agreement, which provided for withdrawal of forces and provisional boundaries. This was the last of a series of such agreements that catapulted Bunche into world renown and won for him the coveted Nobel Peace Prize. At Rhodes I had many conversations with Ralph Bunche, usually in his hotel suite where he conducted his negotiations. He was usually in his dressing gown, his normal attire for receiving, separately, the Arab and Israeli representatives. They would not meet together.

I became a great admirer of Bunche, with whom I developed a close relationship. He spent a weekend with Cecilia and myself on our farm in Middleburg. Bunche had gained a great deal of practical experience about the Middle East which he gave me full benefit of. Although he was not at that time dealing directly with the refugee problem, he knew all of the pitfalls. When I later became Assistant

Secretary for the Near East, South Asia and Africa, it was only because Bunche had turned down President Truman's offer of the job. I was not in the slightest bit embarrassed to be considered second to Ralph Bunche.

The Israeli representative at Rhodes was Col. Moshe Dayan, who later became chief of staff of the Israeli armed forces and was to rise to Israeli secretary of defense and foreign minister. Although the Arabs and Israelis officially refused to meet together at Rhodes, I often saw Dayan and Arab representatives walking hand-in-hand in the gardens, in the Arab custom. Dayan told me about his youth in prewar Palestine and the action he participated in during the war as part of a British-Jewish Agency joint operation against the Vichy French, that resulted in the loss of his left eye.

Dayan was a gentle, kindly man, with his years of great responsibility and prestige still ahead. He always retained, however, that quiet demeanor and shy half-smile, along with his black eye patch. Our paths were to cross again in future years. His death was a great loss to the Arab-Israeli peace-seeking process. In his memoirs he tells of the secret behind-the-scenes negotiations he had conducted on March 23, 1949, with King Abdullah, from which he had only just returned when I met him, and which resulted in the successful cease-fire agreement completed on April 3.

In Damascus I stayed with U.S. Minister James H. Keeley, who was valiantly trying to maintain relations with an unstable Syrian government. Jim was of great help in arranging my meetings with Syrian officials. The Syrian reaction to any assistance to the refugees was, however, predictably and entirely negative. The Syrians, whose great oasis and city of Damascus has been one of the most important centers of Islam for over a thousand years, could not be persuaded to yield on such a basic issue. This was very disappointing to me since, in our first look at the possible absorptive capacities of the various Arab states, we had high hopes for the relatively vacant but fertile Jazirah region of northern Syria. My memories of Syria are still influenced by this unsuccessful visit, and by another in March 1951, when my bedroom in our legation was blown to bits by dynamite in my absence.

When I arrived in Baghdad our minister was away; however, our legation provided valuable assistance. In deference to British primacy in Iraq, I called on the British chargé d'affaires, then the young Humphrey Trevelyan, a relative of the famous historian, who was himself to go on to the highest ranks in the British service and a peerage. I have the report he made to the Foreign Office of our discussion, as well as the minutes taken by Crawford of our Embassy.[6] Trevelyan tried to talk me out of approaching the Iraqi government at all on the subject of refugees, since he knew Iraq was the most adamant of all the Arab states against accepting them. In his view the question could not even be discussed in Iraqi circles in view of Iraq's categorical refusal to negotiate with the PCC until Israel agreed in principle to permit the refugees to return. Iraq was rabidly anti-Zionist, was threatening retaliation against Iraqi Jews, and wanted no part in settling the refugee problem.

I replied that the refugee problem existed and some workable solution had to be found. The U.S. and the U.K. were the only countries that could do it. I urged a linkage of refugee settlement with the large-scale economic development schemes being sought by Iraq and other Arab states. Trevelyan did not believe that refugee settlement should be linked with Iraq's current request for flood-control projects before the International Bank. Development schemes for refugees should be clearly labeled as such. The British reasoned that refugee resettlement would be automatically furthered if the right projects were undertaken.

Trevelyan did not agree either with my suggestion that the PCC be assigned responsibility for surveys and negotiations with the Arab governments. He felt that any organization connected with Palestine would be suspect by the Arabs. Although we were not in full agreement, my discussions with Trevelyan were most helpful. He was of course right in his analysis of the Iraqi position. I found that no Iraqi official was willing to consider taking refugees.

I enjoyed greatly my first visit to Amman, capital of Transjordan, where I stayed at the old Philadelphia Hotel. The Roman amphitheater opposite was full of Arab refugees who had made it their home. Wells Stabler, our young chargé, had excellent relations with King Abdullah, who gave him a horse on his departure. Wells, whom I jokingly called "the law East of the Jordan," was fulfilling extremely well responsibilities that would normally have fallen to a more senior officer. Wells arranged for me to meet with King Abdullah and his Finance Minister. The King understood the refugee problem very well and promised to do all he could to help, if proper inducements were forthcoming. I had received the same impression in my earlier talks with his Prime Minister, Tawfiq Pasha, at the PCC meeting in Beirut.[7] Although Tawfiq took the common line with other Arab officials in meetings, he had expressed to me an awareness of the resettlement problem and a willingness to consider concrete proposals. Such a parallel approach he did not feel worked against the Arab states, and was a help to the PCC in working out overall solutions to problems.

The situation was that the Palestinians, most of whom had, under the British Mandate, received a higher education and more political experience than other Arabs, would in fact be hard for Jordan (as Transjordan became known in April 1949) to assimilate. Abdullah undoubtedly understood that they constituted a possible danger to his old-fashioned Hashemite regime. As a result of receiving so many displaced Arabs, Jordan was already threatened with becoming a poorhouse for refugees. Abdullah was, however, tempted by the additions to his population the refugees would represent and the economic assistance that he might receive for taking them. We were a little concerned that Jordan would take more refugees than it could absorb.

While in Amman, I also had an interesting meeting with E. C. Bryant, field director for the League of Red Cross Societies. He took me to a refugee camp which the league was operating near the city. The refugees appeared to be reasonably well housed and fed, but merely milled around without anything to do or any hope for the future.

I did not enter into any discussions with the Israeli government on refugees at this stage. The number of refugees they would be willing to repatriate and the compensation they would pay were the key problems, which were being considered at the highest level.

I did not, either, during my 1949 visit, have any discussions on refugees with the Lebanese government. With more than 250,000 refugees, Lebanon was strained to capacity. They fully understood the economic and political problems this posed for their future. The later emergence in Lebanon of the Palestine Liberation Organization (PLO) and their terrorist activities based in Lebanon were not yet apparent, although they might have been anticipated. In any event, it was clear that Lebanon needed to be relieved of some of its refugee burden, not given any more.

Later, both before and after I became Assistant Secretary of State for the area, three opportunities arose which, if they had succeeded, would have virtually resolved the refugee problem. On one occasion Israel offered to take a total of 250,000 refugees as part of a general settlement.[8] Since there were at the end of hostilities about 125,000

Arabs in Israel, and Israel had already repatriated 25,000, this meant an additional 100,000. This was 150,000 less than the estimated 400,000 in the territory they originally occupied, and 100,000 less than the 200,000 we had urged Israel to take. The Arabs responded with a counter-offer of acceptance if Israel would take a total of 500,000 (250,000 more than offered). Israel, however, declined to raise the ante. The game of numbers of refugees continued.

Ethridge had received another interesting probe on refugees from David Ben Gurion, Prime Minister of Israel, as early as April 18.[9] The Israelis would take the 250,000 refugees in the Gaza Strip, occupied in the war by Egypt, in return for ownership of the strip itself. This proposal seemed to us to offer good possibilities for a breakthrough, since the number of refugees involved was greater than the 200,000 we had been urging. We asked the Egyptians to give the Israeli offer careful consideration, but they turned it down. Egypt did not want to be accused of trading land for refugees in overcrowded Egypt proper. Perhaps they also felt they would end up with the refugees anyway, and lose the strip in the bargain.

As early as April 29, Minister Keeley reported that the mercurial General Husni Zaim, military ruler of Syria, would accept 250,000 refugees for settlement in Syria, if enough economic assistance could be provided.[10] We in the department were elated and tried to pin him down. Subsequently, Zaim had great difficulties in working out a ceasefire with Israel and felt he could not make concessions on refugees without a quid pro quo from Israel. These were not forthcoming and time ran out on him. He was assassinated on August 14 by a group of his officers because of personal grudges.

I have often thought how drastically the course of Middle East history would have been changed if one of these possibilities had materialized, and wondered if there was not something we could have done to push one of these proposals through. Certainly there was nothing more Ethridge could have done. Starting late in March, he organized the PCC conference in Lausanne, Switzerland, largely to get movement on the refugee problem. As early as May 16, Ethridge reported that the Arabs had admitted privately that they would have to take refugees.[11] The Israelis, however, even under the extreme pressure of one of the strongest diplomatic notes I have ever seen, sent by Truman to Ben Gurion on May 28, refused to make any definitive statement on refugees or to separate the question from a general peace settlement. Truman wrote to Ben Gurion that if Israel continued to reject the General Assembly Resolution of 1948, "the

U.S. government will regretfully be forced to the conclusion that a revision of its attitude toward Israel has become unavoidable." Ben Gurion refused to budge. The Israeli representative in Lausanne, Eytan, who by chance had, as Walter Ettinghausen, been my good friend and classmate at Queen's College, Oxford, offered no meaningful concessions on refugees. Despite heroic efforts by Ethridge and others, the Lausanne Conference finally foundered on this issue.

On May 2, my office prepared a memorandum for Secretary Acheson for a meeting with the President which, among other recommendations, suggested consideration of holding up the remainder of the $100 million Export-Import Bank of Washington (Ex-Im Bank) loan to Israel, which was $49 million, to put pressure on Israel to take at least 200,000 refugees. I do not know whether the Secretary raised the issue with the President at that time. On June 10, following rejection by Israel on May 29 of our latest proposal on refugees, a memorandum was sent to the President which among other recommendations urged that the Ex-Im Bank "should be immediately informed that it would be desirable to hold up the allocation of the $49 million as yet unallocated of the $100 million earmarked for loan to Israel." [12]

I was advised by the Department that this recommendation had been approved and that I should inform the Israeli Ambassador. I asked the Ambassador to lunch with me at the Metropolitan Club and put our decision to him in the most tactful and objective way I could. In light of the costly military demands made on Israel to defend itself against the Arabs, whose enmity arose mainly from the failure of Israel to carry out the UN resolution on the refugees, Israel would not be able to make effective use of the Ex-Im Bank loan unless this issue was defused by Israel's taking at least 200,000 refugees.

The Ambassador looked me straight in the eye and said, in essence, that I wouldn't get by with this move, that he would stop it. There was other conversation, but I had got the point. Within an hour of my return to my office I received a message from the White House that the President wished to dissociate himself from any withholding of the Ex-Im Bank loan. I knew of the President's sympathy for Israel, but I had never before realized how swiftly the supporters of Israel could act if challenged.

But I must get back to the Middle East. Before leaving the area after my tour in early April 1949, I visited as many of the refugee camps as possible, talking with the refugee leaders, the valiant UN officials who were coping as best they could with overwhelming problems, and the dedicated representatives of the Quakers and other private relief groups. In all the camps I saw the utter despair of people living in tents or on the ground with only elementary nourishment and meager health facilities. They were underfed, bewildered, and embittered. They asked why they couldn't go home. In many cases they could see their farms across the barbed wire. Whoever had been responsible, it had not been those poor people. One would be hard put to find a more poignant example of human misery.

On my way back to Washington from the Middle East I participated in a series of meetings in London with Foreign Office and Treasury representatives on the refugee problem.[13] It was obvious that the cooperation of the British, who had only recently exercised a mandate over Palestine and still held strong positions in the Arab states, would be the key to any refugee program. I was ably assisted by my good friend Lewis Jones, who was in charge of Middle East affairs at the embassy. Lewis, a delightful, unabashed Anglophile, was a focal point for U.S.-U.K. cooperation on the Middle East for many years. Quiet and soft-spoken, he kept the most difficult discussions on a low and friendly key.

Our meeting on April 13 was presided over by Michael Wright, British Assistant Under Secretary of State, who was later to be my opposite number as Assistant Secretary and with whom I maintained a close association until his recent death. On this day we were joined by John McCloy, president of the International Bank for Reconstruction and Development (World Bank), who happened to be in London. We and the British had high hopes that the bank could play an important role in refugee resettlement.

Wright opened the meeting on April 13 by saying that Foreign Office information indicated that the total number of refugees was close to 900,000 and that we were all faced with the problem that present relief efforts would end the next fall (December at the latest). The U.K. was anxious to pass from the stage of relief to that of resettlement. Wright stated frankly that the U.K. was very distressed at the possibility that all aid to the refugees would be given through UN channels. He did not think the UN was a particularly efficient body for such work. The UN approach might permit the U.S.S.R. to obtain a foothold in the Middle East through participation in the UN organization. Also, in whatever form financial help was given, the major contribution would still have to come from the U.K. and the U.S.

I replied that the U.S. was anxious to see the refugee problem solved and was willing to do its part in a settlement. However, we wished to avoid direct responsibility, which would indicate the necessity for a UN or PCC façade. I summarized the conclusions I had drawn from my recent visits. Regarding financial aspects, I said it must be recognized that under existing authority the U.S. could supply only small amounts for technical assistance under our Point Four Program; that in addition to foreign exchange, any refugee program we develop together must include provision for local currency required.

The best approach to the Arab governments, in my judgment, would be to stress development for their benefit, not just for the refugees. On the other hand, any increase in the standard of living in each Arab country would be the index of its ability to absorb refugees. The U.S. was also concerned that emphasis on development might turn out to be a kind of Pandora's box, leading to a flood of similar demands from South American and other countries.

McCloy spoke next, saying that the World Bank did not deal in relief matters; its sources of supply would immediately dry up if it tried to do so. The bank must have reasonable prospects for repayment and "it takes a good deal of imagination to see such prospects in the Middle East." One idea that had occurred to him, however, which might tip the scales in favor of certain projects in the Middle East, was a consortium of the U.K., U.S., and France to underwrite the bank's loans. McCloy urged that we not organize the making of another report. Both Wright and I explained that we had in mind only a survey to bring existing reports up to date in an authoritative way so international support could be obtained.

Following my return to Washington on April 15, I made a preliminary report to Webb and Rusk.[14] There followed intensive staff work directed by the departmental officers who had been concerned with Palestine affairs over many months: Dean Rusk, both as Assistant Secretary for United Nations Affairs where he was ably assisted by Robert W. McClintok, and later as Deputy Under Secretary; Joseph W. Satterthwaite, Director of the NEA Office, and his deputy Raymond A. Hare; and Frazer Wilkins, Stuart W. Rockwell and Samuel K.C. Kopper of NE (Near Eastern Affairs). This was a devoted and tireless group, dealing with a fluid and complex situation constantly in crisis.

There resulted from those studies an agreed Departmental memorandum "Palestine Refugee Problem".[15] I presented a report of my trip to the Secretary, and recommendations based on this memorandum, on April 27. I said that the disposition of the refugees was now a political issue of the highest order between Israel and the Arab states. Neither side would consider it strictly as a refugee problem. This situation would probably continue until there was a general peace settlement. In the meantime, pressure would have to be exerted on both Israel and the Arab states, if their agreement to repatriation and resettlement, respectively, was to be secured.

With the exception of Jordan, which viewed refugees as an opportunity to improve its position, the Arab states were reluctant to accept them permanently for political as well as economic reasons. They, on the one hand, had taken the position that Israel and, to a lesser extent, the UN and the U.S., had created the problem and were responsible for its solution. The Arab states felt that this should be through repatriation, in accordance with the General Assembly resolution of December 11, 1948. The Israelis, on the other hand, were reluctant to repatriate any large number of refugees because they needed land on which to settle Jewish immigrants. The Israelis contended that the problem was created by the invasion of the Arab states, who should solve it by resettlement.

I advised the Secretary that agreement by Israel to repatriate at least a token 200,000 refugees was necessary for any satisfactory solution of the problem. This was needed to persuade the Arab states to accept refugees. There had up to that time been no appreciable absorption of refugees into the economies of the Arab states, nor could there be without increased unemployment, lower living standards, and deterioration of political stability.

The present number of refugees could not be supported by the Arab governments, or by voluntary relief organizations either in or outside the Arab states. The refugees should whenever possible be on a work rather than a relief basis, even though the initial cost per refugee would be greater. This would help check the serious deterioration in morale among the refugees, assist resettlement, improve the local economy, and reduce the need for outside assistance. Absorption of the refugees could only be achieved through increased productivity of arable land, development of new industry, improvement in transportation, etc. Apart from political considerations, Syria, Iraq, and Jordan offered significant possibilities for resettlement, while Lebanon offered much less. Egypt and Saudi Arabia could take only token quotas.

Overall responsibility for the refugee problem should, I urged, be placed squarely on Israel and the Arab states. All possible outside assistance should be utilized under the auspices of the UN. In order to secure the cooperation of the Arab states, any solution should be formulated within the broader framework of the interests of the countries concerned. Since the development projects required for solution of the refugee problem would probably absorb most of the external financing available for the Middle East during the next few years, the questions of economic development and the solution of the refugee problem were indivisible.

I proposed to the Secretary a plan which, in addition to certain actions of a holding nature, involved the creation of an Economic Survey Mission to be set up under the authority of the PCC as soon as political conditions permitted. The mission would, in cooperation with the states concerned and others interested, examine the refugee situation using existing surveys and recommend measures to overcome economic dislocations created by the recent hostilities; provide necessary assistance for refugees and for their reintegration into the area on a self-sustaining basis; and foster development projects required to achieve this, while increasing the economic potential of the countries concerned.

At an appropriate stage in the work of the Economic Survey Mission, a more permanent refugee agency would be created to carry out the approved program. The agency would, whenever possible, utilize the states concerned, other UN members, and international and private organizations. It would coordinate and facilitate technical and financial assistance, and exercise general supervision.

The most important recommendation in my report was obviously that for the Economic Survey Mission. I proposed that it be headed by a triumvirate consisting of a British, an American, and a Turkish representative. When I was asked about rumors in the Middle East of a McGhee Plan, I always replied that the McGhee Plan was to get Clapp to make the Clapp Plan.[16] From the beginning, Gordon Clapp, head of the Tennessee Valley Authority, who then widely symbolized the conservation and proper use of water, was foremost in my mind as U.S. representative on the survey group I hoped to form. Secretary Acheson and the President agreed and Clapp was asked to come to Washington. He spent the evening before his meeting with the President at my farm and we went over the whole project. After Clapp had accepted the President's offer I asked him when he would like to leave for the Middle East to join his Turkish and British colleagues. It was characteristic of Clapp that he merely responded, "I am ready to go now." No packing or leavetaking. "Now."

The Economic Survey Mission made its first Interim Report to the PCC on November 16, 1949. The report emphasized the seriousness of the refugee situation and the continuing stalemate between Israel and the Arab states it created. It argued that relief provided by the UN should be phased out and responsibility left to the countries of the area to provide work as soon as that could be financed. The report recommended that a new agency be set up to direct programs of relief and public works. During the Istanbul Chiefs of Mission conference held in March 1950, the Interim Report was considered, with Clapp present, and strongly endorsed.[17]

On May 9, Secretary Acheson directed to President Truman a memorandum I had prepared estimating expenditures to repatriate and resettle 700,000 Arab refugees on a self-sustaining basis to be $250–$275 million over three years.[18] The U.S. share was set at $40–$50 million a year, not to exceed 50 percent of the total, after taking into account all sources, which included only $15–$50 million from the International Bank for Reconstruction and Development (IBRD) and the Ex-Im bank. Responsibility would remain with Israel and the Arab states, with outside aid under UN auspices.

On May 23, I accompanied Assistant Secretary Ernest A. Gross to a meeting with Senators Arthur H. Vandenberg and Tom Connally on the refugee problem.[19] Their reaction was not enthusiastic. Vandenberg, in particular, questioned the validity of the program, and both he and Connally asked how we could underwrite a situation brought about by the taking of houses and land from the Arabs by the Israelis. Gross and I explained that we had no new program to propose to Congress at that time. The meeting highlighted the importance of an appropriate Israeli contribution if we were to be successful.

The final report of the Survey Mission was made on December 28, 1949.[20] It did not deal directly with refugees but noted that the obstacles to economic development were similar to those hampering rehabilitation of the refugees. The two, the Mission felt, were inseparable. It said:

> There is no substitute for the application of work and local enterprise to each country's own resources. Help to those who have the will

to help themselves should be the primary policy guiding and restraining the desire of the more developed areas of the world to help the less developed lands.

In accordance with this principle the Mission, abandoning its original hopes for large land and water development projects as being premature, recommended limited pilot demonstrations in Jordan, the West Bank, Lebanon, and Syria, which could be undertaken promptly. These would employ labor, lead to settlement of families, provide experience in planning and technical teamwork, and could be completed in a few years as a basis for larger projects. The UN Relief and Works Agency for Palestine was established on December 8. Under it, work relief was to be shifted to the local governments and merged with the pilot development projects as soon as possible.

President Truman signed into law on June 5, 1950, a bill authorizing $27.45 million for aid to Palestine refugees. The President said, in part: "I am especially glad that the Congress had taken action with respect to the problem of the Arab refugees from Palestine. The program authorized in this bill carries out the recommendations of the United Nations Economic Survey Mission for the Near East, headed by Mr. Gordon Clapp. This program had been drawn up in the light of the serious problems facing the Palestine refugees, and with the economic potential of the Near East in mind." The organization to deal with the refugee problem was now financed and in place. Let us see how it carried out its mission.

The United Nations Relief and Welfare Administration (UNRWA) has over the years provided relief in the form of direct sustenance to the refugees, who now number over a million and a half, double the original number. Although the oil prosperity of a number of the Arab countries, particularly Saudi Arabia, has offered job opportunities for the skilled, the UN programs calculated to change the status of the remaining refugees from relief to work have been limited by resources. Efforts to create work opportunities through large-scale irrigation projects, as originally hoped by Clapp and promoted enthusiastically for many years by Eric Johnston, former head of the U.S motion-picture industry, and others, have not materialized. Efforts made by Joseph E. Johnson, distinguished head of the Carnegie Endowment for International Peace whom I persuaded to try to resolve the refugee problem through political negotiations, all failed after a valiant try.

As for the present state of the refugees, Palestinian representatives claim that there are now approximately 4.4 million Palestinians resident in Israel, Israeli-controlled territories, and neighboring Arab countries.[21] Their estimates show that 530,000 of these are Arabs living in Israel and holding Israeli citizenship. About 820,000 are on the West Bank and 475,000 in Gaza, many of the former and most of the latter being part of the 700,000 Arab Palestinian refugees created by the 1948 war and their offspring. Nearly 1.2 million Palestinians are located in Jordan, where they form the greater part of the population: 350,000 are in Lebanon; 275,000 in Kuwait; 220,000 in Syria; 125,000 in Saudi Arabia; more than 100,000 in the Gulf states; 50,000 in Egypt; 25,000 in Libya; and 20,000 in Iraq. (These figures are based on 1980 estimates.) Another 250,000 are scattered throughout the rest of the world, about half of them in the U.S.

Broadly defined, all Palestinians, except Israeli Arabs and most West Bank Arabs, are refugees, inasmuch as they do not live in areas that they or their families occupied in pre-1948 Palestine, or they call "home" somewhere other than the place where they presently live. Narrowly defined, about 1.8 million are refugees officially designated so by UNRWA, which is responsible for their maintenance. About one-third of the official refugees in Jordan, the West Bank, and Gaza, and a somewhat higher percentage in Lebanon, are quartered in UNRWA-supported camps. Although they may vary widely in size and conditions, these camps are characterized as being crowded, and the quality of housing is low, with sanitation and lighting below standard. About half of official refugees still receive some portion of their food through UNRWA, and, taken as a whole, their diet is adequate.

Most of those accounted as official refugees are poor villagers and small farmers and their descendants, who fled from land that was their sole source of income. Most urban and middle-class Palestinians, who amounted to an elite and were better educated and more skilled than comparable sectors in other Arab countries, have reportedly become integrated in their countries of refuge. Palestinians in Jordan, for instance, are Jordanian citizens, although they may still retain a Palestinian identity. As a group, the Palestinian diaspora has been highly successful and plays a decisive role in the professional and economic life of countries like Jordan and Kuwait.

The prospects for any drastic change in the status of the official refugee group cannot be considered hopeful. Efforts to get an agreement on the status of an autonomous Palestine state, which after the collapse of the four-power Geneva approach was pursued actively by

President Carter at Camp David in 1978, have not been successful. The possibility of any political agreement which could assist in alleviating the plight of the Arab refugees seems minimal.

The present situation represents a great human tragedy for the millions of homeless and stateless Palestinians involved. No matter how one interprets events leading to their loss of lands and homes, the individuals concerned were mostly farmers and peasants—not involved in political decisions but innocent victims of the 1948 war. The outside nations involved—including the U.S. who, because of our large-scale support for Israel and UNRWA, had the greatest opportunity—have done little to assist in any real solution to the problem in its present form, after thirty-four years of coping with it in its various phases.

5

Nehru's First Visit to Washington

October 11–13, 1949.

It is, I believe, appropriate now to describe our first official contacts
with the leaders of the new states of the Middle World. As Assistant
Secretary of State I managed Pandit Jawaharlal Nehru's first official
U.S. visit as Prime Minister of India in October 1949. The visit seems
to me worth reporting in this volume since it represented Nehru's
first encounter with our American leaders. Arrangements on the Indian side were made by the Indian ambassador, Nehru's sister,
Madame Vijaya Lakshmi Pandit. She had only recently arrived in
Washington, after the preparations had started.

The arrangements had been facilitated by the excellent background information provided by our Ambassador to India, Loy W.
Henderson. Loy Henderson, a man for whom I have always had
great respect, is often cited as the outstanding Foreign Service officer
of his time. A native of Arkansas, Loy graduated from Northwestern
University and later took his degree in law. After duty in the First
World War, he entered the Foreign Service at thirty-two and had
tours of duty in Moscow, European Affairs, and preceded me in Near
Eastern and African Affairs, before going on to important ambassadorships in India and Iran. I was happy to attend the dedication of a
conference room in the Department in Loy's honor. Loy's evaluation
of Nehru and his advice on how to handle him were in the extensive
briefing papers our bureau prepared for Secretary Acheson and President Truman. Nehru had acquired an admiration for upper-class
English culture, manners, and society from his years at Harrow
School and Cambridge University and from his contacts with the
British colonial administration as a member of a leading Indian family. This had apparently resulted in his tendency to deprecate most
things American as being inferior to British standards.

Nehru came to America with an apparent chip on his shoulder toward American high officials, who he appeared to believe could not possibly understand someone with his background. He appeared determined to appeal to the American people over the heads of their government. Needless to say, he did not accomplish this, but only succeeded in making himself so unpopular with Americans generally that it would later prove difficult to muster support for helping to meet India's urgent need for wheat. Nehru and Truman didn't hit it off at all. Rumor has it that, in his first informal meeting with the President, he was offended by Truman's extended discussion of the merits of bourbon whiskey with Vice President Alben Barkley of Kentucky, who was one of the invited guests.

In Nehru's official meeting with the President and Secretary Acheson on October 13, Indian Foreign Minister Sir Girja Bajpai was the only other participant.[1] Secretary Acheson's memorandum of the conversation at that meeting is as follows:

> The President received Prime Minister Nehru at 4:30 this afternoon. Sir Girja Bajpai and the Secretary of State were present. The interview lasted three quarters of an hour.
>
> The President hoped that the Prime Minister was enjoying his visit, expressed his desire that he should have a real opportunity to see and know the people throughout the country, and assured him that he would have a warm and enthusiastic welcome. The Prime Minister spoke feelingly of the impression which the visit was making upon him.
>
> The President referred to his deep concern for the welfare of the Indian people and of the people throughout Asia who were facing problems of the greatest magnitude. He spoke of the difficult transition being made in Indonesia, throughout Southeast Asia, and in India, and expressed the earnest hope that this transformation could be made peacefully and speedily.
>
> The Prime Minister noted that a great change had come over all the Asian peoples. They no longer accepted poverty and misery with resignation and believed that an organized effort was capable of improving their situation. All of this great change was being expressed politically through the growing nationalism in Asia. It was this nationalism which had completely outmoded the colonial status. Wherever that obstacle was removed, progress was possible although other difficulties still existed. The President observed that we in this country had been through the same experience. We had found that the solution of

the colonial problem was not the end. It had taken a great civil war to teach us that we must live peacefully together and it had taken involvement in two world wars to bring home to us that we could not be independent of peoples beyond our shores. He devoutly trusted that the people of India would not have to repeat our experience.

The Prime Minister agreed and asserted his determination that the problems which confronted India must be solved without conflict. He stated that perhaps the most pressing of the Indian problems had to do with the relation of people to the land. He said that over the past few decades both the total number and the percentage of people living on the land and living by agriculture had increased, and that it was necessary to reverse this trend to increase industrialization and to increase the productivity of agriculture. He thought that the critical time was in the next few years, and he mentioned he had spoken to the Secretary of State last evening about the Indian desire to acquire a stockpile of approximately one million tons of wheat. The importance of this was both to reassure the people that the food supply was secure and also to bring about a reduction in the price of wheat which had a controlling influence on all other prices in India.

The President observed that twenty years ago half of our population lived by agriculture whereas now only twenty-nine percent did so. However, we had increased both the production rate and the total agricultural production in excess of the present purchasing power in the world. He mentioned that if the peoples of India and China could purchase an amount of cotton equal to one ounce per person there would be an actual shortage of cotton. He said that we would be glad to cooperate with India in our mutual interest in the matter referred to by the Prime Minister.

The President referred to the Kashmir situation as one of the problems which he hoped fell within the Prime Minister's determination to solve without conflict. The Prime Minister assured the President that this was so. He reviewed the circumstances which led to his belief that an important and perhaps basic element in the Kashmir situation was to solve this problem on other than an adherence to one nation or another on a religious basis. He thought that determination on a religious basis would have a deeply unsettling effect upon the Moslems living in India and upon the Hindus living in Pakistan. He discussed the Indian conception of the secular state which the President said was thoroughly in accord with American institutions and ideas. The President again stated that his only concern was to be of assistance in the common aim of maintaining the peace and obtaining a just settlement.

The conversation then turned to the situation in China. The Prime Minister expressed his view that the basic situation in China was that the agrarian revolution, which had begun many years ago but had been intensified in 1911, had been so mishandled by the Kuomintang that power had fallen by default in the hands of the Communists. He thought that they were not desired in China but were accepted in the absence of any other apparent force interested in dealing with the problem. He thought that Communism was alien to the Chinese mind and that foreign domination would be deeply resented. He believed that the course of events would restore Chinese nationalism as a governing force and would weaken the subservience to Moscow.

In regard to recognition, he thought that India's proximity to China put India in a somewhat different position from that of other countries and indicated a leaning toward early recognition. The President hoped that this was a matter in regard to which the non-Communist countries could consult and if possible concert their action. The Prime Minister agreed that there should certainly be consultation.

After Secretary Acheson's elegant dinner for Nehru at Anderson House on October 12, arrangements had been made for the Secretary to receive Nehru privately in his house in Georgetown. The following is taken from Acheson's account of the evening as given in *Present at the Creation*.[2] It is so important, I believe, in revealing Nehru's philosophy, that I believe it is worth quoting Acheson's own inimitable prose.

I had hoped that, uninhibited by a cloud of witnesses, we might establish a personal relationship. But he would not relax. He talked to me, as Queen Victoria said of Mr. Gladstone, as though I were a public meeting. Beginning with his desire to establish a stockpile of a million tons of wheat, he told me of his plan to reduce the price of wheat in relation to other prices in India. He hoped for help from us in selling them wheat at less than world prices. We were already at work on the problem, which I told him would require legislation, and hoped to have favorable action shortly.

Pandit Nehru also found the French experiment in Indochina with Bao Dai hopeless and doomed to failure as the "Emperor" lacked the character, ability, and prestige necessary to succeed and was not given adequate scope by the French. I was inclined to agree but expressed doubt about any visible alternative. Nehru saw it in the nationalist movement, although he was convinced that Ho Chi Minh was a Communist. However, to believe that the Communists would use a popular-

front government to liquidate their opponents was, he thought, to mis-
apply Eastern European experience to Asian countries. In India and
Burma, Communists had begun as the left wing of the nationalist
movement, then attempted to take over the movement and failed.
This, he hoped, would be repeated in Indochina. To me this was a
clearly specious idea, since, as the experience of both France and Italy
showed, the attempt to take over would be inevitable and the outcome
would depend on the strength of the other side. With the leadership of
the nationalist movement already in Ho's hands, the outcome in Indochina would seem pretty clear.

Thus far Nehru had kept the talk on the failings of the Dutch and
French. I wanted, as innocently as possible, to get him to talk about
one of his own. First of all, however, he went off on recognition of the
Communist regime in China, where his views were of some interest
because they obviously stimulated Bevin's [Ernest Bevin, British Foreign Secretary]. Bevin was not likely to let India take the lead in setting
a recognition policy for the Commonwealth. Nehru's views, which he
also expressed the next day in his meeting with the President, were
that there was now no alternative to the Communists in China, since
the Kuomintang had completely failed to handle the agricultural revolution. But communism as a doctrine was alien to the Chinese mind,
and the foreign domination inherent in Moscow's role among Communist states would be deeply resented in China. India's proximity to
China "indicated a leaning toward early recognition." The President
hoped, as I had, that countries deeply concerned in Asian affairs would
consult before recognizing. Although the Prime Minister agreed, I felt
that we had had our consultation.

When, finally, I urged Pandit Nehru to help me by a frank discussion of a practicable solution of the trouble over Kashmir, I got a
curious combination of a public speech and flashes of anger and deep
dislike of his opponents. The first part of it was a legalistic exposition
that the first hostile act, and hence the aggression, was Pakistan's.
From this it followed that India could not, and the United Nations
should not, proceed with the merits of the problem until the aggression
had been purged by the complete withdrawal of all Pakistani and
tribesmen from Kashmir. This was interspersed with bitter denuncia-
tion of Pakistan deception and intrigue. Both Nehru's ideas of proce-
dure, which seemed to preclude negotiation, and his notions on the
dispute itself made any possibility of settlement dim indeed. A profound ideological issue, he said, was presented. Pakistan conceived of
the foundation of its state as religious and claimed Kashmir because its

inhabitants were largely Moslems. Such ideas, Nehru insisted, struck at the very basis of stability in the Indian subcontinent. In India the state was wholly secular. Religion was neither a qualification nor disqualification for citizenship; it was irrelevant. There were some thirty-five million Moslems in India, many in high office. To accept a religious basis for the adherence of provinces to either state would be profoundly unsettling everywhere, and a plebiscite campaign on such a basis would be most inflammatory and disastrous.

By this time, having talked from ten-thirty to past one o'clock in the morning after a strenuous day, my guest had clearly earned a rest. For my part, I was becoming a bit confused. We therefore adjourned this interesting talk. It made a deep impression on me. I was convinced that Nehru and I were not destined to have a pleasant personal relationship. He was so important to India and India's survival so important to all of us, that if he did not exist—as Voltaire said of God—he would have to be invented. Nevertheless, he was one of the most difficult men with whom I have ever had to deal.

In her memoirs Madame Pandit refers to the difficulties of the visit and the disappointing aspects of it.[3] She had, she said, after her arrival as ambassador, found Acheson preoccupied with the Cold War. Everything was to him, she thought, either black or white and the arch enemy was Communism. Nehru's nonalignment was to Acheson a peculiar concept. She considered Acheson's knowledge of Asia and India limited, because of disinterest. She knew the concentration on Communism would annoy Nehru during his visit and tried to steer him to more congenial people whom he would like.

According to Madame Pandit, Nehru felt warmth in the reception accorded him by many but was so offended at the emphasis on the wealth of the various guests during a luncheon tendered by bankers, that he did not seek their aid. He was also critical of the lavishness of a banquet given at the Greenbrier by Col. Lewis Johnson, who had met Nehru during an early mission to India. She said that Nehru's reactions to these events were not typically Indian, but Nehru's. They would seem an inappropriate response to hospitality extended to do him honor and help India. Madame Pandit considered the official talks, which were left to Sir Girja, were not important, except for providing Nehru an opportunity to explain India's stand in the UN, which often sided with the Soviets and was generally unpopular in the U.S.

Madame Pandit said that her favorites in Washington were Wal-

ter Lippman, Justice Felix Frankfurter and later the new senator
from Minnesota, Hubert Humphrey. Soon after his arrival the brash
young senator, whom I later came to admire very much, asked me to
call on him. "McGhee," he said, "I find that people get along on the
Hill by specializing. I want to specialize on India. You arrange for me
to get invited to the Embassy, maybe a trip to India. I can help you
up here when matters arise affecting India. I want to be for India
what (Congressman) Walter Judd is for China."

I held out my hand and said, "Senator, you just made a deal."
The arrangement, which was a sincere expression on his part as a
genuine friend of India, proved very helpful to Madame Pandit and
to India.

I found Madame Pandit an attractive, warm person. When she
arrived in Washington as ambassador, she seemed to have assumed,
as Nehru's sister and because of India's importance, that she would
deal only with President Truman. Unfortunately for her, it didn't
work out that way. After her initial White House call, she did see
Secretary Acheson occasionally, but sought no contacts with me or
our Bureau. At a reception I expressed regret that the President had
been unable to see her, and invited her to come in and chat with me
about matters coming up in the next session of the UN General Assembly. She called and we had an hour's friendly talk which I considered most helpful. Later she came in often and we developed a good
relationship. One of the most pleasant official duties I can recall was
to receive from Madame Pandit, with a formal tongue-in-cheek
speech, the gift of a baby elephant presented by India to our National
Zoo. Perhaps because I knew her better, I was disappointed that it
was not she who was chosen by Nehru as his successor. She would, I
believe, have been much more open in her dealings with us and the
West. Indira Gandhi has proven to be too much like her father.

Later I will give accounts of my two visits to India as assistant
secretary, both of which involved long and unsatisfactory talks with
Prime Minister Nehru. It is a sad fact of history that there has not yet
been a negotiated conclusion of the Kashmir dispute which dominated the discussions during Nehru's 1949 visit. India still retains military control over this lovely, unhappy vale.

6

British-American Middle East Relations

Washington, D.C., November 14–17, 1949.

Soon after assuming my responsibilities as Assistant Secretary of State, I had sought a meeting with my opposite number in the British Foreign Office, Michael Wright, British Superintending Under Secretary of State for Foreign Affairs, to discuss the problems of the Middle East and to seek to develop a common policy. Although I was no doubt influenced by my respect for the British, I fully understood that the Middle East up to this point had largely been a British show. It was a critical area in the developing Cold War. We were heavily engaged in Western Europe, Greece, Turkey, and elsewhere. We wanted the British to hang on in the Middle East as long as possible. We didn't want to have to replace them. We hoped to use whatever influence we had to help bolster them, even while keeping the option open of relieving them, as in Greece, if it became necessary.

In June of 1949, British Foreign Secretary Ernest Bevin had asked Acheson if the U.S. thought it would be useful for Wright to come to Washington to discuss the Middle Eastern question.[1] The reply was positive, and on October 11 I suggested that Wright be invited to Washington prior to a meeting of the American Chiefs of Mission in Arab countries and Israel proposed for November 22. Important developments were taking place. There had been no U.S.-U.K. talks on the Middle East since November 1947.

I had met Michael (later Sir Michael) Wright during my several visits to London as coordinator for aid to Greece and Turkey and special representative for the Secretary of State on the Arab refugee problem. I had found him not only knowledgeable and articulate as a Foreign Office representative but friendly and cooperative, with an ever-ready wit and great charm. Over the years we developed a friendship which I valued highly: he often visited me on my farm in Middleburg, and I saw him when I was in London.

On October 24, I wrote Wright a letter outlining my thoughts for the future.[2] I suggested that it would be helpful to both our governments if we could meet again to discuss matters of common interest in the Middle Eastern area, particularly in the political and economic fields. Although I had prepared no precise agenda, I suggested we might discuss the activities of the Economic Survey Mission (the Clapp Mission on the Arab refugee problem), whose preliminary report would be available; the U.K.'s longer-range development proposals for the Middle East; and such political questions as the Syrian-Iraqi union movement, the status of the Arab League, and the Italian colonies question. At that point we preferred not to deal with military or strategic problems as such, except as they might bear on other topics.

We met in Washington on November 14, 1949, with a large group of State Department and Foreign Office officials; I was mainly supported by my valued deputy, Raymond Hare.[3] In our opening meeting we stuck to general remarks. In evaluating Anglo-American relations, I said that it was obvious that both countries sought stability in the Middle East and in the attitude of its leaders toward the West. The U.S. had no desire to compete with or to hinder the U.K. in carrying out its policy in the Middle East. We were limited by our traditional policy of noninterference in the affairs of other nations and the difficulty of making ad hoc decisions in the absence of a general policy.

Wright agreed in general but stressed that the U.K. viewed the Middle East as a key to the overall struggle between the West and the Soviet Union. If Western influence were to be removed from the Middle East, either voluntarily or by force, Communism would certainly fill the vacuum left. Communist control would bring alarming results affecting the U.K.'s relationship with Asia; it would also prejudice the future of Europe and pave the way for Communist domination in Africa. The triumph of Soviet ideology in the Middle East and Africa would certainly secure a tremendous strategic prize for the U.S.S.R., and the loss of the Middle East to Communism would have a devastating economic effect on the U.K. Postwar recovery would be prejudiced and, deprived of Middle East oil and to a lesser extent cotton, the U.K. economy would be irretrievably damaged. It was to our common advantage that the U.S. should concern itself increasingly with this problem. Wright pointed out that Britain had no desire to persuade us in this matter; it was entirely our decision, but the U.K. considered our presence in the Middle East to be to the common advantage.

I replied that the importance of the Middle East to us was determined to a considerable extent by its importance to the U.K. We had no positions in Africa and Asia comparable to those held by the British, whose defense depended on the Middle East. We were not so dependent as the U.K. on Middle Eastern oil. Nevertheless, our interests in the area were great, and it was important to us because of its strategic position and control of air routes. The pervading problem from the American side was how far we should go in accepting new responsibilities and playing a more positive role in the area.

It was not sufficient, I continued, just to ward off Communism in the Middle East; it was also necessary to assist the states there in improving living standards and social and political institutions and to help them acquire self-respect and a sense of their proper place among the nations of the world. While the U.S. had found it generally advantageous to back nationalism against Communism, nationalism was not necessarily friendly to British and American interests. I pointed out that we should help put the Middle East countries on their own feet, in hopes this would induce them to cooperate with the West. The real question, then, was how far we could go in achieving these objectives. As European colonial interests declined in the Middle East, our encouragement of nationalism posed less of a problem for our relations with the British and the other European powers involved. This did not, however, in all cases—India, for example—result in improved relations between the Middle East and South Asia and the West. In the case of Pakistan and Iran, initial favorable reactions had turned sour because of unexpected events.

Wright agreed that support of nationalism could be used effectively against the spread of Communism. But nationalism and Communism could not be fought together. It should be our objective to convert the nationalism of the Middle East countries into a friendly force. France, Belgium, and the Netherlands did not yet wholly share this view.

In the same meeting, we discussed a Palestine settlement. I said that it was U.S. policy to keep the solution of the Palestine question within the guidelines of the UN. We had decided that it was neither desirable nor possible for us to propose any overall solution. The U.S., therefore, supported the continuation of the Palestine Conciliation Commission under the UN. In my view there was no quick solution;

our delegate to the PCC would, however, urge the commission to seek a solution in every way possible, including encouragement of direct talks. Even so, if the U.S. was to take a positive role in the economic development of the Middle East, we must be associated with the solution of the Palestine problem, otherwise congressional support would not be possible. No other policy or legislative basis for U.S. participation in the development of the Middle East existed at that point, except for the Point Four Program, which was limited to technical assistance.

Wright then raised the question of the incorporation of the West Bank into Jordan. The British Foreign Office felt that the present state of uncertainty was bound to introduce an unnecessary element of instability into the area. The incorporation, besides removing a cause of instability, would be a material factor in solving the refugee problem. The Arab League appeared to be reconciled to the step, and it seemed unlikely that the Israelis would object.

I replied that when Bevin had raised this question recently with Acheson, we considered the moment not ripe for incorporation. This might lead to a similar declaration by Israel about her occupied territory, which would be resisted by the other Arab states. New factors had now been introduced. Israel had asserted title to the territory she occupied and had stated there would be no cession of it. We had accepted the principle of incorporation of the West Bank with Jordan and were concerned only with the question of timing.

Wright suggested that sometime after the UN General Assembly meeting Jordan should, by proclamation, incorporate the area. The U.K would raise no objection, and he hoped we would follow suit. The Anglo-Jordanian Treaty would automatically be extended to the enlarged area. He agreed with Raymond Hare that the move would solve the area's principal territorial problem and would be a marked step forward. I promised to discuss the point with our representatives at the coming meeting in Istanbul.

The discussion then turned to the report of the Economic Survey Mission. In particular we focused on the proposal of the mission to set up a new agency for the administration of relief and relief works projects. The Foreign Office presented a series of criteria for carrying out the mission. The transition from relief to relief works programs was to be made as soon as possible. Any new agency set up should not be administered or controlled by the Secretariat of the UN. The new agency, Wright said, should not include Slav or other undesirable membership and should, if possible, be composed of British, American, French, and Turkish representatives (i.e., the same membership as the Economic Survey Mission). Also the local governments should be made responsible as far as possible for the execution of the program. The new agency should not, at that stage, be made responsible for all development in the Middle East area as a whole. The proposed arrangement should not make any government directly responsible for the handling of relief funds raised under UN auspices; and finally, the U.K.'s contribution could be in nonconvertible sterling only.

We agreed with these guidelines and I emphasized our anxiety to avoid national responsibility for the distribution of funds derived from international sources. At that meeting we also discussed Arab unity. Wright expressed the British view that one of the reasons for Arab bitterness against Western countries was the territorial settlement after World War I, which they felt created artificial divisions. There existed among the Arabs a deep-seated desire for some sort of union, but so far it found expression only in the Arab League, whose record was on the whole unsuccessful. The policy of the league had been extremely nationalistic and anti-Western, though it was no longer so strongly biased.

Wright felt that if the West blocked every move toward Arab unity, the Arabs would revert to their earlier extremism. Certainly there was a strong desire for change in the Middle East. In Arab minds, social, economic, and political reform or change were linked. Thus, any attempt to block political change was automatically interpreted as an attempt to block economic and social change. Like us, the U.K. was opposed to change by force but could not oppose change brought about in a peaceful and constitutional manner. Unlike the French, though, the U.S. and the U.K. had no desire to retain the status quo at all costs.

It was agreed by both sides that much of the instability in the Middle East arose from a feeling of national insecurity in the countries concerned. We discussed generally how far this could be relieved, and several key points emerged. The Egyptian proposal for a general Arab collective security pact was in too elementary a stage to judge. The Anglo-American attitude toward it should for the time being be noncommittal. A Middle East pact based on the NATO model was excluded by present U.S. policy and, in any case, would not by itself meet U.S. strategic requirements. Bilateral treaties between the U.K. and Arab countries were still necessary because of their stabilizing effect. In light of the Palestine situation, we agreed that we must maintain a balance in the favors we extended to the Arab states and Israel. The U.S. military assistance program could not now be extended to any Middle East countries except Iran and Turkey, although we might later add Saudi Arabia.

Wright said that U.S. support of the existing Anglo-Arab treaties would help the U.K. and would increase Middle East stability. We agreed to consider the extension of U.K. treaty obligations to additional Arab countries. We thought the maintenance of the U.S. air base at Dhahran was a stabilizing influence. A revision of Arab League activities toward economic development should be encouraged. And both countries agreed not to obstruct political changes in the Middle East brought about in a peaceful and constitutional way.

The discussions also included the disposition of the former Italian colonies, long-term economic development of the Middle East and Ethiopia, and various boundary and other technical questions in the Persian Gulf. A feeling of cooperation, based on the assumption that we were dealing with common problems and had no desire to take advantage of one another, pervaded our meetings. Happily this feeling continued for the remaining two years that I served as Assistant Secretary, including the period after Sir James Bowker succeeded Michael Wright. Bowker also became a good friend. Our relationship during this period was strained only by the Anglo-Iranian oil crisis and the Anglo-Egyptian Treaty.

It is interesting to review the subsequent course of U.S.-U.K. relation in the Middle East, which have gone through various vicissitudes. The defense requirements of Britain and the U.S. in the area had in 1950 appeared to be very similar, even though there were occasional divergencies in political and economic interests. Although cooperation between the two countries had been close, there were occasional suspicions that U.S. policy was based on different priorities not always consistent with the British position. This view was accentuated after the Conservatives returned to power in Britain in 1951.

In 1955 the British joined Iraq and Turkey in the Baghdad Pact. Lieutenant Colonel Gamal Abdel Nasser, who had become Premier in 1954, spared no effort in rallying Arab support against the pact, directing his propaganda campaign against Britain. The U.S. refrained from providing Egypt with military assistance because Nasser refused to accept military advisory personnel, and we were reluctant to sell arms in exchange for cotton as suggested by Cairo. In 1955, Nasser turned to the Soviet bloc for the military equipment he had originally sought from the U.S. Britain and the U.S. attempted to limit Soviet influence in Egypt by offering to finance jointly—with the World Bank—Nasser's twentieth-century pyramid, the Aswan Dam. In July 1956, however, the two Western powers called off the loan abruptly, according to British Foreign Secretary Anthony Eden at the insistence of Secretary Foster Dulles, who turned against Nasser because of Nasser's increasingly close association with the Soviets and the Communist bloc.

The cancellation of the loan set in motion the chain of events that led to the Suez crisis of October-November 1956, and ended finally Britain's special involvement in the Middle East. When Nasser threatened to nationalize the Suez Canal in retaliation for the Anglo-American action, Eden and Dulles collaborated in calling a conference of maritime countries whose vessels were canal users. In September, Nasser rejected recommendations made for international control of the waterway. Eden and French Premier Guy Mollet determined that the situation required armed intervention; an Anglo-French expeditionary force was mounted and air attacks were launched from Cyprus against targets in Egypt.

But the decisive phase of the intervention, a landing at Suez, was not delivered until the first week of November in collusion with Israel, whose forces had entered the Sinai and were advancing toward the canal. Although the Suez Canal Zone was occupied, the operation failed to achieve the political goal—an end to Nasser's regime and influence in the Arab world. The Anglo-French action was roundly condemned by world opinion. The U.S., who had advised the British of their strong opposition to the action, voted with an overwhelming majority in the UN calling for a withdrawal of the expeditionary force.

Jordan denounced the British action against another Arab state and canceled its defense treaty with Britain. In July 1958, an army coup, led by nationalist officers, overthrew the Iraqi monarchy and replaced it by a government with a policy of nonalignment. Events in Iraq seemed to trigger a chain reaction in the region. British troops were dispatched to Jordan to bolster King Hussein, whose regime was threatened by pro-Nasser elements. Although Britain continued through the 1960s to maintain garrisons in the Persian Gulf area and in Aden (South Yemen), by the end of the 1950s Britain had clearly surrendered the political initiative in the Middle East. Sudan became an independent nation on January 1, 1956. The last British troops were removed from the Suez Canal Zone on schedule in June of the same year.

From all outward appearances, the special relationship between the two English-speaking powers was as evident during the years Prime Minister Harold Macmillan was in office as it had been at any time since the war. Much of that was due to the personality of the Prime Minister himself and his close ties with Presidents Eisenhower and Kennedy. The general line of British foreign policy and the presumption of a special relationship with the U.S. continued under two Labour governments led by Harold Wilson, and under Edward Heath's interim Conservative government, in the 1960s and 1970s. Two departures, however, were the Labour party's abandonment of an "East of Suez" commitment and Britain's admission, in 1972, to the European Economic Community (or Common Market), after which British foreign policy was coordinated more closely with what represented a consensus of its Community partners.

7

The Shah's First Official Visit
to Washington

November 18–19, 1949. Visit to Teheran, December 4–6, 1949.

I will now describe the first official visit of the next Middle World head of state to arrive in Washington after I became Assistant Secretary, the Shah of Iran.

The unexpected collapse of the regime of the Shah in 1979 and his forced exile focused world interest on his rejection by the Iranian people. Why was it not anticipated? Could the U.S., as his principal supporter and ally, have done anything to avert it? Why was it critical to the U.S. to support the Shah as long as we did?

Iran, once called Persia, is a land of snow-capped mountains, green valleys, and barren deserts. Its population in the 1950s was just under 20 million. The first civilization in the area was that of the Elamite Kingdom in southeastern Persia starting around 2000 B.C. Iran was conquered by many races including the Medes and the Persians and by the Persian Achaemenid, Cyrus the Great, who in the sixth century B.C. extended his rule over all of Asia Minor and Egypt as well. This empire reached its peak under Darius, who in the fourth century B.C. ruled from Greece to India from his twin capitals of Persepolis and Susa.

Later, Persia was to be conquered by Alexander the Great in the fourth century B.C., and in the seventh century A.D. by the Arabs, who gave it the Shiite branch of Islam as its religion. After further subjugation by Turks, Mongols, and Afghans, parts of Iran during the nineteenth and early twentieth centuries came under the influence, and often the control, of both Russia and Britain. In the early 1900s a British company was given the oil concession for southern Iran.

Reza Shah Pahlavi was a military officer, who in 1921 became dissatisfied with a weak Iranian government, marched his troops to

Teheran, and took control. In 1925, he forced the abdication of Ahmed Shah. And, with the approval of the Majlis, the legislative body elected under the constitution, Reza Shah developed a program to modernize Iran and free it from foreign influence. He attacked the Imams (religious leaders) and confiscated property left as religious endowments. Considerable progress had already been made before the outbreak of World War II. Reza Shah announced his neutrality in the war, but when he refused to allow the use of the Iranian railways for supply to the Soviet Union in 1941, the Soviets and British occupied Iran and forced his abdication.

The postwar period witnessed Soviet withdrawal from Azerbaijan under U.S. pressure, denial of a Soviet oil concession in the north, and the emergence of a strong nationalist movement supported by the Communist Tudeh party directed against all foreign interference in Iran, particularly by the British.

The son of Reza Shah Pahlavi, Mohammad Shah Pahlavi, with whom we had enjoyed good relations since his accession to the throne on September 23, 1941, had never paid an official visit to the U.S. Educated in Switzerland, an avid sportsman particularly in skiing and flying, he appeared thoroughly Westernized. His future seemed bright. Although not prepossessing in appearance, he had an intensity and an air of self-importance that gave him a kingly aura. At thirty, after nine years of experience as ruler, he seemed promising as a monarch, with a reformist and modernist view, a liberal and an open mind. He seemed sincerely interested in educating his people and breaking up large estates to distribute land to the peasants.

Starting in January 1942, the Shah had sought large-scale military aid and an expansion of trade with the U.S. The Millspaugh Mission, whose purpose was to explore how we could aid Iran, had ended in failure in June 1944. But we had cooperated in furnishing military aid in the form of surplus equipment in 1947. Our military and police missions in Iran had done good work. However, Iran's Seven Year Plan of internal development, which had been headed by Max Thornburg, formerly of the State Department, had been too grandiose. After an assassination attempt in February 1949, the Shah attempted to ban the Communist Tudeh party and curb the power of the Majlis. His difficulties and frustrations, however, only increased. And his expectations of the U.S. had reached unrealistic proportions.

At the invitation of the President, the Shah made an official visit to the U.S. starting November 16, 1949. We wanted to expose him to our national leaders, find out what sort of man he was, and try to influence him along constructive lines. He arrived on President Truman's personal plane, the *Independence,* and stayed at Blair House. I was in charge of the arrangements for the visit and attended all meetings except that with the President. Iranian Ambassador Hussein Ala and I had seen to it that ample opportunity would be afforded the Shah for talks with the President and with Secretary Acheson. It was also planned that on the day of his arrival Deputy Under Secretary Rusk, Assistant Secretary Thorp, and I would accompany the Shah to a meeting with General Omar Bradley and the Joint Chiefs of Staff, of which Bradley was chairman.

In my briefing memorandum to Secretary Acheson of November 17, I advised him on the topics that would likely be raised.[1] The Shah would be preoccupied with his obsession of building up his country's military strength. Considering himself a military expert, he had gone into the question of Iran's requirements in great detail. The Shah would probably describe his strategic plans in the event of a Soviet invasion and his consequent need for an army larger and more elaborately equipped than was possible under both Iran's present budgetary position and our plans for military assistance.

We felt that the Shah should be listened to sympathetically but without any commitment being made. If he asked questions concerning the present status of military equipment to be furnished, he might be told the program was not sufficiently far advanced for the presentation of any detailed lists at this time. It could be pointed out that our military assistance to Iran was limited by the fact that for effective use military equipment must fit the military budget, and any increase in Iran's budget would have serious repercussions on its Seven Year Plan for economic development. Moreover, we must take into account our own security requirements and limitations on our resources.

I also conveyed to the Secretary the importance the Shah attached to his ambitious program of economic development. He would probably raise the question of economic assistance for Iran's Seven Year Program, requiring expenditures of about $650 million. The financing of this program, which involved agricultural, irrigation, highway, railway, industrial, public health, and educational projects, now depended primarily on oil royalties.

I warned that the Iranians might also ask the International Bank for Reconstruction and Development (World Bank) for loans up to $250 million to provide additional funds. The immediate goals of the program included raising standards of education and public health, improving agricultural methods and transportation facilities, and reforming the administration. Earlier that fall, in September 1949, in answer to a specific Iranian request for an economic grant of $147 million, the department had replied that no authority existed for a grant, and that it would be impossible to obtain such authority from Congress since Iran had a favorable foreign-exchange position.

I suggested to the Secretary that he might wish to describe to the Shah in general the part that our recently announced Point Four Program might play in assisting Iran in its Seven Year Plan. I reiterated the program's emphasis on technical rather than financial assistance and stressed the role that private capital must assume. The first step that Iran could take in preparing the way for its Point Four participation should be the negotiation of a Treaty of Friendship, Commerce and Navigation with the U.S., which would include suitable clauses on investment guarantees.

I also emphasized the desire of the Shah to formalize U.S. commitments to Iran, which did not then seem feasible. Ambassador Ala had suggested that, upon the departure of the Shah, a joint statement be issued reaffirming the principles of the Teheran Declaration on Iran, promising Iran further military and economic assistance, and extending the Truman Doctrine to include Iran. I advised the Secretary that if the Shah raised this point, it might be pointed out that our position regarding the maintenance of the independence and territorial integrity of Iran was well known, that we would consider a public reiteration of it in connection with his visit here, but that we could not make any commitments toward further financial, military, or other aid.

I told the Secretary that if the Shah suggested a regional Middle East defense pact, with or without a guarantee by the U.S., he might tell the Shah that our government was not in a position to give consideration to any other pacts until the ramifications of the North Atlantic Pact became clear. "It is important, however," I added, "that you avoid the impression that if Iran were attacked she would be left to her own resources."

The climax of the Shah's visit was, of course, his meeting with the President at the White House. The President had been shown my briefing memorandum and had discussed the issues that would be raised with the Secretary. The key point was to try to slow down the Shah in his military and economic demands. The Shah, as we were to discover, was not content to make progress slowly, but continued to press his demands with all who would listen.

Truman's meeting with the Shah took place on November 18, 1949. Also present were Ambassador Ala and the Secretary of State. Since I was not there, I have relied on the memorandum of conversation drafted for the Secretary by Lucius Battle of the Executive Secretariat of the State Department.[2]

The Shah opened by observing how much he admired the strong spirit of patriotism in the U.S.; his own country was also strongly patriotic. He described the long history of Iran, its ups and downs and the extent of the Persian Empire under Darius the Great. He then spoke of the long periods of foreign influence Iran had been subjected to and the current dangers from the Soviet Union. This led him into the main theme of his talk.

He proceeded to describe the situation as he saw it in the Middle East, alluding to Iran's vulnerability to the U.S.S.R. In any defense against the Soviet Union, Greece constituted the left flank, Turkey the center, and Iran the right flank. The Shah spoke of our support for countries willing to resist foreign domination, and the large sums which we had spent strengthening the left and center flanks in the Middle East. From a military point of view this effort would be largely wasted if the right flank remained so weak as to invite attack. The Shah acknowledged that our reply might be that Iran was not yet ready to absorb large quantities of military equipment. This might be true; however, it was necessary to make a start, and it should be done now.

President Truman assured the Shah that his ideas would receive the most respectful attention. This would be carefully discussed with his military advisers and with the Secretary of State. The President pointed out that he was necessarily operating under budgetary limitations. The Congress, which held the purse strings, had, after considerable debate and in the face of some opposition, passed a Military Assistance Bill, but one much smaller than the President would have wished.

The Shah then turned to the economic situation. He spoke of Iran's desire to develop its great natural resources, of his Seven Year Plan, and of the setback caused by the bad harvest in the past year. The income from oil royalties, which was to be used for the Seven Year Plan, must also pay for certain other current necessities. This left the military requirements and certain other economic needs unprovided for. He hoped some way could be found, either through the barter of strategic materials which the U.S. needed or through some form of lend-lease program, to procure current consumable items like wheat. He also mentioned new equipment for the railways. If the needs of the oil industry were subtracted, the capacity of the railroads for all other requirements was only seven hundred tons per day. This he wished to increase to sixty thousand tons per day.

Truman, in reply, made no commitment, but left the door open by promising that if Iranian representatives would present us with specific requests we would give them careful and sympathetic consideration within the limits of the authority provided by law.

This concluded the interview, which lasted a little over a half hour.

The Secretary called on the Shah at our official guest house, Prospect House, later on the same day—together with Assistant Secretary Willard Thorp; Jack Jernegan, director of the Office of Greek, Turkish and Iranian Affairs; and myself—in order to give the Shah an opportunity to discuss privately some of the major questions in which he was known to be especially interested.[3] During the course of the meeting, which lasted about an hour and twenty minutes, we touched on a number of subjects. The bulk of the conversation, however, addressed the Shah's desire to obtain both economic and military assistance quickly and in substantial quantities.

The Shah considered it vital that the military strength of his country be increased promptly to prevent its being overrun or subverted before economic improvement plans could have their effect. The next three or four years, he felt, were critical, and he wanted to develop the military strength of Iran to approximately one-half that of Turkey. This would mean an army of 150,000 plus 30,000 frontier guards. He did not consider that this was "shooting too high," since one-third of the number at any one time would consist of raw recruits of no use in combat and another 30,000 would be engaged in rear-echelon activities, leaving a maximum army of 70,000.

The Shah argued that such a force, equipped and trained by the U.S., was essential so that Iran, if threatened, could put up a fight for her independence. If Iran could resist an attack for two or three months it would be a great help to the Western powers in a general war. The Shah hoped very much that the U.S. could increase the amount of military assistance we planned to give his country.

Acheson agreed with His Majesty that some increase in Iranian military strength was probably desirable, but emphasized the fundamental necessity of giving priority to economic and social development. All nations in the free world face the same problem, Acheson explained. If we all attempted to build up our military establishments to the level of the Soviet Union, we would wreck our economies and be so weakened that we would collapse without even being subjected to military attack. The best way to prevent war, which was after all our real objective, was not by military preparations but by so developing our free economic and social structures that the Russians would be deterred from attacking.

The Secretary cited Nationalist China as an example of bad results from a wrong policy. At the close of World War II, Chiang Kai-shek had been on top of the world; he had large and well-equipped forces enormously superior to the military forces of the Chinese Communists. President Truman and General Marshall had strongly advised him to concentrate on improving the economic and social condition of the Chinese people, but he had chosen to attempt a purely military solution. The result was that the Chinese people had lost all confidence in the Nationalist government. Even in the military field, Chiang had been defeated because his soldiers, lacking confidence, would not fight. All the vast quantities of American military equipment poured into China had merely gone to arm the Chinese Communist armies as a result of the mass surrenders of the Nationalist forces. (It is interesting that our relations with the People's Republic of China have now developed to a point where we can consider arms assistance to them.)

Now, Acheson continued, it was Southeast Asia that faced Communist pressure. While the countries of that area would need some military equipment, we believed that our greatest effort there should be made in the field of economic progress so that the new national governments could gain the loyalty of their people. After all, our resources were limited and we had to utilize them in the manner that would be most effective.

The Shah observed that China's downfall was largely due to corruption, and that Turkey was putting large resources into its military program and still was able to maintain its internal stability. Some Iranians had called him a Communist because he wanted social reforms. He was opposed to the absentee-landlord system and to the exploitation of labor, but even if he took away all the wealth in the hands of the landlords and factory owners it still would not amount to very much in light of Iran's needs, and, he implied, would not compensate for the misfortunes that would result from military unpreparedness.

In view of the present-day discussion of the role of the Shah's reforms in the ultimate downfall of his regime, Secretary Acheson's response is interesting. The Secretary replied that he had not meant to suggest immediate sweeping social reforms of the sort mentioned and he agreed with the necessity for a certain degree of military preparedness. He emphasized the importance of striking a balance, and in answer to the Shah's specific request for increased military aid, he suggested that the Shah discuss this especially with General Bradley when he saw him later in the afternoon. We would see what adjustments, if any, could be made. Acheson's comments can be interpreted as a note of caution to the Shah against drastic social reforms, although he left it to the Shah to "strike a balance." His suggestions regarding military aid reflected the general U.S. view of skepticism over the Shah's grandiose plans (which we gave in to during the Nixon administration).

On the subject of economic development, the Shah emphasized the importance of the Seven Year Plan, which, he said, was fully appreciated by the people of Iran. In this field, too, he hoped for direct American aid. Could we not find some way to extend financial assistance on the pattern of the European Recovery Program? Could not the President make a public statement that he would request congressional authority for such a move with regard to Iran? The Secretary replied that this would be very difficult in light of our other commitments. Acheson, Thorp, and I all pointed out that Iran had a favorable balance of payments, which made it a good credit risk for loans from the World Bank. Congress would expect Iran to exhaust its credit at the bank before appealing for direct aid.

The Shah observed that Iran's dollar resources were not, after all, so great as people seemed to think. The oil royalties, which were the primary source of dollars, presently amounted to only £7 or £8 million yearly, around $20 million at the existing rate of exchange, and even if doubled by the new agreement with the oil company, would still not amount to an enormous sum. Iran had already been in touch with the World Bank, which had indicated its willingness to extend credit of some $35 million for certain projects, including a cement factory. The bank was planning to send a mission to Iran in December to study these particular projects. However, $35 million was a small amount in comparison with what was needed and the bank would have to take a broader view if it was really to be of help in the Seven Year Plan.

Toward the end of the conversation, the Shah explained that the

Iranian public expected a great deal in the way of American assistance to result from his visit to this country. He could not return empty-handed. Was there not something more that we could do, whether in the economic or military fields? Could we not issue a statement re-emphasizing our support for Iran and promising further assistance?

The Secretary replied that we could issue a communiqué, preferably in the form of a joint statement by the President and the Shah, reiterating the public statements of support for Iranian independence made previously. Acheson did not think, however, we could say anything new. In the economic field, we would examine carefully points which had been discussed in conversation and see what could be done in providing railroad equipment, bank credits, etc. With respect to direct aid outside of the Military Aid Program, we simply had no authority.

In conclusion, the Shah emphasized Iran's determination to make economic progress. Iran had always faced the Russian menace and had, figuratively, "fought Russia with her bare hands" to protect her independence. With or without American help, if anything happened in Iran her course of action would be the same. The meeting terminated on this note. The Shah appeared to understand that he had not made his case.

The Shah, along with Brigadier General Mohammed Mazhari, called on the Joint Chiefs of Staff at the Pentagon at the end of the same day.[4] Jernegan and I accompanied them. The Shah now had his chance and poured out the details of his strategic plans in the event of a full-fledged Soviet attack on Iran—particularly Iranian needs for tanks, tank destroyers, trucks, and small-arms ammunition, and for the training of Iranian military personnel in the U.S. The chiefs listened in silence, raising few questions. The situation became embarrassing.

General Bradley eventually replied that the Joint Chiefs would be glad to consider what military equipment could be made available to Iran under the Military Aid Program. It was obvious, however, that the chiefs did not consider the Shah's plans to constitute a basis for supplying military equipment. These were grandiose and unrealistic of achievement against an all-out Soviet attack, which appeared in any event unlikely. In the event of a general war, the Soviets would not attach a high priority to such a remote and difficult terrain. The same might be said for the Shah's economic plans, which were far ahead of Iranian capabilities.

Following the official meetings with the Shah, a behind-the-scene tussle went on as to the concrete results of the meetings and how they should be described in the joint communiqué which it had been agreed would be released after the Shah's departure. In a breakfast meeting with the Shah on November 19, Jack Jernegan, who had borne most of the burden of preparations for the visit, advised him that our differences were mainly a question of timing.[5] "We were not ready to go so far or so fast as His Majesty wished," Jernegan later reported. The Shah had not seemed critical of the U.S. attitude but had pressed for tangible results which could reassure the Iranian people. He told the Persian legend of Sohrab and Rustum. Rustum mortally wounded his son Sohrab without knowing who he was, and then sought medicine to save his life when it was too late.

The State Department, in its comment to the Department of Defense on Iranian military aid after the meetings, emphasized the importance of boosting the morale of the Shah, which would be a key factor in assuring Iranian resistance to Soviet pressures and Iranian willingness to fight a delaying action in event of war. Our dependence on the Shah became increasingly the key element in our policy toward Iran through the years, until his fall from power in 1979.

After much U.S. resistance, in which Deputy Under Secretary Dean Rusk took part (he refused to accept the principle that the Shah must have something tangible to take back with him, saying that it set a bad precedent),[6] the communiqué was released on November 30.[7] It reaffirmed the three-power declaration at Teheran December 1, 1943, in which the U.S. had "made clear its desire for the maintenance of the independence and integrity of Iran." This the U.S. "intended to continue," we said. The President expressed appreciation of the importance of the Iranian Seven Year Plan and offered support for justifiable loans from the World Bank and grants from Point Four funds, with Iran offering inducements to private investment. As part of its policy "to help free people everywhere in the maintenance of their freedom wherever the aid which it is able to provide can be effective," the communiqué stated, the U.S. is prepared to offer "certain military assistance" and would "bear in mind" Iran's future needs.

Since the final collapse of the Shah's regime can be attributed largely to excessive military and development expenditures after the large increase in Iran's oil income in 1973, we were probably right to hold him back in 1949. In any event we did not have the money. We

were not able to help the Shah obtain from the U.K. an increase in
Iranian oil income, obtain a loan from the World Bank, or find any
source of large-scale U.S. aid. The Mutual Security Act, with the first
funds for which Iran would be eligible, did not come until 1951. The
visit of the Shah, at the beginning of what seemed such a promising
regime, was from any viewpoint a failure. He did not get the assistance he wanted and we were not able to persuade him to lower his
military and development sights. He was bitterly disappointed.

In *Present at the Creation,* Dean Acheson refers to the Shah's
visit as being the result of the pressure of the NEA Bureau upon him
and his pressure, in turn, upon the President:[8] "This seemed a good
way to help the prestige of the young ruler at home and let him learn
at first hand the realities and limitation of American aid." Acheson
recalls, however, his intense dislike of summit meetings of this type,
which he felt those in regional bureaus never learned to understand
but continued to advocate. Usually the visitor insists on being given
something to make his trip a success, is disappointed in what is offered him, and goes home empty-handed. To this indictment I plead
guilty. In the Shah's case, Acheson pointed out that his program was
an ambitious one and that the Shah wanted American help for all of
it. Had we given the Shah large-scale aid, this would in turn only
have intensified Soviet propaganda and Tudeh party activity against
him.

Acheson deplored the failure of the Department to find a solution
to the problem of how to aid the Shah. He felt we were always too
little or too late, always finding excuses to let the British or the World
Bank do it, always pressing the Shah to scale down his economic
program and plans for his army. I have often wondered whether, if
we had been able to find a realistic basis of support in 1950, and used
it as a lever to influence the Shah constructively while he was more
malleable, the course of Iranian history might have been changed. I
don't know.

In any event, the future was not to hold any greater success even
after, at my recommendation, we moved Henry Grady, our ambassador most experienced in extending aid, to Iran. Both the Shah and
our embassy thought, as a result, that more money would be available
than actually was, and our relations with Iran steadily deteriorated.
On November 4, 1950, the Soviet-Iranian Trade Agreement was announced and cooperation with the U.S. came to a halt. When Prime
Minister Ali Razmara was shot by religious extremists on March 7,

1951, a whole era had come to an end and the Mossadeq era began.

I was to see the Shah on several occasions in the future. The next time was after the assassination of Razmara, when the Shah was dejected, unable to form a government, and cowering in his palace. I saw him again in 1974 when a business associate and I had an hour with him in his palace at Teheran. He was then at the peak of confidence, full of ambitious plans for the future. It is such a tragedy for Iran and the world that the reign of this promising young man, who came to Washington with such high hopes in 1949 and who could have achieved so much for his country, was to end in total collapse.

What went wrong? In retrospect we know that the Shah's aspirations for himself and his country were far too ambitious. He attempted to justify his insatiable appetite for military equipment by Iran's strategic situation as guardian of major oil reserves and the approaches to the Persian Gulf. However, he expected more than this from his military expenditures. They were also to him a source of prestige to strengthen his regime; a way to assure the loyalty of his army; and a means of catapulting Iran into being not just a Middle Eastern power, but, as he was to claim, an Indian Ocean and African power. To those unrealistic ends he sought the very latest in aircraft, tanks, and naval vessels.

The scope of the Shah's plans increased faster than Iran's income. This was true even after 1973, when it rose to $20 billion a year. With the blank check given the Shah by the Nixon administration, in my view a great mistake, he purchased billions of dollars worth of military equipment, most of it too sophisticated to be maintained and operated by the Iranians. The Shah's economic and military programs not only exceeded Iran's infrastructure and available trained manpower but helped the conservative Iranian religious hierarchy rally discontent against him.

The Iranian people, who had never been consulted about the Shah's plans, were not enthusiastic followers. No effort was made by the Shah to develop a political base or any participation in government by the middle class he had created. Instead of pressing for human rights, President Carter should have encouraged greater political participation by the Iranian people and a decrease in corruption. If this had been done, Iran's National Intelligence and Security Organization (SAVAK) in the form it ultimately took would not have been necessary. The Shah withdrew more and more into a shell, accepted little advice, and resorted increasingly to dictatorial and repressive measures based on his SAVAK intelligence apparatus. He engaged in and permitted wide-scale corruption by friends and family. In the end his whole faulty structure fell because it had no underlying support among his people. They had not been educated in Europe, which was the Shah's spiritual and intellectual home.

A little over two weeks after the Shah's departure from Washington, I made a get-acquainted visit to Teheran, which had been planned for some time. My wife, Cecilia, and I arrived in Teheran by Air Force plane from Baghdad on December 4, 1949. The plane, which was assigned to the embassy in Teheran, was called *The Magic Carpet*. The officers and crew were most enterprising. They had made very imaginative preparations for their passengers, offering a bewildering variety of dishes and delicacies, including twenty Dagwood-style sandwiches, ten kinds of hors d'oeuvres, and ten condiments. They put on a good show. We were met by U.S. Ambassador John Wiley and his wife, Irena, and other members of the embassy staff, as well as by Ali Gholi Ardalan, Assistant Secretary of the Ministry of Foreign Affairs.

We were taken to a picturesque old palace, originally occupied by a member of an earlier royal family, which served as the embassy residence. It had huge windows with dramatic views of the snow-capped mountains surrounding Teheran. There was an outdoor swimming pool, which could be used eight months a year. The embassy was part of a large walled compound, guarded by Marines, where all the embassy staff worked and lived. The residence itself was set in a large, beautifully-landscaped park through which ran a constant stream of water, man-made and locally called a *ganat*. These streams, which are conveyed by underground tunnels built by hand with frequent shafts reaching the surface, collect the water high on a mountainside and are sloped to carry it, as if in a large underground pipe, to the outskirts of the city. The digging and maintenance of these *ganats* is a hazardous undertaking.

Ambassador John Wiley was a man of striking appearance—tall, handsome, and rugged, with silver-trimmed glasses and an attractive smile. John, born in France of American parents, attended Georgetown University Law School and entered the service at twenty-three. After tours of duty at many European posts, he served as Ambassador to Columbia and Portugal before his final assignment to Iran. John had a wealth of experience in difficult Foreign Service posts. He was often outspoken, given to statements which he intended to be slightly shocking. Dealing with the Iranians, he said, "is like eating soup with a fork." His wife, Irena, of aristocratic Polish origin, was a very talented artist and linguist, not to mention a perfect hostess. She was a sculptor and painter and spoke at least six languages. The Wileys were charming and amusing. The atmosphere of the old palace provided a perfect backdrop for our visit, despite the cramped quarters and primitive plumbing.

In the absence of the Shah, who was still in the U.S. following his official visit, my most important meetings were to be with the Prime Minister and Foreign Minister. My visit to Teheran was merely to get acquainted with the officials of the Iranian government below the Shah and to learn more about the background of the issues which had been discussed with the Shah in Washington, particularly the overriding problem of U.S. aid.

U.S. relations with Iran had developed slowly since the end of the war. Iran had traditionally been in the British and Russian spheres of influence. This had been both a cause and a result of the Anglo-Iranian Oil Company's (AIOC) concession, which represented Iran's one most important asset and which so far had produced little benefit for the country. The annual income to Iran from the company was currently only some $30 million a year, which the Iranians said was less than their expenses in providing security for AIOC installations. In the meantime the AIOC was making a very large profit, all based on Iranian oil, which was, at the time, the company's only source. An agreement between the AIOC and Iran had been concluded which would have more than doubled Iran's income, but the Iranian Majlis refused to ratify it, holding out for much more.

The British Embassy in Teheran was, in many ways, the real source of power in the country. The Embassy and the AIOC largely controlled the press and the Majlis. Although the U.S. had been thrust by the Second World War into a position of some responsibility in Iran, and had provided the necessary support to the Shah to force withdrawal of the Soviets from Azerbaijan, we did not want to rock the British boat. Britain was an important ally. We had too many newly acquired responsibilities elsewhere to want more. Our open intervention to help resolve the issue between Iran and Britain over the AIOC concession, which had already arisen and would intensify, was to come later.

However, we considered U.S. security interests in Iran of great importance. On July 21, 1949, the National Security Council had made a report on Iran.[9] Because of Iran's resources, strategic location, vulnerability to armed attack, and exposure to political subversion, it was to be regarded as a continuing target of Soviet expansion. Loss of Iran to the U.S.S.R. would provide the Soviets with advance bases for further subversion or aggression against other Middle Eastern countries; afford bases much closer to potential U.S.-U.K. lines of defense; give the Soviets control over important oil resources; and constitute a threat to other oilfields in the area. It would also provide means of harassing air and sea routes to the West, and so undermine the will of the Middle East countries to resist other Soviet threats. Loss of Iran would thus jeopardize all of the Middle East, which was vital to U.S. security. The Security Council concluded that we should continue to support Iran, both with our military mission there and diplomatically.

On Monday, December 5, I called on Ali Asqhar Hekmat, Foreign Minister, and Mohammad Sa'ed, the Prime Minister. Both calls involved a general review of the Shah's recent visit, about which they knew little, and of current U.S.-Iranian relations, particularly the troublesome problem of aid. This had been complicated by the controversial position taken by Abol Ebtehaj, head of the Bank Melli, during his visit with me and other U.S. officials in Washington in September. He had taken the position that Iran was not in need of economic grants or loans, only military aid.

After luncheon at the embassy, I had a briefing session with the embassy staff. Later, at a cocktail party at the Iranian Officers Club, which was an elaborate establishment, we met most of the top Iranian officers as well as our own attachés and military mission members. We were shown the room reserved for the Shah, where the uniform he was wearing when he was shot five times the previous year was displayed. The worst shot went through his neck. All of the bullet holes were marked to show just where they entered the garment. The Shah had not been seriously injured.

The Foreign Minister gave a formal dinner for us that evening with about forty guests, in a large mirrored dining room. The many interesting Iranian dishes were perfectly served by waiters in white tie. After dinner the Foreign Minister made a flattering welcoming speech, comparing my visit to the one just made by the Shah to our country. I responded with a few off-the-cuff remarks. Later, I was taken aside for a conversation with Lieutenant General Ali Razmara, commander of the Iranian army, who was accepted as the probable next Prime Minister. Razmara's star had been rising for some time as a result of strong British and American backing. Little did I realize as we chatted about the current situation in Iran, particularly the delicate oil problem, the important and tragic role Razmara was soon to play. A slight wiry man with a deadpan face, he talked quietly and soberly. I was impressed and was prepared to recommend U.S. support when he was proposed for Prime Minister.

Cecilia and I arose the next morning at 6 A.M. to accompany Mr. Ney of the Near East Foundation on an inspection trip of his work with Iranian villages. The roads were so dusty we almost choked. We went about thirty miles out of Teheran to a little village which Mr. Ney was "managing" as an experiment. The village water system had been purified. Tractors, latrines, improved seeds, and poultry had been introduced, and the villagers were being trained to use them. We looked into one of their houses and saw a strange-looking contraption, a type of brazier, which was used both for sleeping and sitting. A large square frame, like a big coffee table and about the same height, had at its center a little charcoal brazier covered by a quilt. There were pillows around the four sides of the frame to lean back on at night. During either day or night feet would be tucked under the quilt to get warmed. One wondered how many toes were burned.

As well as we could observe, the experimental village was working admirably. Mr. Ney explained to us that success was primarily a matter of gaining the villagers' confidence. For example, at first they did not want to have their houses sprayed with DDT to kill mosquito infestations. But by getting the mullah, the local religious leader, to give permission to spray his house, Mr. Ney was able to get the others to agree. Malarial incidence was, as a result, reduced by 50 to 70 percent. Other villages whose inhabitants witnessed the success of this trial initiated similar programs to the extent possible. Mr. Ney was limited in expanding his program only by the lack of funds and materials. The Near East Foundation, under Mr. Ney, also maintained elementary and teacher-training schools, which we visited.

Apart from her admiration for the effort and vision required to carry out such enterprises, Cecilia was impressed by the fact that all of the girls had hennaed hair, and tiny children could write in Farsi. Along the way we saw many fat-tailed sheep, a particular variety which occurs in a belt all across Asia and into China. Their fat tails, which cover their entire rear end, range in weight from eight to twenty-five pounds. As a repository for fats and oils the tails are of great value for human consumption, or to be drawn on by the sheep when food is scarce.

Later I met with Prince Abdorreza, who received me on behalf of the royal family in the absence of the Shah.

I lunched at the embassy with Ambassador Wiley and the British Ambassador Sir John Le Rougetel, while Cecilia lunched with Le Rougetel's wife. As usual it was important for me to check with the local British representative in a British sphere, or former sphere, of influence. The British were always very correct during such visits in their attention to protocol. They knew that their influence was declining and were happy to have us share some of their former responsibilities. We knew this also. Still, having assumed so many postwar responsibilities so fast, we wanted the British to maintain their position in Iran as long as they could. We did, however, hope they would prod the AIOC to provide the Iranians a greater return from oil production and worked quietly toward this end. I was always impressed with the British ambassadors I met during this period. They still had the training, confidence and cool demeanor of men born to rule, and in the most gentlemanly way. My wife and I have maintained warm friendships with many of the British ambassadors and their wives whom we got to know during this period.

In the afternoon, we visited the Archeological Museum, where I indulged my addiction to Luristan bronzes. The Luristan culture represents a self-contained civilization of the Lurs people in the mountains of western Iran near the Iraqi border, which reached its peak around 850 B.C. It had only been discovered about ten years before my visit. Luristan artifacts, most of which were taken by vandals from funeral mounds, cover the full range of utilitarian objects, from safety pins to knife sharpeners to symbolic horse bits, as well as many votive symbols. Their particular attraction is the variety and ingenuity of their ornamentation, specializing in laughing antelopes and imaginary animals of all types.

I had learned to appreciate these bronzes from an earlier meeting with John Wiley in Ankara, where he had brought some Luristan artifacts for Ambassador George Wadsworth. I acquired a number of good pieces in the shops of Teheran on this visit, which was quite legal in those days. I maintained contact with many of the shops, particularly the Hajji Baba, and continued to make purchases of Luristan bronzes and Persian ceramics as long as they were available, with the result that I have in my home a sizable collection, a source of great enjoyment. Quite by accident I was a few years ago provided an aerial view of Luristan from a helicopter while visiting oil wells being drilled by a company of which I was a director. I talked to many of the workers on the wells but, alas, they knew nothing about bronzes. Alas, also, the wells all turned out to be dry.

Our visit to the museum was short as Ebtehaj had arranged for us to see the royal crown jewels, kept in a vault in the Bank Melli, where they served as the backing for the Iranian currency. Ali Baba could not have seen one-tenth as much when he incanted "open sesame" and entered the robbers' den. There were walls covered with ropes of pearls, and showcases piled high with unset diamonds, rubies, and emeralds. There was an exquisite little box lined with diamonds and covered with large emeralds. A French jeweler who had come to appraise it had found it impossible to estimate its value. There were gem-covered scabbards, a gem-encrusted globe of the world, watches, rings, tiaras, and stomachers. The displays staggered the vision, imagination, and cupidity. Cecilia's favorite article was exhibited in a high back wall case: a cerise bumbershoot lined with electric blue silk. On the end of the stick (the part you would thump on the floor) was a flat round emerald; the rest of the handle was diamond-studded and each of the little rib ends sticking out was covered with diamonds.

That evening the Wileys had about sixty guests in for a supper. There were Iranians, Americans, French, and British. An extensive buffet was followed by bridge. In the morning we departed very early on *The Magic Carpet* for Isfahan, which unfortunately we didn't reach because of bad weather. Instead we proceeded directly to Karachi, Pakistan.

My first visit to Iran had been disappointing. I left with the same unsatisfactory lack of any coherent grasp of the country that others have experienced. The centerpiece for the U.S. in Iran then was the Shah. In his absence Iran revealed its natural fragmentation into many component elements: the civil servants, the army, the mullahs, the landowners, the peasants, and the cultivated Teheran sophisticates. Without the Shah they simply didn't fit together. It was not so much that we were eager to rely on the Shah and support him under any circumstances. It was obviously a risk to put all of our eggs in one basket. Americans have always had a tendency to deal with de facto governments, even when they are not friendly. It usually seems to us surreptitious to deal directly with the opposition, not the gentlemanly thing to do, particularly when the government shows its displeasure. Even when the Shah was weak, as when I saw him in the crucial days of March 1951, there still seemed no alternative for us but to try to help him regain his strength.

Later, we were to have the choice of dealing with Mohammad Mossadeq, during the years he was in power starting in 1951. But our lack of trust both in his motives and abilities, and fear of offending the British—who considered him an enemy—kept us from any close association. It is claimed that in the end we helped overthrow Mossadeq;[10] however, even if this were so, we were still faced with the same dilemma. Unable to perceive any alternative to the Shah, whether we wanted one or not, we seemed destined to support him—blindly and on his terms—until we both went down in Iran together. It is difficult to see how our present very bad situation in Iran can be reversed.

8

Middle East Chiefs of Mission Conference

Istanbul, Turkey. November 26–29, 1949.

One of the most profitable practices of the Department of State in organizing the conduct of U.S. foreign policy is, in my judgment, the holding of regional conferences of our diplomatic and consular representatives, to meet with key departmental officials and focus on regional problems. Held usually in an attractive and isolated setting, these meetings make possible a thorough discussion and analysis of key issues, with recommendations for future policy. The conferences are preceded by careful preparation and the officers involved, almost all career men, are of high caliber. This chapter describes the first such meeting over which I presided after assuming my new duties.

On October 7, 1949, I sent a memorandum to Under Secretary Webb proposing the further elaboration of U.S. Middle East policies and their coordination with the U.K.[1] I pointed out that, separately and together, the U.S. and the U.K. faced a number of specific problems in the Middle East. Important developments were taking place that required continuous study and consultation between the two governments and our missions in the field.

I cited as an example the Economic Survey Mission, which had been established on our initiative by the UN General Assembly's Ad Hoc Political Committee, acting through the Palestine Conciliation Commission, on September 1, 1949. A meeting of U.S. Chiefs of Mission in the Middle East was needed to discuss the preliminary findings of our representative on the Survey Mission, Gordon Clapp, to advise him on his longer-range report, and determine how our Chiefs of Mission could help carry out the recommendations of the Survey Mission.

I also referred to the U.S.-U.K. combined military planning which had been going for a year under Rear Admiral Richard Conolly, commander-in-chief of U.S. naval forces in the Eastern Atlantic and Mediterranean. Our Chiefs of Mission should be briefed on this planning and discuss how it could be carried out. The meeting might also consider the proposed Iraq-Syria union, which would have widespread repercussions in the area. I suggested that we schedule a meeting on or about November 22 on a U.S. naval vessel to be boarded from Cyprus; that Admiral Conolly be asked to brief us; and that we ask Michael Wright, chief of the Middle East Section of the British Foreign Office, to visit Washington for an exchange of views prior to the meeting.

Webb approved my recommendations, with the exception that, on the suggestion of Deputy Under Secretary Dean Rusk, the Conolly briefing was deleted in light of the fact that the Secretary and Under Secretary had not yet had such an opportunity. Michael Wright came to Washington for meetings from November 14 to 17.[2] The Department had agreed to holding the U.S. meeting in Cyprus; however, the British Colonial Office advised us on November 1 that this might lead to increased Communist activity there, which in turn could lead to embarrassment to both countries. As a result we decided to hold the conference in Istanbul.

Although I have been to Istanbul many times over the years, including my visits earlier as coordinator of Greek-Turkish Aid and later as Ambassador to Turkey, I have never failed to be moved by the aura of this ancient seat of empires. Beneath its modern drab exterior, Istanbul hides more history than any other city in the world except Rome. Constantine made it the new eastern capital of the Roman Empire in A.D. 330 on the site of the Greek city of Byzantium. It is said that he lured fifty thousand Roman bureaucrats to the new Constantinople by promising them villas comparable to the ones in which they lived in in Rome.

For the next 1,123 years, until the Ottoman Turks came over its hitherto impregnable land walls in 1453, Constantinople was the capital of the Byzantine Empire, for most of this period the most important empire in the world. Although little of the Byzantine city remains, and much of the Turkish capital is in ruins or disrepair, an air of power and mystery hangs over the city. This seemed particularly true during the drab, overcast days of November 1949, with cold winds coming up from the Bosphorus, when the U.S. Chiefs of Diplomatic Missions of the Middle East met in conference.[3]

I was chairman of the conference. Burton Y. Berry, the newly-appointed director of the Office of African and Near Eastern Affairs, and Gordon H. Mattison, deputy director of the office, accompanied me to Istanbul. U.S. diplomatic representatives who attended the conference included the American ambassadors Jefferson Caffery (Cairo); Henry F. Grady (Athens); John C. Wiley (Teheran); George Wadsworth (Ankara); James G. McDonald (Tel Aviv); Edward S. Crocker (Baghdad); and J. Rives Childs (Jidda). The American ministers also present were Lowell C. Pinkerton from Beirut, and James H. Keeley from Damascus; A. David Fritzlan, the American chargé d'affaires at Amman; and William C. Burdett, Jr., the consul at Jerusalem.

Press coverage of the conference was extensive. The arrivals of the various participants, particularly Gordon Clapp who had come from Beirut, were highly publicized. Prior to our meeting there had been much speculation as to its purpose. The favorite subject of this speculation was a so-called Mediterranean Pact, vague ideas concerning which had been bruited about in the Middle East for some time. A shopping list of nine possible subjects, which was quoted in a number of newspapers, included: Soviet propaganda activities; disagreement between Israel and the Arab states; the U.S. Point Four program; the effect of U.S. policy on two recent Syrian coups d'état; the effect of a probable union between Syria and Iraq; Soviet pressure on Iran and the status of Iranian oil; oil productive capacity of the Middle East to meet the probable war; a security system to protect Middle East oil; and whether U.S. economic and military aid to Turkey would be adequate to resist Soviet pressures.

In order to defuse these speculations, I issued a short press statement soon after my arrival, explaining that the meeting was a routine gathering of top U.S. officials in the Middle East to discuss any and all subjects of interest, but not any particular subjects. No press releases or leaks occurred during the meeting despite great pressure from the journalists. The meeting took place in the splendid old Istanbul consulate general building overlooking the historic Golden Horn. From the consulate one could see, rising from the hills of ancient Constantinople, one of the most important architectural monuments in the world, the sixth-century Hagia Sophia. One could also see the great Turkish mosques of Sinon, which although influenced by Hagia Sophia, added a new dimension to architecture.

George Wadsworth, veteran Foreign Service officer, a bachelor, charming, gracious, and witty, was our host. We worked so hard we seldom left the consulate, except for those who lived in the nearby art nouveau Pera Palas Hotel. We were never, however, without food and drink and good company. All of the ambassadors present, except McDonald, were ranking career officers with long Middle East experience. They knew each other well and worked harmoniously together within the conference.

Although we were diligent, there were a few diversions. I had several pleasant duties as chairman. One was to pay a call on Dr. Fehrettin Kerim Gokay, Governor and Mayor of Istanbul and once president of Istanbul University, who later returned my visit. Gokay, a medical doctor, was one of the world's leading psychiatrists. He was short, dynamic, and balding, with a Turkish mustache and eyes that danced in excitement. He was a political figure of national importance. Then, and during my tour of duty as ambassador from 1951 to 1953, Gokay proved a staunch friend of the U.S. After my visit he reported to the press that I had promised that my colleagues and I would help solve the social problems of Istanbul, and that I had said that Marshall Plan aid was fully justified in Turkey because the best results were being obtained there. I didn't recall saying it just that way, but I had no objection.

Together with Consul General La Verne Baldwin, I also paid a call on Athenagoras, Patriarch (or Archbishop) of Constantinople of the Holy Orthodox Catholic Apostolic Eastern Church, usually referred to as the Greek Church or the Greek Orthodox Church. I had known Athenagoras for many years, since the time he served as Archbishop of the Metropolitanate of New York. Historically, the church has represented the successors to the Catholic churches of the ancient East, where the religion originated, but which were separated from those in the West when Constantine split the Roman Empire in the fourth century. The two branches grew further apart from the fifth century until the final schism in 1054, when Pope Leo IX excommunicated the entire Eastern Church.

Athenagoras, in his modest ancient seat, the Fenar, in one of the rundown sections of the city near the Golden Horn, was the titular head of his church as the "first among equals." The church, which included the patriarchates of Constantinople, Alexandria, Antioch, and Jerusalem, was governed by a Holy Synod consisting of twelve metropolitans. Tall, handsome, with a white beard, a black headpiece, and long black robes, Athenagoras exuded spirituality, sincerity, and brotherly love. He played well his precarious role as leader of the fifty thousand Greeks in Istanbul, otherwise, apart from a few

Armenians, a totally Islamic city in an Islamic country. He maintained excellent relations with the Istanbul authorities and, through regular visits, with the government in Ankara.

I often called on Athenagoras, both before and after my 1949 visit, and always found my meetings with him a pleasant ritual. There was first a warm embrace and kiss on both cheeks, the tasting of honey from a pot into which a spoon was dipped, and then the sipping of wine. Eventually I came to know most of his close associates. Athenagoras would ask me about America and tell me about his problems with recalcitrant patriarchs and metropolitans. While I was ambassador he arranged a memorable ten-day visit for me to the monasteries of Mount Athos. Athenagoras's return call at the consulate, where all the ambassadors joined me in receiving him, was a highly publicized event.

The Chiefs of Mission conference lasted four days. In my opening remarks, I described the background of events which had led to the calling of the conference. The Middle East was emerging as a key area in the world-wide struggle between the West and the Soviet Union. The U.S., as a latecomer in the area, needed to coordinate its efforts with those of the British to prevent the creation of a vacuum which could be exploited by the Communists.

I said that we must help minimize the severe dislocations created by the Arab-Israeli War and the problem of the Arab refugees by supporting the findings of the UN Economic Survey Mission. Gordon Clapp had joined the conference to give us his preliminary findings and seek our advice as to the final report. In addition, we must deal with the problem of emerging nationalism in the Middle East and how to channel it in our favor. We must seek to increase the security of the area by helping the U.K. keep its troop and base rights there and by increasing the military strength and stability of the states of the area.

I will not attempt to summarize the vigorous discussions that ensued. The conclusions that finally emerged from the conference were these: the basic objectives of U.S. policy in the Middle East must be the maintenance of peace through the development of area economic stability and security; the enhancement of U.S. prestige; and the orientation of the area to the U.S. and the Western powers and away from the U.S.S.R. To achieve this we must maintain an active interest in the area, within a framework of strict impartiality between the Arab states and Israel. At the meeting of the Arab League Council on

October 22, 1949, a resolution had been adopted calling for a collective security pact among the Arab states. We felt that the proposed pact would not likely have any significant effect, and did not require a definite position by the U.S.

We felt that our primary objective was to prevent the Soviets from gaining control of any of the Middle East countries by subversion short of actual war. To states bordering the Soviet Union we must extend military and, where necessary, economic aid. We must encourage strong popular resistance to Communist aims. For countries not contiguous to the U.S.S.R., military preparedness, except that required for internal stability, was not considered an important factor. Technical and financial assistance should be given to achieve political and economic stability. We agreed that we should not attempt to negotiate multilateral or bilateral security pacts with the Middle Eastern states until we were prepared to commit the military forces required to carry out our guarantees. We should, however, continue to develop particularly close relations with Saudi Arabia.

We agreed that Soviet Communism was seeking to dominate the Middle Eastern states through subversion. Economic and social conditions, particularly among the Palestine refugees, were ripe for such a movement; however, as a result of police and other repressive measures the situation seemed under control. There was agreement that the refusal of the older political cliques in the states of the area to permit the introduction of young liberal elements into their governments might result in a growing susceptibility to Communist propoganda. We should take notice of the Soviet technique of playing upon the nationalist feelings of tribal and other minority elements, as for instance the Kurds, to create trouble. In Iran, for example, where organized terrorism for political ends appeared to have Communist connections, the conference felt there was grave danger that a successful attempt on the life of the Shah, or other leaders, could lead to anarchy.

Clearly the time had come for the U.S. to indicate to the British that we had no objection to the early incorporation of Arab Palestine into Jordan, if accompanied by appropriate steps to ensure fair representation of Palestinians in the Jordanian legislature. The conference did not recommend the extension of military assistance to Middle Eastern states not included in the present Military Assistance Program, except to allow Saudi Arabia to obtain arms on a reimbursable basis, when authorization could be obtained from Congress.

The conference felt that the Economic Survey Mission's interim report displayed an excellent grasp of the situation and it was heartily endorsed. It was feared, however, that it might be handicapped at the start in certain states because of ESM's connection with the PCC and the Palestine problem. The proposed UN Work and Relief Agency recommended by the interim report was approved. It was in no way to be connected with the PCC. We felt that we should not encourage the extension of the U.K. treaty system to other countries, and that every effort should be made to increase the prestige of the UN in the Middle Eastern area. The U.S. should encourage direct negotiations between Israel and the Arab states, but should not abandon publicly our principles on refugees and territories. We should not, however, advocate any precise terms of settlement, leaving this to be determined by the relative bargaining positions of the parties. The conference urged that our representatives in Middle Eastern countries should, as far as possible, assume a positive role in urging more representative and democratic forms of government.

On November 30, after the Mission Conference was over, I held a press conference at which I issued a short release emphasizing that our primary objective had been to support President Truman's policy announced at the time of Gordon Clapp's appointment to the UN Survey Mission to the Middle East. I explained that to traditional U.S. cultural interests in the Middle East had been added increased economic ties and a recognition of the area's strategic importance. This, in turn, had resulted in our increased interest in the welfare of the Middle East governments and peoples. We sought no special privileges; however, we recognized an obvious community of interests.

I said that we agreed with the interim report of the Survey Mission that economic and social development offered the best hope for area stability, toward which we hoped Point Four assistance could contribute. Fortunately Communist agitation and propaganda were not yet a problem in the Middle East. "These states have become their own masters. We see no present need for U.S. association with any regional military or mutual defense pacts to assure greater protection against aggression." Reporting on the conference, the Istanbul daily Vatan of December 3 said: "It may be asserted that the shortcomings of the exclusion of the Near and Middle East countries from the Atlantic Pact have been eliminated by the steps taken to improve their economic situation and reinforce their resistance." The failure of the conference to recommend a security pact was not missed.

The conference did not result in any startling policy recommendations. It is included mainly as a point of reference to our changing attitudes toward the Middle East. While recognizing the Communist threat, and the increasing security interest of the U.S., our approach was cautious. It would take another year and a deepening of the Cold War threat to the Middle East before the U.S. would come to the point of offering a place in NATO to Greece and Turkey and large-scale economic and military aid to the other Middle Eastern states. Our emphasis on strengthening ties with Saudi Arabia and our approval of the incorporation of Arab Palestine into Jordan were faint glimmerings into issues which were destined to develop great importance.

9

Invitation to Liaquat

Visit to Karachi, Peshawar, and Lahore, Pakistan. Prime
Minister Liaquat Ali Khan. December 6–11, 1949.

I was, of course, keen to visit the countries in my area of jurisdiction
in the department and to talk with their leaders. Following the Istanbul conference, I made arrangements for a series of familiarization
visits to Iran, India, Sri Lanka, and Burma.

The peninsula of southern Asia, which after the Second World
War was divided between India and Pakistan, is normally spoken of
as the Indian subcontinent. This is because of its size, being about
equal in area to all of Western Europe, and the fact that it is cut off
from the rest of Asia by the Himalaya Mountains. Present-day Indians are a mélange of various invading races, at least seven of which
can be identified: the Scythians and Dravidians from Western Asia,
the Mongoloids from the Northeast, the Indo-Aryans from the Northwest, the Turks and Mongols from Central Asia, and the Persians. Of
the seven major religions in India, the most important are Hinduism,
Islam, and Buddhism, in that order. There are reputed to be some
220 distinct languages in India, and many more dialects.

Civilizing influences began in India with the invasions of the
Indo-Aryans around 2400 B.C. Evidence of urban life dates from this
period. Written history in Vedic literature exists from about 1500 B.C.
Alexander the Great invaded India around 326 B.C. Although India
has over the centuries spawned a variety of local dynasties, the true
Indian empires were created by Muslim invaders, including Arabs,
Iranians, and Turks, starting about A.D. 1000. India was sacked by the
Mongol Tamerlane in 1398, and the great Mogul Empire created in
1526 by Babur of Kabul lasted into the early eighteenth century,
when Europeans gained control over important coastal areas; first
came the Portuguese, then the Dutch and the British, through the
East India Company. After many local and border wars, India came

under the rule of the British Crown in 1858 and was ruled until 1947 by a British Viceroy.

After World War II, the U.K. understood that India must be granted independence. India had at that time a population of about 350 million, 85 percent Hindu. The Indian nationalist leader, Mohandas Gandhi, apostle of nonviolence, had been leader of the Indian National Congress since 1919. Independence was granted in 1946 by British Prime Minister Clement Attlee, subject to the working-out of practical details. The partition of India in 1947 resulted in separating the predominantly Hindu and Muslim areas. It was a bloody episode, and produced ten million refugees. The Dominion of India was created on August 15, 1947, but was unfortunately soon deprived of its leader when Gandhi was assassinated in 1948. The Indian constitution was passed by the parliament in November 1949, and formally adopted in January 1950, when India became a republic within the Commonwealth. Pandit Jawaharlal Nehru, a follower of Gandhi and leader of the Congress Party, was named India's first Prime Minister. Nehru's party won a sweeping victory in the country's first general elections concluded in March 1952, confirming his government in power.

In the meantime, Pakistan was undergoing a parallel evolution. Following creation of the Muslim League in 1930, its president, Mohammed Ali Jinnah, headed a movement to found an independent Muslim state. The Dominion of Pakistan was created on August 15, 1947, with Jinnah as the first Governor-General. With partition, between six and seven million Hindus and a smaller number of Muslims were exchanged between the two countries. Tension between the two was exacerbated in 1947 by difficulties arising over Indian retention of control over Kashmir, which was predominantly Muslim. After armed clashes in 1948, the UN was asked to settle the dispute.

This was the background in Pakistan and India when I first visited there in December 1949, a scant two years after their independence. India had just accepted a new constitution. Both states had been paralyzed by post-partition clashes, particularly those over Kashmir, which were continuing. Pakistan faced the almost insurmountable problem of taking care of many millions of refugees, and neither country had the resources required to alleviate the sufferings of their masses. Substantial assistance from the U.S. and other Western nations had not yet been initiated; the U.K. was doing its best, but was severely limited by its own economic difficulties. Tensions between the two countries mounted as Nehru led India into a policy of neutralism in the Cold War. Pakistan saw an opportunity emerging to obtain substantial U.S. assistance by taking a position favorable to the U.S. and the West. Nehru was not willing to compromise his neutrality, although he did seek grain from us.

Cecilia and I arrived in Karachi by Air Force plane on December 6. Bad weather had forced us to return to Teheran without landing for a planned visit to Isfahan, which was a great disappointment. We had taken off again at 10 A.M. and had flown straight to Karachi over the desolate wastes of eastern Iran and Baluchistan, along the path of Alexander's army returning from India. From the air, the parched, mountainous expanse was appalling. We were met at the airport by our chargé d'affaires, Hooker Doolittle, and his wife, and by Counselor and Mrs. Merritt Cootes, whom we were later to see much of in their retirement home in Florence. We dined with the two couples quietly and went to bed early. There was, however, little sleep. We were beset by mosquitoes and could hear varied noises all night from the thoroughfare in front of the house. My wife identified some of them as camels' bells, turkeys in chorus, Muslim chants, crows, boys flying kites, and song birds. At dawn we were able to observe the passing scene.

Most of the women to be seen were in purdah, veiled from head to foot, often in black with an eye slit of heavy net. Women in complete purdah, we were told, did not go out at all and were not allowed to meet anyone, not even other women. By contrast many women, including the Prime Minister's wife, were completely emancipated and were active in politics and civic affairs. Camels were much in evidence, pulling wagons with rubber tires while maintaining complete dignity. Many men were pulling bicycle rickshaws. We saw men who had dyed their beards red.

At dinner that night there were about twenty guests. My wife was impressed with the service, which was performed by eight "bearers" wearing picturesque red fezzes with brass pins of the American eagle emblem upon them. One could only guess how many more bearers, the term applied to all servants except "sweepers," were in the kitchen.

The purpose of my visit was to extend an invitation to Prime Minister Liaquat Ali Khan to visit America. The Prime Minister was, however, in Peshawar visiting the Governor of the Northwest Frontier Province. Although I did not wish to delay my mission, I did want to take advantage of my first visit to Karachi to meet with key officials, particularly Mr. Ghulam Mohammed, Minister of Finance, who had been a frequent visitor to Washington seeking aid for the new state. He had visited Cecilia and me on our farm in Middleburg, where he had made fast friends with our young son Michael.

My most important meeting, therefore, was with Ghulam Mohammed at his residence at noon on December 9.[1] He took the occasion to discuss his greatest interests. First, he referred to a recent conversation in Delhi with Sir Girja Bajpai, the Indian Minister of External Affairs and Commonwealth Relations, during which Bajpai had proposed that, regardless of how difficult it seemed for the two governments to find solutions to such problems as Kashmir, water rights, and evacuee property, they should announce their determination not to resort to war in any case. Ghulam Mohammed then showed me Pakistan's reply, agreeing to refer the problems Bajpai had cited to a third party for either mediation or arbitration, on the condition that the decision of such third party should be accepted as final. Pakistan would then be willing to agree to a joint declaration that there would be no war.

The Minister referred to the forthcoming visit to the U.S. of the Pakistani Prime Minister. It was of the utmost importance that he should be accorded a reception equal to that received by Nehru. I replied that as far as all official arrangements were concerned there could be no question about this, but that I was obviously not able to give any assurances as to the reaction of the press or public.

After some discussion concerning Pakistani sterling balances, Ghulam turned to the subject that was undoubtedly uppermost in his mind, namely, the International Islamic Economic Conference, called the Exposition—and the formation of a permanent organization to continue the work of the conference. He gave me copies of his inaugural address at its first meeting. The Minister noted that in his speech he had strongly denounced Communism. He did not refer to his attack, in the same speech, on both the U.S. and the UN. He said that he had been bitterly criticized by Russia for the speech, but that he had considered carefully certain developing trends and had become convinced that the time had arrived for plain speaking. He accepted the responsibility for being the prime mover, on a private basis, for an Islamic bloc, an idea originally introduced by Jinnah. Although the delegates to the conference had been private citizens, he assumed that they had attended with the approval of their governments.

I pointed out that the economies of the Islamic countries were not complementary. What could be accomplished from an economic standpoint by cooperation between nations producing more or less the same materials from primitive agricultural economies? The Minister believed it enormously important to establish some mechanism for a closer union and interchange of ideas between the Muslim countries. He pleaded for U.S. support in the establishment of an Economic Commission for the Middle East under UN auspices, similar to the Economic Commission for Asia and that for the Far East. I replied that, although we would give the matter serious consideration, I did not believe that religion in itself provided a basis for a separate economic grouping; furthermore, a regional bloc, if formed, would have to include the new state of Israel.

My discussions with the other Pakistani officials were fruitful. U.S. relations with Pakistan were at this time on the upswing. Pakistan, particularly because of the pressure of its rivalry with India, was courting us assiduously. In seeking aid, particularly arms aid, Pakistan took pains to disassociate itself from Indian neutralism, and promised that its forces would be at our side in the event of Communist incursions into South Asia. They offered for us an attractive alternative to the somewhat truculent Indian neutralism. Their spokesmen, particularly Ghulam Mohammed, were persuasive.

I held a press conference in the afternoon in the library of the U.S. Information Service, in which I asserted that "the U.S. is becoming increasingly aware of the importance of Pakistan and of our relations with Pakistan."[2] I pointed out as evidence our support of Zafrullah Khan as one of the Vice Presidents of the UN, the inclusion of Pakistan in the Far Eastern Commission advising the UN Supreme Commander in Japan, and our support for Pakistani membership on the UN Economic and Social Council. I promised Pakistan full consideration in the allocation of Point Four funds then being debated in Congress. This was before the first large-scale appropriation of U.S. aid funds under the military/economic Mutual Security Program. Although the amount involved globally under Point Four initially was small—only $25 million a year—countries like Pakistan, which were so desperately in need, saw it as a foot in the door. Having little else to offer, I stressed our meager exchange-of-persons program. And in closing I said, "We encouraged you in your struggle for independence, and will furnish such assistance as is within our power to your new and progressing country."

The *Pakistan Times* of December 9 featured a cartoon depicting me, a Yankee with a black top hat smoking a cigar, as a spider in a web attracting poor Pakistan leaders to their fate. I was quoted as saying, "America is becoming increasingly aware of Pakistan importance." The *Civil and Military Gazette* of the same date shows me as a cigar-smoking (which I was then) Uncle Sam offering the Prime Minister an empty hat labeled "Foreign Policy," while with my other hand behind me I offered another hat full of arms and dollar bills to India, with scrolls labeled "Trade Agreements" and "Dollar Loans."

Ghulam Mohammed gave a dinner in our honor for about fifty at his residence. It was a large old-fashioned house in the Indian style with ghastly modern furniture. We sat and drank fruit juices for hours and then ate many very hot Pakistani dishes with lots of curry and too much grease. There was present a congenial group of high- and medium-level Pakistani officials, all British trained and very enthusiastic about the creation of their new state. It was still too early for disillusionment to have set in. The problems that they were to face as a poor divided country, locked by history and the dispute over Kashmir into a bitter rivalry with a much more powerful India, were not yet seen in full perspective.

We arose early for a 6 A.M. flight to Peshawar, arriving there at 11:30. We were met by the aide-de-camp and secretary to the Prime Minister, Aga Abdul Hamad. There was much picture taking by newsreel photographers before we were taken to Government House, the residence of the Governor of the Northwestern Frontier Province, where Prime Minister Liaquat and his wife, the Begum, were staying. I carried with me the invitation from President Truman for them to visit Washington in May. After Nehru's visit the previous October, we felt under some obligation to balance with a Liaquat visit. Liaquat, as second only to Jinnah in his party during the pre-independence era, was, since the great Jinnah's death in 1948, the unchallenged leader of his country. He was a big, strong, confident man with considerable international stature. We wanted him as a strong anti-Communist ally in the subcontinent, for his country had strategic territory on both the northwest and northeast borders of India.

Arriving at Government House, Cecilia and I were immediately received by the Prime Minister and his wife. They were a friendly and attractive couple, he brimming with smiles and she bursting with energy and exuberance, which had earned her the nickname "Tiger in Silks." Before Pakistan radio and a television recording, I gravely presented the President's letter. The Prime Minister read it and asked me to thank the President. He accepted the invitation. I liked him, as a man you could do business with.

There followed a delightful luncheon for eighteen, the most entertaining meal we had had since we left home. The Begum was in good form and Liaquat laughed easily. The atmosphere created was completely unconstrained. The Begum demonstrated clearly why she was such a vital force in Pakistan, particularly in women's rights. She was impatient with the women in purdah and the men who kept them, or let them stay, there. She was very quick with the tongue; this had, of course, resulted in criticism which I am sure bothered her very little.

After lunch Cecilia and I were driven up the Khyber Pass to the Afghanistan border, fulfilling a long-held desire. The pass, which starts twenty miles west of Peshawar, had always conjured up for me romantic images. It cuts through dramatically rugged hills and has been used as a route of invasion by many conquerors, including Alexander. It traverses an area called Pushtunistan, the land of the Pushtu-speaking peoples. The Pushtus, who include many feuding tribes, are known as warlike, undisciplined individualists, who were paid off but never conquered by the British. Although most had pledged their allegiance to Pakistan, they continued to lead quite independent lives.

The Pushtus had been awarded to Pakistan on separation, but the issue still arose as to whether they should not, as many Pushtus desired, have an independent state of Pushtunistan. This had created a severe problem between Afghanistan and Pakistan, still going on, which we were making a major effort to resolve in order to prevent the Communists from using it to their advantage. Moreover, an independent Pushtunistan would not, in our view, have been a viable state, and there was no one to pay for it except us.

We stopped at a military post for tea and were received by the political agent of the Khyber Agency. Later we were joined by a number of tribal chiefs, obviously reliable ones assembled for that reason. They were critical of us for allowing India to keep territory in Kashmir they considered conquered from their fellow tribesmen. If the Indians did not give the land up blood would flow. They were an interesting lot in their variegated mountain garb, guns showing. They were obviously ready to fight at the drop of a hat. I couldn't help sympathizing with them.

We arrived back at Government House in time to dress for a big dinner. We were pleased but rather surprised to be served the same main-course partridge, with a delicious and distinctive sauce, that we had had for lunch. Liaquat and the Begum were as convivial as before, but the Governor, whose wife was in purdah and could not receive visitors, proved to be a Pakistan prototype of a farcical British Colonel Blimp.

After dinner we all went to a nearby army camp, where a program of tribal dancing had been arranged around a huge bonfire. A large audience of soldiers was waiting when we arrived, to be ushered into a huge tent with lovely Afghan rugs on the ground, braziers of coal for heating the chill mountain air, and comfortable chairs and lap robes. We were served sherry, coffee, tea, and cigarettes in regal style.

The dances were terrific. The music was barbarically rhythmical, the tunes on rather a minor scale, almost atonal to the Western ear, with many unresolved phrases. The motions of the dancers, all men, were violent, yet amazingly graceful. There was much rapid jerking and whirling of heads, many with long hair. The effect was savage and exciting. There were fourteen dances, each performed by a particular military unit, descriptively designated in the program as 6 RFFRIF 2/15 Punjab (MG), 100 and 101 BDE, and 2 FFRIF. The names of the dances were also picturesque: Balbala, Qawali, Balbala Tawala, American Doctor, Laila, Masuol's Dance, Ghumar (Cis-Indus Dance), Ghuiaar (Cis-Indus Dance), Bhangra-sword and Bragzuna.

Later we visited the mess hall of the army camp, which seemed just as it had been when left by the British. Only men were invited to sign the guest book. When the Begum discovered that the ladies had been ignored, she addressed some withering remarks to the poor post commander, suggesting that women might as well leave as remain there on sufferance. This was Cecilia's reaction to finding her name omitted from the write-up in the Karachi papers under pictures of our arrival at the airport. Women at that time had a long way to go in Pakistan. Before my departure the Governor presented me with an attractive brocaded wool coat similar to those he and others had worn to the dancing, which still reminds me of the evening.

Returning to Government House I conferred with members of our embassy in Kabul, who had flown to see me for this purpose. Because of the tense situation between the two countries, a visit to Afghanistan was not considered appropriate at that time.

The next morning we arose very early for our departure by plane to Lahore in northern Pakistan. When asked the previous evening what we would like for breakfast, we had agreed to what we understood was to be porridge. Imagine our dismay when the large silver-

covered dishes were brought in by turbaned bearers at the prear-
ranged hour, to lift the cover plates and discover partridge again,
which we had eaten every meal we had had in Peshawar.

Lahore we found to be a very pretty town, brilliant with bougain-
villaea and chrysanthemums. We took a short tour before lunch, visiting the old walled city, the impressive fort built by the Moguls, and
a beautifully proportioned mosque that could hold many thousands
of people. We also went to the Shalimar Gardens, not the ones of
"Pale hands I loved" fame but reputed to be even more beautiful,
with reflecting pools, fountains, little carved "pleasure palaces," and
beautiful formal gardens, just as laid out six hundred years ago. One
could almost visualize the dancing girls who once graced them. The
platforms in the center of the pools, where dancing took place, had
runways leading to the banks. After a hasty lunch at the consulate
general, which was the usual residence of the Doolittles, we departed
Pakistan by plane for New Delhi.

We were both delighted, the following May, to receive the Prime
Minister and the Begum when they came to Washington for their
official visit. Not being a great world figure, Liaquat did not attract
the same attention that Nehru had commanded from our media.
However, his talks with the President and the department were of a
more substantial character, including assurances that Pakistani forces
would be available in the event of a Communist military threat to
South Asia from the north. Progress was also made on the Pushtunistan and Kashmir questions.

The Prime Minister and his wife made a great hit in Washington.
"Came and Conquered" was the headline of the social page of the
Washington *Times-Herald* of May 5, 1950, describing the "brilliant"
white-tie dinner given the couple by Secretary and Mrs. Acheson at
Anderson House. My wife gave a luncheon for the Begum at our
Kalorama Road residence. The Prime Minister, in addition to his
meeting with the President and Secretary of State, met with Secretary of Defense Louis Johnson and the Joint Chiefs of Staff. (An
embarrassment occurred when Secretary Acheson and I waited in
vain after the state dinner for a private meeting I thought I had
arranged between the two at my residence. The young department
officer in charge of the Prime Minister's schedule, although aware of
the meeting plans, had done nothing to get Liaquat there because he
considered his responsibility was only for formally scheduled events.)

When Liaquat and the Begum went to New York City to address
a local group and make an appearance at the UN, my wife and I

accompanied them on the train, for old times' sake. After the four of us were settled in our compartment, I asked Liaquat if he would like a drink before lunch. He suggested an orange blossom, which consists of orange juice and gin. This concerned me, since I didn't know how much, as a Muslim, he drank, or whether he knew how strong a drink he had asked for. When he asked for a second orange blossom, I really began to worry, having in mind his reception committee and speaking commitment immediately after arrival. I had underestimated him. He gave no evidence of having had anything to drink at all.

Liaquat, during his U.S. tour, raised a few unfriendly questions concerning U.S. policy, probably to assuage his country's neutralists. At a University of Chicago Round Table on May 6, he declared that the people of Asia were under the impression that the U.S. was interested only in the possibility of a war with the U.S.S.R. and not in the peace of the world. The U.S. would not be doing all that it should do unless it assured that the condition of the people in the East was made better and their economies developed. "On that," he continued, "depends the peace of the world." Liaquat called on the U.S. to play a more active role in Kashmir, which he characterized as "the most dangerous dispute facing the world today."

When the Prime Minister and his wife appeared on Eleanor Roosevelt's television show over the NBC network, I was asked to participate. Liaquat reiterated his view that the peace of the world depended on peace in Asia. I characterized the understanding reached between Liaquat and Nehru as one of the outstanding examples of statesmanship in modern times.

Liaquat's tragic assassination in 1958 had disastrous results for his country, which has not produced a comparable leader since. The Begum was subsequently appointed Pakistani Ambassador to The Hague, where we saw her during a visit in 1963 while I was serving as U.S. Ambassador to Bonn. She was still her same dynamic, smiling self, "The Tiger in Silks."

I came away with a very favorable impression of Pakistan and its leaders. Starting with Ghulam Mohammad, and certainly with Liaquat, I was impressed with their forthright positive approach. They understood how much help they needed if their new state was to survive their keen competition with India and make a go of it. They openly sought our aid on our terms, promising support in our efforts to build a defense against the Communist threat. Compared with the wishy-washy neutralist Indians they were a breath of fresh air.

10

Encounter with Nehru

Visit to New Delhi, India, Prime Minister Nehru, December 11–14, 1949. Visit to Colombo, Sri Lanka, Prime Minister Senanayake, December 17–20, 1949. Visit to Rangoon, Burma, Prime Minister Thakin Nu, December 22–24, 1949.

Cecilia and I arrived in New Delhi on December 11. We were met by Ambassador Loy Henderson and his wife, Elise, who were old friends from Washington, and by O. V. Ramsdurai of the External Affairs Ministry. We were greeted by a large showing of the Indian press.[1]

After I had exchanged a few words with the press, we were rushed immediately to the embassy residence to change clothes and proceed to Government House for a reception for some six hundred guests, given by His Excellency Shri Chakravarti Rajagopalachari, Governor-General of India (in effect, President). After traversing what seemed miles of marble entrance hall, we were introduced to the diplomatic corps. I was the only man there who was not an ambassador. We received warmly by the Governor-General, a distinguished-looking man who closely resembled Gandhi, with a similar spiritual quality. The whole group was then ushered out to the gardens, where the remaining guests had assembled. We passed through lanes of splendid, immobile, beturbaned, be-lanced guardsmen in scarlet coats. Fountains were splashing, a band was playing, and flowers were blooming in a tremendous formal garden. It was a fine sight after our dreary journey.

Later we returned to the embassy for a reception given in our honor by the Hendersons, to which two hundred guests had been invited. The key to the success of my visit was the fact that Prime Minister Nehru, whom we had met during his visit to Washington in October, was there with his daughter, Indira Gandhi, as was Deputy Prime Minister Sardar Vallabhbhai Patel. All fifteen members of the

cabinet had been invited and most came, including the most interesting lady Minister of Health, Raj-kumari Amrit Kaur. Also present
were the Chief Justice of India and General K. M. Cariappa, Chief of
Army Staff and Commander-in-Chief of the Indian Army. It is interesting to note that the Commander-in-Chief of the Indian Navy was
a Vice Admiral W. E. Parry and that the Indian Air Force Commander was Air Marshal Sir Thomas Elmhirst. Since 75 percent of
the officers in the Indian armed forces before independence had
been British, many were seconded to continue until they could be
replaced. There was much conversation that gave me a valuable insight into the mood and preoccupations of the Indian government
hierarchy.

The following morning we were given an introduction to problems of managing a household in India. We had put in our breakfast
order the previous day, including time of call and style of eggs. At
the appropriate time a series of bearers trouped in to set up an elaborate table with syrup, honey, preserves, and butter, all the trimmings,
but only trimmings, except some prunes. As we sat down Cecilia
asked the bearer if there was some coffee or tea. He replied, "Yes,
yes, lady sahib," and hastened away. We ate the prunes and waited.
Bearers kept coming in and out to rearrange forks and perform other
tasks. We inquired again about the coffee and were reassured. Suddenly a bearer arrived with two large dishes of porridge, which he set
down with a flourish. Since we had not ordered porridge we declined
it, to his consternation.

All of this took time, and I was getting concerned because of my
early appointment with the Deputy Prime Minister. Just as Loy
called through the door, "George, we must go," the scrambled eggs
arrived. Still no coffee. I leapt up and left and so did the eggs; they
were quickly whisked away. Eventually Mrs. Henderson rescued Cecilia with coffee she had brewed herself.

When we called on Sardar Patel, Deputy Prime Minister, at his
residence, at nine on the morning of December 12, we found him
and his sister sunning themselves on his front porch. Patel almost
immediately launched into a rather lengthy exposition of India's attitude with respect to Kashmir and other outstanding issues between
India and Pakistan. I took the occasion to stress how important it was
to us—and should be to India, Pakistan, and all of South Asia—for
both countries to iron out their differences in a conciliatory spirit.
Patel agreed but insisted that the fault lay with Pakistan. The conversation also touched briefly on economic relations between the U.S.

and India. I said that American investors did not consider the present investment climate favorable in India.

Later that morning, I attended the opening of the Indo-American Conference by the Honorable Dr. Syama Prasad Mookerjee, Minister for Industry and Supply, at the University of New Delhi.

I was received by Prime Minister Nehru at noon in his office in the Council House.[2] He was in the midst of a busy day and understandably seemed a trifle preoccupied. This was the main meeting of my visit. As a junior official, although I was told I was the ranking American to visit India up to that time, I could scarcely expect Nehru, the world statesman, to tell me anything he had not been willing to tell the President two months before. I had carefully prepared the points I wished to make with him following up the discussions in Washington. At his suggestion, I spoke first.

In attempting to outline our general policies with respect to India, I emphasized that the U.S. was not endeavoring to persuade India to enter into any kind of a power bloc, although it normally looked to India for cooperation among the democratic members of the UN in discouraging aggression and other violations of the UN Charter. In describing the conditions under which American private capital might be willing to enter India, I pointed out that we were not trying to pressure India to pursue any particular economic policy. We would like to see American private investors contribute to Indian development. I felt I was performing a service to both countries in describing the kind of environment which might induce American private capital to enter India, and devoted considerable time to describing our policy toward Greece as an illustration of our aiding countries without taking advantage of them.

When Nehru's turn came he said, "Mr. McGhee, I am sure you would like for me to be very frank with you. I will." With that he proceeded to ramble all over the lot in his own well-known form of double-talk. I kept waiting for something of substance that I would be able to report. There was nothing. Ambassador Henderson later reported that Nehru "while friendly, was, as usual, rather reserved and he evaded in his rather lengthy replies any discussion of the rather concrete matters touched on by Mr. McGhee." Others have had the same experience with Nehru. Whether it was preoccupation, straight evasion because he didn't consider the conversation worth his effort, or a difference between the inner workings of the Indian and Anglo-Saxon minds I will never know. In any event, it was a very unsatisfactory experience for me and, although continuing to respect

Nehru for his leadership qualities, I was disappointed in his unwillingness to discuss important issues with me. I was pessimistic that we would ever be able to establish any real basis of understanding with Nehru. Except for the "smooth talk," there was nothing he said you could come to grips with.

Later Nehru gave a small luncheon for Cecilia and me which was presided over by his daughter Indira Gandhi. Little did we realize then that she was to become Prime Minister herself. Conversation was in a light, general vein.

At six o'clock in the evening of December 12, I had a conference with American correspondents in Delhi at the embassy. This was largely an off-the-record discussion of U.S. policies toward India, and Indian-American relations in general. I thought it would be a mistake for us to make any grants to India, at least not until India had exhausted the possibilities of obtaining credits from the World Bank and through American private investments. It was up to India to create conditions which would attract American investors. I expressed the view that the extension of direct American financial aid to India, in the form of grants or credits, would not be of political benefit to the U.S.

Later in the visit, I called on Governor-General Rajagopalachari in Government House.[3] In his opinion, our government was devoting too much energy to opposing Communists outside the U.S. It seemed to him that by permitting Communists in the U.S. a relatively free hand to carry on their activities, we were partly responsible for the American animosity toward the Communists. If our government, like that of India, would take effective measures to squelch the Communists in our own country, our fear and anger over international Communism could not be so great. I pointed out to Rajagopalachari that the U.S. was devoting its energy not so much to fighting Communism as to opposing Soviet aggression. I cited Greece as an example of the need for cooperation among the democratic powers, in order to protect small countries from Communist aggression.

Luncheon on the 11th at the embassy was an official affair, including the Deputy Prime Minister for Industry and Supply, Minister of Commerce, Minister for Defense, Foreign Secretary, and other officials, most with wives. The luncheon plan footnotes listed the vegetarians, also those who did not take butter, eggs, spices, and alcohol. On the top rung of each dining-room chair was a different-colored thread to indicate to the servants what could be offered the occupant. Pity the poor hostess.

In the evening, K. P. S. Menon, who was at that time in charge of the Ministry of Foreign Affairs, and Mrs. Menon, gave a magnificent formal dinner for us at Hyderabad House. There were perhaps fifty guests. It was so good I kept the menu. Borscht à la Russe was followed by Filet de Sole à l'Ambassadrice with Pommes Nouvelles Vapeur, later Délices de Perdreaux Lucullus with Bouquet de Primeux des Indes and Salade à l'Orange followed by Châlet Suisse Mont Blanc and Courbelle de Deuceurs and Demitasse. In responding to Menon's welcoming toast, I gave Montesquieu's quotation that friendship represented the highest degree of perfection in society, as being relevant to the budding friendship between the U.S. and India.

The next day provided an interesting afternoon of sightseeing. We went to the Red Fort, built by the Mogul emperors during the sixteenth and seventeenth centuries. The Red Fort constituted, in effect, a great walled city for the Emperor, his soldiers, and his court. There were mazes of halls, temples, and courtyards for the Muslim ladies in purdah, beautiful marble screens, paved walks, pools, and fountains. It was quite an impressive display, surrounded by a great high wall from which the Emperor watched elephants trained to fight.

Cecilia took a particular interest in the religions of India, so we visited one of the great mosques of Old Delhi, similar to others we had seen, and the recently built Birla Hindu Temple, the likes of which we had never seen before. There was one huge main temple connected to several smaller ones by runways or courtyards. The buildings were all red and white with flowers and bell-shaped cupolas and whatnots piled on top, looking like something a child would make with blocks.

Scattered throughout the garden were statues of elephants, monkeys, cobras (as fountain pieces), tigers, and crocodiles. All are sacred animals and fit somewhere into the vast panorama of myth and religion embraced by Hinduism. There were idols of richly dressed gods and people of wealth to whom the worshipers prayed, also Vishnu with the four arms and Krishna with six. There was an elephant-headed god and a monkey-headed one. And all around were children playing and screaming in the halls, and bells ringing, as the evening chants began.

There were in pre-partition India two main religions, Hinduism and Islam. After partition, Pakistan became a Muslim state, India a secular one. Many Muslims continued to live in India even after the exodus of millions of Muslim refugees. The differences between the two cultures are enormous. On a superficial level, Muslims will eat all meat but pork: Hindus eat little meat, never beef. The cows, which are holy to the Hindu and protected by them, are a miserable-looking lot. Holiness does not protect them from labor. They are worked very hard and when old are turned into the streets to fend for themselves. Occasionally, a priest will choose a calf and declare it particularly sacred. We saw one large black bull which had the distinction of being so designated, which had a beautifully embroidered mask and coat. People paid the priest to worship it, as he led it down the street.

The Hindus are the dominant religious group in India, with Brahman their passive universal world spirit. An active triad of deities— the trimurti—includes Brahma, the creator; Vishnu, who preserves his creation; and Siva, who destroys it. Cecilia found that the Sikhs, whose religion was founded in the fifteenth century and is a blend of Hinduism and Islam, had abolished idolatry and the caste system. She was particularly interested in a religious group, the Jains, who will eat no living thing. Believing in transmigration they fear eating a relative. When they discovered the existence of microbes they were so afraid that they might swallow one that they tied cloths across their mouths. Gautama Buddha was born in India in the sixth century B.C. The number of his adherents has been swollen in recent years by Untouchables, who have sought through conversion to escape the onerous Hindu caste system.

That evening we were invited to another reception by the Governor-General at Government House for the participants of the Indo-American Conference. This was held inside, and the stairs were lined with the same scarlet-coated lancers who had been in the garden two days before; they looked straight out of Hollywood. We enjoyed chatting with members of the conference about their impressions of India. Herbert Elliston, then editor of the Washington *Post*, was there with his wife, Joey, and Kay Halle from Washington. I was glad to see Dr. Arthur Holly Compton, the world-renowned nuclear physicist, and his wife Betty. I had studied under Dr. Compton at Oxford.

Cecilia and I chatted amiably with Nehru. I suddenly realized how short he was. Cecilia had the feeling that he had for some reason given her a disapproving look. Earlier, before leaving the residence, Elise Henderson had tactfully suggested she wear a shawl over her evening gown; we would be going on to a formal dinner. Cecilia, not knowing why the suggestion had been made, had decided not to. Later she discovered that it was not considered proper for a lady to expose so much of her shoulders in public. Nehru, she concluded, didn't approve, and I'm sure she was right. In a picture taken at the reception of me with Nehru which appeared in the *Indian News Chronicle,* he appears to be glaring fiercely.

We went directly to dinner at the residence of His Highness the Nawab of Pataudi and the Begum Sahiba, at 5 Barackhamba Road. Before dining we reclined on cushions on the floor, and later at dinner we also sat on cushions covered with brocades, at very low tables, and ate with our fingers. The whole repast was placed on the table at once: each person had a large round silver platter containing about six smaller silver bowls, each with a separate dish. As our hosts were Muslim, we had beef, chicken, dal and other legumes, rice, and for dessert, a farina pudding with paper-thin silver-leaf coating. The bread was a flat wheat cake that resembled a Mexican tortilla and the rice was difficult to handle until one learned to mold it into a ball and pop it into the mouth. Vintage champagne flowed freely all during the dinner.

Back in the drawing room, again on cushions, we were given a draw off a hookah, a water pipe, which Cecilia did not like at all. Then came the dancing girls. A beautiful young nautch dancer from the south, in a flimsy green costume and ankle bells, did a stylized but most exciting series of dances. She used her hands to tell the story, and did it quite gracefully. Another dancer, a very young girl from the north, did a rowdier sort of dance. The rhythm was great but the music was difficult to appreciate, being not only atonal but high and whiny, hurting our unaccustomed ears. The whole evening was really superb and we left feeling grateful to our host and hostess for having gone to such great pains to show us life as it once was among the Indian aristocracy. It represented a style which was not to continue much longer.

The following morning was free for us, as I had declined a shooting expedition in favor of sightseeing and shopping. We lunched with General K. M. Cariappa, Commander-in-Chief of the Indian Army, at his residence at 4 King George's Avenue. The General was a charming and attentive host, but so British it was hard not to laugh. He smoked black Russian cigarettes, talked much about cricket, and peppered his conversation with such anglicisms as "I say! Jolly good show, what?" One expected to hear "Pip, pip, cheerio." He gave us an excellent Indian lunch and insisted that Cecilia take some papier-mâché mats she had admired. Cariappa had a reputation of being an excellent soldier and commander-in-chief.

In the afternoon we shopped and went sightseeing with the Ellistons. We were shown the fantastic jewelry available from sales by the

Maharajas. At one store the proprietor brought forth a series of large boxes, each of which he opened. One contained a set of perfectly matched amethysts, so deep a purple as to be almost black, set in diamonds. The box also contained two impressive necklaces, to be worn together, the longer one with a large pendant; earrings made of several stones; a large bracelet for each arm; two or three rings for each hand; and an optional tiara for more formal occasions. There were similar sets with rubies and emeralds and several of the Mogul rose, or crude-cut diamonds, and other stones, mounted in gold. The reverse side was beautifully encrusted even though to be worn next to the body.

That evening we attended a dinner given by Dr. S. S. Bhatnager, Secretary of the Department of Scientific Research, and his wife. Arthur Compton and other American physicists attending the Indo-American Conference were among the honored guests, along with several Indian physicists. The Indian food was strong and delicious but the conversation of the more prosaic scientists was a little sticky after our evenings with nawabs and ambassadors, and we were glad to be able to leave early.

On the morning of December 13 I held a press conference for Indian journalists at the U.S. Information Service Library.[4] I had prepared a statement expressing my pleasure at being in India and my satisfaction that the friendliest of relations existed between our countries. Americans, who had strongly sympathized with India's desire for independence, were becoming increasingly aware of India as a vital force in the world. The recent visit of Prime Minister Nehru had been most helpful. We were assisting Indian representation in international bodies, and increasing numbers of Americans were visiting India. We had hopes that India would benefit from U.S. technical assistance under the Point Four Program then under consideration by Congress. Since the amount under discussion was only $45 million (later reduced to $25 million) worldwide, India obviously wouldn't get very much. However, at that juncture it was all of the "trade goods" I had to offer. There were many questions.

Reaction from the press was varied. The *Indian News Chronicle* published a cartoon labeled "One by One," showing me as a cowboy on horseback (I assume because I am a Texan) attempting to lasso a bull labeled India, while Ceylon looked on. Below it said, "Mr. McGhee, Assistant Secretary of State, explained the Point Four Program at a Press Conference in New Delhi."

The *Nation* interpreted my visit as an effort to assess the strength of the Nehru government, and whether Nehru could make good his promise that there would be no nationalization of property for at least ten years. The *Nation's* editorial of December 14 expressed the pervading fear of foreign domination still remaining from the colonial era. "India's neutrality had already been bartered away to the British Commonwealth. American dollar aid and the infiltration of American private capital could only confirm India's partisanship in favor of the Western powers. An India in the embrace of the Four Point Program was no more neutral than a Marshallized Europe."

Many papers, including the *Indian News Chronicle*, commented on my Point Four remarks, noting the program's inadequacy in the face of the tremendous needs of the developing countries. Some emphasized my hope that U.S. private investment would come to India. I had attempted to assure them such investment was entirely on its own and no political exploitation would result. Most papers reported my statement and my answers as I gave them, although one commented that my remarks about American interest in India sounded like what I had said in Karachi a few days before. After reviewing my papers I concluded they were right. I had not foreseen being reported in New Delhi.

On the morning of December 14, after farewells to the Hendersons, we took off in the embassy plane for visits to Agra, Madras, and Calcutta. My first visit to India had been a most interesting and rewarding one despite my disappointment with Nehru. He was a complicated man who evoked a variety of images. I was to see him in several moods: the cool, handsome, aristocratic, ascetic-appearing intellectual; the revolutionary aspiring for world leadership of the newly liberated countries with his concept of neutralism; and the idol of the liberal West.

For me there was also another side. Nehru spoke easily and sonorously, but the words that came out really had little meaning to me. They sounded fine if you didn't have to report or analyze them, but if you had a mental pencil poised to record his thoughts, nothing worth jotting down came through. In the end I had nothing to report. I would not say that he was being deliberately duplicitous or evasive or insincere: his mind just did not go from cause to effect, or progress from *a* to *b* to *c*, as mine did or, I believe, as most Westerners' would. Perhaps the Indian mind, particularly after centuries of coping with conquerors, has adopted a more cautious and circuitous line of reasoning than prevails in the West.

There is no question that Nehru was devoted to his country, and to the Indian people, but he approached the masses aloofly as a member of the ruling class. I had been with him outside of official U.S. groups on a number of occasions during his first U.S. visit. As a relatively junior officer, I had melded into his own entourage. I had seen him act so rudely, even brutally, with members of his staff, over some real or imaginary dereliction, that I was embarrassed for both him and them. His constant aide and prompter, always at his side, was his daughter Indira, who appeared to be in competition with Nehru's sister, Madame Vijaya Lakshmi Pandit, Indian Ambassador to the U.S.

We departed from India on December 17 for our first visit to Ceylon, now Sri Lanka.

Sri Lanka (the original Sinhalese name, which in 1972 replaced the European designation of Ceylon, will be used where possible, although this is difficult since it was in 1949 called Ceylon) is a large and lovely island, set like a jewel in the Indian Ocean off the southern apex of the Indian subcontinent. The Tamils from southern India conquered the northern part of the island in the thirteenth century and established in the arid part of the island one of the most elaborate irrigation systems ever created by man. Sri Lanka has throughout history been a frequent object of conquest by outside powers. It was ruled successively by the Chinese, Portuguese, and Dutch, until the arrival of the British in 1795. As a crown colony, Sri Lanka underwent considerable development, largely under the plantation system, created and owned by the British, which produced rubber, tea, coffee, cocoa, and coconut.

Because of its location with respect to India and the shipping lanes of the Indian Ocean, Sri Lanka has considerable strategic importance. On March 24, 1949, the U.S. Joint Chiefs of Staff had determined that it would be in our national interest if South Asia (Afghanistan, Pakistan, India, Burma, Nepal, and Ceylon) could be oriented toward the U.S. and other Western democracies and away from the U.S.S.R.[5] We should meet any deficiencies in the military equipment of the South Asian countries required under British strategic plans. In short, Ceylon was considered important to us but we preferred to let the British continue to assume primary responsibility for its security.

Since our arrival in Ceylon was on a weekend, my official calls on the government were set for Monday morning. It was natural that I did not delay my call on the British representative of the Crown. At

6:30 p.m., Cecilia and I paid our duty call at Government House on the Governor-General of Ceylon, Lord Soulbury, and his wife. They were a delightful couple, whom we were to see again on our second visit to Ceylon in 1951. We later became good friends with their son Sir Peter Ramsbotham, who, with his delightful wife Frances, served with great distinction as British Ambassador to Washington in the 1970s.

On Sunday we visited the celebrated Buddhist shrine at Kandy and the world-famous Peradeniya gardens. On Monday morning I attended the staff conference at the embassy and made a call on the British High Commissioner (Ambassador) at the Chancery. At noon I called on the Prime Minister, D. S. Senanayake. He was an impressive man, with a large frame, a long, grave, rugged face, and gray hair and mustache. His selection as his country's first Prime Minister reflected his leadership in Ceylon's independence movement.

My meeting with the Prime Minister involved few points of political significance. Although an independent country, Ceylon was still under strong British influence. I wanted to assure Senanayake of our interest and friendship, and to back up the British. We had no desire to take their place: we did, however, want to be in a position to help fill any vacuum that the British might leave. I referred to our important business interests in Ceylon, particularly our importation of their agricultural products and our sales to them of oil and miscellaneous manufactured goods. We hoped, in connection with Point Four technical assistance, that U.S. investment could be increased. I inquired about Ceylon's attitude toward China, which was at that time very much in our minds.

The Prime Minister welcomed me and expressed interest in developing relations between our countries. He thought that Communism in China was not at present aggressive and would require considerable time to consolidate its country's forces. He did not consider Ceylon endangered by Communism from outside, or by the small local Communist elements. He expressed interest in the introduction of U.S. capital in partnership with local capital. Later the Prime Minister attended a luncheon given for us at the embassy residence. In the evening there was a large reception at the Ambassador's residence attended by Ceylonese officials and leading citizens.

Before our departure the following morning for Calcutta, the embassy issued a press release containing my comments on our visit. It was a public-relations move to let Ceylon know we had been there and that Americans wanted to be their friends. We had enjoyed meeting the high officials of the country and were gratified that Ceylon continued its Commonwealth ties. I said that the U.S. was becoming increasingly aware of the importance of Ceylon in South Asia. We appreciated her wartime contribution. We valued the tea and rubber and other important products we bought from Ceylon. If a climate could be created there which American investors found conductive to making profits, I felt confident they would want to invest there. In the meantime our government offered Ceylon technical assistance under Point Four.

My statement was reprinted without comment the following morning in the local *Daily News* and the *Times*. We left Ceylon with a most agreeable impression and the feeling that the island had good prospects for the future.

Burma has always represented to me a complete enigma. My superficial contacts with this fascinating country have intrigued me, but have failed to explain it to me. The present inhabitants, numbering some 33 million, are divided into numerous ethnic groups, the largest of which are the Burmans, accounting for about 70 percent of the population, who are descendants of tribes who migrated to Burma in ancient times from Tibet. The country came under British rule in stages, the last part being incorporated in 1886 as a part of India. It was given limited self-government in 1922, becoming a British colony in 1937. Burma was occupied by Japanese forces from 1942 to 1945. It became an independent republic outside the Commonwealth on January 4, 1948, with U Nu (Thakin Nu) as Prime Minister.

Cecilia and I arrived in Rangoon from Calcutta. On the morning of December 23, I paid my official call on Prime Minister U Nu, as he is normally called, who was a very religious man.[6] Shortly before our arrival he had announced that he was temporarily giving up his wife, somewhat in the way a Christian gives up something for Lent. He announced that during his period of absence from the family bed he would live in a bungalow on the grounds of his residence. I visited him at his residence, not the bungalow, and we had a pleasant chat.

After preliminary courtesies I asked the Prime Minister if he did not think that Burma was facing a very grave crisis, meaning the recent insurgency on the part of the Karen minority, who sought to create a separate state. He replied that he felt Burma had passed the worst part of its crisis, but that he was disillusioned after his unsuccessful effort in April to negotiate with the Karens. He did not propose to negotiate again with the leaders or any group of them until they had laid down their arms. He gave no indication that the government proposed to make a peace offer. There was some discussion about the Karens and whether the danger from Communist China was not increasing. As usual I emphasized the Communist threat.

We then discussed the Point Four Program. I told U Nu we hoped Burma would be interested in receiving technical assistance under the program, part of which would be carried out through the UN. I pointed out the importance of internal stability if Burma hoped to attract private investors. The management of American companies was guided by the interests of their stockholders, in deciding whether or not to invest abroad. Stable conditions and the assurance of a fair return were essential. I explained that there was still a great field for investment in the U.S. and that many of our companies were reluctant to invest abroad. When they did, however, they were willing to accept modest returns.

The Prime Minister expressed surprise that business firms would be guided solely by the prospect of an assured return on their investment. He thought, naïvely, that they would have an interest in undertakings which would help contain the spread of Communism. I replied that our government might support undertakings for political reasons, but not private companies.

I don't believe, however, that I really succeeded in establishing contact with U Nu. Smiling all the time, he was shy and noncommittal. I attempted to persuade him that we wanted to be friends with Burma, and that we had no desire to draw him into any bloc or tell him how to run his economy which had, since independence, been highly socialistic.

Later the Prime Minister and his wife received Cecilia and me at luncheon. U. E. Maung, the former Minister of Justice, whom I had entertained in Washington, gave us a candlelight reception in a picturesque courtyard surrounded by government buildings. I was received by the Acting Foreign Minister, Sao Hkum Hkio, who was new at his job.[7]

The Minister said that he recognized insurgency as Burma's immediate major problem requiring early solution, but did not anticipate any increase in insurgency after the rice harvest. He did not seem concerned about a possible invasion from China, or elsewhere. Burmese history had recorded continuous border raids. He did, however, acknowledge the danger of Communist penetration through minorities. The Minister emphasized Burma's urgent need for financial assistance, and expressed impatience at the delays which had occurred in receiving it. Burma would not consent, no matter how badly off it was, to a loan with strings attached. When I inquired how this could be reconciled with the need of the lending country to have some assurance that the money would be used for agreed purposes, the Minister merely reiterated that the Burmese were strongly against any conditions.

Before my departure I released a statement to the press. I paid tribute to the country and its people and to the Prime Minister, Foreign Minister and U. E. Maung, expressing appreciation for their hospitality. I emphasized America's keen interest in Burma, and our hope that Burma would overcome its current internal difficulties. We supported Burma's nationalist aspirations, I said, and hoped Burma would continue to strengthen its Commonwealth relations. We wanted to be helpful to Burma without imposing ourselves or our political or economic ideologies. I pointed out that we had friendly relations with many socialist countries, including, at that particular time, Britain. Our only concern was that Burma be allowed to "work out its own destiny without being overwhelmed by the new Communist imperialism which, under the guise of a leftist economic doctrine, had engulfed one country after another."

We had, I said, no desire to create a bloc of nations to struggle for world power. We recognized, however, our responsibilities in assisting other nations to resist aggression, and hoped Burma's internal difficulties, which were of concern to all of its friends, would not prevent Burma from paying close attention to the world situation and the dangers which Burma might face from the outside. I was only able to cite Point Four as a possible form of U.S. assistance. Knowing full well that Burma would not be attractive to American private investment under present conditions, I said only that future interest would depend on the policies of the Burmese government and the degree of security and stability that could be achieved there, in which endeavor I wished Burma well.

It is interesting to be able to read in the British Records Office the dispatch to the Foreign Office of the British Ambassador, James (later Sir James) Bowker, who became my opposite number in the Foreign Office as Superintending Under Secretary of State, and a good friend over the years.[8] I had, naturally, since Burma was in the British sphere, established contact with him on my arrival, and he and his attractive wife Elsa had given a pleasant dinner for Cecilia and myself. I assured Bowker that we recognized British primacy in Burma and wanted to help them. In return he outlined the program of financial assistance planned for Burma which, considering the British financial situation, I felt was generous. His report to London, which was flattering, indicated appreciation that I had in my press conference gone out of my way to express pleasure at Burma's cordial relations with the Commonwealth, and had stressed our close ties with the U.K. which, like Burma, had a socialist government. My cooperation with the British in Burma seems to have paid off.

Burma, unlike India and Pakistan, opted to receive its independence outside the Commonwealth. Its parliamentary democracy withstood both Communist insurgency and ethnic separatist movements. In 1958, however, a split in the ruling Anti-Fascist People's Freedom League, itself a loose coalition of individuals and interest groups, precipitated a serious political crisis, causing Prime Minister U Nu to call on Army Chief of Staff Ne Win to head a caretaker government empowered to restore order.

Elections in 1960 returned U Nu to power, but, despite the sweeping parliamentary majority won by his newly formed Union Party, the perennial Prime Minister's government proved ineffective in dealing with Burma's pressing social and economic problems. Ne Win intervened again in 1962 to depose U Nu. Marking out the "Burmese Way to Socialism," the General's revolutionary government suspended the constitution and instituted authoritarian control over the country and its economy through the Burma Socialist Program party. All other political organizations were outlawed. Ne Win introduced a rigorously centralized government and proceeded to nationalize the economy as part of his planned transformation of Burma into a "democratic socialist" state.

Ne Win's regime remains supportive of Burma's prevailing Buddhist religion, patronizing the monasteries in much the same way that the Burmese kings did in former days. Insurgent ethnic movements, spearheaded by the Shans and the Karens in their opposition to centralization, have joined in a common front to carry on resistance to the government. Many Burmese Muslims have fled to Bangladesh to escape persecution. Indigenous Communists have received aid, including arms, from China.

The road to socialism has been a rocky one for Burma. Although rich in resources and blessed with fertile soil, Burma's economic growth has been slow, barely keeping pace with its population growth. Despite the government's emphasis on agricultural development, productivity has also been low, considering the available resource base, and attempts to diversify have largely been unsuccessful. Burma's trading position has likewise deteriorated with the decline of the market for its rice exports, curtailing as a result the inflow of consumer goods and the investment capital essential for development. Unemployment has become a way of life for large segments of the urban population. The old managerial and professional class has become virtually extinct. Buildings, public and private, have been left to decay, utilities in advanced disrepair are unreliable, and the country's transportation infrastructure has all but broken down.

My early visits to India, and particularly to Ceylon and Burma, were very much under the shadow of the British. The question arises as to whether I should have been more aggressive in proposing new concepts or in establishing contacts with individuals and groups not sponsored by the British. In retrospect, I think not; even if we had we would have had limited opportunity to change future events. The leaders of these countries trusted the British and were all still busy sorting out their affairs with them. Our resources already stretched by massive aid to Europe and the Middle East, Americans were reluctant to undertake new responsibilities toward hundreds of millions of strange people on the far side of the world. Better let the British bear their burdens as long as they were willing and able, before their inevitable retirement.

11

Developing an African Policy

February–March, 1950. East-West African Conference of U.S. Diplomatic and Consular Officers. Lourenço Marques (now Maputo), Mozambique. February 27–March 2, 1950.

It is not surprising that, in 1950, no comprehensive U.S. policy had been formulated for Africa south of the Sahara. We had few national interests of importance in that area, most of which we recognized was the responsibility of the European "metropolitan" powers, who regarded our activities there with suspicion. World-wide we were at that time concerned primarily with our Cold War with the Soviet Union, which had reached crisis proportions with the Korean War. In meeting the Communist threat, the cooperation of our European allies was essential.

Yet, there was obviously a need for a U.S. African policy. The only independent countries were Liberia and Ethiopia. It was already clear, however, that the general trend toward self-determination would result in increased world interest in progress being achieved in Africa. The new majority in the UN, swelled by the newly-independent countries of Asia and with strong support from Latin America and the Communist countries, was pressing to speed up decolonization. Furthermore, we were engaged in building up the economies of our European allies, and economic development in Africa could serve this, as well as the African interest.

There was also another set of factors involved which is more difficult to set forth, that peculiarly American combination of humanitarianism and self-interest. We were interested in American economic opportunities in Africa, while at the same time maintaining a genuine concern for the welfare of its peoples. Both objectives could easily coexist in our minds. There was also the looming threat of Soviet Communism to the African countries once they achieved independence. This would raise the question of military security. It became clear that we must make up for lost time, that the development of an African policy was not only timely but overdue.

The immediate focus for such an effort was the convocation of a conference of American diplomatic and consular representatives in Africa scheduled to be held in Lourenço Marques, in Portuguese Mozambique, on February 27, 1950. There had never been quite such a conference before. There was enthusiasm on the part of our officers in Africa, who had tended to consider themselves neglected if not forgotten men, and were surprised that an Assistant Secretary was coming.

Since our Point Four Program was to be discussed, the British Embassy in Washington was eager to provide us full information on arrangements for technical cooperation in Africa. This was, in effect, to obtain our support in defeating the proposal of the World Federation of United Nations Associations for an Economic Commission for Africa. From the British archives, I find that the Foreign Office had advised their representatives in Africa of my visit, saying that I was "a good friend of the U.K. and that any courtesies shown me would amply repay themselves."

Prior to the conference we had invited to the Department a group of American experts on African affairs to discuss the agenda.[1] The non-governmental representatives at that meeting were carefully chosen: Dr. Emory Ross of the Foreign Missions Conference; James A. Farrell, Jr., president of the Farrell Steamship Lines; Dr. Robert G. Woolbert of the University of Denver; Dr. Derwent Whittlesey, professor of geography at Harvard University; Dr. Cornelis W. de Kiewet, acting president of Cornell University; Dr. Mark H. Watkins, professor of anthropology at Howard University; Dr. Ralph J. Bunche, director of the Department of Trusteeship for the UN; Dr. Channing Tobias of the Phelps-Stokes Foundation; Dr. John Morrison, professor of geography at the University of Maryland; Juan T. Trippe, president of Pan American Airways; and Ogden White of the Filatures Tissages Africains.

The Department was represented by the top officers concerned: Raymond Hare, my deputy; Burton Berry, director of the Office of African and Near Eastern Affairs; Durward Sandifer from the Office of United Nations Affairs; Leo Cyr, officer in charge of Southern African Affairs; and several others.

I emphasized in my opening remarks the need for a comprehensive U.S. policy toward Africa. For the first time, we had tools in the form of Point Four technical assistance and funds from the Economic Cooperation Administration (ECA). In addition to furthering our traditional economic, humanitarian, and religious-evangelistic interests, we wanted to assist economically our hard-pressed European allies, the colonial metropolitan powers, and assure a proper role for the UN in furthering the development and progress toward self-government of the African people.

During the course of our meeting the outside consultants agreed on the importance of developing an overall African policy in view of the "malleability of the African people" and our influence with the colonial powers. We must, on the other hand, first try to overcome the deficiencies in our knowledge of Africa; to differentiate between Communist infiltration and justifiable local political goals; to avoid the appearance of wanting to create spheres of influence for ourselves; and not to get between the Africans and the metropoles, who were in most cases in the midst of difficult negotiations for withdrawal. Our consultants pointed out that Africa was weak in soil and climate, and that more interest must be given to agriculture than to the extraction of minerals. They urged that we cooperate with the metropoles to improve the skills of the Africans, their education, health, and the local infrastructure, rather than push for early independence.

The conclusions of our meeting, as I later reported to Deputy Under Secretary Rusk, were the first step in developing an African policy. We had agreed that the basic objective of our African policy should be to accelerate development, and that this should be accomplished through cooperation between the European colonial countries, the Africans, and the U.S. With the ECA and President Truman's proposed Point Four technical assistance program available, we were for the first time in a strong position to pursue this objective. American plans for technical assistance should be coordinated by the UN.

The conference agreed that if our aims were to be believed and understood, a statement of U.S. policy was needed at the highest level, not only on policy toward Africa, but on colonial policy generally. Otherwise, we ran the risk of being deliberately misrepresented by our critics throughout the world. We should at the same time work toward a reasonable acceleration of the political evolution of the African peoples, in agreement with our Western allies: Britain, France, Portugal, and Belgium.

In order to attract private American capital to Africa, the group concluded that there must be improvement of internal transportation and conservation of water, the carrying-out of hydroelectric schemes, and the building of hotels and rest houses. Africans should be trained in industrial and mechanical techniques, which the conference thought could be done without dislocation of the local labor force. It was felt unwise to bring a large number of displaced Europeans to Africa. Africa was too poor to support them and it was felt they would tend to exploit the Africans.

The conferees recognized that there was a basic conflict between a clearly enunciated policy aimed at speeding up decolonization and assurances of cooperation with our European metropolitan allies. It was felt that this might be alleviated by a series of conferences, or consultations, with our allies. It was assumed that Africans would welcome American capital and know-how, for how else could they obtain the development they so desired? Yet it was recognized that for American capital to be profitably invested, there would first have to be improvements in infrastructure. This would not be attractive to foreigners, but would have to come from the metropoles. There was as yet no thought of grant aid from the U.S. for this purpose.

The results of the Washington conference were carefully documented so as to be available for the conference in Lourenço Marques, which was attended by forty-two officials.[2] They included representatives from our departments of State, Agriculture, and Commerce and from the Economic Cooperation Administration; our ambassadors to Ethiopia and Liberia; and consular officers from the Gold Coast (later Ghana), Nigeria, Angola, the Belgian Congo (now Zaire), Mozambique, Tanganyika (now Tanzania), Kenya, Madagascar, and South Africa (to provide coverage of the Rhodesias, now Zambia and Zimbabwe), Nyasaland (now Malawi), South-West Africa (now Namibia), and the High Commission Territories (now Botswana, Lesotho, and Swaziland). I served as chairman of the conference.

Our host country, Mozambique, or Portuguese East Africa, had come into the possession of Portugal in 1507, when the Portuguese seized it from an Arab sultanate dating to the tenth century. Covering some 300,000 square miles, the country had in 1950 a population of nearly 6,000,000 blacks and 60,000 Europeans. The principal exports were sugar, copra, sisal, and nuts. Mozambique had close ties with the Union of South Africa, which utilized the principal port and capital, Lourenço Marques. Development of the colony, which suffered from malaria and other tropical diseases, had been limited. The total number of native students at all levels, for example, was less than 100,000.

The report on the political situation in Mozambique submitted by Consul H. Gordon Minnigerode for our conference was as follows:

> So far as it is possible to discover, there is no appreciable agitation for independence or self-government in Mozambique, and no probability of such a movement arising in the near future. This situation is attributed chiefly to the autocratic form of government which prevails, as personified by the dictatorial power vested in the person of the Governor-General, who is responsible only to the Minister of Colonies in Lisbon, and whose rule reflects in the Colony the dictatorship which prevails in Portugal; the situation is also largely due to the almost universal illiteracy and lack of political consciousness among the native population of the country.
>
> The Governor-General exercises executive and legislative functions under the Organic Constitution of the Colonial Empire, issued by decree on November 5, 1933, and his actions and decisions are subject to review only by the Minister of Colonies. Electoral rights are restricted to a small percentage of prominent Portugese citizens who are possessors of property and represent the well-to-do industrial and agricultural classes. There is no legislative assembly, the nearest approach being the small Government Council of ten members.
>
> Under this highly centralized society the authority of the Government has remained unquestioned, and it may be said that politics are non-existent. In view of the illiteracy of at least 95% of the native population, a rigorous censorship of all literature printed or imported, and a highly effective police organization, such a movement is believed unlikely. The probability is that the present system will continue for many years.

Although there was little time for relaxation from our hard work schedule, we were able to visit with our hosts from the Mozambique government and tour the city of Lourenço Marques. Admiral Gabriel Texeira, Governor-General of Mozambique, proved an interesting and able representative of his country in one of Portugal's most important colonial posts. A career naval officer from an old Lisbon family, Texeira ran his colony with an iron hand. There was no local participation in government and there were few amenities for the mass of black inhabitants. Those, however, who by heritage, skill, or hard work had risen to wealth and leadership were at least superficially accepted as equals in the business and social world of the national capital. Several were invited to the excellent formal dinner the Governor-General gave following my initial call. Among the officials present were Agostinho de Torres Fevereiro, the attorney general; Teodusio Cardinal Gouveia, archbishop of Lourenço Marques; and other members of Texeira's government. There were also present some of the local business leaders.

In his after-dinner remarks Texeira said that if a major armed conflict between East and West was inevitable, it was gratifying to be able to state that Portugal was on the "right side of the fence." He stressed the close ties of friendship which existed between our countries. In my reply I observed that the U.S. was a young upstart in comparison with Portugal's five hundred years as a great maritime nation. I welcomed Texeira's use of the colloquial American expression "the same side of the fence," and said that although some might consider us naïve in the new role we were assuming abroad, I assured Texeira that we had only the best of intentions toward Portugal and his government in Mozambique. It did not occur to me that Portugal would retire from Mozambique in my lifetime.

Texeira, in turn, accepted an invitation to dine with our group in our hotel, where he spoke freely about his philosophy of how a colony should be run. During our five days at Lourenço Marques, I got to know Gabriel Texeira well, and found him not only a charming man but a broad-gauged official. A real aristocrat, he bore his almost total authority in Mozambique quite naturally and with good grace. The Portuguese generally had no self-doubts or apologies for their colonial policies. They considered their colonies to be integral parts of Portugal. They were sure that their system, which had endured five hundred years, was the best for both peoples. This undoubtedly contributed later to their being totally unprepared for the collapse of their African regimes. Texeira was later to progress to the highest posts in the government in Lisbon, and I kept up with him over the years through brief notes at Christmas. In parting from Lourenço Marques he gave me a beautiful bronze filigree replica of a Portuguese caravel sailing vessel in a handsome hardwood case, which I value highly.

Our delegation stayed in the delightful Hotel Polona, a resort hotel owned by a Johannesburg family with American connections. We were well looked after and had pleasant times on the broad terrace, surrounded by palm trees, overlooking the sea. I gave one formal dinner followed by dancing on the terrace. Among our group was an attractive young lady Foreign Service officer, Margaret Tibbetts of the London Embassy, who later became our Ambassador to Norway. Also among the group was Ambassador to Liberia, Edward Dudley, whom I had visited on the way to the conference. We had traveled together to Johannesburg and Lourenço Marques. In Johannesburg, at my insistence, he stayed in the consulate in my stead, in order to avoid the indignity of not being able to use the common rooms of the hotel, because he was black. When traveling by car through the Union of South Africa to Lourenço Marques we had a tense moment when we went into a restaurant in a small Transvaal town for lunch. The proprietor was obviously shocked and hesitated for a moment, not knowing what to do. Eventually, however, he served us with good grace.

An amusing incident happened one evening at La Polona while we were having drinks on the terrace. A subject of discussion at the morning meeting had been what was characterized as the "Hey, boy" attitude of many white colonialists toward blacks. Obviously this served to aggravate race relations unnecessarily. Suddenly in the midst of our cocktail conversation, when it became apparent that we needed another round of drinks, we heard a clear voice boom out, "Hey, boy." We looked around to see who had said it. It was one of our black participants. We were convulsed with laughter.

An important part of the conference program was a country-by-country analysis by our representatives of the threat of Communism and of attitudes toward the U.S. in their areas. These reports, which are summarized in the following pages, are enlightening to read in the light of subsequent events. Our preoccupation with the Communist threat is self-evident:

Ethiopia. Contrary to rumors given currently abroad, personnel of the Soviet Legation in Addis Ababa do not exceed fifteen. Few Ethiopians are employed in the legation. It has an exhibition center, but it is temporarily closed. However, it is possible that Soviet literature is being distributed elsewhere in Africa by the legation. There is a Soviet-operated hospital. The attitude of Ethiopians toward most U.S. foreign policies has, in general, been somewhat negative. Much of the population is illiterate and there are few newspapers in the country. The Ethiopians are appreciative of the help we have given them but are disappointed with our stand on Italian Somaliland. They do not feel, however, "that we have let them down." They are reluctant to go along with our anti-Communist campaign because they are afraid of Russia and do not want to get themselves into a difficult position. In case of war they would not want to be on either side.

Liberia. Communism is not much of a problem. There is no evidence of a tie-up with Moscow. Government officials, entrenched as they are, do not want it. The native is too illiterate to be receptive. There is some evidence that the Firestone plantation strike (see Chapter 12) may have been stimulated from Nigeria or the Gold Coast. Conditions do exist, however, that could certainly play into the hands of Communist agitators. The general attitude toward American foreign policy is extremely favorable in Liberia. Our actions in the UN and our anti-Communist crusades are well regarded. We have been called upon for technical assistance in areas not usually sought by other governments. American lawyers are used in the drafting of legislation; also U.S. census experts. With respect to Point Four, the Liberians are very much interested in the technical assistance given so far and would like to have more. Liberia is disappointed that it has not been included in Marshall Plan aid, which neighboring colonial territories have received.

British Central Africa (Northern and Southern Rhodesia and Nyasaland). There is little evidence of Communism in these territories at present. Conditions do exist, however, that could make them a fertile field. Tribal differences militate against Communism. The governments are favorable to our anti-Communist campaign since they regard Communism as one of their greatest dangers. The ruling group are British, who are very conscious of the fact, and want to remain in power. Since their fate is closely linked to Britain, they welcome any assistance we can give to Britain. The territories are financed almost completely from Britain, American capital participating to only a modest degree. The governments do need our technical assistance and capital for development, but are reluctant to accept benefits which might lead to a growth of U.S. influence, on the theory that "where capital goes, influence goes."

British East Africa (Kenya, Uganda, and Tanganyika). Communism is not understood in East Africa. There is a spirit of nationalism and a tendency to consider anyone against the government as a Communist. Officials agree that Communism *per se* does not exist. A possible danger exists, however, in the lack of sympathy and understanding on the part of officials and Europeans generally toward Africans and Indians, and in efforts to maintain white supremacy. There are some agitators among foreign-educated persons but the number is very small. Some Europeans connected with the ground-nut scheme, the raising of peanuts on a large scale in Tanganyika, may be Communists. The recent riots in Uganda against the government resulted from ineptitude and absence of force to deal with the situation. Officials approve U.S. anti-Communism.

The East African authorities are still living in the age of Queen Victoria. They do not realize how much the British need us or how close our cooperation has already developed. They are only mildly aware of our anti-Communist stance; the blacks not at all. Marshall Plan aid is regarded with mild interest. There is no great interest in the Atlantic Pact. The UN and U.S. attitude toward dependent territories is not regarded favorably. Most Britons in East Africa feel that the U.S. is interfering with something that is not our business. Tanganyika is regarded by the blacks as a British territory, where independence is being delayed by the U.S. attitude toward trusteeship.

Belgian Congo. There is little evidence of Communism among natives. The police are vigilant and all immigrants to the Congo are carefully vetted. Tight security exists. The natives themselves are not receptive to Communism. Possible sources of future danger are infiltration by Communists from French Equatorial Africa, the Czech Consulate in Leopoldville, and the Czech Bata shoe plant. The general attitude of Belgian officials toward our foreign policies is favorable, although there is suspicion of our impatience to hasten economic development and native education. Officials are sympathetic with our anti-Communist campaign and feel that we are working with them to that end. The press, however, has a tendency to speak of the U.S. and Russia in "parallel columns," as powers fighting against each other. They hope Africa may escape that conflict.

Belgians in the Congo are generally cold toward the Marshall Plan. They suspect that this is merely another means to gain an economic foothold in the Congo. Recently, however, their attitude has changed somewhat because the colonies surrounding the Congo are asking for aid. The Belgians in the Congo will no doubt follow the French lead on the Atlantic Pact, but consider themselves in a strategic position should war come. They are building a transportation system across the Congo partly for strategic reasons. They are suspicious of us in the UN because our attitude in the Trusteeship Council could lead to a vote against the Congo.

Nigeria. There is evidence that Dr. Nnamdi Azikiwe (known as Zik), one of Nigeria's foremost indigenous leaders, is a Communist, although he says he is for any country that would assist Nigeria in attaining independence. Nigerian students are befriended by Communists in the U.K. and could be susceptible on their return. The government is concerned at increasing amounts of Communist literature coming into the colony. It is difficult to draw the line between Communism and nationalism in Nigeria. As yet there is no Communist party.

Gold Coast. Kwame Nkrumah, who engineered the recent general strike, in now in jail. There is no Communist party as such, only two known Communists in the territory. There are some indications, however, that Communist literature is coming in from the Ivory Coast. There is no native awareness of our anti-Communist movement. Americans are very popular with the natives who became acquainted with us during the war. There is little interest in Marshall Plan aid. The colony now benefits from the Colonial Development and Welfare Fund, is very rich, and does not require large development aid. Only assistance in road building has been requested. Officials in the Gold Coast are inclined to be suspicious of our Point Four Program. They would not like the idea of our technicians working independently there.

Angola and Mozambique. No Communist activity is tolerated here. About 95 percent of the natives are illiterate and there is no organization among them. A few Communists may, however, have infiltrated from the Union of South Africa. Angolan authorities carefully guard against infiltration from French Equatorial Africa and the Congo. Until recently the government of Angola censored information on the Marshall Plan. There is a negative official reaction toward the UN and especially the activities of the Trusteeship Council.

French West Africa. There is well-organized Communist activity inspired by the Rassemblement Démocratique Africain (see Chapter 19). An intensification occurred in January of 1950 in the Ivory Coast and culminated in the burning of homes and other acts of violence directed at native deserters from ranks of the RDA. The party once considered the Ivory Coast its stronghold; however, a new line of penetration along Latitude 14°, which separates the sedentary habitable part of West Africa from the nomadic strip next to the Sahara, has apparently been adopted. (End of Summary Reports.)

After these presentations to the conference, there was a full discussion, which formed the basis for a conference report. The report was noteworthy, first of all, for what it did not contain: There was no hint of boldness with respect to the promotion of decolonization. Nor was there any hope or expectation of "greater cooperation in the political field among the powers having interests in the area." The focus of the report was on stimulating cooperation in the economic field, "particularly in anticipation of the expiration of the ECA program," and on the possible provision of Point Four technicians and the use of good offices in Point Four programs, with a body that might be set up jointly by the metropoles and South Africa. No bold new departures here.

However, when discussion turned to the Cold War, new perspectives opened up immediately. It was as if this theme removed some of the inhibitions resulting from our desire not to get ahead of the metropoles. When it came to protecting our vital interests in countering Communism, there emerged in the conference a spirit of activism. On this subject, the conference report was clear.

> Positive efforts should be made to counter Communism through Point Four, ECA, Educational Exchange and the US Information Service. Every effort should be made to distribute widely appropriate material extolling the dignity and worth of the individual and pointing out that Communism is at complete variance with such a concept. All government agency representatives should report on genuine Communist activity, clearly distinguishing it, however, from other activity directed toward improving the lot of the natives.

There was one important phrase in the otherwise mild report. While we emphasized the importance of the dignity and worth of the individual, there was nothing said to connect it with the dignity of national self-expression. At the same time, however, our representatives wisely warned against accepting the tendency of some colonial powers to tar with the Communist brush movements that merely sought emancipation from colonialism. Thus we talked about the necessity to identify "genuine Communist activity."

An interesting sidelight with respect to decolonization was provided by the fears voiced at the conference that the decision to entrust Italian Somaliland totally under a trusteeship system calling for independence in ten years might be harmful to decolonization elsewhere. "If Somaliland becomes independent and the experiment failed, the movement towards self-government in other parts of Africa might be set back many years." As it happened, Somalia was one of the first countries to become independent in Africa, but its development toward independence had no influence on the trend of events on the continent. This was another case of a clouded crystal ball.

The report also called for cooperation with UN activities in Africa, and discussed local attitudes toward U.S. foreign policy.

Fear of Communism and of Soviet penetration is so strong in the area among the ruling group that there is little doubt of the area's basic sympathy for this aspect of US policy. There is considerable interest in US aid among officials and businessmen in places where actual deliveries have occurred, an interest which also extends to neighboring countries as yet unaided. There is some misunderstanding as to the nature and scope of the Point Four program.

As one reads this passage today, there can be little doubt that references to "the ruling group" and "officials and businessmen" refer, except perhaps in the case of Liberia and Ethiopia, to nationals of the metropoles. There is no evidence that African attitudes, i.e., those of the future rulers, were dealt with. Yet there are vague references to African—as distinguished from metropolitan—opinion, as for instance in the following recommendation:

While concluding that the reaction of a large part of Africa to American foreign policies is determined primarily by the attitudes of the European metropolitan powers, the conference nevertheless recommended that US foreign policies be depicted in Africa in terms of African interests, African limitations, and the capacities of African channels of mass communication. Policy presentations keyed to European interests and levels of sophistication have only a limited appeal in Africa.

So much for the official proceedings of the conference. On a more private level, it brought me an excruciating experience that I shall never forget. At one point I envisaged my resignation as Assistant Secretary as the result of a sensational press disclosure which could have been traced directly to me.

This story has to do with our mania for security. The conference dealt, of course, with many sensitive subjects, for instance, our attitudes toward the metropolitan powers. The conference was the subject of particular interest on the part of the world press, whose African representatives had converged on Lourenço Marques for the meeting. The Portuguese authorities might also have been expected to make special efforts to learn about our proceedings. So delicate did I regard our discussions that I forbade anyone to take notes when any evaluation was being made of the rule of the various metropolitan powers. I made my own notes in longhand on ruled yellow paper, which I carried with me outside the conference.

We permitted ourselves only one break during conference hours, a tour of the city before lunch on the last day. When we returned to our task, I reached into my inner pocket and found my yellow note paper missing. I was filled with apprehension. On the one hand, if I had lost them and the Portuguese authorities had found them, they would have been angry at some of the references to their colonial rule but they would have been quiet about it. On the other hand, if the press found the papers, they would make world headlines. I turned the chair over to someone else and sought out our security officer, who was from our Cairo embassy. I explained my predicament and asked him to accompany me back to the hotel, where the security officer inquired discreetly and I made a thorough search of my room, to no avail. I let him drop me off at the conference but asked him to retrace the route of our sightseeing and search for yellow papers. I resumed the chairmanship of the meeting but my mind was not on it. I was mentally drafting a telegram of resignation to the Department.

An hour later, the security officer drew me aside to lay some yellow sheets before me on the table. "How many did you say you had?" he asked. "Thirteen or fourteen? In any event I have thirteen." He explained that when he had stopped at the cathedral, which our group had visited, he had asked a maid in the yard of a house opposite if she had seen some Americans in a bus. She had. Had she seen any yellow papers? Yes, a lot of them were blown along the road. What happened to them? They were picked up by a Portuguese soldier who had stepped out of ranks from a squad marching by.

The security officer explained that he had not gone to the authorities but directly to the soldiers' barracks. He went from room to room asking each soldier, "Did you see any yellow papers when you marched by the church today?" At last one man reached into his blouse and pulled out the papers. He was given the equivalent of $10. We had the papers. If I could have, I would have promoted the security officer on the spot. Just to be sure we hadn't missed one page we continued our search of the church area the rest of the day.

Upon my return to the U.S., and after making my report to the Secretary, there remained the question about how to make a public statement on American policy toward Africa, which had been the goal of the Washington and Lourenço Marques meetings. There is a tried and true method for stating such a policy, and that is in a public speech.[3] An occasion to deliver such a speech arose when I was invited to address the Foreign Policy Association of Oklahoma City in May. The speech was, of course, cleared by appropriate authority, and although it said nothing earthshaking about any new departure in our policy, it brought together a more comprehensive statement of African policy than any previously given by a high American official. My lead-in was, predictably, in connection with the Cold War:

> In these troubled times, it is gratifying to be able to single out a region of 10 million square miles in which no significant inroads have been made by Communism, and to be able to characterize the area as relatively stable and secure. Yet, if one carefully distinguishes between efforts on behalf of normal political and economic aspirations, and agitation inspired by Communist elements, that is basically the case. It is difficult to judge whether the failure of Communism to make progress is due to resistance or disinterest on the part of the African peoples, to the results of constructive efforts by the governments concerned or their effective vigilance towards Communist propaganda and agitation, or whether the Soviet dominated Cominform has been so occupied elsewhere that it has not yet devoted its maximum efforts to the penetration and subversion of the African continent.
>
> Advantage must be taken of this period of grace to further the development within Africa of healthy political, economic, and social institutions, to create an understanding on the part of the Africans of the forces of Communism which are disturbing the peace and security of hundreds of millions of peoples elsewhere in the world, and to inspire a determination to resist these forces.

I realize that, in retrospect, this passage will seem excessively preoccupied with the Communist threat, yet I make no apology. It provided a way of enlisting American interest in Africa. It was, I believe, truthful as to the existing situation. It was foresighted in that it warned against the storm that was to come. And it served as an introduction to a broader statement of our interests in the African peoples.

Speaking first of American attitudes toward Africa, I sought to address the great ignorance of our people about that continent, the historical background of American humanitarian efforts there, and our general interest in assisting underprivileged peoples to raise their living and educational standards. I concluded, however, that "despite our humanitarian interests and our desire to be of assistance to underprivileged peoples, the present scope of our world commitments was creating a growing desire on the part of the American people to assume as few additional world responsibilities as possible." That was to change later, as the Cold War intensified, but it was an accurate description of the limitations under which we then operated.

I then referred to African attitudes toward the U.S., noting pointedly the effect which racial discrimination in our country had on the way Africans looked at us. Next, I acknowledged the limitations posed for our policy by the overriding necessities of our relations with the European metropoles, saying:

> An important factor affecting the nature and direction of our African policy is the attitude of the European powers themselves toward us, which is at the same time friendly, critical and suspicious. By virtue of the European Recovery Program and the Mutual Defense Assistance Program, the Western European powers, which are also the leading metropolitan powers in Africa, have a closer and more intimate relationship with us than at any time in history. This is a reciprocal relationship for defense and for economic recovery which none of these powers wishes to disturb. Moreover, with specific relationship to Africa, they welcome ECA assistance which enables them to build mutually advantageous economic relations with their African dependencies.
>
> On the other hand, these powers are fearful of what they regard as an apparent tendency to give indiscriminate and uncritical support to movements toward self-government or independence without adequate consideration of the experience and resources of the peoples concerned. The administering powers are fearful lest too much encouragement to peoples who are politically immature and whose economies are still primitive, will result in political and economic chaos.

The reader today will have noted, as perhaps the reader would have in 1950, that there was no endorsement of the views attributed to the colonial powers. These were described, and our close relationship with them stressed, but there was no acceptance of the existing view that independence must await economic, social, and educational progress.

"It is necessary," I pointed out, "to keep in mind that we are not in a position to exercise direct responsibility with respect to Africa. We have no desire to assume the responsibilities borne by other powers and, indeed, our principles, our commitments, and our lack of experience all militate against our assumption of such obligations."

Against this background, I defined American objectives in Africa under four headings: First, we have a major interest in seeing that the peoples of Africa advance in the right direction and in accordance with the principles of the United Nations Charter. We favored the progressive development of the peoples of Africa toward the role of self-government or, where conditions are suitable, toward independence.

A second major objective, which arose out of our relations with the metropolitan powers and with the peoples of Africa, was our desire to assure the development of mutually advantageous economic relations between them, in the interests of contributing to restoration of a sound European economy and in the interests of fulfilling the aspirations of the African peoples.

Third, the United States needed to preserve its rights of equal economic treatment in the territories of Africa (the non-discrimination point which had been stressed in the Lourenço Marques report), and to participate, itself, both commercially and financially, in the development of this great continent, along with other nations of the world. America had, in the previous year, exported to Africa products to a value of $616 million and had imported products worth $338 million. In addition we must continue to have access to Africa's vital reservoir of minerals.

And, finally, an equally important objective of United States foreign policy was to assist in providing an environment in which the African peoples would feel that their aspirations could best be served by continued association and cooperation with the nations of the democratic world, both in their present status and as they advanced toward self-government or independence in accordance with the provisions of the United Nations charter.

As I look back on that speech, it is the second objective which I believe contained the nub of what we were trying to say. We did not wish to draw Africa to ourselves, but whether dependent or independent—and we hoped for the latter—we wished to see the continent aligned with the free world for its own benefit as well as ours. Though then timidly stated, this is still the broad thrust of American policy toward Africa. The only basic difference is that the African countries are now independent, and that the Cold War has meanwhile come to Africa.

Innocuous as it might now appear, the sensitivity of the colonial issue resulted in more widespread comment on my Oklahoma City speech on Africa than on any other I ever made. From Johannesburg, the *Forum* of June 3 quoted most of the speech which it called "of considerable importance."[4] It cited my interpretation that "no significant [Communist] inroads have been made [in Africa]" as at variance with the views of many South Africans. The article warned that, in the clash between the master-servant ideology of the South and emancipation as followed elsewhere in Africa, American influence would be on the side of emancipation.

The *Eastern Province Herald* of Port Elizabeth, South Africa, said, "Our attitude like that of other European powers in Africa—toward America's policy as seen by Mr. McGhee—is at the same time friendly, critical and suspicious. All are fearful of . . . American tendency to give indiscriminate and uncritical support to movements toward self-government or independence without adequate consideration of the experience and resources of the peoples concerned."[5]

The *East African Standard* of Nairobi said that the Americans "are treading where they have no real right to be,"[6] while the Indian-owned *Kenya Daily Mail* praised the speech. M. Jean Letourneau, Minister for Overseas France, commenting on my speech from Paris, is quoted as saying, "Political autonomy or independence for African territories was unthinkable, because it would mean only the 'Balkanization of the Dark Continent.'"[7] He did not regard "the McGhee statement as reflecting final State Department policy—France has had more experience in both Africa and Asia than certain other countries." Our embassy in Paris was asked to explain my speech to other French officials to deter similar reactions.

Le Courrier d'Afrique of Leopoldville saw in the speech assurances of cooperation with the Belgians in the Congo.[8] Sir Roy Welensky, a leading Rhodesian politician of Northern Rhodesia, according to our Consul-General in Salisbury, took exception to my statement favoring "the goal of self-government or where suitable towards independence." In saying there was not necessarily a conflict between the European powers and legitimate African aspirations, he believed that I "placed less emphasis on the safeguarding of European interests than was warranted."[9]

Let us take a look at what happened in Portuguese Africa. At the time of the Lourenço Marques conference, Portugal's colonial stake in Africa seemed secure for the foreseeable future. In the following year, the Portuguese presence was confirmed when Angola and Mozambique were made overseas provinces. But reality proved to be different from appearances, which mistakenly reassured the Portuguese of the permanence of their "civilizing mission" in Africa.

By the mid-1960s, liberation movements in both territories had challenged Portuguese authority. Although colonial forces, recruited largely in the territories themselves, held the upper hand over the guerrillas, Portugal's long-term commitment in Africa and to its settler communities there strained its resources and created dissension in the armed forces. A military-led coup in April 1974 overthrew the authoritarian regime that had been in power in Lisbon for more than forty years. This set in motion the process of decolonization that would bring Angola and Mozambique to full independence, along with Guinea Bissau, Cape Verde, and São Tomé, the next year.

In Angola, the coalition transitional government composed of rival liberation movements fell apart before formal independence was achieved in November 1975. The Soviet-backed Popular Movement for the Liberation of Angola (MPLA) unilaterally proclaimed a people's republic, calling for Soviet and Cuban aid against the Western-favored National Front (FNLA) and Jonas Savimbi's National Union (UNITA), which subsequently gathered support from South Africa. Limited South African armed intervention in the civil war that ensued presented the opportunity for introduction of Cuban combat units and Soviet advisers, who remain in Angola in large numbers more than six years later, ostensibly to protect the country from South African aggression. In 1977, the MPLA was transformed into a Marxist-Leninist vanguard party whose politburo controls the country on the Soviet model through a revolutionary executive council. Savimbi forces, with South African aid, continue to resist the Marxist government in Angola and its Cuban allies. Reports confirm that UNITA controls the countryside in most of southern Angola, where it has the allegiance of ethnic groups that predominate in that area.

Under similar circumstances, the Marxist-oriented Mozambique Liberation Front (FRELIMO) came to power at independence under the leadership of Samora Machel. As in Angola, a one-party socialist state was established with FRELIMO as the base. Although Mozambique has intimate political ties with the Soviet bloc, it retains its economic links with South Africa. Ideological differences have caused severe cleavages within Mozambique's Marxist organization, and dissidents have joined formerly pro-Portuguese groups there in opposition to the Machel regime. They conducted guerrilla operations, probably with South African support, against government forces.

It was unfortunate that I was not able, during my visit to Africa in 1950, to meet any of the African leaders. In the view of most of the colonial powers at the time there were no native leaders, and they had no desire to encourage any outside of purely tribal responsibilities. My first opportunity came when an African protégé of the British, the first power to initiate the training of talented natives to assume political responsibilities, made an official visit to our country under British auspices.

Kwame Nkrumah, who in 1950 was 41 years old, had attended Lincoln University in Pennsylvania and the London School of Economics. He had led the drive for independence in Ghana since 1947, and had often come in conflict with the British. When he came to Washington, he held the appointive position of Leader of Government Business. The British had spotted him as a comer and had helped him by giving him the most important position available to a native, although it held little power. Nkrumah was an attractive, fluent man with a winning smile. He was accompanied on his visit by Mr. Kojo Botsio, the Minister of Education and Social Welfare. I received Nkrumah in my office on June 8, and we discussed the progress being made in Ghana toward independence. He was hopeful for the future and made no serious complaints against the British conduct of the colony. Later I gave a luncheon in his honor at the Mayflower Hotel, including subcabinet representatives of other government agencies. My after-luncheon remarks were carefully calculated to give him an accurate expression of our view toward British policy and the future of Ghana and Africa.[10]

Freedom, I said, is closely bound to progress. The only limitation to freedom is that it not interfere with the freedom of others. Progress must come by peaceful means and by the exercise of free choice. Traditionally the U.S. had supported orderly movements toward self-government and we were pleased with the constitution that had come into effect in Ghana on January 1 of that year. It had established popular elections and granted broad competence of Africans over their own affairs for the first time. Although some had misgivings, we were confident that this bold British experiment in African administration would succeed. It must succeed. The eyes of the whole world would be focused on the Gold Coast. I wished Nkrumah every success with his government and assured him of our continuing friendship for Ghana.

It is indeed sad that Nkrumah, who in 1950 looked so promising as the future leader of a free Ghana, should have later failed so completely, with a great setback for his country. Named Prime Minister when self-government came in 1951, and again when independence came in 1957, Nkrumah embarked on an ambitious development program, building hospitals, schools, cocoa-storage elevators, and the Volta River hydroelectric and aluminum project. The program threw Ghana heavily in debt. Many projects, such as a grandiose meeting center for the Organization of African Unity, reflected Nkrumah's personal ambition to become leader of the emerging African states.

Accused of favoritism, personal extravagance, and corruption, Nkrumah arranged in 1964 a referendum which gave him dictatorial powers and set up a one-party socialist state patterned along London School of Economics lines. As his vanity and isolation increased, the once-promising economic situation in Ghana steadily worsened. Nkrumah was finally overthrown in 1966 by a police-army coup. His political inclination in the Cold War is indicated by the predominance of Chinese and East German teachers and technicians there who were expelled. Although elections were held in 1969, Ghana was not to return to civilian rule until 1979. Meanwhile its economy continued to deteriorate.

Nkrumah's example has unfortunately been replicated by other leaders, most notably in recent years by General Mobutu Sese Seko, President of Zaire. My disappointment with Mobutu parallels that with Nkrumah. I met him first in 1963, when, as Under Secretary for Political Affairs, I went out to the Congo to negotiate with Moise Tshombe, head of the Katanga government, to carry out the UN's so-called "U Thant" plan, which we had developed in the Department to end his secession. While in Leopoldville I met Mobutu, then head of the Congolese army under Prime Minister Joseph Kasavubu and Prime Minister Cyrille Adoula. I attended a convivial Sunday breakfast at Mobutu's farm near Leopoldville and had long talks with him about the future of an independent Zaire.

Mobutu had started out well, coming to power with strong U.S. and Belgian backing following the defeat of the secession of Tshombe in Katanga, and of the leftist "People's Republic" in Stanleyville in 1965. With enormous mineral resources, Zaire had excellent prospects. Mobutu's extravagances and dictatorial rule, plus widespread corruption, caused a deterioration which was exacerbated by the nationalization of foreign-owned business and a decline in the world price of copper. Today, Zaire's economy is completely dependent on its foreign creditors, as Mobutu continues his one-man rule. How sad that Nkrumah, and Mobutu after he succeeded Lumumba, leaders of two African countries with such promise for development, should have proved so unequal to the task. They were not able to resist the corrupting effect of power and popular adulation, and set a bad precedent for other African states.

12

Our Next Friend, Liberia

Visit to Monrovia, Liberia, President Tubman,
February 21–25, 1950.

I had long had the desire to visit Liberia, which had been founded by the American Colonization Society in 1822 to settle freed blacks from the U.S. As one of the two independent black African countries south of the Sahara at that time (the other being Ethiopia), I thought Liberia should provide some insight into how the new African states expected in the future might develop. Liberia stretches some 370 miles along the southwest corner of the African coast's western bulge, and extends up to 160 miles into the interior. Of the million and a half population in 1950, the fifteen to twenty thousand descendants of the first settlers constituted a ruling class.

Liberia has a humid climate and heavy rainfall along the coast. Its fertile soil grows a variety of crops, including rice, bananas, cocoa, coffee, cassava, and sugar. In 1926, the government granted a one-million-acre ninety-nine-year lease to the Firestone Tire and Rubber Company, which, together with several independent firms, produced about 50,000 tons of rubber a year. The Liberia Mining Company mines the rich Bomi Hills iron ore reserve under an eighty-year lease granted shortly after the war. Under wartime lend-lease, the U.S. built a modern harbor for Monrovia, which was opened as a free port in 1948.

William V. S. Tubman began his first term as president in 1944. The National Unification Program sponsored by his administration purported to stress the common nationality of all Liberians, and the elimination of all distinctions between tribal elements and descendants of black American colonists. Tubman had based his foreign policy on close relations with the U.S. In many ways both countries looked on Liberia more or less as another U.S. state. President Tubman maintained close personal relations with U.S. presidents and officials. The U.S. responded by sending a Public Health Service Mission and an Economic Advisory Commission, and by other forms of assistance.

At the time I visited the country, on my way to the Lourenço Marques Conference, Liberia was undergoing a transition expected to have profound and far-reaching effects on the whole of Africa. Ambassador Edward R. Dudley analyzed this for us in our conference in Lourenço Marques as follows: Once condemned by the colonial powers as the horrible example of black self-rule, Liberia promised to set a pace which the colonial powers would find it difficult to follow. Because of the strong American moral and financial support given its early settlers, Liberia's government had, almost without exception, been strongly pro-American. This did not mean that Liberia had always blindly followed our lead in all matters. They had often shown surprising independence and political astuteness. For one hundred years, however, they had regarded America as "next friend." This relationship had resulted in constant demands upon us for help along many lines.

America, in turn, profited. Liberia had provided a friendly base for our operations on the West Coast of Africa, and had welcomed American business enterprise on favorable terms. Since Liberia admitted only persons of African descent to citizenship, it had not had racial problems encountered elsewhere in Africa. In the past there had been a distinct class cleavage between the minority Americo-Liberian ruling class and the indigenous native population. The present administration, however, had for the first time admitted native people into the government and granted them the right to vote.

Each of the three so-called hinterland provinces had a tribal chieftain sitting in the lower house of the Liberian legislature. This did not, of course, change things greatly. Complete illiteracy still prevailed among the tribal people. It represented, however, a new trend which was appreciated by the native people. It would appear, therefore, that no serious strife was likely to occur in the near future between the native people and the Americo-Liberians. (The serious strife was to occur just thirty years later.)

I arrived in Roberts Field, Liberia, via Pan American Clipper in the early evening of February 21, 1950. Roberts is a large, well-equipped airfield which had been built for U.S. use during the Second World War. I was met by Assistant Secretary of State M. Dukuly for the Liberian government and by Ambassador Dudley, whom I was to get to know quite well during the next several weeks, as we traveled together to Johannesburg and Lourenço Marques. He was accompanied by his attractive and vivacious wife, Rae. Ed Dudley was indeed a remarkable man. A native Virginian, he received his law degree at St. John's University and was, within a year, appointed Assistant Attorney General of the New York State Department of Justice. Later he served as counsel for the National Association for the Advancement of Colored People (NAACP) and for the Virgin Islands government. In 1948 he was appointed Ambassador to Liberia, where he did an outstanding job. Later he held an important judicial post and served as president of the Borough of Manhattan.

There was much to talk about as the three of us drove the long trip to Monrovia in the dark: news from Washington, my visit, and the forthcoming conference. The next morning I was awakened early by the bright sunlight shining on the sparkling Atlantic. The embassy residence, of gleaming white stucco, was perched atop a hill over-looking palm trees, a sandy beach, and the sea. Monrovia is an important port.

My first appointment the following morning was with Secretary of State Gabriel L. Dennis, a stout, balding, dignified man with rimless glasses. Very friendly, he was a member of the Americo-Liberian aristocracy. He extended me a warm welcome and invited me to take a boat trip to visit his plantation the afternoon of the following day. I took up with him the various items on the agenda which had been prepared in Washington for my visit.[1]

The U.S. had, in December 1949, suggested to President Tubman a five-year Economic Development Program for Liberia, based on recommendations by Oscar Meier, chief of the Economic Mission to Liberia. The U.S. Export-Import Bank had indicated willingness to consider a variety of projects: road development, rice production, Monrovia water and power distribution systems, an agricultural credit corporation, repair of river landing facilities, and an agricultural extension program. It had been estimated that these projects might require loans of $1 to $2 million the first year, and that other projects could also be considered. Terms offered were twelve years at 3.5 percent.

I stressed to Dennis the importance of this program for the future of Liberia and the stability of its government, and expressed the hope that it would be considered favorably. For our part, the Ex-Im Bank was ready to proceed. Dennis responded that the proposed program was still under consideration by the Liberian cabinet, which should make their decision shortly. As a result of a suggestion made to me by Juan Trippe, president of Pan American Airways, I had on February 14 requested the Secretary of the Air Force, whose department was spending $5 million annually for the maintenance of Roberts Field, to modernize the road from Monrovia to the field, which was in poor condition. I expressed to Dennis the hope that this request would be approved. I congratulated the Secretary on the profit made by the port in the preceding year. It was our hope to strengthen both our Economic and Public Health missions in Liberia if funds were available under Point Four, by providing additional personnel and equipment. We believed that priority should be given to housing.

I expressed the hope that the strike that had begun in December on the Firestone Rubber plantations could be ended. In our view the Liberian government needed to take a more positive role in helping end the strike, which would not only hurt Firestone and the Liberian economy, but would also discourage additional private investment. We were attempting to find a suitable U.S. lawyer to assist in the codification of Liberian laws. We could send a census expert whenever the Liberian government would indicate willingness to pay his expenses. Dennis expressed gratification at the progress being made in our various efforts to assist Liberia. He said that President Tubman would raise with me the question of military assistance.

I was received by the President at 11 A.M. According to my schedule, I was granted an audience, as with royalty.[2] Tubman was a jovial, gregarious man, obviously a skilled politician. He, too, received me warmly. I presented a letter from President Truman which emphasized generally our desire to assist Liberia and maintain close relations.[3] President Tubman expressed appreciation for President Truman's letter. He promised to give me his reply to the questions I raised. I went over the various matters I had taken up earlier with Secretary of State Dennis; the President expressed approval, adding that there was one more matter he would like to go over with me after the luncheon he was giving in my honor in two days.

I had been invited to a lunch that day given in honor of Colonel Lansdell R. Christie, discoverer of the Bomi Hills iron-ore mine and founder and principal owner of the Liberia Mining Company. Christie was an extraordinary individual who served during the war in Liberia as an American army officer. While there he had traveled about the country studying it carefully. He had read old U.S. Geological Survey reports on iron-ore occurrences at Bomi Hills. More far-sighted than the large international steel and ore companies, Christie negotiated a concession with the Liberian government, and with the help of a $4 million Ex-Im Bank loan raised the necessary capital, and brought the mines into production. Later he was to sell his minority interest to Republic Steel for $12 million. His early death was a great loss.

The luncheon, given by Attorney General C. Abayumi Cassell, was an elaborate affair which I feel is worth describing. After hors d'oeuvres we were served mock hollandaise soup, then fish and potato casserole followed by roast turkey with prune dressing and vegetables. Then came ham and salad followed by butterscotch pie and ice cream. There were three vintage French wines. That evening I was invited to cocktails with Secretary of State Dennis. I scarcely needed any dinner.

The following day I visited the Bomi Hills mine. I observed the tremendous boost to the local economy given by the hard-surfaced road which had been built connecting the mine with the port of Monrovia. Farm produce that hitherto had had to be carried by hand or on animals was rushed along the new road with every kind of truck or vehicle. This was the most important result, so far, of the iron-ore project, which was just getting underway.

President Tubman gave a luncheon in my honor on February 24 at the Executive Mansion, to which cabinet members had been invited. It was a very pleasant affair. The President paid careful attention to all of the niceties of the occasion. There was a friendly exchange of toasts. After lunch, President Tubman took me aside and said he wanted to request our government to send a military adviser, at Liberian expense, to train their army.[4] Liberia also wished to purchase American arms and equipment. He referred to the state of martial law in effect at the Firestone rubber plantation. Recently violence had broken out there after workers had rejected a two-cent-a-day wage increase, following three months' negotiations. Liberia, he said, was vulnerable to foreign doctrines. The company offer did not seem to me to match the importance of the strike.

I replied that I fully recognized the need for basic security forces in Liberia. Such protection against agitation would give Liberia confidence in proceeding on its development programs. I would press for an early assignment of a military adviser. Our exchange was reported by the New York Times. In March 1950, Colonel West A. Hamilton, retired, was selected by both governments to make a survey of Liberia's military needs.

I was very impressed by Tubman. He was obviously a man of

great capacity and was pushing for the development of Liberia according to his concepts. That this did not reach the mass of the people, whose lives remained unchanged, may have contributed to the overthrow of the ruling class on April 12, 1980. The grandiose palace Tubman built at great public expense certainly did not help. I found him, personally, however, a warm, friendly man with a strong attachment to the U.S.

After lunch, I was picked up by Secretary of State Dennis and taken by launch to his country estate. This outing gave me a welcome insight into the life of the governing group. The early settlers, having come from the U.S. South where they had been slaves on typical Southern plantations, had tried to recreate the life there. Having been shut off from their African origins, it was the only life they knew. The rivers were named after Southern rivers. We went up the Mississippi. The Dennis country place was a large, aging red brick neo-classical structure of excellent proportions. We sat at ground level on a brick terrace under white columns, just like those of an antebellum home on the real Mississippi. Dennis had invited some of his neighbors to join us for a dinner of Southern snacks.

I will always regret that I did not get to attend the surprise birthday party which President Tubman gave for his wife at the Executive Mansion the last evening I was in Monrovia. I had heard about President Tubman's parties. Apparently they usually got really going around midnight, the guests sipping the best scotch, and lasted to the wee hours. I have always found that Africans create during their social occasions a convivial atmosphere which is contagious. Unfortunately, the press of my schedule in Monrovia and our early departure the next day forced me to decline President Tubman's invitation.

My other regret was that I did not have an opportunity during my stay in Liberia, indeed during any of my visits to Africa, to establish contacts with the indigenous tribal peoples. In Monrovia a successful man would occasionally be pointed out as coming from local stock. However, once he became assimilated in the Americo-Liberian community, the same gulf opened between him and his people upcountry. I lost the opportunity to find out what sort of people they were, and to gain some insight into their customs, way of life, and aspirations.

I also missed the chance to discover their art and its religious symbolism. In a tour of Africa Cecilia and I made in 1974 I was delighted by the masks and ancestral figure carvings of the West African tribes and started a collection which I have added to since.

One of my prize pieces, which I obtained in London, is from the Bassa tribe of Liberia. It is a delightful helmet mask with a large, beautifully-carved coiffure and a most artistic face, distorted by a small puckered mouth and pinched nose. How I regret that while I was in Liberia I was not exposed to the wealth of art and tradition of the native Liberians, who lived in quite another world from what I saw in Monrovia.

After my return home I kept up a personal correspondence with President Tubman on matters pending between the two countries, reassuring him of our interest in Liberia. He had become irritated at the seeming delay by the Ex-Im Bank in approving funds for certain development projects: water and sewerage facilities for Monrovia and a hydroelectric project. In my letter to him of February 7, 1951, I pointed out that the bank had advanced $5 million to Liberia for roads and that our Technical Assistance Program and Military Training Mission were doing well. Further loans were held up only because Liberia had not furnished the necessary technical data. I assured him that our purpose was to help Liberia develop its economy for the benefit of its people and that Liberia had many friends in our country.

A brief summary of subsequent events in Liberia would, I believe, be appropriate. The Americo-Liberian elite, to which I have referred, had cultivated a typical settler mentality in Liberia not unlike that of European colonists in other parts of Africa. They had traditionally seen it as part of their civilizing mission to maintain control over the local inhabitants. For more than a century, this small, tightly knit group of families of American origin had succeeded in that aim. Although economic growth was noticeable in the postwar period and cosmetic attempts made to integrate the African population by degrees into the mainstream of Liberian political life, it was obvious that whatever benefits Liberian society and the country's narrowly based economy could produce were still reserved largely for the elite.

When President Tubman died in 1971, he was succeeded by William R. Tolbert, who for nearly thirty years had served as his Vice President. Although most Liberians continued to identify Tolbert's administration with the elite, he made great efforts to enhance the country's image as an African nation, nonaligned, and active in the Organization of African Unity. The new President even took to wearing African dress on public occasions although it is doubtful if this helped greatly in establishing himself as a man of the people. In 1978, the government, for the first time, allowed an opposition group to criticize its policies in an open forum. The opposition movement was subsequently organized as the Progressive People's Party, which grew rapidly and soon challenged the monopoly held on Liberian politics by the True Whig Party since 1883.

Unwittingly, Tolbert had let the lid off a long-stewing pot. Food riots, strikes, and demonstrations in support of the PPP led to bloodshed in 1979, and gave an excuse for the arrest of opposition leaders and student activists. Intense antigovernment and anti-oligarchy sentiment boiled over in 1980, when a military coup, led by twenty-six-year-old Master Sergeant Samuel Doe, toppled the Tolbert regime. Tolbert and a number of government officials were killed in the coup, or brutally executed later after drumhead trials on charges of treason and corruption. Although ostracized initially by the OAU, whose members were shocked by the coup's violent course, Doe seems to have established himself securely as head of the People's Redemption Committee, a junta that operates de facto as Liberia's government. Martial law, imposed at the time of the coup, was lifted in April 1982 on the second anniversary of the military takeover. Although Doe promised "wide participations of the people" in future government decison making, democratic institutions have not been restored in Liberia. Doe, meanwhile, has been promoted to the rank of major general.

13

Introduction to Apartheid

Visit to Capetown, Union of South Africa, Prime Minister
Malan and General Smuts, March 3–9, 1950.

Following the conference of Lourenço Marques, I paid an official
visit to the Union of South Africa during March 3–9. Although the
Union was not under my jurisdiction, the department wanted me to
take advantage of my presence in the area to engage in discussions
with Prime Minister D. F. Malan and his government. Malan's policies were under severe criticism in the U.S. and the UN. There was
no policy-making official in the department who had served in South
Africa or was personally acquainted with the government officials or
their problems.

South Africa is a rich, beautiful, but troubled country, lying in
isolation in the lowermost part of the African continent, surrounded
on three sides by oceans. It was discovered for Europeans in 1487 by
the Portuguese Bartholomeu Diaz, of the great school of seamen
founded by the Portuguese pioneer in the science of exploration,
Prince Henry the Navigator. At that time the Table Bay area was
occupied by the Hottentots. Two English captains claimed it for
James I in 1620, but the area was first colonized by the Dutch East
India Company in 1652. Dutch immigration to the Cape area continued, with interruptions, until its conquest by the British in 1795 in
behalf of the deposed Prince of Orange. Coincident with European
settlement in southern Africa was the migration of Bantu-speaking
peoples into lands beyond the Great Fish River. Here they made
their first tentative contacts in the eighteenth century with the Boers,
who were immigrants from Holland.

British control of the Cape became permanent after 1806, inau-
gurating settlement by British colonists. Cape Colony, as it was
called, also provided security for the route to India. The abolition of

slavery by Britain in 1833 and the threat they perceived to their way of life in Cape Colony, prompted the Boer farmers to undertake the Great Trek into the Orange River country and the Transvaal. Here in the 1830s they established independent republics that were stoutly defended against British intervention. The discovery of diamonds and later of gold in the Transvaal brought unwelcome outsiders to the Afrikaner arcadia, which also lay athwart the British-controlled route that Cecil Rhodes envisioned stretching from the Cape to Cairo. The bloody Anglo-Boer War of 1899–1902 ended the independence of the Boer republics and embittered Afrikaners against English-speaking South Africans.

Mr. D. duPlessis, Union Consul-General in Lourenço Marques, had extended me an invitation from his government to visit the Union, and had made arrangements for me to be taken in a Skymaster plane from Johannesburg to Cape Town. Colonel Sandenberg, warden of Kruger National Park, had also invited me and Ambassador Dudley, who was traveling with me, to see the park and be his guests at the park headquarters in Skukusa, en route to Johannesburg. Our visit to the park was the first time I had ever seen African wildlife under conditions of complete freedom. Visitors were instructed to stay in their cars and keep to the road at a speed no greater than twenty-five miles per hour. The park covered some eight thousand square miles, the largest in the world. Colonel Sandenberg made excellent arrangements for us.

We saw lions, which would come right up to the car. There were elephants, which stayed in large herds and avoided the roads. There were zebras, certainly the most photogenic of animals. It is almost impossible not to take their picture. There were giraffes, jackals, wild dogs, leopards, spotted hyenas, chacma baboons, lizards, vervet monkeys, dignified sable antelopes, roan antelopes, elands, steenboks, gray duikers, waterbucks with horns over three feet long, reed bucks, tsessebe, kudu, buffalo, graceful impala, blue wildebeest, warthogs, crocodiles, and cheetahs. There were also over 320 indigenous species of birds, as well as eight migratory species. A martial hawk eagle I saw had a seven-foot wingspan. The hornbill family was well represented, and the giant ostrich. I have never seen such a bewildering variety of wildlife. It was an extraordinary visit.

We then proceeded to Johannesburg, where I was guest of honor at a very pleasant cocktail party extended by Consul-General Sydney Redecker. J. Mincer, the Mayor of Johannesburg, and his wife, were among the guests; also representatives of the Department of External

Affairs, the Federated Chamber of Industries, the Chamber of Commerce, the Transvaal Chamber of Industries, the local university, and the American and South African business community. I was amazed at the progressive spirit and dynamism of the Johannesburg businessmen. New skyscrapers and industrial plants were much in evidence, creating an atmosphere more like Chicago than Africa. Indeed, there was nothing else in Africa like it. I was reminded of a similar impression when in Brazil, in the 1940s, I had visited São Paulo, which remains unique in Latin America. Europeans, given the right ingredients, can create an industrial complex anywhere in the world. Fortunes were obviously being made in Johannesburg.

When I visited the nearby city of Soweto, however, where the half million blacks working in Johannesburg lived—commuting by crowded bus rides to the city—I was apprehensive for Johannesburg's future. I found there only ramshackle wooden dwellings and meager utilities, shops, and recreational facilities. I witnessed the operation of the identity-card system. The Johannesburg papers were full of reports of breaking and entering and major crime: even in those days the white residents of Johannesburg did not feel secure.

There was no U.S. Ambassador in the Union at that time, North Winship having resigned the previous November. I was received on my arrival in Cape Town at noon on March 5 by the chargé, B. C. Connelly, a capable veteran Foreign Service officer. He and his wife were most hospitable and helpful.

The National Party of Prime Minister Malan had only recently come to power in coalition with Minister of Finance N. C. Havenga's small Afrikaner party. In the election, Malan, running on a platform of apartheid (or segregation under a white supremacy system), had received only 45 percent of the votes, narrowly defeating by six seats the United Party of General Jan Christiaan Smuts. Since taking office, Malan had faced continual black unrest. On February 17, three weeks before my visit, Consul-General Redecker had reported serious rioting in Johannesburg—the most serious up to this point against the established European authority of South Africa. On June 8, 1950, three months after my visit, Connelly reported from Capetown that the riots in Johannesburg of May 1 were uglier in mood than any in the recent past. The United party, which had up to this point supported the government's precautionary measures, launched an all-out attack on the "apartheid-mad" nationalists.

In the briefing papers he prepared for me, Connelly had emphasized three points of sensitivity which I would encounter.[1]

The question of native representation and rights was the single most important problem in the country. All political parties were essentially in agreement on this question in principle, although they argued over degree and definitions. The whites basically despised the blacks, even though few really knew them except as servants, and they feared them in terms of white survival. They resented internal criticism, which they believed to be based on hopeless idealism, and foreign criticism. They felt that advice from the U.S. was particularly based on ignorance. In the U.S. view, there was apparently little native adherence to Communism and no serious threat to white supremacy.

The second area of concern was Afrikaner nationalism. The Afrikaans-speaking South Africans then comprised 60 percent of the white population. Descended from Dutch and Huguenot settlers who had come to the Cape in the seventeenth century, they considered themselves to be the authentic South Africans, excluding English-speaking whites along with the black majority and the mixed-race coloreds. The Afrikaner had a strong desire for a republic, and a nationalist drive based on anti-British and patriotic emotions.

A third problem which preoccupied the South Africans was how to develop their mineral-rich country in the face of grave problems: soil depletion and erosion, antiquated agricultural methods, inadequate use of black manpower in skilled and semi-skilled jobs, and a lopsided dependence on revenues from gold. These had led to a large adverse balance of payments.

The general attitude of South Africans toward the U.S. appeared to be a friendly one, although our relations were not extensive. There was, however, resentment against our failure to support the Union on South-West Africa and on racial issues in the UN. The U.S., for its part, was highly desirous that South Africa remain a strong member of the British Commonwealth, and that it modify its view on the question of dependent peoples generally, in order to help avoid Communist exploitation.

A serious issue between the Union and the UN had arisen out of the Union's administration of its mandate from the League of Nations over South-West Africa. The Union held that the UN had no jurisdiction in the matter. In December 1949, however, the General Assembly had asked the International Court of Justice (ICJ) for an advisory opinion on South-West Africa. On July 11, 1950, four months after my visit to Cape Town, the ICJ had declared that the

Union could not unilaterally alter the international status of South-West Africa and must submit reports of its administration to the UN. This opinion was approved by the General Assembly on December 13, 1950, and a five-member committee was set up to negotiate compliance with the Union.

I had long had a keen desire to visit the Union for several reasons. It is an area of great natural beauty: the view of Table Mountain which looms over Cape Town is unforgettable, as are the rocky coasts and lovely farming area with quaint Cape Dutch architecture to the south. I also felt a sympathy for the South Africans for their extremely difficult racial problem. Although I did not think they were doing well in solving it, I felt, as a Southerner, that I understood it, and hoped progress could be made there.

And, finally, I was keen to see the country of Cecil Rhodes, to whom I owed a debt of gratitude as a Rhodes scholar for three years at Oxford. Rhodes, the frail son of an English minister, had gone to Durban in Natal in 1870 as a young man to seek his fortune. Between 1873 and 1878 he divided his time between the Kimberley diamond fields and Oriel College, Oxford, although he did not graduate. He conceived of the Rhodes scholarship as a means of unifying the British Empire and bringing the U.S. closer to England. When he died at age forty-eight, he had made several fortunes, opened up vast areas in Africa for colonization and incorporation into the Empire, served in the highest positions in the government of his adopted country, and was recognized as a world statesman.

An official of the Ministry for External Affairs had kindly suggested to Connelly that I might wish to see former Prime Minister Jan Christiaan Smuts, leader of the opposition United Party. It was made clear that the ministry preferred that Connelly make the arrangements. Smuts, world-renowned South African general and political leader, easily the most famous of living South Africans, was born in 1870 near Riebeeck West in Cape Colony. Although also eminent as soldier, philosopher, and botanist, the Oubaas (old master), as he was called, was thought of in his own country primarily as a politician. He was educated at Stellenbosch and at Cambridge in England, where he had a brilliant academic career. He was admitted to the Cape Town bar in 1895 and became a political ally of Cecil Rhodes. After the ill-fated raid led by Dr. L. S. Jameson, however, Smuts moved to Johannesburg and transferred his loyalties to the Transvaal. During the Boer War he led the Afrikaners in the Cape.

Together with Louis Botha, Smuts founded Het Volk (The People) party, and emerged as the leading Afrikaner exponent of reconciliation between Boer and Briton in South Africa. He subsequently was appointed to Botha's cabinet in a self-governing Transvaal, and was a minister in the first Union government formed by Botha in 1910. World War I projected Smuts into world prominence as a military commander in East Africa and as a member of the Imperial War Cabinet in London. Smuts represented South Africa at the Versailles Conference and contributed significantly to the creation of the British Commonwealth and the League of Nations. He became Prime Minister for the first time in 1919, brought South Africa into World War II during a second tenure in office, and returned to London to serve in Churchill's war cabinet. At the time of my visit, his party, the United Party, which drew most of its support from English-speaking whites, had just been defeated at the polls by Malan's Nationalists, largely on the apartheid issue. He was opposition leader at the time of his death in May 1950, only three months after I saw him, hailed abroad as an elder statesman of considerable stature.

In our after-dinner conversation of about an hour and a half on the day of my arrival, General Smuts presented his views on Africa and the world scene.[2] Smuts was an impressive man with white hair and a neatly trimmed moustache and goatee. He had a natural dignity but was friendly and expressed himself openly. He made no partisan reference to internal South African issues, however. He told me that in his view the present world situation was more serious than at any other time in his career, and that we faced one of the real crises of history. The only hope for the world, he felt, was in the West, which had borne the burden of world responsibility for hundreds of years. The West could survive only by working more closely together; the UN had, in Smuts's view, been rendered ineffective by the U.S.S.R. He did not, moreover, believe that any closer political union among the Western powers was possible, except through closer economic cooperation.

It was Smuts's belief that all of the free European countries could make a contribution toward relieving the present situation. He felt that the U.K. had less to offer under the Labour government, however, than it had under Churchill. The burden must therefore rest principally upon the U.S. The success of U.S. efforts in the postwar period, particularly in Greece, showed us capable of meeting these responsibilities.

As a result of losses to Chinese Communism and Indian neutralism, he felt the West must look more to Africa for the resources required for the inevitable struggle with the Soviets. Africa, although not rich in agriculture, had untold mineral resources, including the ferro-alloys, coal, and uranium. Africa should be developed by Europeans, as Smuts felt the black African was content with his life. There was no serious threat of Communism in Africa, or any other seeds of instability which could not be coped with in our lifetime. There was ample time to build on Africa as a base.

Smuts was confident that America could play an important role in Africa, both with private investment and through the Point Four Program. In his view there was no basis for a new approach to the U.S.S.R. Any Western overtures now would be considered a sign of weakness by the Soviets. Only when there was some fundamental change, such as a break-up of the U.S.S.R's unwieldy political structure, would a new approach be possible.

In the General's view, the forces at play in the Far East were still beyond Western control. He had been convinced that General Marshall's mission to China would fail. Even if Southeast Asia fell to Communism, which he considered probable, there would ultimately be a break-up of Communist domination, possibly through economic failure. Anarchy and chaos might then exist for an extended period, during which no outside efforts would be effective. India was a source of special concern to Smuts. He was pessimistic about the country's future, as the present leaders of India were really like Europeans, without any real hold on the people. There was little that America could do to help except to be friendly.

Although my part in the conversation was mainly to put an occasional question to Smuts and draw him out on key issues, I was entranced by the breadth and sweep of his views, evolving as they had from years of participation in international affairs as a world leader. The objectivity and clarity of his analysis of the world scene impressed me. Happily much that he predicted has not taken place.

Prime Minister and Mrs. Malan gave me a luncheon, attended by Minister of Finance N. C. Havenga and the Administrator and Secretary for South-West Africa, and their wives. It was held at Groote Schuur, Rhodes's house, which he had left to the government as the prime minister's official residence. The house is a pleasing structure in the Cape Dutch style. Its broad back terrace ascends toward Table Mountain, which we could see through an avenue cut in the lush

Cape vegetation. In browsing through the library left by Rhodes, I found many volumes of the Greek and Roman classics which he had had translated and bound in typed form. Later, I visited Rhodes's farm and the humble house by the sea at Muizenburg where, just before his death from tuberculosis, the roof was partially removed so he could breathe better. Later, I saw his grave in Southern Rhodesia, a territory first settled by British pioneers at his instigation in 1890 and a land to which he felt a close attachment.

I did not, from my first encounter, obtain a favorable impression of Malan. A large, stolid, impassive man of seventy-six, he seemed to epitomize the stubborn, dogmatic attitude of the Boer, much like that of their ancestors in Friesland in the Netherlands. Dr. Malan had been educated in theology and had served as a minister of the Dutch Reformed Church. Although he expressed himself well, he was considered more a politician than a thinker, a man who maintained his position by political manipulation. He tried hard to appear disarming, to give the impression that he was truly concerned with the human aspects of the grave issues he was dealing with. But he was not, to me at least, convincing. In his discussion of race issues he appeared to revel in apartheid as a desirable end in itself, not something which was forced on him and that he accepted reluctantly. Mrs. Malan was a pretty, slightly plump lady, much younger than the Prime Minister, over whom she apparently exerted a considerable influence. She made an effort to lighten a luncheon that was otherwise a rather stiff affair.

In my official conversations with Malan later, the topics of major interest for me were related to security: where the Union would stand in the event of East-West hostilities; the threat of Communism in Africa, which had so far not been serious; and the question of apartheid, the issue on which his party had come to power and which caused much concern in the U.S.[3] I did not want to appear either approving or unfriendly, but I wanted to draw him out.

I expressed appreciation for the government's invitation to visit Cape Town. The Prime Minister told me that he considered South Africa's relations with the U.S. to be very friendly. Just as events in the U.S. created world-wide interest, today the Union was in a somewhat similar position with respect to Africa. In the event of an East-West conflict, the Union would be able to provide supplies to allied vessels and furnish other assistance. Whether the Union would be able to send troops abroad was dependent upon her ability to maintain internal order and on other circumstances.

Dr. Malan referred to the Union's desire, voiced both in parliament and in the press, to join the North Atlantic Pact (NAP). He was sure that this was well known to us and the British. He understood, however, that the NAP applied to the North Atlantic area. I pointed out that the NAP was but one regional pact, and did not exclude similar arrangements for other areas. I advised him that no Far Eastern pact was then being contemplated. Actions to be taken under the NAP were still not complete. For example, we needed to know the extent of the European contribution before our commitments could be determined. I remarked that the Turks were also very much interested in a similar pact. Connelly later told me that he had not been advised either by Malan or any other member of the government, since his arrival some four months previously, of any South African interest in joining a regional security pact. He did not understand Malan's reference to having communicated his views to the U.S. In my later meetings with other Union officials no one mentioned a pact.

The Prime Minister, continuing, said that his government was trying to prevent Communism from making any headway among the natives, who were susceptible to Communist propaganda. He believed that the Soviet Consulate General in Pretoria, which was vastly overstaffed by Russians who kept exclusively to themselves, was the training school for Communist agents. The Prime Minister pointed out that the Europeans in the Union were outnumbered one to four by non-Europeans, which made segregation an absolute necessity. The government was endeavoring to separate the whites and non-whites into individual residential areas. This did not involve sending all nonwhites back to the native reserves, but rather putting each race together in its own area or areas. The native would then be able to live in accordance with his own tribal customs. Dr. Malan stressed that his policy was to treat the native with justice. All whites in the Union were in favor of white supremacy. More and more members of the opposition in the parliament agreed with the government's native program, he told me, which he believed was making progress. I was skeptical.

I left Malan with many misgivings. I did not believe his policy of apartheid, as he described it, would work. I had doubts that his views were flexible enough to deal with the enormously difficult problem he faced. I was deeply troubled by the moral issue involved.

On March 6, I called on the Minister of Finance Havenga, for a discussion of economic matters.[4] Mr. Havenga, a hero of the Boer

War and disciple of the late General James B. M. Hertzog, was considered next in line for Prime Minister. According to the Minister, adequate private capital was available for the Orange Free State gold mines. However, the Union's total development program of £60 million a year required continued private loans from the U.S., Switzerland, and England. The postwar shortage of dollars had forced the imposition of import controls, much to their regret. He added that this could have been avoided if the U.S. Ex-Im Bank had granted their request for loans. I pointed out that the Union had not been able to meet the bank requirements for identifying specific projects under their loans. He made it clear, with a touch of bitterness, that he planned no further request.

Later in the day I met with Dr. E. G. Jansen, Minister of Native Affairs, a lawyer by profession and a respected elder statesman of the Nationalist Party.[5] He pointed out the numerical inferiority of the 2.5 million Union whites to the 8 million nonwhites, also the great differences in education, which complicated the problem of handling the blacks. They had picked up the vices of the white man but not his virtues. The illegal entry of blacks from Nyasaland and Rhodesia greatly complicated the Union's problem, since few were willing to work on farms, and when found, had to be deported. Jansen confirmed that education of the blacks was entirely in the hands of the churches, although a study was underway which might result in a more active government role. I found this situation shocking.

Jansen referred to the great differences between the various tribes. Temporary mine workers created no problem, but housing and training for urban workers was inadequate. The government was endeavoring to have employees pay for a share of the costs to meet these deficiencies. The European trade unions prevented blacks from taking the jobs of Europeans. In another conversation on the same day, Dr. T. E. Donges, Minister of Interior and Mines, pointed out the great problem created by the several hundred thousand Indians in the Union who had proven unassimilable. He feared additional pressure for further Indian immigration and possible repercussions in the Union from the inevitable reaction against Indians in East Africa. Donges looked toward the bright prospects of the Orange Free State gold mines, which would start yielding large returns in a few years.

I had an interesting meeting at Connelly's residence with Sir Evelyn Baring, the British High Commissioner to South Africa, at his request.[6] We discussed mainly the position of the blacks. Sir Evelyn considered that the previous Smuts government had made an earnest effort to find a solution to the non-European problem. They had created an investigating commission which had in March 1948 produced the Fagan Report, rejecting total separation. The urban black's life was economically intertwined with that of the European, and he was there to stay.

The Smuts government had, however, been defeated before the report could be carried out, and was succeeded by the present nationalist government with its policy of apartheid. Although Sir Evelyn disclaimed knowing the final answer to the racial problem, he did not believe the present government was going about it in the right way. Apartheid in the universities doubled the teachers' burden, resulting in less teaching for both races. In answer to my query, Baring said he did not consider possible the emergence of a single native leader in Africa. For example, despite his ability and interest in his people, Tshekadi Khana, the former Regent of the Bamanguato tribe, was not of high enough caliber to get continent-wide support.

I had my longest discussion with D. D. Forsyth, Secretary for External Affairs.[7] As a professional diplomat he was not involved with party matters, but the policy of the Malan government affected everything he did. Naturally, he had his own point of view. Although I was not in a position to expound U.S. government policy on the issues involved, I helped draw him out on the Union's problems with the UN, its relationship with the Commonwealth, and the results from the application of its apartheid policy.

Forsyth felt that South African relations with the U.S. were of the very best. However, the two did not always see eye to eye. The U.S. often took what he termed a juggling attitude, which referred to such issues as the Union's regime in South-West Africa, which we strongly opposed, the failure of our Ex-Im Bank to grant the Union's $100 million loan application on technical grounds, and our attitude toward the Reverend Michael Scott, an Anglican clergyman who had appeared before the UN Trusteeship Council in 1949 to testify on behalf of natives in South-West Africa and against the South African administration there.

Forsyth mentioned, in an offhand way, that he believed there was some uneasiness throughout the world in regard to U.S. aims. We were pouring money in everywhere. He did not consider us imperialistic but asked, "For what purpose is this being done?" South Africa, according to Forsyth, felt very strongly that if the UN continued its present course of interference in the domestic affairs of member nations, it would fail. Recent developments, such as UN mixing in

South-West African affairs and UN investigating bodies going to other non-self-governing areas, were actions which had never even been thought of by the framers of the UN Charter at San Francisco in 1945. This "interfering" process was the result of action by smaller nations, particularly in Latin America, who were in no way concerned directly in Africa. They were, however, sufficiently numerous to outvote the major UN members who were directly responsible, and who were opposed to such steps.

Forsyth had served fourteen years in South-West Africa and felt that he could speak with authority on the area. The Europeans there had their own administration, officials, and House of Assembly and would shortly have representation in the Union Parliament. A white could not cross the borders from the European section into the native reserves without a special pass. The blacks in the reserves ran their own affairs, in separate areas. There were a number of different tribes with different customs and organizations; their chiefs could request the administration's advice, but it was given only in an advisory capacity.

I knew Forsyth had attended the recent Colombo Conference, and asked what impression he had of Prime Minister Nehru. Forsyth replied he could not at first make him out, but had come to the conclusion that Nehru was an extremely able and ambitious man who was, above all, an opportunist. Nehru wanted to head a group of Asian states with India as the principal member. India had remained with the Commonwealth only because Nehru considered that best suited his purpose at the present time. However, Nehru had not taken any clear stand against the Soviets. Forsyth felt that if Nehru could achieve his goal by playing along with the Communists, he would certainly do so.

Forsyth expressed concern over Indian expansionism. He said that South Africa had a serious problem in their Indian residents, and gave the impression that he thought they might serve as an eventual fifth column. Since the annual increase in India's own population could not possibly be absorbed in the Indian economy, many Indians would have to emigrate. One of the Sinhalese ministers at the Colombo Conference in Sri Lanka had said to him, "We, like you" (meaning we would like to immigrate to you). Forsyth added that he thought the Colombo Conference had been worthwhile, for Southeast Asia had to be strengthened against the Communist advance.

I said that we felt the Commonwealth was a powerful force for world peace and prosperity and we hoped South Africa would remain in it. Forsyth replied that talk of establishing a South African "republic" was, in his opinion, for local consumption only; South Africa had no intention of leaving the Commonwealth. The English-speaking nations, the U.S., and the Commonwealth, were the only safeguards against a Communist-dominated world. We had the same language, the same traditions, the same way of life, and the same aims. We had to stick together. Forsyth's over-simplified generalization was not, I thought, altogether correct.

Forsyth remarked that he had once asked Dr. Malan what he conceived as the ultimate goal of apartheid. The Prime Minister's reply was that it meant complete separation of whites and nonwhites. The nonwhites would be given help in improving their lot, economically and socially, but they would have to live by themselves. For example, in higher education the natives would receive instruction identical to that of the whites, given by the same teachers, but would be taught in completely separate buildings. Some of the extreme enthusiasts of apartheid even had in mind complete native states run exclusively by the natives. He had interpreted well the future that apartheid was to take.

Forsyth gave a luncheon in my honor at the Civil Service Club on March 7. He made a particular point of seating me next to the Union administrator for South-West Africa, who happened to be in Cape Town. Later Forsyth wanted to know what I thought of him. It was as though he was saying, "Look, he's a very decent fellow. Our policy in South-West Africa can't be so bad." Actually he was a big, bluff, rather pleasant man, who seemed about what one would expect for a colonial administrator.

After a day of sightseeing and photography in the Cape area, I departed on the morning of March 9 in an Air Force plane for Victoria Falls. Although I had enjoyed my discussions with my South African hosts, had appreciated their hospitality, and had every good wish for them in facing almost insurmountable problems, I once more was filled with grave misgivings. I tended to agree with Sir Evelyn Baring that the Nationalists were not going about solving their problems in the right way. Although their basic attitude differed little from that of General Smuts, they tended to extol as a virtue a policy forced on them by the great disparity between the numbers of blacks and whites.

The National Party had come to power in 1948, clearly aiming at the creation of an Afrikaner-dominated state. In 1960, South Africa was declared a republic, in a move opposed by most of the country's English-speaking whites, and withdrew from the Commonwealth. The Afrikaner politicians had succeeded, where the Boer generals at the turn of the century had not, in isolating their people and their country.

Soon after it came to office, the Nationalist government began putting into practice its designs for apartheid, literally "separateness," according to which complete segregation on the basis of racial designation would be instituted in every aspect of life in South Africa. Over the years, apartheid has been embodied in an edifice of repressive legislation that has denied the nonwhite majority basic human and political rights. By its very nature, accompanying security legislation meant to enforce apartheid, has curbed the civil rights of whites as well, and silenced much liberal opposition to government policies. Parliamentary opposition to the Nationalist government is too small to be effective. More salient than anti-apartheid forces in the political process has been an emerging opposition to the right of the Nationalists, protesting what it views as Nationalist moderation in racial matters.

Meanwhile, the tempo of resistance to apartheid and white control in South Africa has increased, manifested in the growth of African political pressures, activity in South Africa by incipient guerrilla organizations, and sudden outbursts of violence like that at Soweto in 1976 and in recent large-scale bombings. South African whites continue to equate African nationalism with international Communism. The so-called "White Redoubt" in southern Africa has shrunk over the past decade as Angola, Mozambique, and Zimbabwe won their independence, leaving South Africa without a buffer against infiltration from the north by hostile forces. General Smuts' vision of a white-dominated Africa was not fulfilled. There is little doubt, however, that militarily South Africa has the capability to deal with internal subversion and external enemies for the foreseeable future.

South African forces are actively engaged in military operations against guerrillas in Namibia, formerly South-West Africa, which South Africa has continued to administer as a mandated territory. South Africa intends to complete the transition of power to an elected Namibian government, closely tied to the Republic and including representatives of the resident white minority. South Africa has, however, thus far excluded recognition of the militant wing of the South-West Africa People's Organization (SWAPO), which remains in a state of insurgency, conducting raids out of bases in Angola. The OAU regards SWAPO as the "only legitimate representative of the Namibian people" and insists that transfer of power in the country should be made directly to its representatives.

South African authorities point out that SWAPO draws its support primarily from only one tribal group, the Ovambo, and is not representative of the people of Namibia. In the interest of South African security, they likewise refuse to consider a withdrawal of forces until assurances are made of a corresponding Cuban pullout from Angola. The Angolans in turn consider a Cuban presence necessary for its defense as long as South African forces are stationed in Namibia. The U.S. participates in a Western "contact" group, along with Britain, Canada, France, and Germany, in an effort to bring about an agreement by the concerned parties on terms for Namibia's independence.

As part of its total strategy, South Africa has put forward a plan for creating a "constellation" of states in southern Africa, committed to political, economic, and military cooperation. In this arrangement, the white republic would be associated with ten independent homelands based on traditional tribal territories carved out of South Africa but containing only a small fraction of the country's black population. When carried through, the homelands policy will deprive most of the country's blacks of their South African citizenship, replacing it with citizenship in the tribal homelands to which they have been assigned, often on an arbitrary basis. Blacks remaining, many of whom may never have seen their assigned homeland, could thereafter be regarded as guests in South Africa, subject to deportation for infringements of apartheid laws or security regulations.

I am not convinced that South Africa will be able to "make it" in the future without painful readjustments. The only hope, it would appear, is that the younger leaders of the ruling National Party will be willing to face up to the dire consequences of a continuation of apartheid, before the point of no return is reached in the struggle. Any government of South Africa must still face the same organizing dilemma: to continue present policies will almost inevitably result in revolution; to compromise on participation in government will probably result, as in Zimbabwe, in majority rule. As in Zimbabwe, this would necessitate for most white South Africans a drastic, perhaps for many an unacceptable, change in their way of life.

14

Other African Visits

March 9–14, 1950.

Since I was proceeding to Ethiopia I wanted to take advantage of the invitations I had received to visit some of the dependent African territories. I realized that I would not meet any African leaders, only white settlers and colonial officials. It was, however, a unique opportunity for an American official. I departed from Cape Town early in the morning of March 9 in an Air Force plane heading for Bulawayo in Southern Rhodesia. From there we would proceed to Livingstone to visit the Victoria Falls. This trip was made possible by the kindness of Lieutenant Colonel Edwin A. Bland, Jr., the air attaché at the American Embassy in Pretoria, who also provided invaluable knowledge of the areas we visited, as well as good company.

On February 22, in Lourenço Marques, C. Edgar Vaughn, British Consul-General there, had extended me a cordial invitation to visit Victoria Falls, Salisbury, and Nairobi, following my stay in the Union of South Africa. All possible assistance was offered, in addition to a package of books on Africa sent out by the Foreign Office. Arrangements had also been made in my behalf through the Belgian government for a brief stop-off in Elizabethville in the Belgian Congo. At Bulawayo I visited the grave of Cecil Rhodes on a bald, windswept, rocky mound of the Motappos, at a spot he, himself, had chosen. I stood in silent respect for this great man, to whom I personally, and all who are a part of the English tradition, owe so much.

Victoria Falls, rivaled only by Niagara Falls for impressiveness, is a drop by the Zambezi River ranging from 80 to 240 feet, involving 62 to 100 million gallons of water per minute. The river is here at its widest, over 1,860 yards, and the fall is abrupt, breaking onto the opposite wall of a narrow chasm only 100 feet wide. The water then flows 130 yards before emerging in a zigzag trough called the Grand

Canyon. The tremendous pressure of the water in this confined trough creates a perpetual mist above the falls, which can be seen in a plane from a great distance. The 400-foot drop in the canyon below the gorge extends for some 40 miles. The falls, which lay in Rhodesia, were discovered by David Livingstone in 1855. The surrounding land was preserved by the Rhodesian government. The Cape-to-Cairo railway crosses the Zambezi River at a minimum height of 420 feet just below the deep Boiling Water Pool marking the outlet of the Grand Canyon gorge.

We landed in a nearby airfield and spent several hours observing the many fascinating aspects of the falls, including the spectacular sloping cataract called Leaping Water. This is one of the four segments of the falls created by islands on the precipice, which normally break the flow of water over the crest of the falls. The river at high mark flows as one unbroken expanse into a seeming crack, with walls of equal elevation. One escarpment of the falls is covered with a rain forest of great trees.

After dinner and a good night's sleep, we departed from Livingstone early on the morning of March 10 and arrived in Elizabethville, in the Katanga province of the Belgian Congo. We were met at the airport by J. G. Ziegler de Zeigleck, Governor of Katanga, a group of local businessmen, the consular corps, U.S. Consul J. Brock Haven, and his consular staff. We had lunch at the home of Consular Attaché Thomas G. Murdock, who had been present at the conference in Lourenço Marques. He was a mineralogist by training and his reports on mining activities in the Katanga had been most helpful.

This was my first visit to the Belgian Congo. I had imagined it to be strange and exotic, and had pictured a mysterious Congo River, impenetrable forests, restive natives, and cities dominated by colonial intrigue. I was surprised to find the few Belgians there living in quite modern cities, running efficient mines and related industrial plants. As a professional geologist I knew that the province of Katanga had one of the most important concentrations of industrial minerals in the world: tin, diamonds, gold, radium, enough cobalt to control the world market, and, most importantly, a copper production of 200,000 tons a year. The richest copper fields became in 1911 a monopoly of the private Belgian company Union Minière.

Interest in Central Africa was stimulated by nineteenth-century discoveries in the Congo Basin by the world-famous explorers David Livingstone, Richard Burton, and H. M. Stanley. The Congo Free State was taken over by the Belgian King Leopold II as his personal property in a formal declaration of sovereignty in 1885. After a tumultuous history, including the Arab War, charges of exploitation, and a commission of inquiry, the Belgian Parliament annexed the area as the Belgian Congo in 1908. When I visited it in 1950 it had a population of about 11 million blacks, and was administered by some 35,000 whites, mostly Belgians under contract, who did not establish permanent residence. It was ruled by a Belgian Governor-General reporting directly to the Minister of Colonies in Brussels.

I had been well prepared by reports at Lourenço Marques from our consulate at Elizabethville.[1] Colonial Belgians were reported to suspect that we sought to accelerate the advancement of backward races, and that this was reflected in our policies toward trusteeship territories such as theirs. At that point, the Belgians were also seeking to raise the economic and social standards of the natives, but had no intention of handing over governing power until the natives had become more advanced. They did not believe European higher education or the creation of an elite class to be in the best interests of the Africans.

The Belgian colonial administration was trying to steer a middle course between British native policy in Kenya and North Rhodesia on the one hand, and South Africa on the other. The Belgians placed no emphasis on independence for the Congo. They believed strongly that it was useless to consider autonomy until the blacks were economically and politically sophisticated enough to govern themselves. Despite their superior attitude, the colonial Belgians appeared, however, to be kindly disposed toward the indigenous population. They stressed vocational education and placed emphasis on medical care and hygiene, and the training of nurses, laboratory assistants, and medical aides. Salaries were low, a fact they admitted. They felt there was no useful purpose served by increasing wages without a corresponding increase in productivity.

After lunch I paid a courtesy call on the Governor and visited Louis Wallet, general manager, and other officials of the Union Minière de Haut Katanga. They took me through the company's welfare center for black employees, which included the hospital, schools, and social center. I was impressed with the scale of their copper production and smelting operation, employing thousands of blacks. Everything was run with typical Belgian efficiency: by any standards, this was one of the most important extractive mineral operations in the world.

During the latter part of the afternoon a reception in my honor was held at the consular residence. The guests numbered about seventy and consisted of a representative cross-section of the city's leadership, including the Governor, ranking members of the provincial government, bank managers, officials of the Union Minière, publishers, representatives of American firms, etc. The event turned out to be an open forum in which I held the floor under a friendly but frank barrage of questions regarding U.S. policy. Special interest was expressed in our Point Four Program, which could have an important bearing upon the Katanga, as a major source of strategic raw materials. The Department's action in establishing the Elizabethville Consulate had contributed somewhat to this speculation.

The *Essor du Congo* of March 9 carried my full biography and said, "It is the first time such a distinguished American personality has visited Elizabethville." Poor Elizabethville, not to have done better. My visit provided an interesting insight into the closed world of one of the most tightly run colonies in the world. The authority of the Governor and Union Minière was complete. I saw no blacks except those working as laborers. Moise Tshombe was later to tell me, when Prime Minister of Katanga, that his father, as a local chief of means, had tried unsuccessfully to get permission from the Beligans to send him abroad for education. The blacks who worked for Union Minière received family housing (as contrasted with bachelor establishments in the Johannesburg gold mines), elementary schooling for their ten thousand children, and health facilities much better than the natives in the bush. However, they had no rights or status whatever.

The subsequent history of the Congo, now Zaire, has been on the whole a disappointing one. Belgium attempted in 1958 to introduce a policy of gradual decolonization that was intended to shift political control to Africans under Belgian tutelage while leaving Belgian interests in control of the economy. The promise of elections spurred the emergence of black leaders, among them Patrice Lumumba and Moise Tshombe. While Lumumba challenged ethnic and regional interests with his call for centralized government, Tshombe, from his base in the Katanga province, campaigned for a federal system that would recognize regional autonomy. The electorate in 1960 failed to give any single party a working mandate in the new Congolese parliament. Under strong pressure by the Congolese delegates at the Round Table Conference held in January 1960, the Belgian government set June 30 of that year as the date for independence, which was obviously too soon.

When Lumumba was named to form a coalition government,

Tshombe, with Belgian backing, declared independence for the Katanga. If successful, the secession of Tshombe's mineral-rich province, which was the source of 80 percent of the Congo's wealth, would have deprived the country as a whole of its economic viability. The UN supplied military assistance to the Lumumba government, but would not allow its peacekeeping force to intervene to restore Katanga by force. Lumumba's appeal to the Soviet Union for aid led to his dismissal from office by his political rival, President Joseph Kasavubu. When Lumumba refused to step down as Prime Minister, he was arrested and killed. The country slipped quickly into anarchy, and over the next several years the burden of restoring order and ending recurring attempts at secession by disaffected regions fell first on UN forces, later on Belgian troops and the national army commanded by General Joseph Mobutu. The Tshombe secession was ended by UN forces when the opportunity was offered by a riot of Tshombe's troops in Elizabethville. As Under Secretary of State for Political Affairs during this period, I was deeply involved.

After an abortive attempt by Tshombe in 1964 to form a national government, Mobutu stepped in and assumed all executive authority at the head of a narrowly-based regime. In 1967, he assumed the presidency of the country, renamed Zaire, under a new constitution. The authoritarian nature of his regime was paralleled by its inefficiency and corruption, and by the sheer difficulty of governing so large and diverse a country. In recent years, Mobutu has bankrupted the once wealthy Zaire, its economy having largely been taken over by its foreign creditors. The positive effects of Mobutu's announced policy of "democratization" have yet to become obvious. The creation of stability in Zaire, a large country with vast resources, situated at the fulcrum of black Africa, remains one of the top priorities of American African policy.

Our group departed from the Congo for Salisbury, where I received a warm welcome from the Right Honorable Sir Godfrey Huggins, C.H., K.C.M.G., F.R.C.S., Prime Minister of Southern Rhodesia. Huggins was a physician by training and had been Premier for sixteen years. It was an important occasion for him, since he had just been given an official house and been granted the right to have me as his first guest. Before, I would have been the guest of the British Governor-General. Huggins had scored an important victory in the long process of achieving self-government for Southern Rhodesia.

Southern Rhodesia, which was separated from Northern Rhodesia by the Zambezi River, had a population of approximately 1.5 million blacks and 75,000 whites, who occupied an area of 152,000 square miles. A part of the South African plateau, it has a temperate climate well suited to mixed farming and ranching. The creation of the Rhodesias was entirely the result of the vision and determination of Cecil Rhodes. Rhodes in 1888 successfully disputed a Portuguese claim to a mining concession from King Lobengula, and won it for his British South Africa Company, which was granted a royal charter to settle and administer the region. In a referendum in 1922, white settlers rejected joining South Africa. The next year, Southern Rhodesia was formally annexed by the British crown as a self-governing colony. Under its constitution, legislative power was vested in the Crown, represented by the Governor, an executive council under the Governor, and a legislative assembly of thirty members elected by whites in eleven districts, but without final power in foreign affairs or legislation affecting natives.

Again, I had been prepared at Lourenço Marques for what to expect.[2] The three territories of Northern and Southern Rhodesia and Nyasaland were geographically contiguous and landlocked. Their economic development depended mainly on common transport and labor-supply problems. Certain development schemes required joint action by the three governments. But there were basic differences among these territories. Southern Rhodesia had status in the British Commonwealth almost equal to that of a dominion, and dealt with the Commonwealth Relations Office. The native policy of Southern Rhodesia was based on the idea of permanent white supremacy with parallel development of the two races. In practice the interests of the Africans were subordinated to those of the Europeans.

In February 1949, an unofficial conference at Victoria Falls passed a resolution advocating a federation of the Rhodesias and Nyasaland "under a constitution which would create a federal parliament, with such powers as are surrendered to it. The British government rejected the proposal, believing it would in effect turn the affairs of Northern Rhodesia over to Southern Rhodesia. The impasse reflected a basic conflict between the British government and the European elements of Central Africa on native policy, as well as differences over the future of all white settlement in Central Africa. The British were not willing to abandon their own commitments to the natives of the northern territories.

My stay in Salisbury was short. I called on Sir Gordon Munro, the British Governor-General, at his official residence. He expressed re-

gret at not having me as his guest. He queried me about our Lourenço Marques conference, about which he had already received reports.
He discussed with me Southern Rhodesia's prospects for the future,
which he considered bright. I was driven about Salisbury and taken
to one of its white clubs. It was a small town, teeming with activity,
with ranchers in typical ranch dress bustling about doing their shopping and socializing. It reminded me of the sheep country around
San Angelo in west Texas where I had worked as a young geologist.
The people I met were friendly, open, and confident for the future.
They felt sure that they could work out their relationship with the
natives. Little did they realize that Southern Rhodesia would, within
thirty years, be a black republic called Zimbabwe.

In the evening, the Prime Minister gave a dinner in my honor to
which all of the members of his government were invited. Our discussions were wide-ranging. The government representatives talked
principally of the future of Southern Rhodesia, already off to a good
start. They were proud that the white farmers and ranchers were
doing so well, and saw immense possibilities for the future which
would assure a continuation of their good life: there was plenty of
land and space for all. They saw no insuperable problem of getting
along with the blacks, who, up to that time, had been quite docile.
They said there would be no trouble unless outsiders stirred them up
with premature talk about native participation in government. There
had been a broadcast over the BBC recently stating that this was the
aim of the British government: the Rhodesians condemned such
statements as being ambiguous and giving false hopes to the natives.
They felt the native was doing well in Southern Rhodesia, and they
did not wish to set back the progress being made.

My hosts expressed warm friendship for the U.S. and solidarity
with our anti-Communist policies. I enjoyed my stay in Salisbury: one
could not help but like these friendly, gregarious people and their
open frontier outlook. They could not know that their pleasant way
of life, based on white supremacy, would be swept away so soon.

The next morning I flew to Nairobi, Kenya, which had in our
Lourenço Marques conference been characterized as the last stronghold of British African imperialism. It was evident, we were told, that
the indigenous populations of East Africa were slowly awakening.
That process would undoubtedly be more rapid under the right leadership; however, this was not yet available. Dissension among the
various tribes prevented the Africans from confronting the European

element as a strong, united group. When given the opportunity, Africans were eager for education, I was told, but wanted even more to become financially successful. Education also increased the Africans' desire for self-government, which had been aroused in part by British promises made during the war. The failure to fulfill these commitments had caused frustration, which, if unsatisfied for a protracted period, would most certainly lead to trouble.

The population of Kenya was growing at a rate which would soon create a shortage of land available for food production. The blacks resented the fact that the British residents in Kenya had most of the best agricultural lands, in the so-called White Highlands, which had formerly belonged to the tribes. In addition to the animosity the Africans felt toward the white settlers because of their dominating position, they increasingly resented the Indians, with whom they came into even closer contact, since Indians controlled the distribution of most merchandise in Kenya.

The *East African Standard* of March 14 announced my arrival as a part of my tour to contact local officials and inform myself. I had said that I was greatly impressed by what I saw in Kenya, by the spirit of the people, the potentialities of the country, and its great possibilities for the future. Nairobi appeared to be a good place to live, and East Africa, with its broad spaces, again reminded me of Texas.

I was taken sightseeing by Consul-General Edward Groth, who had been in Lourenço Marques. We visited a game preserve just outside Nairobi, where we sat in our car, surrounded by numerous small cars packed with Indians, and watched the lions come and go and sun themselves, oblivious of our presence. We visited some Kikuyu villages in the neighborhood, which were already showing signs of overpopulation. Their well-built reed huts and simple way of life were appealing.

In the evening I was entertained at dinner by Major General Sir Philip Mitchell, C.M.G., M.C., Governor of Kenya. We had a broad discussion of the colony and the future prospects of the British settlers there. This was long before the era of the Mau Mau and Kenyatta, and there were no serious problems, although the settlers must have known that their comfortable, colonial existence would not last long. Unfortunately, as in the other colonies, I had no opportunity for discussions with any native Kenyans. If I had, I would, of course, have gotten quite a different story.

Although I saw little of Kenya at the time outside of Nairobi,

Cecilia and I were to have the opportunity in 1973 to return for a visit to see and photograph the animals in the great game lodges of this lovely country. This included the Mount Kenya Safari Club, the Samburu Game Lodge, Ngurman Lodge and young Richard Leakey's new lodge overlooking the Rift Valley near Nairobi. We had the luxury of being flown by a petite young British girl pilot named Heather, who took Cecilia and me to one lodge and then, by appointment, reappeared after two days to fly us to another.

Nairobi, with its round Hilton Hotel, had become a most attractive city. Kenyatta had exceeded all expectations as a national leader and the white settlers were still holding on. We stayed with our old friends, U.S. Ambassador and Mrs. Robinson McIlvaine, who told us about their many trips about the country and their interest in wildlife. We visited the Masai and Kikuyu tribes in their native environments, and I was lucky enough to get a number of their artifacts and ceremonial objects for my African collection. Kenya remains one of the most interesting countries in Africa for the average Western tourist. The photographic safari has taken the place of the "white hunter." If present efforts to save the elephant from the ivory hunter, and preserve other game animals, are successful, Kenya, which depends so much on tourism, should have a bright future.

In an address to the South African parliament in 1962, Harold Macmillan reminded the members of that body of the "winds of change" that were blowing across Africa. The term has become part of our international political vocabulary. Macmillan was referring to a reality that the British government had recognized and was responding to in its process of decolonization of British Africa. After transitional periods of internal self-government under British tutelage, this process had brought full independence to Ghana in 1957, to Nigeria in 1960, to Tanganyika (renamed Tanzania after its subsequent merger with Zanzibar in 1964) and Sierra Leone in 1961; to Uganda in 1962; to Kenya in 1963; to Zambia and Malawi in 1964, and finally in 1966, to Botswana.

Ghana started out as a model of orderly transition and stability whose good example the others were expected to emulate. President Nkrumah, however, soon engaged in constructing a cult of personality that obscured for a time the ineptness and venality of his regime. Eventually it alienated members of the elite, particularly in the military, who wanted to maintain order and preserve national unity. Nkrumah was ousted in 1966 by a military coup. General Joseph A. Ankrah, who assumed command, pledged to end abuses of power, and restore democratic government. His efforts were discredited, however, when his government was accused of election fraud. General Ignatius Acheampong, leader of a second military coup in 1972, likewise failed to establish a viable civilian government, and it was left to those of yet another coup to ban the old political parties and prohibit the old politicians from participating in new elections that were supposed to give democracy a fresh start.

Shortly before the scheduled elections, junior officers, led by Flight Lieutenant Jerry Rawlings, seized control of the country, tried former civilian and military leaders, and executed a number of them, including Acheampong. A civilian parliamentary regime was reinstituted with instructions from the young officers, who stepped down to make way for it, to make haste in cleaning house. In 1982, however, economic development, which in Ghana had seemed so promising a quarter century earlier, still languished. Renewed charges were heard of corruption in high places. In response to the failure of the civilian politicians, Rawlings came out of retirement to remove President Hilla Limann from the office in which he had placed him and to reimpose military rule.

Nigeria, black Africa's most populous country and, because of its oil reserves, potentially its richest, presented a different format for a similar pattern of military intervention when the political process in Nigeria seemed on the verge of breaking down. The country itself is a mosaic of ethnic groups, although the decisive cleavage is between the conservative Muslim north and the more progressive, but sharply divided, non-Muslim south. A military coup in 1966 overthrew the parliamentary regime of Prime Minister Abubakar Tafawa Balewa, but disagreement among the regional commanders over the structure of Nigeria's federal system contributed to the secession of Biafra, which was predominantly Ibo, the following year. A ruthlessly fought civil war, costly in lives and in property in the best-developed region of the country, was ended in 1970 with Biafra's defeat and reintegration into a federal system intended to de-emphasize the ethnic identification of its constituent parts. Delay by military leader General Yakubu Gowon in returning the country to civilian government led to his replacement by disaffected high-ranking officers, who put into effect a new constitution. Following elections, Lieutenant General Olusegun Obasanjo turned over the reins of government to civilian President Shehu Shagari in 1979.

The political evolution of former British colonies in East Africa was, on the whole, less traumatic. There, with the exception of Uganda, the role of the armed forces was confined to national defense, and responsibility for government remained in the hands of able and popular leaders: Jomo Kenyatta of Kenya, Julius Nyerere of Tanzania, Kenneth Kaunda of Zambia, and Hastings (later Kamuzu) Banda of Malawi. They had all led their respective countries to independence. In each case, the establishment of a one-party state channeled tribal rivalries, conflicting personal ambitions, and the clash of ideologies into closely-controlled party conferences, rather than the arena of parliamentary politics. There has resulted considerable success in economic development.

Kenya, for example, as a capitalist economy, has enjoyed sustained growth. Kenyatta, once anathemized as the guiding spirit behind the terrorist Mau Mau, proved to be a leader of probity, fairness, and moderation. Following his death in 1978, power passed in an orderly transition to his vice-president, Daniel arap Moi, the member of a minority tribe, whose peaceful accession to the presidency was seen as a triumph over ethnic differences. Meanwhile, Tanzania has achieved political stability under President Nyerere. His brand of "African socialism," however, which stresses cooperative and communal activity within a planned economy with state participation, has not been so successful.

Uganda's lot was less fortunate. A year after independence, Prime Minister Milton Obote deposed the federal President in a bloody coup and established a unitary republic, abolishing traditional political structures and banning all opposition parties. Obote proposed to introduce a socialist economy and to remove the tribal element from politics. In 1971, however, his government was overthrown in a military coup led by Idi Amin Dada, who established a barbaric dictatorship based on the support of an army composed mainly of mercenaries and recruits from Amin's own tribal group. Tanzanian forces intervened on the side of Ugandan exiles in 1979 to defeat the Amin regime. A provisional government pledged to return democracy to the country proved incapable of dealing with the existing chaotic conditions. Pressure was brought to bear by Tanzania for Obote's restoration to Uganda's presidency under Nyerere's patronage. Retention of a sizable Tanzanian military presence has been required to assure the regime's security. The infamous Amin is in exile.

However strongly they may have blown in other parts of British Africa, the winds of change of which Macmillan spoke bypassed Southern Rhodesia, where the prosperous white settler community, who were never more than 5 percent of the population, continued to exercise their right to self-government, excluding the black majority from the political process. The Central African Federation, which came into being in 1953 with Huggins as federal Prime Minister, lasted for ten years and was dissolved when Northern Rhodesia (Zambia) and Nyasaland (Malawi) seceded to become independent black-majority-ruled countries. Meanwhile, the Rhodesian Front, led after 1964 by Ian Smith, had come to power in Salisbury on a platform demanding full independence. The British denied approval, however, until evidence was given that the government intended to move toward eventual black majority rule, a condition unacceptable to Smith and his Rhodesian Front.

Terminating negotiations with London, the Smith government made a unilateral declaration of independence (UDI) in 1965 that was regarded by the British government as an act of rebellion. All attempts to reconcile Salisbury and return the colony to legality failed. By the mid-1970s, liberation groups supplied by China and the Soviet Union were waging a guerrilla war against the white regime from sanctuaries in Zambia and Mozambique. Rejecting Anglo-American initiatives to reach a ceasefire leading to the lifting of UN sanctions against Rhodesia, Smith opted instead for an internal settlement with black nationalist groups, led by Bishop Abel Muzorewa, who were willing to negotiate. The settlement, which did not include the militant groups under Robert Mugabe and Joshua Nkomo that were allied in the Patriotic Front, led to the creation of a supposedly black majority regime sharing power with Smith's Rhodesian Front, with Muzorewa as Prime Minister. The intensification of the guerrilla war by Patriotic Front forces after the internal settlement in 1979 brought Muzorewa to the conference table with Mugabe and Nkomo at Lancaster House in London. Here the British government imposed a new constitution that would assure genuine black majority rule and allow for the colony's restoration to legality. Elections in February 1980 gave Mugabe an overwhelming victory over Nkomo and Muzorewa, and in April the country became independent as the Republic of Zimbabwe.

Mugabe is a self-professed Marxist committed to a socialist economy as well as to single-party rule, but he is also regarded as a pragmatist willing to bide his time. Although a sizable number of Europeans have left Zimbabwe, many remain and actively participate in the political process. The government relies heavily on the services of white civil servants, military officers, and technicians. Existing businesses, for the time being, remain intact, and a multiparty parliamentary government continues to function on the Westminster model in Harare, as Salisbury is now called.

15

Into the Lion's Den

Visit to Addis Ababa, Ethiopia. Emperor Haile Selassie.
March 14–18, 1950.

Ethiopia is the real Middle World. Flying in over the rugged mountains and plateaus of Ethiopia evokes an aura of great age and mystery. One conjures up images of empire and of the legendary Queen of Sheba, whose union with Solomon gave rise to generations of Ethiopian noblemen. The Ethiopia I visited on March 14, 1950, however, was a unified country under the leadership of an astute emperor, Haile Selassie, who was to hold the reins of power for nearly half a century.

When I arrived at the Addis Ababa airport from Kenya, an impressive array of Ethiopian officials were present to greet me: Foreign Minister Ate Aklilou Habte-Wold, Haile Selassie's personal secretary Ato Taffaro Worq, and Chief of Protocol Birhanou Tesseme. Also on hand were American Ambassador George R. Merrill, British Ambassador Daniel W. Lascelles, and Indian Minister Sardar Sant Singh.

Addis Ababa, the capital, is located in the center of the 457,000-square-mile country, which borders on Kenya, Sudan, and Somalia, and faces Saudi Arabia across its five hundred miles of Red Sea coastline. But until the 1890s Ethiopia was largely undisturbed in its highland isolation. Today there are approximately 32 million Ethiopians. They comprise one hundred ethno-linguistic groups, about half of whom are Amharic-speaking. About half are Christians, an island in Muslim-dominated North Africa and the Horn of Africa. As early as A.D. 300 Syrian missionaries converted local rulers to a form of Christianity practiced by the Coptic Church, which provided a long line of Ethiopian emperors with a basis for stability and continuity.

Ethiopia was unified within its present borders in the late nineteenth century by Menelik II, who also extended Ethiopian rule over the Somali-inhabited Ogaden. World events made their first heavy impact on Ethiopia in 1896, when Italy unsuccessfully attempted to establish a protectorate over the country. Italy had earlier occupied neighboring Eritrea, which, after World War II, was assigned to Ethiopia. The thorny problem of Eritrean and Somali independence continues to threaten the country's unity today.

Following nearly two decades of internal power struggles after the death in 1913 of the ruler Menelik II, Haile Selassie (until then known as Ras, or nobleman, Tafari) was crowned as the sole Emperor of Ethiopia in 1930. His full title was Haile Selassie I, Conquering Lion of the Tribe of Judah, Elect of God, and King of Kings of Ethiopa, a mouthful in any language. Five years later Italy once again intervened in Ethiopia. Mussolini attacked the country in 1935 and seized Addis Ababa the next year. Haile Selassie and his family were forced to spend the war years in England, but when British and Ethiopian troops drove out the Italians in 1941, he returned to the throne. He initiated a series of reforms, including the abolition of slavery. At the time of my visit, the country was, except for Eritrea, relatively stable. There had, however, been reports, particularly from French sources, that Addis Ababa was being built up as the head-quarters for Communist propaganda and other activity in Africa.

Since the war, the U.S. and Ethiopia had maintained good relations, which had been strengthened by Ambassador George Merrill, my host for this visit. After exchanging friendly greetings at the airport, he took me to his residence. I found it to be in an old palace of one of the members of the royal family, which had been modernized just enough to make it comfortable, without spoiling its original charm. A sweeping terrace, where we had tea, had been built in the shade of a huge tree.

George, a bachelor, was a veteran of almost thirty years in the service. He went on to Afghanistan as his last post. He was a skillful diplomat and a good host. The first evening, armed with martinis in a thermos and a hamper of hors d'oeuvres, we drove to a plateau high over the city to witness a magnificent sunset. From the heights we could see the royal palace, the Coptic churches, and other stately reminders of what was the world's oldest remaining empire. The scene made a deep impression on me; I felt that I was somehow a part of its thousands of years of history.

Later, I was to take up recent history with the Emperor, and in preparation Ambassador Merrill filled me in on the details. He told me that since 1945 the all-important interest of Ethiopia had been the question of the disposition of Italy's former colonies in East Africa. Ethiopia had been keenly disappointed by the action of the fourth session of the UN General Assembly in recommending that Italian Somaliland be placed under a ten-year trusteeship, with Ethiopia's traditional foe Italy as the administering authority. The Ethiopian government had registered its disappointment with this decision by making an official protest about its legality to the Secretary General of the UN.

Ethiopia, Merrill told me, was also engaged in reorganizing and increasing its military potential, apparently following suggestions made a few years earlier by the British military mission to Ethiopia. There was no doubt that a more effective military force would go a long way toward stabilizing the Ethiopian government's hold on the country. There had always been a certain amount of defiance by local authorities of orders issued by the central government. At times civil disorders had broken out against land taxes, and there had even been open rebellion. Merrill's report was helpful for my conversations with the Emperor, the first of which took place that same evening. I had been honored with an invitation from the Emperor and Empress to a dinner with them in my honor at the Imperial Palace: it was certainly not an invitation to be ignored. It read "By Command of his Imperial Majesty Haile Selassie I."

I entered the palace through a passage lined with cages of lions, which seemed to provide a most appropriate introduction to an emperor known as "the Lion of Judah." The lions were turning in their cages as I approached; I could see their eyes flashing in the light of the torches of the palace yard. I felt again a deep sense of the historic situation in which I found myself. Although my invitation called for white tie and decorations, I unfortunately had only the white dinner jacket I had worn in Lourenço Marques, and no decorations, to display. I entered the throne room and was presented to the Emperor and Empress.

The Emperor was a small man, but striking in appearance. He had a long, aquiline nose, a black beard, and close-cropped black hair. He possessed great natural dignity and self-assurance. The Empress was equally impressive, taller than the Emperor, with typical Ethiopian jet-black hair and a full face. She wore a light white fur jacket over a black satin dress. A Coptic cross hung from her neck.

There were between thirty and forty guests at the palace that night. Preceding dinner, champagne was served very formally by waiters dressed in European attire. I chatted with members of the cabinet and the diplomatic corps, before being seated at a table for sixteen, on the right of the Empress. On my other side was the couple's eldest son, the Duke of Harrar, who later was involved (apparently against his will) in a plot to overthrow his father. On the far side of the Empress sat the second son, with whom I was able to converse as well. The conversation focused on hunting and the rich wildlife of Ethiopia. The family's wartime stay in England had given them the opportunity to learn our language well.

After dinner, I was taken to sit by the Emperor for a get-acquainted talk. He answered my questions about his hopes for his country, most of which, unfortunately, he was never able to accomplish. He told me that he had something he particularly wanted to take up with me but would reserve it for our meeting the next day. After a suitable period, another guest was brought to take my place. Observing the animated discussion that ensued, I asked who my successor was and was somewhat taken aback to discover that he was the Russian Ambassador. The Emperor, it seemed, was keeping his options open. After dinner there were drinks and small talk to a rather late hour, when the Emperor and Empress retired.

The following morning the Emperor and I engaged in official discussions, which I opened by presenting him with the following letter from President Truman:[1]

> Great and Good Friend: I am sending you this letter by Mr. George McGhee, Assistant Secretary of State in charge of African Affairs, who is making a visit to your country as a representative of this government.
>
> The excellent relations which presently exist between our two countries are most gratifying to me. I take this occasion to reaffirm to you the whole-hearted desire of my Government to maintain and strengthen these relations.
>
> We in the United States have followed with interest and admiration the continued progress of your country, since the end of the war. I have been particularly impressed with your personal interest and success in expanding the educational facilities of Ethiopia. In this regard, I am informed that a new university is now in the process of being established. You have my sincere best wishes that upon the completion it will serve as a monument to your splendid efforts in this field.

I avail myself of this opportunity to wish you much continued success and good health.

Faithfully yours, (Harry S Truman)

The Emperor did all of the talking for his side, despite the presence at the meeting of Minister for Foreign Affairs Aklilou.[2] It was obvious that he did not just speak for Ethiopia; he *was* Ethiopia. It was also obvious from the beginning that his primary concern was Eritrea, most of which was being claimed by Ethiopia now that Italian colonial rule of the area had ended. At the time Eritrea had a population of just over a million people (now 2.2 million) who occupied some 45,000 square miles of mountain and coastal area along the Red Sea. Christians predominated in the western part of the country, and Muslims in the south and central areas as well as along the coast.

In November 1949, the UN General Assembly had approved a resolution placing former Italian Somaliland under a ten-year trusteeship, with Italy as administrator, and had established a commission to examine the future of Eritrea. It was well known that Ethiopia opposed Italian reentry into East Africa, but would probably acquiesce in the Somaliland trusteeship if the quid pro quo were Ethiopian control over Eritrea. The U.S. supported the Ethiopian position, but at the time of my visit no final solution had been negotiated. Haile Selassie described the situation in great detail for me.

According to the Emperor, conditions in Eritrea had changed even more clearly in Ethiopia's favor since the problem was first studied in 1947 by the Commission of Investigation of the Four Great Powers. The UN commission subsequently found that supporters of federation with Ethiopia were a clear majority. According to Haile Selassie, the opponents of federation, who under Italian pressure had united in the so-called "Democratic Front," had by 1950 realized that they had been duped by the Italian government, to further Italian interests. Muslim Eritreans had recently withdrawn from the Front and established a new Muslim League. The Front was also weakened by the withdrawal of certain Christian members, called the Liberal Progressives. Bribery and acts of violence by the Italians had sparked these defections, according to the Emperor, which demonstrated the overall indignation of the Eritrean population at Italian machinations.

Haile Selassie described to me three factors contributing to the tense situation in Eritrea: the increase of trade-union movement there, the presence of Italy in Somaliland (called Somalia after the war), and Italian activities in Eritrea in support of its independence. He told me that such a state of tension had been created that, if the UN failed to recognize the realities in Eritrea by June, he believed the situation would become intolerable. Because of the long delays and frustrations a general uprising of the population, now fanatic in their demand for union with Ethiopia, was almost certain. This was, of course, not a disinterested view.

Haile Selassie expressed his gratitude for the support shown thus far by the American government for Ethiopia's stance on Eritrea, which he said was all he could have desired. He noted, however, that our January proposals had been rejected by the Italian government. Italy must be made to recognize the consequences of her actions, Haile Selassie said, and the situation settled in favor of Ethiopia as approved by the majority of the UN commission, consisting of Norway, Burma, and South Africa.

Haile Selassie also raised the question of loans to Ethiopia by the Ex-Im Bank and economic assistance under Point Four. Until now, Ethiopia had been able to maintain a sound currency. After the war, the U.S. had become the largest importer of Ethiopian goods, but the country needed to expand its means of production and its transportation network. America was in a position to offer needed assistance in the form of technical expertise and capital. Already the Sinclair Petroleum Company was drilling for oil in Ethiopia in complete freedom. In addition Ethiopian Airlines, under American administration, had acquired an enviable reputation abroad. The Emperor hoped that through the Ex-Im Bank and Point Four assistance, Ethiopia could begin a period of great economic development. The problem had been fully studied by American experts over the past five years, and detailed plans had already been submitted to the U.S. government.

In closing, the Emperor reiterated his keen satisfaction with the cordial relations existing between our two countries, and his appreciation for the support given by the U.S. to Ethiopia dating from the dark period of Italian occupation, when we were one of the few countries refusing to recognize the Italian regime. Since then our friendly attitude had been demonstrated through the Lend-Lease program and our support at the UN. I assured Haile Selassie that the U.S. would continue to support the cession to Ethiopia of all of Eritrea except the Western Provinces, which we believed should be annexed to the Anglo-Egyptian Sudan. I pointed out, however, that since the UN General Assembly had established a commission to investigate the Eritrean issue and submit a report, we would have to take its conclusions into consideration.

The State Department, I assured Emperor Selassie, would continue to support Ethiopian requests for loans from the Ex-Im Bank to fund projects which met the bank's standards, and Point Four assistance for Ethiopia was already in our plans. I also commented on the good relations between Ethiopia and American firms operating there, and expressed hope that the climate for U.S. investment would be further improved through the negotiation of a Treaty of Commerce and Friendship between our two countries.

In addition, I promised the Emperor that the State Department would reexamine Ethiopia's request for fighter planes, and help to find suitable aircraft through commercial channels and the granting of export licenses. I reiterated the importance we attached to Ethiopia as a stabilizing influence in the Horn of Africa and our desire to assist Ethiopian economic development.

During our meetings Haile Selassie conducted himself with great dignity and in a statesmanlike manner. He was fully familiar with all the facts and figures concerning the matters we discussed. I liked him and hoped we could help him. In retrospect, he might be criticized for not having taken steps to project his country more rapidly into the modern era, through mass education and political involvement by the Ethiopian people in their own government. Habits of a thousand years are not, however, easily overcome. The Emperor could, like the Shah, have tried to go too fast. Haile Selassie's conduct during the war, his determined effort to save Ethiopia from Italian domination, and his success in federating most of Eritrea during the postwar period, even though many consider that he treated it as annexation, were all very much to his credit. His overthrow and repudiation in 1974 must have come as a great humiliation. I believe that he deserved better.

In my meetings with government officials during my stay in Addis Ababa I had become aware of another interesting facet of Haile Selassie's rule: he had a very liberal policy toward accepting foreigners as advisers. A knowledgeable American historian was adviser to the Foreign Office, a Dutchman served with the Ministry of Agriculture. The chief of the Ethiopian Air Force, Count von Rosen, a Swede, treated me to a fascinating flight in the Emperor's personal plane over a lowland area teeming with game. I visited the Lake

Tana area where Ethiopia had such great hopes for development. Four full days in Addis Ababa had permitted me to complete my mission there, as well as to visit some outlying villages and shop for Coptic artifacts that became the basis for another collection. Ambassador Merrill gave a formal dinner in my honor on my second evening, which was preceded by a cocktail party given by the Foreign Minister in his new ministry on, curiously enough, King George VI Street.

On the morning of the 18th I departed en route to Saudi Arabia for Asmara, for a brief visit to the U.S. Army radio station, Radio Marina. I visited with General Drew, commander of the local British contingent in Asmara, to discuss U.S.-U.K. cooperation in operating our vital communication and radio-intelligence facilities there. For many years Asmara was to play a key role in world-wide U.S. military communications and as a monitoring point for Soviet radio. The importance of the station decreased, however, when Turkey was admitted to NATO in 1952 and permitted us to build intercept stations there.

Six weeks later, after the completion of my journey and return to Washington, I received a letter from Emperor Haile Selassie on some of the matters dealt with during my stay in Ethiopia. It read:

The Imperial Palace
Addis Ababa
28th June, 1950

My dear Mr. McGhee,

We have received through your Embassy your most thoughtful and useful gift [an early electronic recorder]. It is indeed considerate of you to have recalled so pleasantly your visit to Addis Ababa. We are particularly pleased that your gift will not only be most helpful in lightening our work but that it will so characteristically reflect the ingenuity and efficiency of your great nation.

We have noted with considerable satisfaction that the matters which were discussed during the conversations which attended your visit are developing very largely as was expected at that time. We have, however, noted with some regret that the proposed purchase of training aircraft for the Air Force Training Station at Bishoftu does not appear to be meeting with success.

Apparently, in spite of the most considerable assistance of your office and your Embassy here, Mr. Golien of the Ethiopian Air Lines who has been authorized to act in this matter, is informed that the only naval aircraft available are Curtiss-Helldivers, and he reports that they are neither particularly suitable, nor in good condition. We would be most appreciative of your efforts to obtain the release of a limited number of planes of a more suitable type.

With the expression of our high regards,

HAILE SELASSIE I
Emperor of Ethiopia

In the meantime progress had been made toward the settlement of the Eritrean question. In December 1950, after difficult negotiations, especially with the Italians, the UN General Assembly had adopted a federation plan for Eritrea. Eritrean unity and self-government were to be assured by making Eritrea an autonomous unit federated with Ethiopia, under the Ethiopian crown. Haile Selassie was quite pleased with the decision.

My involvement in Ethiopian affairs was resumed when Foreign Minister Aklilou made an official visit to Washington on December 11. Cecilia and I entertained him and his wife at luncheon at the Carlton Hotel. In my meeting with him later in the State Department, he expressed appreciation of the U.S. role in settling the Eritrean question, particularly in opening up communication between Ethiopia and Italy.[3] I told him that the settlement had given me renewed confidence in the resolution of disputes through negotiation, and congratulated him and the Emperor.

Aklilou also raised with me the perennial question of planes for Ethiopia. I pointed out that the high cost of reconditioning surplus planes, which made them prohibitively expensive for Ethiopia to purchase, was beyond our control. Fortunately, I noted, Ethiopia was at peace, and we must accord higher priorities to countries under attack. Thus, I was not able to give Aklilou any real encouragement about aircraft. Later, of course, as the Cold War developed, we did supply military equipment to Ethiopia on a considerable scale, and a large U.S. military mission was established in Addis Ababa.

During our conversations in Washington, I reminded the Foreign Minister of the draft Treaty of Commerce and Friendship that we had submitted to Ethiopia, in the belief that it would encourage U.S. investment. Aklilou promised to expedite its consideration, as well as that of the Point Four Program, within his government. I also reiterated the importance we attached to the continued operation of Radio Marina in Asmara. Sometime before the Eritrea federation was carried out, we wanted to discuss the construction of a telecommunications center in Asmara and an air and naval base at Massawa on the Red Sea for use during emergencies. Aklilou agreed to these discussions.

Without making it a condition, I sought to link the granting of these important U.S. facilities to our assistance to Ethiopia on the Eritrean question. Eritrea was federated with Ethiopia by UN action in 1952. In 1953, a mutual defense treaty was signed between the U.S. and Ethiopia, and we were given control over the Asmara military base after the British withdrawal. The U.S. became Ethiopia's major military ally and its principal trading partner, buying some 40 percent of the country's coffee and providing about 20 percent of Ethiopia's imports. In 1955 Haile Selassie proclaimed a more liberal constitution, which gave Ethiopians the right to vote. These were good years for U.S.-Ethiopia cooperation.

In later years, the memory of Haile Selassie's brave defiance of Mussolini during the war obscured from the rest of the world the backwardness of an autocratic regime that had kept Ethiopia mired in poverty and inequality. Despite his early reforms, he lacked a longer-range plan for economic development. Few advances were made in education, and land reform was stymied by the opposition of feudal landowners. A Shoan aristocracy largely dominated the political life of the country.

The Emperor narrowly survived an attempted palace coup in 1960. Persistent but ineffective opposition continued to come from a small modernizing elite, who saw the cure for Ethiopia's backwardness in the introduction of Western-style parliamentary democracy. Senior military officers were uncomfortable with the evidence of growing disorder, and were concerned with heavy losses against secessionists in Eritrea that threatened to undermine the morale and prestige of the armed forces. Junior officers, meanwhile, complained of poor pay and limited opportunities for professional advancement. Even members of the government administration were disturbed by the aging ruler's inability to come to grips with the country's problems. His view of the events taking place around him was narrow.

My friend Aklilou rose from Foreign Minister to Prime Minister, a position he would hold for sixteen years. He was not, however, able to put into effect economic and political reforms long overdue. He faced drastic inflation, a severe famine, and widespread corruption, which resulted in growing unrest among urban interest groups. In early 1974, the opposition converged as students joined striking workers in Addis Ababa and army units mutinied to protest conditions of service. A number of plots to seize control of the government were incubating within the armed forces, the plotters ranging from conservative generals anxious to restore order to radical junior officers bent on revolution.

It was a group of the latter, organized in a revolutionary committee that came to be known as the Derg, who preempted the field and by degrees brought down the government, with the backing of military units won over to their cause. In September, Haile Selassie was formally deposed, Aklilou was forced to resign, and a military government, socialist in orientation, was established in Addis Ababa. Members of the royal family, officials of the imperial government, and rival military officers were imprisoned in the reign of terror that followed the Emperor's death in custody. On November 15, 1974, fifty-nine political prisoners, including Aklilou Habte-Wold, were executed.

Ideological conflict and personal competition for power within the Derg resulted in the rise and demise of a succession of leaders before Mengistu Haile Mariam, a lieutenant colonel who had served as the Derg's liason with units in the field, climbed over the bodies of his fallen colleagues into the ruling committee's chairmanship. Mengistu dealt ruthlessly with traditional leaders and the secessionist movements that had sprung up in nearly every part of the country. His most determined enemies, however, were found among Marxists opposed to continued military rule, who had taken a position to the left of the Derg for several months in late 1976 and early 1977. Fighting between government vigilantes and the leftists raged nightly in the capital, and several thousand real and suspected opponents of the military regime, many of them schoolchildren, were slaughtered in what was dubbed the "Red Terror."

In February 1977, the U.S. cut off military assistance to Ethiopia, citing flagrant violations of human rights by its government. Mengistu reacted by beating a path to Moscow, soliciting Soviet aid against the budding Somali intervention in the contested Ogaden region. In a few months, the Soviet Union pumped more than $1 billion worth of military hardware into Ethiopia, more than that country had received in twenty-five years from the U.S. Stiffened by the introduction of Cuban combat units and Soviet advisers, well-equipped Ethiopian forces routed the Somalis in early 1978 and then turned their attention to the war in Eritrea, where secessionists had gone on the offensive.

Ethiopia has, under Mengistu, made some improvements in education and health care, but at the cost of living under a totalitarian regime, which is in large measure mortgaged to the Soviet Union. Mengistu, whose political objectives have more to do with remaining in power than with ideological concerns, has resisted Soviet promptings to form an Ethiopian Communist party linked to the Kremlin, to replace military rule. Political opposition, particularly from the radical left, still lurks behind a façade of apparent stability, while for four years the Eritrean war has continued in deadlock. The Department of State has reported a gradual improvement in human rights in Ethiopia and has sought to improve relations with Addis Ababa as a means of persuading Mengistu to step back from the Soviet embrace.

I personally find it very sad that the good beginnings of U.S.-Ethiopian relations in the postwar years were terminated by such a complete breakdown. I consider it a tragedy that the Soviets have, with the assistance of their Cuban surrogates, built on the ruins of the ancient Ethiopian empire, long presided over by our one-time friend Emperor Haile Selassie, a base for influence in this strategic area. It is particularly disappointing when I recall my visit to the Emperor in 1950, and the great hopes he had, which I shared, for the future of his country. He just didn't make it.

16

Negotiations with the King of Oil

Visit to Jidda and Riyadh, Saudi Arabia. King Ibn Saud
and Prince Faisal, March 18–25, 1950.

The Arabian Peninsula is in a very real sense an island, surrounded
by seas except to the north, where it is cut off from the fertile Mediterranean coast by the Arabian desert. The hot, dry desert land of the
interior is inhabited largely by nomadic Bedouins, people famous for
their domestication of camels, which were used for transport of goods
across the desert and raids on neighboring tribes. The earliest evidence of their civilization on the Arabian Peninsula dates back to
5000 B.C. For centuries the Bedouins were largely undisturbed, but
the vast reserves of oil discovered on the peninsula in the early part of
the twentieth century have propelled their country into world prominence. Saudi Arabia is the most Arab of the Arab states: it was on
what would become Saudi Arabia's territory that the prophet Mohammed founded the Islamic faith about six hundred years after the
birth of Christ; the holy cities of Mecca and Medina are located
there.

In early days the Arabian Peninsula had been divided into two
distinct types of civilizations. In the Yemen in the south, along the
well-watered coastal areas of the Red and Arabian seas, a confedera-
tion of tribes and kingdoms had dominated the important trade
routes between India and the Horn of Africa. Other Arab kingdoms
of the south emerged in the first millennium B.C. Innovations in navigation and a decline in the market for frankincense and myrrh, for
many centuries the region's most sought-after exports, contributed to
the gradual decline of this civilization. By the time Mohammed had
conquered the northern parts of the peninsula, the deterioration in
the south was complete.

Northern Arabia, the land of the Bedouin, developed more

slowly, its principal advantages being its mineral wealth and control of trade routes. Arabia was unsuccessfully invaded both by the Romans and the Ethiopians. Starting from Medina in the seventh century, Arabs, inspired by Mohammed, launched a series of invasions and conversions that by the eighth century gave them control of lands stretching from the Punjab in India to Spain. Mohammed died in 632, only two years after his conquest of Mecca, the wealthiest and most advanced city on the peninsula. Although he had attempted to impose unity over Arabia, his rule was too short to establish lasting peace. Over the next thousand years life in Arabia reverted to its former state of tribal warfare, with occasional periods of conquest by foreigners. Although Mecca remained the spiritual center of Islam, the centers of political and economic power had shifted elsewhere.

Mecca and Medina lay in the region known as the Hejaz which, starting in the sixteenth century, was until 1926 part of the Ottoman Empire. The Turkish hold, however, was never strong there. The wilder interior of the Arabian peninsula was the scene of religious upheavals that, in the mid-eighteenth century, witnessed the rise of the Wahhabis, a puritanical sect bent on reforming Islam. An alliance between its founder, Mohammad ibn Abdul Wahhab, and the prominent House of Saud, enabled the Saudis to contest rival chieftains for control of the Arabian peninsula in the name of Islamic revival and to launch raids as far afield as Syria and Mesopotamia. The Wahhabi movement was set back by the Egyptians in the early nineteenth century, but the Saudis continued to dominate much of the interior region known as the Nejd, absorbed in tribal warfare, incursions into neighboring territories, and confrontations with the Turks.

Some members of the House of Saud were forced into exile during this period, including the family of the young Abd al-Aziz. They took refuge with their Bedouin followers and lived later in Qatar and Bahrain. Abd al-Aziz, known as Ibn Saud, returned to join his family's struggle to regain their power and, in 1902, captured Riyadh from a rival amir. By the eve of World War I, Ibn Saud could claim the allegiance of most of the Arab tribes in northern Arabia. During the war, the British courted both the Sauds and the Hashemites, who had ruled Mecca since the eleventh century, to enlist their support against the Turks. The Hashemite leader Sharif Hussein proclaimed Arab independence in 1916, drove the Turks from the Hejaz, and significantly aided British military operations in Palestine. In launching the Arab revolt against the Ottoman Empire, Hussein had also presumptuously declared himself "king of the Arabs," but even his title to the Hejaz was rejected by the tribes in the region. When Hussein attempted to assume the mantle of caliph, formerly worn by the Ottoman sultans, Ibn Saud retaliated in force in 1924. In 1926 he seized Mecca, and was proclaimed king of the Hejaz and Sultan of the Nejd and Dependencies, thus uniting into a single state the major part of the Arabian peninsula. In doing so, he won both the allegiance of the Arab tribes and British recognition. In 1932, he announced the creation of the United Kingdom of Saudi Arabia, making his capital at Riyadh in the Nejd, the Saudi heartland.

All through this turbulent history, the Bedouins of the desert lived out their lives in very much the same fashion as had their ancestors, moving with their goats and camels, following the cycles of growth, living in black mohair tents, and using the same simple rugs and utensils. Unfortunately, Bedouin life is now changing rapidly and may not survive. Many Bedouins are seeking employment in the cities and oilfields. In an attempt to preserve the Bedouin way of living, the Saudi government subsidizes the tribal peoples, furnishing feed for animals and, ironically, a Toyota for each tribal chief. The desert sands are now streaked with their tracks, which somehow seem to resist erasure by the winds.

I arrived in Jidda late in the afternoon of March 18, 1950, on a U.S. Air Force plane from Asmara. The flight over the Red Sea had been exciting: the deep blue of its water contrasted with the barren brown coast, often formed by mountains coming down to the sea. One felt a sense of moving from one ancient seat of civilization to another in isolation from the modern world that lay beyond. I was met at the airport by my old friend J. Rives Childs, U.S. Ambassador to Saudi Arabia, and members of his staff. It was my first visit to a country that had always intrigued me—the desert, the Bedouins, the heart of Islam, Mecca and Medina, and now the vast oil reserves. It promised to be a fascinating visit.

En route to the embassy, Rives filled me in with the plans for the week I would spend in Jidda, Riyadh, and Dhahran. It was good to see Rives again: a typical Virginian from Lynchburg, a graduate of Randolph-Macon and Harvard, he combined Southern charm and grace, with a natural wit and an inquiring mind that had brought him success in two professions. Starting out in life as a journalist and a scholar in French literature, Ambassador Childs had already written a number of excellent books on literary subjects before commencing a successful diplomatic career. This had included a number of key

Middle East posts. Rives told me whom I would meet at the reception for forty-five he was giving before dinner, described recent events in Saudi Arabia, and gave me descriptions of the high Saudi officials I would meet later, as well as the key princes and King Ibn Saud himself.

Life in the rambling old residence at the edge of the desert was intriguing. At the reception there were ministers from other Muslim countries, as well as from Italy and France, and the British Ambassador, Alan Trott. Also present were a number of Saudi, American, and British officials and businessmen, including Robert Henry, the local Arabian-American Oil Company (ARAMCO) manager; Gary Owen of ARAMCO; Stribling Snodgrass, vice-president of Bechtel International, a leading American engineering firm which had undertaken a number of construction projects in Saudi Arabia; several American advisers to Saudi government ministers and mining and oil enterprises; a few key Saudi businessmen, including Sheikh Mohammed Alireza, president of the Jidda Chamber of Commerce and representative of a leading Saudi family; and the Saudi Deputy Ministers of Foreign Affairs and Finance. Later, at dinner for ten, we were joined by Sheikh Abdullah Sulaiman, who as Finance Minister was very close to the King and one of the most powerful men in Saudi Arabia.

After dinner I had a long talk with Rives Childs and his top staff about my meeting the next morning with Prince Faisal, second son of the King and then Foreign Minister. Already he had shown the brilliance and steadiness that were to mark his subsequent career until, as King and at the height of his powers, he was assassinated by a demented relative in 1975. Although my meetings with King Ibn Saud in Riyadh would be the climax of my visit, Faisal was the key to its success, even more important than Crown Prince Saud, viceroy of the Nejd region.

American policymakers had long recognized the importance of Saudi Arabia to our interests and had sought to strengthen the close ties that had developed between us. We understood the importance of assuring Saudi economic progress as a whole, which would not only improve their oil-producing capabilities but would contribute to the nation's political stability. We also understood the preoccupation of the King with the security of his regime and his country, and had already responded by sending a military mission to Saudi Arabia.[1]

Close relations between Saudi Arabia and the U.S. date from the historic meeting already referred to between President Roosevelt and King Ibn Saud on board the destroyed U.S.S. *Murphy* in Egyptian waters on February 13–14, 1945. For his meals Ibn Saud had brought his own lambs, which were killed on the decks of the destroyer. In *Reilly of the White House* by Michael Francis Reilly,[2] the visit is described as follows:

> The Murphy had put into Jidda to pick up His Majesty Abd-al 'Aziz ibn-'Abd-al-Ramān al-Faisal ibn-Su'ud, King of Saudi Arabia. Before going aboard, His Majesty suggested a few minor alterations in the Murphy's make-up. He wanted awnings put up on this trim destroyer's fo'c'sle. He sent the awnings aboard with a lot of expensive rugs that were to be scattered over the decks. Huge earthenware jugs of water from the Holy Wells of Mecca were also carried past the pop-eyed watch officer of the Murphy. Finally, there remained but one more addition to the Murphy's oriental reconstruction. This addition consisted of a herd of sheep which were driven aboard and pastured aft on the fantail. They were to grace His Majesty's table.
>
> When the rugs, the awnings and the sheep were aboard, ibn-Saud came on, accompanied by forty-seven assorted relatives, guardians. (In addition to a support staff of 26 the king had: 10 guards, 3 valets, one for each royal prince, and 9 miscellaneous slaves: cooks, porters, and scullions.)
>
> Ibn-Saud came aboard, limping badly. He was a huge man, well over seventy years of age and badly crippled. His vision was greatly impaired by cataracts, but in his flowing black robes and red and black turban with gold head ropes he was certainly the most impressive foreign statesman I have ever seen.
>
> I don't think the meeting was a diplomatic success. The boss and the giant Arabian argued the problem of Palestine, and Ibn Saud could not agree with him.

Saudi potential oil reserves were already recognized at the time of this meeting as among the greatest of any country in the world. The first major oilfield in Saudi Arabia was discovered in March 1938, just before World War II, but the war had limited its development. Since oil was not then in short supply except where limited by transport, scarce steel could not be made available to Saudi Arabia for drilling equipment. During the war Harold Ickes, Secretary of Interior and the Petroleum Administrator for War, had sent a technical mission to Saudi Arabia to evaluate the oil reserves there and their potential for the future. This mission, which was headed by the distinguished geologist and my father-in-law, Dr. Everette L. DeGolyer, reported the presence of at least 4 billion barrels of proven reserves, with possibilities for much more. Compared with present Saudi reserves of 175 billion barrels, with more still yet to be discovered, this early figure seems small, but it was a startlingly large figure for that day. As a geologist myself, I was fully aware of the importance to U.S interests of Saudi oil, which had been developed by the American-owned ARAMCO.

Although I hoped to help resolve some of the immediate Saudi oil problems, particularly the question of royalty payments which the Saudi government considered inadequate, the major developments affecting Saudi oil during the period I served as Assistant Secretary arose later and I was to be deeply involved. The decision to offer the famous fifty-fifty profit-sharing agreement, which would set the stage for twenty-two years of uninterrupted oil production under a partnership between ARAMCO and the Saudi government, was made in my office in the State Department by the ARAMCO parent companies in November 1950.[3] My main hope at the time of my present visit was to lay a sound basis for U.S.-Saudi relations, in order to assist ARAMCO in maintaining its position as the sole developer of Saudi oil.

Although in 1950 the American government was mainly preoccupied by the necessity to contain the expansion of Soviet Communism, we believed that Communism posed little threat to Saudi Arabia. There was nothing in the Saudi Arabian background that would make Communism understandable or attractive to its people. We also considered exaggerated the Saudi apprehension over a possible threat by King Abdullah of Jordan or the Regent acting for young Faisal II in Iraq. The sons of Ibn Saud's traditional Hashemite enemy, Sharif Hussein, Abdullah and Faisal II's father, Faisal I, had been given these territories following World War I in return for their father's loyalty to the British.

I was later to encounter a corresponding concern on the part of Abdullah, whom I visited in Amman in March of 1951, over possible hostile action by Ibn Saud. Defusing this mutual distrust had been one of our main objectives, over and above a contribution to the solution of the Arab-Israeli conflict, in launching the Tripartite Declaration (U.S., U.K., and France) in May of 1950, as will be described in the following Chapter. The blanket guarantee by the declaration of existing frontiers, although it was vague as to how this would be carried out, helped hold Middle East rivalries in check and calm fears of aggression.

The central goal of the Saudis in 1950 was to gain U.S. protection, and for assistance in enlarging and modernizing their armed forces. A mission headed by General Richard J. O'Keefe had been in Saudi Arabia in 1949 for two months to study their military requirements. Although their report was submitted to the Joint Chiefs of Staff on January 3, 1950, and the Chiefs had sent an abridged copy to the State Department on April 18, the department decided not to give the report to the Saudis because "it would only give us headaches we need not have." One of the objectives of my visit was to allay Saudi suspicions at the delay in receiving the report, and to reach agreement on how we would proceed in helping meet their military needs.

Saudi Arabia was drawn to the U.S. for protection both because of the Saudi leaders' distrust of British motives (largely due to the British alliance with the Hashemites), and because the Saudis had confidence in ARAMCO's ability to develop Saudi oil. The British, with ample oil reserves in Iran, had turned down the Saudi oil concession, a move which they would later severely regret.

I met with Prince Faisal for three hours on the second day of my visit.[4] With him were Sheikh Sulaiman, Minister of Finance, and both of their deputies. In addition to Ambassador Childs I was accompanied by two other members of the embassy staff. I asked Faisal if I might start by summarizing the various issues we saw in our relationship with Saudi Arabia, after which I would welcome his comments. I spoke from notes, to which I had given considerable thought, and the time for translation helped me to formulate my remarks.

I described our relationship as being in a class by itself, based on a firm friendship that had begun with the meeting between President Roosevelt and King Ibn Saud. There had developed between these leaders a strong rapport and mutual respect. Roosevelt had been greatly impressed by the King and had sought closer ties with him. These had since been strengthened, both at the official level and by the Saudi relationship with ARAMCO, to which had been entrusted sole responsibility for developing Saudi oil. The close bonds that had arisen between our countries over the years, combined with the obvious U.S. interest in developing Saudi oil, were much more reliable than a treaty, I suggested. We had an obligation to try to understand the problems of Saudi Arabia and, as a friend, to assist her within the limits of American capabilities in solving these problems. Cognizance had to be taken of what the Saudi Arabia government considered its problems, not just what we perceived them to be.

I told Faisal that the U.S. felt that the only important security threat facing the world was the aggressive designs of the U.S.S.R. We had, I continued, accepted this view reluctantly, and hoped that history would prove that we had made every effort in the postwar period to cooperate with the U.S.S.R. and establish friendly relations with her. Even though it was against our traditions, we had, where necessary, to preserve the independence of nations threatened by the Soviets, given large-scale military assistance, first to Greece and Turkey, and now to Western Europe under the North Atlantic Treaty. I pointed out that this reflected our conviction that the security of the North Atlantic area, with its great industrial potential, was vital to the free world.

Saudi Arabia was fortunately not directly menaced by the Soviets and had no internal Communist problem. We understood that Saudi Arabia would, in the event of a shooting war, have to face the problem of its own defense, including defense against possible Soviet intervention. We also understood that Saudi Arabia was apprehensive about her neighbors, Jordan and Iraq. I had discussed this question with the British Foreign Office, as well as with all of our Middle East ambassadors, at the Istanbul Conference held the previous November. We did not feel that Saudi Arabia was threatened by its neighbors: we had analyzed the situation in the following way, which I thought should be reassuring to Saudi Arabia. In the first place there appeared to be little basis for joint action on the part of Iraq and Jordan. Both had special treaty arrangements with the U.K., providing for U.K. control of national forces and bases. Both were dependent on the U.K. for military equipment, personnel, and leadership. The British were capable of restraining any aggression on their part against Saudi Arabia, and had assured us they would do so.

I noted that, while Saudi Arabia was, of course, entitled to its own security forces, the only ultimate security any nation had was its internal political and economic strength. Saudi Arabia was fortunate that it could devote a large portion of its resources toward economic development. I recounted the events which had led us to send the group headed by General O'Keefe to investigate the military needs of Saudi Arabia. I understood that the Saudis had studied O'Keefe's preliminary report and were in agreement.

As the President had written to His Majesty in the letter[5] which I would deliver to him in Riyadh, our Joint Chiefs of Staff were presently studying General O'Keefe's report. They would determine whether the recommendations were the best possible for Saudi Arabia in light of its military situation and the equipment available. After further study by the Department of State, the final decision would be made by the President, who would seek from the Congress what additional authority and funds were needed.

We would then renew discussions with Saudi Arabia for a long-range agreement on the Dhahran air base. We attached the greatest importance to the utilization of this base, both from the standpoint of Saudi security and our own. We wanted Saudi Arabia to feel that it had in the U.S. a strong friend who would assist it in time of adversity. If at any time Saudi Arabia was menaced by aggressive or subversive activities by any country, I concluded, we would take strong action.

Prince Faisal replied that all who were sincere in their feelings toward Saudi Arabia had been well pleased to see U.S.-Saudi friendship strengthened. He was eager to see the further cementing of this friendship. Even though differences in points of view might arise, he hoped they would not have an adverse effect on our relationship. He was acquainted with the report submitted by General O'Keefe's survey mission, which Saudi Arabia considered a bare minimum. "We need more," said Faisal, "but not less than that." Faisal went on to point out that security could be divided into several stages: internal stability, complete security from aggression or menace from a neighboring country, and lastly, security from a menace to the whole world.

Saudi Arabia must make preparations to face these threats. Its situation, Faisal noted emphatically, was unique. Did I have any idea what a force just to maintain internal stability would involve? The security and peace prevailing all over Saudi Arabia were not the result of its police force, he reminded me, but of the wise manner in which the King governed the country. Some dissidents, he said, were building up a campaign against Ibn Saud, alleging that he was an absolute monarch who wasted his money, neglecting important projects. He was not spending money on a luxurious personal life or to augment his own wealth, his son said. On the contrary, he was spending it on gifts to those who if they had no money to feed themselves would be a threat to internal stability. If the history of the Arabian Peninsula was reviewed, Faisal said, it would be found that most of the tribes had done nothing to guard the security of the country, but Ibn Saud had spent money in certain areas to keep them quiet and prevent a menace to the security of the whole country.

Faisal declared that if the dispute with the Hashemites had been left to the parties alone to resolve, without interference by foreign powers, Saudi Arabia could have settled it easily. But, he said, Saudi

Arabia's neighbors were supported by a great foreign power. Although he understood that that power had no intention itself of threatening Saudi Arabia, he pointed to an indirect threat through support of his country's neighbors. Meanwhile Saudi Arabia had been deprived of arms. Despite the current high prices for arms, which Saudi Arabia could not meet, the Saudis wanted to receive as much military assistance as their neighbors, Faisal continued. He concluded that, although Saudi Arabia maintained friendly relations with the British, Saudi leaders had decided to place more of its interests in the hands of the U.S. Foremost among those interests at present was a serious effort to improve Saudi defense forces and promote social and economic development. So the Saudis expected that, as our new allies, they should be able to depend on the U.S. for increased support.

I replied that I fully appreciated the factors which had been mentioned and understood Saudi Arabia's need for security forces. Because of the special friendship he had referred to, I told Faisal, the U.S. would assist Saudi Arabia in developing its military. Concerning economic development, we desired to help Saudi Arabia. We would assist her through Point Four technical assistance, Ex-Im Bank loans and private investment. In order to facilitate this, I told Faisal, we wanted to negotiate with the Saudi Arabian government a Treaty of Friendship, Commerce and Navigation that would serve as a basis upon which our business in Saudi Arabia could be conducted. The treaty would, of course, correspond to Ibn Saud's wishes and did not need to be complicated. We felt it would symbolize the close and friendly relations between the two countries.

Prince Faisal said he was pleased with my assurances that we would assist Saudi Arabia economically in the ways I had mentioned. Since the King would ultimately determine the final points of such aid, it was not his wish to go too deeply into economic questions. Assurance that the U.S. government was ready to help Saudi Arabia was sufficient.

We then turned to a discussion of the Arab refugee problem. Faisal pointed out that if the refugees took residence in other countries, there would be no one to return to Palestine. In the case of earlier UN resolutions involving partition of Palestine, he said, the Arab nations had been forced to accept UN terms. Israel, however, had flouted UN Resolution 75 by not permitting the refugees to return. I replied that we deeply regretted this, and that our notes to Israel urging compliance were known to His Royal Highness. Faisal ended by stating that he would not like to see us give Israel any more loans or financial assistance. I gave no such assurance.

We had at last come to the inevitable, and apparently insoluble problem of the Saudi attitude toward Israel, a matter about which the Saudis, as the "Keeper of the Holy Places," the "Most Arab of the Arabs," felt particularly strongly. They have not, however, let the issue dominate U.S.-Saudi relations, nor did they in these early years threaten to stop the flow of oil. I was pleased that my talk with Faisal had ended on an amicable note in spite of our differences over Israel.

Later that day I visited the new pier at Jidda. Trucks and all sorts of machinery and construction materials were being unloaded. Jidda had begun as a mere entry point to Mecca, which was located fifty miles away. It had since emerged as the Saudi economic hub and point of contact with the outside world. I had a chance to stroll among the picturesque houses of the city, which had a distinctive style, featuring multistory white plaster construction with delicately designed screened wooden balconies covering their façades, to afford privacy for the harem and shade from the glaring sun reflected off the Red Sea. In a visit to Jidda in the fall of 1979, I was disappointed to see that most of these lovely residences had been replaced by modern construction. Fortunately a few of the finest traditional houses are being saved.

At four o'clock Prince Faisal received me for tea at an attractive villa in nearby Hadda. I observed him carefully. He had a narrow, sharp face with a hawklike nose. His eyes flashed. In our talks he had shown a mastery of the situation and a moderation in his views which foretold the later capacity he demonstrated as a statesman. The more relaxed atmosphere gave me a better opportunity to size him up, and I was very favorably impressed. Also present was Sheikh Sulaiman, Finance Minister, who was later to take a very hard line with us on oil royalties. This afternoon, however, he was in gay spirits. I suspected that he had had more to drink than tea.

In the evening there was a quiet dinner at the embassy in anticipation of an early-morning departure for Dhahran. Rives Childs and I went thoroughly over the ground covered with Prince Faisal, since we would be reviewing the same matters with the King in Riyadh. In my meeting with Faisal and on several other occasions I was greatly assisted by a personable young Saudi employee of the embassy. He was an excellent interpreter, guide, and friend. On one occasion, to my surprise, he confided in me the difficulties he and his wife were having with their slave. The slave, a young girl, did little work, was protected against any infringements upon her rights, and was proving more costly than a servant. Slavery, I found, was at that time still common, particularly on the part of the royal family. I was deeply shocked.

The trip to Dhahran, headquarters of the U.S. Air Force Command and of ARAMCO's main offices in Saudi Arabia, took nearly five hours. Appropriately, given Dhahran's role, Ambassador Childs and I were met at the airport by U.S. Air Force Commander General O'Keefe and three ARAMCO executives, as well as a Saudi government official. I lunched at the ARAMCO Executive House: it was agreeable to me to be back with oil men, many of whom were old friends, and to receive answers to the many questions I had about the Saudi oilfields. What was the best idea they had of reserves? Were pressures holding up? Was there a good water drive in the oil reservoirs? What were gas-oil ratios? Had they mapped some good new structures to drill? How best could production be stepped up? All of my questions were answered very frankly.

Afterward, Consul-General Parker T. Hart gave me a tour of what they called the "Quonsulate." Not only was the American consulate housed in a metal Quonset hut, intensifying the blazing Saudi sun, but so were homes for staff members and their families. When I returned to Washington I helped obtain better living quarters for the staff and a wall around the embassy compound. Pete Hart, a graduate of Dartmouth, Harvard, and an international institute in Geneva, was to become a close friend with a strikingly parallel career. He followed me both as Assistant Secretary and Ambassador to Turkey, before his retirement to accept an important executive post with Bechtel International. Later General O'Keefe gave a cocktail party for me, and Pete and Jane Hart hosted an excellent dinner, their guests including a congenial group from the consulate staff and their families.

The following day, after a guided tour of Dhahran, I rode the Saudi-Iranian railroad to Ras Tanura, where I inspected the refinery, terminal arrangements, and camp. I lunched with local ARAMCO officials, who told me about their facilities, which were handling 500,000 barrels a day. Little did we realize that this would rise, by 1979–80, to over 10 million barrels a day. That evening I was given dinner in the ARAMCO guest house at the Dammam field.

Early the next morning Rives Childs and I were taken by Air

Force plane to Riyadh, where we were to remain for two days. Riyadh has been the capital of the Saudis since the destruction of their old capital, Al-Dhira'iyyah, by Mohammed Ali of Egypt in the early nineteenth century. We arrived shortly after 9 A.M. and were met by Saudi officials, who took us through the largely unpaved streets of what appeared to be essentially a new city of palaces and public buildings, superimposed on the old fortified town. I was quartered in a spacious apartment in a palace built rather hastily for a state visit of the King of Afghanistan, who had just departed. Welcoming banners for him were still in place. The palace itself was sparsely decorated. The plumbing facilities in my apartment, although crude, were a particular source of pride for my hosts, since such modern conveniences were rare in Riyadh. During a recent visit to Riyadh I was disappointed to find that this palace had been torn down. I would have liked to see it again.

A delicate problem arose which was handled magnificently by the tactful Childs. Would I object, he asked, to wearing Arab dress while I was in Riyadh? My initial reaction was that it would not be appropriate for me as an American official. It might be the subject of criticism even though there were no press representatives there.

"It's for you to decide," said the wily Ambassador. "However, it could be considered a matter of respect toward an older man. It would also make easier his problem with the populace of having you, as a nonbeliever, here in a holy city. In London, our ambassadors wear knee breeches when they are presented to the King. Moreover, Ibn Saud wants to present you with fine winter and summer robes and headdress if you will just let his tailor measure you. Saudi robes are quite elegant and would make nice mementos of your visit." He had me. I wore Arab dress.

In all I met with the King five times. Usually the precise time of meeting was not revealed until the moment arrived. There were changes in times set. Between meetings with the King there were numerous visits by Fuad Bey Hamza, adviser to the King, and Sheikh Yusef Yassin, Minister of State. I had the vague impression that they were playing cat and mouse with me, sounding me out in preparation for my meeting with the King, returning to ask additional questions he probably required. I was told by Rives Childs that this was typical of the reception accorded an emissary in an oriental court. Normally they would not accept a two-day visit, such as mine, but insisted on at least a week for sounding-out and preparation. He recalled a visit to the Yemen when his meeting with the King had been postponed day by day for a week, each time with unconvincing explanations. On the eighth day he packed his bags and asked permission to leave, whereupon he was promptly given his audience.

Shortly after our arrival we were received by the King for the usual exchange of courtesies.[6] He extended warm greetings, recalling his meeting with President Roosevelt. I was not quite prepared for his overpowering appearance. Ibn Saud, whose full name and title were Abdal-Aziz Bin-Abd-al-Rahman al-Faisal ibn-Saud, was a big man with a large face and a large nose. He had a jet-black mustache and beard, and kept his eyes half-closed as if he were protecting them from the sun. He smiled easily and was friendly, open, and pleasant in manner.

Before my next meeting with the King, I had a brief conversation with Sheikh Yusef Yassin,[7] in which I tried to persuade him that Saudi Arabia should exert more influence on the Arab League to become a source of stability in the Middle East. Sheikh Yusef agreed that, although Saudi Arabia was not as wealthy or powerful as other Arab states, nevertheless, in the Arab League meetings the representative of Saudi Arabia always had the final say.

Sheikh Yusef gave indications that he would try to persuade the Arab League to cooperate in carrying out the program of the United Nations Economic Survey Mission for the Middle East headed by Gordon Clapp. He appeared to accept my assurance that no political commitment was involved. His response was entirely negative, however, to any suggestion of encouraging or even permitting any Arab country to make peace or establish normal relations with Israel. The Arabs, he said, considered Israel a great menace with unlimited territorial ambitions, including Syria, Jordan, and more. He asserted that the Arabs had no aggressive designs against Israel but intended to treat that state as if a wall surrounded it. Saudi Arabia had no basis for trade with Israel and could easily isolate itself from Israel.

In the afternoon, I met with the King, his two advisers, and Prince Faisal.[8] An aide translated the letter I had brought the King from President Truman.[9] It read:

> Your Majesty: I am sending this letter by Mr. George C. McGhee, Assistant Secretary of State in charge of Near Eastern Affairs, who is making a visit to your country as a representative of this government.
>
> You will recall that I wrote you on May 23, 1949, with regard to the negotiations which were then taking place with respect to the Dhahran Air Base Agreement, and that shortly thereafter agreement

was reached providing for renewal of the previous agreement for a period of one year. Subsequently, Brigadier General O'Keefe of the United States Air Force, at your invitation, visited your country for the purpose of studying the military requirements of Saudi Arabia. I understand that he has already discussed his recommendations with you.

General O'Keefe's report is being studied by competent agencies of the United States Government. It is expected that this study, which is an essential prerequisite to a decision as to future courses of action, will be completed shortly. I am sure you will understand the necessity for the most careful consideration by the United States Government in such an important matter.

I have studied with great interest the remarkable development of Saudi Arabia under your enlightened leadership. Your country stands as a bulwark to peace in the Near Eastern world. It is gratifying that your leadership extends not only through Saudi Arabia but also generally through the Near East.

The United States has always attached the greatest importance to the ties of friendship and understanding which bind us with Saudi Arabia. I assure you that it is our hope and belief that these ties will always continue.

I avail myself of this opportunity to wish you much continued success and good health. Faithfully yours, (Harry S Truman)

I repeated a shortened version of what I had told Prince Faisal two days earlier about our proposed response to Saudi security needs. If the independence or integrity of Saudi Arabia was threatened, we would take most immediate action. The King would understand, however, that, in light of the probable complexities of the situation that might arise at any given time, it was not possible to state in precise terms what action might be taken.

His Majesty discussed at some length his problem with the Hashemites, an issue that evidently was foremost among his concerns. He said that the two Hashemite rulers had been imposed on their respective countries and had never been accepted wholeheartedly by the people. Their military power was entirely derived from British support, without which they would represent no threat. Saudi Arabia on the other hand had no such outside support.

His Majesty said that he had at one time offered the oil concession of Saudi Arabia to the British but they had refused it. He, himself, was well aware, on the basis of information given him by the Turks, which they had obtained from the Germans before the First World

War, that Saudi Arabia was potentially one of the richest oil countries in the world. Although the British had been given first refusal of the oil, they had always resented the fact that the concession had been given to America, and his difficulties with the British had begun from that time. Accordingly, he pointed out, Saudi Arabia had every right to expect that we would approach its security needs with sympathy.

The King mentioned his boundary difficulties and described the British position as very unreasonable. They were a people of "but." They made statements and gave assurances and then, always at the end, there was a "but." His Majesty said that he would like me to meet with Sheikh Yusef Yassin and Fuad Bey Hamza to continue and amplify our discussions.

In the evening the king entertained me at a state dinner. I would estimate that there were fifty guests, mostly princes, sons of the King. Dinner, except for the dishes given the King, was served in Western style: cold soup, fried fish, sauce tartare, turkey with vegetables, mutton and rice, bouche of chicken, cream chocolate, and seasonal fruit. This represented a very recent innovation in Riyadh, which greatly disappointed me since I had looked forward with anticipation to Arab food. Since I was sitting on the King's right I asked him, through the interpreter, whether I might not share his Arab dishes. He readily assented.

During dinner Ambassador Childs asked the King if he would tell us the story of his capture of Riyadh from the ruling Amir.[10] I asked him if any other Arab ruler had ever controlled the Arabian Peninsula, as he now did. His Majesty replied that a member of his family, coincidentally with the same name, had established brief control over the Arabian Peninsula about 250 years ago. This constituted the only previous union of the entire area, after which his family had ruled only over minor villages.

In response to Childs's request, the King recounted that he had been assisted in his conquest of Riyadh by only forty followers. They neared the city on camels and then walked the final four hours to Riyadh, arriving after dusk. The King knocked on the door of a house that was at the edge of the village and constituted a part of its outer fortifications. The door was opened by a woman, who refused him admittance. He advised her, however, that he was a servant of the Amir and that if she did not admit him he would see that her husband would be killed by the Amir, whereupon she acceded. When he entered the house she immediately recognized him, since he was apparently well known. When he was recognized by the other members of her family, they acclaimed him and agreed to support him.

In order to prevent the woman from disclosing his presence, Ibn Saud locked her in her room and he and his followers proceeded over the rooftops to an adjoining house, where he found a man and his wife sleeping in bed. He also locked them in a room so that they would not sound an alarm. He then proceeded to the home of one of the Amir's wives, whom they found sleeping with her sister. She, when awakened, advised that the Amir was in his palace but warned Ibn Saud that he could not overcome the Amir, whereupon he locked them up. At this juncture, since it was still several hours until dawn, he and his followers prepared coffee and slept. At dawn, as was his custom, the Amir emerged from the palace, which was well defended, along with seven of his guards. The gate to the palace was opened and they entered the courtyard in front.

Ibn Saud and his followers, who had been lying in wait, attacked the group, and the seven guards fled back into the palace with the Amir following. Ibn Saud grabbed the Amir from behind and arrested his flight. The Amir in turn kicked Ibn Saud and pushed him down, whereupon Abdullah Saud bin Jiluwi hurled a spear at the Amir, killing him. The group then attacked the palace, which was defended by two hundred soldiers, and took it with the loss of only two rebels and fourteen wounded, after killing fifteen of the Amir's defenders. Within two days some four thousand men had rallied to Ibn Saud's support. Ibn Saud said that the conquest of Riyadh had been difficult, especially since it was the first, but there had been worse battles. On two occasions all of his followers, eight or nine hundred people, were killed, and he alone escaped to recruit more support. The King said the best account of the capture of Riyadh was that given in Rihani's book.

After dinner Fuad Bey and Sheikh Yusef came with Rives Childs to our quarters in the new palace to probe our position.[11] I repeated the proposals I had made to Faisal and the King. They said that the King really wanted two things, arms on a grant basis and a military alliance. They urged that we try to bridge the gap between us.

On the morning of March 23 we were received by Crown Prince Saud[12] instead of the King, who they said was fatigued. I suspected, however, that he was trying to put pressure on me through his representatives. Young Saud was not as impressive as his father or his brother Faisal, and was not very successful as a monarch when he succeeded his father in 1953. He received me cordially and advised me confidentially that he had persuaded his father not to press for a treaty of alliance, but to accept the basis for future relations I had proposed.

In a later meeting with the King,[13] I went over the key points again: Treaty of Friendship, Commerce and Navigation; technicians under Point Four; Ex-Im Bank loans; the Dhahran airfield agreement; and military aid pursuant to the O'Keefe report. I assured the King he would be advised before congressional action was sought on carrying out the O'Keefe report. The King expressed full agreement with my proposals and assurances, and he also expressed hope that when the final details of military assistance were worked out someone, perhaps I, could come to Saudi Arabia and review them with him before a final decision was reached.

Later in the afternoon the Crown Prince received us for tea, and then dinner, in a large palace[14] surrounded by a lovely garden, just being completed outside the city. It was reported to have forty rooms and bathrooms. The palace, he said, was a place for him and his family to have picnics during the day, that they never spent the night there. At dinner I was dismayed to see that the first course was a shrimp cocktail. Western food again. Saud, however, was very proud of his kitchen and of his ability to serve Western food. When he showed me the kitchen I saw, to my surprise, the local manager for Bechtel International sporting an apron and acting as chef. Bechtel showed great adaptability to local conditions, by making their manager available for Saud's whims.

In my final talk with the King that same evening[15] I told him how pleased I was with the outcome of our meetings and with the firm expressions of friendship he had voiced for our country. His Majesty also professed satisfaction. He reiterated his strong rejection of Communism, because of its aggressive nature and its opposition to religion, which constituted the basic element of Arab life. The stability of the Arab world was an extremely important factor in safeguarding against the spread of Communism, since any disaffection here would spread elsewhere. He pointed out that Communism had made some gains in the Arab world, particularly in Iraq and Egypt, and urged the U.S. to assist in counteracting these movements. The King gave China as an example of what happens when such inroads go unchecked.

I replied that we sought, through assisting countries in their economic development, to demonstrate that the free world offered more than Communism. I hoped the King would continue to give us advice about the Arab world. He agreed and expressed the hope that we would support the Arab League and unity among the Arab states. I promised to report to the President the generous remarks the King had made about our country and the satisfactory conclusions we had reached. In parting Ibn Saud presented me with his photograph, an antique gold sword, and, of course, my robes. Under departmental regulations I had to deposit such gifts with the Chief of Protocol, until I left the Department.

In retrospect, my meeting with King Ibn Saud was only one of the earliest of a long succession of efforts to strengthen American ties with Saudi Arabia. We recognized it as a key Middle Eastern country but one which, at the time of my visit, had not yet emerged into the modern era. We fully understood the importance of its oil reserves, which were destined to have world significance. Suspicious of foreigners from what they considered unsatisfactory encounters with the British and the Turks, the Saudis had an almost childlike trust in the U.S. They considered us a real friend to whom they could turn for their vital security needs. Over the years our government has not seriously disappointed them, despite complications arising out of our policy toward Israel. It is hoped that this special relationship can continue, since in my view it is absolutely vital to both countries.

Following my last conversation with King Ibn Saud, I left Riyadh early the next day by car and arrived at noon in Hofuf,[16] two-hundred miles east. Hofuf, which then had a population of about eighty-thousand, is the principal city of the largest oasis in Saudi Arabia, Al Hasa, which has been famous for its dates since Roman times. Hofuf was in A.D. 930 the temporary repository of the sacred Black Stone of the Kabah of Mecca. I paid a call on Amir Saud Bin Jiluwi, an attractive, vigorous man, ruler of the Eastern Province. His father, a great warrior and loyal cousin of Ibn Saud, had, as the King had told me, played a key role in the capture of Riyadh. As a reward he had been given hereditary governature over Al Hasa, after Abd al-Aziz took Hofuf in 1913 with six hundred men, from his traditional enemies, the Turks.

Bin Jiluwi gave me a magnificent luncheon, Saudi style, with about fifty guests under a colorful tent. After so many disappointments with Western food I was elated. I was, however, somewhat taken aback, after plunging in to eat with my right hand, to observe my host pick up his knife and fork. It was obvious from the deference paid him that Bin Jiluwi was a powerful man. After lunch I walked about Hofuf and observed the working stalls. At the shop where the famous Hofuf right-angled daggers were made, I attempted to buy one. They cost $500, I was told; however, one would not be available for four months since Prince Faisal had orders covering that period. My disappointment was assuaged when, on my final departure from Riyadh, Faisal presented me with one, which also went to the Chief of Protocol on my return.

Departing from Hofuf we visited the agricultural camp nearby and some of the oasis pools. Pressing on, we arrived at the great Abqaiq oil field, where we inspected the wells, flowlines, and tank farms. Abqaiq, the second field to be discovered in Saudi Arabia, was not produced until after the war. It became the major producer and was in 1952 the first Saudi field to be subjected to pressure maintenance through injected gas. It maintained a production of 285,000 barrels daily without loss of pressure. That evening I departed by ARAMCO plane for Dhahran for a final dinner at the ARAMCO Executive House. On March 25, with Ambassador Childs and Consul-General Hart, as well as a vice-president of Bechtel International and an executive of the Trans-Arabian Pipeline (TAPLINE), I spent the day flying over and visiting other Arab oil sites. We began at Qaisuma, the eastern terminus of the TAPLINE route, where we toured the pumping station, and then proceeded to Ras al Misha'ab, where we briefly inspected the operations by which pipe was welded, moved by what was called a skyhook onto immense trucks and then transported across the desert to Kuwait.

Resuming our flight, we circled over the American Independent Oil Company (AMINOIL) camps and wells in the Neutral Zone along the northern border of Saudi Arabia, and the Kuwait Oil Company's (KOC) camps and new pier. Landing at Kuwait airport, our group was met by several oil company executives and officials from the British and American consulates. In the afternoon we paid a courtesy call on Sheikh Abdullah as-Salni al Subah, who was in line to replace the recently deceased Amir. It turned out to be a rather tense meeting, since on the one hand Sheikh Abdullah had not yet been formally invested with governing power, and on the other, the British government representative who accompanied us, J. A. F. Gethin, was concerned to protect Britain's favorable position in Kuwait and not permit Americans to gain a strong foothold in the country.

Kuwait sits atop the Burgan oilfield, at that time the largest single field in the world, and although one American company, Gulf Oil, was part owner of the KOC, and another, AMINOIL, was developing the Neutral Zone owned jointly by Kuwait and Saudi Arabia, it was the British who had the closest relations with the Kuwaiti government. Understanding the situation, my colleagues and I were very correct in our discussions with the Sheikh, who nervously offered us tea in his modest palace. I assured His Highness that we had no intention of replacing the U.K. in Kuwait.

Before the discovery of its oil riches, Kuwait had been an insignificant byway. Even in 1950 the country had only begun to receive what was to become a rapidly increasing oil income; the influx of Arab refugees and other foreign workers had not yet started; and Kuwait had not begun its phenomenal development program. Gethin confided to us that British influence in Kuwait was not as strong as in Bahrain, which explained why there was no British financial adviser to Kuwait. Later I was able to help Gulf obtain direct ownership of its interests in Kuwait (rather than through the Kuwait Oil Company, which was a British subsidiary) by appealing directly to Sir William Fraser, chairman of the Anglo-Iranian Oil Company, during a visit in London in April 1951 to discuss Iran.

Leaving Kuwait, our group flew over Abadan in Iran, so we could take a look at the Anglo-Iranian Oil Company's refinery there, the largest in the world. We landed at Basra, Iraq. After brief conversations at the airport with U.S. Ambassador Edward S. Crocker, based in Baghdad, and other embassy and consular officials, the rest of my party returned to Dhahran. The next morning I proceeded to the U.S.

In his reporting dispatch Ambassador Childs generously evaluated the results of my visit to Saudi Arabia as follows:[17]

> Mr. McGhee came at a time when for many months the Saudi Government has been seeking more definite reassurances as to our relations than we have been able to give them. During the almost four years that I have been in Saudi Arabia my principal task has been that of conducting a delaying action. As the Department may well appreciate a time comes when delaying tactics cease to be effective and that time had been approaching on the eve of Mr. McGhee's arrival. It is my opinion that Mr. McGhee's visit represents a turning point in US-Saudi relations. He is the highest ranking American official ever to have visited Saudi Arabia and this in itself was interpreted by the Saudi Government as reassuring and evidence of our desire for close friendly relations. The great task as Mr. McGhee now realizes is for us

to deliver and to realize concretely the assurances given His Majesty and officials of the Saudi Arabian Government regarding the lines which our relations are to take in the future.

On April 11, Secretary Acheson transmitted summaries of my conversations with His Majesty and with Prince Faisal to the President. Under Secretary Webb later conveyed the substance of these conversations to Senator Tom Connally, chairman of the Foreign Relations Committee,[18] in one of his regular briefings.

On April 17, I received in Washington the following message from the King:[19]

> It has been a pleasure for us to receive your kind cable after your return to Washington. It was a pleasure, too, to have the chance of your acquaintance which strengthens our belief in the good understanding of each other. No doubt your prosperous visit has emphasized our feeling of trust and confidence in the progress of relations between our two countries and in the consolidation of friendly bonds between us. We are sure that the USA shares our interest in developing and strengthening such relations. Abdul Aziz.

Looking back I believe that the ties King Ibn Saud referred to have been carefully and successfully nurtured during the past three decades. Saudi Arabia has remained closer to the U.S. than any other Arab country and we in turn have provided Saudi Arabia much in the way of armaments, economic aid, technology, and political backing. The sale of F-16 fighter-bombers in 1981 and advance-warning aircraft in 1982 represent only the most recent examples of this fruitful, ongoing cooperation.

There have, however, been some low points in our relations. In 1954, the U.S. Point Four mission was dismissed by King Saud, Ibn Saud's son and successor. Two years later the agreement for leasing the Dhahran air base was up for renewal and King Saud, under pressure from Saudi nationalists, agreed only to renew the lease on a month-to-month basis. But in early 1957, during a visit to Washington, the King agreed to a five-year lease and the U.S. in turn agreed to supply him with arms and development aid. When the Dhahran lease became due again in 1962, the U.S. relinquished its right to the base and handed it over to the Saudi government.

Early in 1964, an ailing Saud turned over power to Faisal, who in November formally deposed the King, taking the regal title and naming Khalid Crown Prince. Faisal, a shrewd and experienced leader

George McGhee with (left to right) Begum Liaquat Ali Khan, Mrs. Franklin Roosevelt, and Prime Minister Liaquat Ali Khan of Pakistan, 1950. *(NBC.)*

The author with Kwame Nkrumah of Ghana.

The author at lunch with President Tubman of Liberia in Monrovia. (*Griff Davis from Black Star.*)

The author with Emperor Haile Selassie of Ethiopia in Addis Ababa. (*T. Boyadjian, Addis Ababa.*)

George McGhee (extreme left) at the swearing in ceremony as Assistant Secretary of State in 1949, accompanied by (left to right) Adrian Fisher, Legal Adviser, Secretary of State Dean Acheson, and Edward Miller, Assistant Secretary. *(Department of State.)*

George McGhee and family after Mr. McGhee was sworn into office as the new U.S. Ambassador to Turkey in 1951. Back row (left to right): Marcia McGhee, Cecilia McGhee, George McGhee, Dean Acheson; front row (left to right): Michael McGhee, Dorothy McGhee, and George McGhee. *(Department of State.)*

King Abdullah of Jordan.

King Ibn Saud of Saudi Arabia.

Prime Minister Jawaharlal Nehru with the author in New Delhi, 1949. *(Punjab Photo Service, New Delhi.)*

King Mohammed Zahir Shah of Afghanistan, 1951.

Egyptian Foreign Minister Salaheddin with the author, 1951.

The Shah of Iran, Mohammad
Reza Pahlavi, 1949. *(Sako.)*

rime Minister Mohammed
Iossadeq of Iran, 1951. *(Fabi-*
n Bachrach.)

The Bey of Tunis, 1950.

Madame Pandit, Indian Ambassador to the United States, with the author, 1950. (*Acme Newspictures.*)

who was genuinely respected, presided directly over his Council of Ministers, involving himself intimately with the operation of his government. The King's daily concerns extended from mediating traditional tribal rivalries to supervising the emergence of a complex modern state in Saudi Arabia to dealing with the arena of international affairs. Numerous agreements and contracts with U.S. government agencies and private firms were made at the time to assist in these efforts. In addition, many Saudi students came to the U.S. to receive technical training, especially in the field of petroleum.

Under Faisal, Saudi Arabia emerged as the leader of the bloc of conservative Arab states opposing Nasser's brand of nationalism. The Saudis were also effective spokesmen for Arab unity and honest brokers in inter-Arab disputes, intervening diplomatically in Lebanon and acting at one point to reconcile Egypt and Syria. Saudi Arabia was also concerned with the security of the Gulf region and undertook to subsidize development in poorer Arab states.

The Saudi approach to the use of Arab oil as a political weapon, however, turned out to be a pragmatic one. In October 1973 in the aftermath of the Yom Kippur War, Saudi Arabia joined the other Arab states in OPEC in imposing an embargo against countries accused of supporting Israel, including the United States. The Saudis asserted their leadership five months later, when they persuaded the oil exporters to resume supplies in order to avoid exacerbating the damage inflicted on the world economy. Possessing an estimated 40 percent of known world oil reserves, Saudi Arabia has consistently sought to moderate demands for increased prices by their oil-exporting partners in the OPEC cartel, and has until the recent oil glut opposed cuts in production levels. Following the embargo the importance of maintaining close ties with the Saudis was underscored for U.S. policymakers. Thus, in June 1974, a U.S.–Saudi Arabia Joint Commission, headed by Secretary of State Henry Kissinger and Crown Prince Fahd, was announced. The work of the commission was to focus on cooperation in economic and security matters.

It was also during the 1970s that other serious problems began to surface between the two countries. As the seemingly never-ending conflicts of the Middle East continued, the Saudis became increasingly unhappy with the strong U.S. commitment to Israel. Likewise, the U.S. was displeased with Saudi Arabia's compliance with the Arab League's boycott of Israel. Just as had been the case in my original discussion with Prince Faisal in 1950, the question of Israel remained the major point of divergence between the two countries.

The assassination of King Faisal in 1975 by a disgruntled nephew revealed the existence of cleavages within the House of Saud, about which outsiders had been largely unaware. His successor, Khalid, was not as forceful or as skilled a ruler as Faisal, nor did he have as firm a grip on the government of his country.

Concern for the future stability of Saudi Arabia and its traditional monarchy was compounded in 1979 by news of the occupation of the central mosque in Mecca by Sunni extremists. There also occurred demonstrations by Shiites in the eastern part of the country, which are believed to have been incited by the overthrow of the Shah. Criticism also surfaced, both from religious circles and centers of political dissent, that questioned the style of the Saudi government, the orientation of economic development, and the pace of modernization in Saudi Arabia. It became generally recognized that political change in Saudi Arabia must keep abreast of economic growth. In 1980, the King promulgated a "constitution" under which a representative assembly would be appointed to advise his government. Its functions, however, were to be entirely consultative and intended to aid the government in keeping a finger on the pulse of the country.

Taking into account the difficult internal and world situation they face, the Saud family appears to have managed their affairs reasonably well. The Saudi people have been permitted to share in their country's wealth and progress, and able men from both within and without the royal family have been given opportunity for education, wealth, and positions of power in the government, the armed forces, and the economy. The transition of Saudi Arabia to a modern state without loss of power by the royal family, appears so far to have been managed better than might have been anticipated.

The ties begun by President Roosevelt in 1945, which were strengthened during my visit in 1950 and on later occasions, have on the whole held firm. The U.S. continues to enjoy good relations with Saudi Arabia.

17

Tripartite Declaration

May 25, 1950.

The Tripartite Declaration of 1950 was an announcement made simultaneously on May 25, 1950, by the governments of Great Britain, the U.S., and France, the principal Western powers with Middle Eastern responsibilities. In essence it stated that the three powers would resume, on a coordinated basis, the supply of arms to the states of the area which had been embargoed by the UN in the aftermath of the May 15, 1948, Arab-Israeli War. This would be for legitimate self-defense and area defense only and not for the development of an arms race. The three powers further announced their intention of preventing any Middle Eastern state from committing aggression against another.

The text of the declaration is as follows:

The Governments of the United Kingdom, France, and the United States, having had occasion during the recent Foreign Ministers' meeting in London to review certain questions affecting the peace and stability of the Arab states and of Israel, and particularly that of the supply of arms and war material to these states, have resolved to make the following statements.

1. The three Governments recognize that the Arab states and Israel all need to maintain a certain level of armed forces for the purpose of assuring their internal security and their legitimate self-defense and to permit them to play their part in the defense of the area as a whole. All applications for arms or war material for these countries will be considered in the light of these principles. In this connection the three Governments wish to recall and reaffirm the terms of the statements made by their representatives on the Security Council on August 4, 1949, in which they declared their opposition to the development of an arms race between the Arab States and Israel.

2. The three Governments declare that assurances have been received from all the states in question, to which they permit arms to be supplied from their countries, that the purchasing state does not intend to undertake any act of aggression against any other state in the area to which they permit arms to be supplied in the future.

3. The three Governments take this opportunity of declaring their deep interest in and their desire to promote the establishment and maintenance of peace and stability in the area and their unalterable opposition to the use of force or threat of force between any of the states in that area. The three Governments, should they find that any of these states was preparing to violate frontiers or armistice lines, would, consistently with their obligations as members of the UN, immediately take action, both within and outside the UN, to prevent such violation.

Our concerns which led to the declaration were centered on the whole troubled Middle Eastern conflict, but particularly on certain problems which had remained following the final Arab-Israeli truce, arranged by the UN on July 18, 1948, which had brought an end to hostilities. At the time of the Arab invasion, the UN had embargoed arms shipments to the entire Palestine area. Although this was lifted by the UN on August 11, 1949, both the U.S. and the British strictly limited arms shipments to those required for internal security and self-defense. Because of the arms vacuum created by the war, considerable quantities of weapons were entering the Middle East, principally from Czechoslovakia. Preoccupied with the Cold War and the vulnerability of the Middle East, the U.S. wanted to stop the flow of Eastern European arms, which could have resulted in increased Communist influence, and possibly total control. We wanted to assure an orderly supply of arms by the three powers for legitimate internal security and self and area defense.

British power in the Middle East was declining; this was typified by the stalemate in their negotiations with the Egyptians over continuation of base and troop rights, which I was to encounter at its worst during my visit to Egypt in March 1951. We wanted to help the indigenous states build up their military strength as a contribution to area defense. They were, moreover, demanding arms on a nationalistic basis, as a price for their cooperation.

We did not feel, however, that we could resume arms supply on a substantial basis without assurances to U.S. and world opinion, particularly to those deeply concerned over the survival of the new embattled state of Israel, that we would prevent an arms race and any aggressive use of the arms we furnished. We also wanted to give Israel as great assurance as possible that we would not tolerate Arab aggression against her ceasefire borders. Although there was considerable backing in the U.S. for firm guarantees to Israel, we did not believe it feasible to obtain Senate approval for a full mutual defense treaty with Israel. What we offered had to be something less than legally binding.

We were also aware of the apprehension on the part of the Arab states that Israel might, with increased arms, attempt to take additional territory, even all territory west of the Jordan. In addition, there were concerns among the Arab states about aggression by each other. As I found in my visit to Saudi Arabia just before the issuance of the Tripartite Declaration, King Ibn Saud was apprehensive that, supported by the British whom he did not trust, King Abdullah of Jordan might attempt to retake the Hejaz, which had been lost to Saud by Abdullah's father, King Hussein. Later Abdullah was to tell me of his desire to reshape the Middle Eastern boundaries in his favor. The effectiveness of the Tripartite Declaration was evidenced by his complaint to me that it restrained him from actions he really desired to take.

We wanted to put to rest all suggestions of possible aggression, whether between the Israelis and Arabs or between Arab states, so that the countries of the Middle East could concentrate on their grave internal problems, including the question of refugees, and seek a permanent peace. We sought the help of the U.K. and France in supplying arms to the Middle East, since we did not want to be the principal arms supplier to Israel, as we have subsequently become. We wanted to keep this potentially explosive issue out of U.S. domestic politics. How could all of these objectives be achieved? They were all turning over in my mind one spring day as I sat at my desk in the State Department.

The Department had been considering the matter for some time. On March 28, Secretary Acheson had received a group of congressmen headed by Representative Anthony Tauriello (N.Y.), who had expressed concern that the large-scale shipments of arms by the U.K. to the Arab states, particularly to Egypt, would upset the precarious military balance between Israel and the Arab states.[1] The Secretary summarized the situation created by the lifting of the UN arms embargoes and the steps we had taken. On the same day, the National Security Council made a draft report on U.S. Policy Toward Arms Shipments to the Middle East.

Among its conclusions this report stated the importance of strengthening the Middle East militarily by supply of arms to the states of the area from friendly sources, and the support of the U.K. position toward this end by such arrangements as the proposed Anglo-Egyptian plans for military cooperation. We would oppose no U.K. arms shipments following such plans; we would keep in close touch with U.K. actions; and we would ourselves export to Israel and the Arab states only that equipment needed to maintain internal order and provide for legitimate self-defense, while refusing to be drawn into an arms race in the Middle East.

At a cabinet meeting on April 13, President Truman found the paper, as revised, was much too one-sided and believed it would cause trouble.[2] Acheson said he believed the problem could be solved if the British, French, and U.S. could get nonaggression declarations from the Middle East countries, which could be announced. The President was reported as being much interested in this idea.

In the formulation of foreign policy—or in other words the devising of a strategy which will make self-reinforcing a nation's various efforts toward the achievement of a given objective—there are seldom any really new ideas. Almost every possible course of action has been thought of before. Breakthroughs occur because the changing world scene permits, at a particular time, something to work which could not have been carried out successfully before. The art of foreign affairs is to sense the opportunity and to make your move, improvising along the way to adapt to the evolving circumstances. I recall the moment the pieces of the Middle East puzzle fitted together in my mind. I arose from my chair impulsively, crossed the intervening room between my office and that of my deputy, Raymond Hare, and burst in without announcement.

"Ray, I have it," I said. "The administration can't get Congress to approve a Middle East treaty, but the three powers can, if we are firm and get together, enforce our views on the states of the area. We are the 'big boys.' The Middle East states are the 'little boys.' All we have to do is to set the rules and say, 'Look here, you little boys, you behave yourselves or we are going to take care of you.' We don't have to say precisely how or under what conditions. If we are really 'big boys' we don't need to. They will mind us. Moreover, they are all so concerned just now about what might happen that they will welcome our assuring them that we won't permit a bully, from whatever quarter, to threaten them. I believe they will welcome our assumption of responsibility. I believe Britain and France will be happy to join us in such a move."

Ray and I sat down and began drafting the various elements of what would, after considerable subsequent pulling and hauling, become the Tripartite Declaration. Cleared drafts looking toward a final decision were submitted by our bureau on April 3,[3] in revised form on April 20,[4] and again on April 28.[5] On May 4, the Joint Chiefs of Staff expressed a dissent, recommending that "the United States neither suggest nor approve a declaration regarding the security of the Middle East, which implies employment, either within or without the UN, of military enforcement measures." This position was accepted in the final draft.

On May 17,[6] the concepts leading to the Tripartite Declaration were recommended to President Truman by the National Security Council. The key new elements involved were that the U.S. would solicit British and French support for public declarations by all three, and that they would not permit the shipment of arms to any Middle Eastern country unless the purchasing country gave to the supplier formal assurance to undertake no aggression against any other Middle Eastern state. Second, we would continue to impress on the British and French the importance of avoiding any danger of a renewal of Palestine hostilities, and seek their agreement to issuance of parallel public statements of determination to take vigorous action both within and without the UN should it appear that an attempt to renew hostilities would be made. Such action would not involve the use of U.S. military forces.

It was not yet possible to achieve the final solution of a peace treaty. But in the meantime we sought to stabilize the Middle East under the prevailing conditions and to give states of the area an opportunity to recover from the war and develop defenses to protect themselves against Communist intrusion.

Fortunately, the task of negotiating the Tripartite Declaration with our British and French allies was given to Ray Hare, who had already contributed greatly to its formulation. Ray, who was one of our ablest career officers, was to go on to a series of increasingly high positions in the Department, two of which, Ambassador to Turkey and Assistant Secretary for NEA, were positions I had previously held. He also served as Ambassador to Saudi Arabia. With so much in common, our association over the years has been a close and friendly one.

The U.S., British, and French Foreign Ministers Conference scheduled for London in late April provided an excellent opportunity for launching our new policy. The U.S. delegation was headed by Philip C. Jessup in its preparatory phases, and later by Secretary Acheson. President Truman reported it as "the most successful international conference since Potsdam." With my strong support, Ray Hare was made delegate for Middle Eastern affairs. Our Tripartite Declaration Proposals were taken up with the British on May 1. One of Ray's first problems was to convince the British that the French should be included.[7] Although of lesser importance in the total Middle Eastern picture, the French still had—and more importantly thought they had—residual influence, particularly in Syria and Lebanon. The French were arms suppliers, potentially on a significant scale, and would be offended and would likely oppose Anglo-American efforts if they were excluded.

In preliminary meetings Hare eventually persuaded the British to admit the French, and quieted their fear that the declaration would foreclose necessary future boundary changes or would not be taken seriously. During the second meeting the British agreed to the draft we had presented them. After a perfunctory display of hurt feelings about not being consulted earlier, the French also approved the draft, and it was transmitted by Dean Acheson, Ernest Bevin, and Robert Schuman for final approval by their governments before announcements in the three capitals on May 25.

The declaration slipped into place in the stream of Middle East policy easily and with few objections. There was some pro forma complaint by the Middle Eastern states that they had not been consulted. Indeed they hadn't. But in private they welcomed the declaration, which had the desired stabilizing effect. The New York *Herald Tribune* of May 26 hailed the fact that the three powers were acting in concert for the first time to prevent renewal of Arab-Israeli warfare and had pledged that they would take immediate action against any state planning aggression. The policy of arms supply to the Middle Eastern states and their assurances that the arms would not be used for aggressive purposes, as embodied in the declaration, received secondary emphasis.

The *Tribune* reported initial Israeli reaction as one of cautious optimism, as "being generally satisfied," and said that American Jewish circles regarded it as an important step in consolidating peace and security in the Middle East. The Israeli Ambassador asked for arms under the terms of the declaration. The Egyptian Foreign Office was favorably impressed.

Editorially the *Tribune* called the declaration:

> Common foreign policy action to some real effect . . . The great powers have in effect agreed to underwrite the peace in Palestine. . . . The guaranty resolves the dilemma which the arms problem presented from the first. It makes it possible to fortify the Middle Eastern states as a bulwark against Soviet expansion without at the same time subsidizing or encouraging a resumption of the war between them. As such it may seem a rather simple act of statesmanship. But it is also a bold one; for neither France nor Britain nor America would have dreamed, a year or two ago, of pledging its men and resources to the guarantee of any kind of peace in Palestine. . . . The joint statement is a good omen for peace and advancement in the Middle East—and on a greater stage as well.

The *New York Times* described the declaration as:

> A great and welcome step in the "total diplomacy" which must be the goal of the West . . . The lack of a unified Western policy on the Middle East has been one of the worst gaps in the battlelines of the Cold War . . . this new move is just and wise, and it will strengthen the West in the global struggle.

Generally favorable reactions were received from Western Europe, South America, and Africa. The Soviets, caught by surprise, were only mildly critical. They predicted the situation in the Middle East would be frozen by the declaration.

The three powers were, of course, most interested in the reaction of the Middle Eastern states themselves. The Israeli Foreign Office spoke "with satisfaction." They welcomed the "break" in the stalemate. Arab reactions were mixed but generally favorable except for Iraq. The Lebanese saw a "freeze" in the status quo. The Saudis, after initial "misgivings," ended up with cautious praise. The British Foreign Office, as I have found from their archives, summarized reactions in the area as follows:[8] Cairo, Minister of Foreign Affairs and press, favorable, palace and government greatly relieved; Beirut, reaction of Prime Minister entirely satisfactory; Baghdad, Nuri Said and others attacked the declaration in the Senate; Damascus, Prime

Minister considers it fundamentally good; Amman, generally favorable; Riyadh, Ibn Saud very pleased, reaction of government one of satisfaction; Arab League, reaction quite moderate.

The Tripartite Declaration appeared to have started out with a generally stabilizing effect on the Middle East. A deterioration occurred in 1955, when Egypt became dissatisfied with its allocations by the three-power committee on arms sales set up in London to administer the declaration, and concluded an arms deal with the Soviet Union through Czechoslovakia. The declaration was further discredited by the Anglo-French-Israeli invasion of Egypt in October 1956.

On October 30, British Prime Minister Anthony Eden told Parliament that the U.K. had conferred with the U.S. over the relevance of the Tripartite Declaration to the British and French action in Suez, implying we had not objected. Actually, the U.S. had, on this occasion, told the British we considered the declaration applicable, and that the invasion was in violation of it. We felt that the Anglo-French-Israeli invasion made a mockery of the declaration. The British, in their confusion over the failure of their efforts, took the position that the invasion was pursuant to their obligations under the Declaration.

Despite the increasing erosion of its credibility, the Tripartite Declaration continued to be cited as a basis for various actions in the Middle East by every American President up to Carter. I have often referred to it as an example of the usefulness of a venerable and ambiguous policy. Such a policy can be revived whenever it can be useful; at other times it can be ignored. All in all, the Tripartite Declaration did, it is believed, have a beneficial stabilizing effect. It relieved apprehension by Israel and Arabs alike about local wars; it provided the most specific assurances given by the U.S. up to that time to protect Israel; it promoted harmony in Middle East policies among the three powers; and it provided a continuous mechanism through the London Committee for a judicious distribution of arms, minimizing the possibility of an arms race.

18

Beginnings of Aid Programs to the Middle East and South Asia

June–August 1950.

Despite the initial encouraging effects of the Point Four Program, I became increasingly concerned about the situation in the Middle East and South Asia and wrote a memorandum to Secretary Acheson on June 7, 1950, giving my ideas as to additional U.S. assistance required for this area.[1] Up to this time we had available for aid programs only a portion of the Point Four fund of $24 million, a pitifully small amount to parcel out among 600 million people.

In my memorandum I said I believed it essential to develop a more positive policy of economic development assistance to the countries of the Middle East and South Asia. Most had only recently achieved independence, had non-Communist governments, faced grave internal political and administrative problems, were weak financially, and were underdeveloped. Even though Communism had made little inroad, all were exposed to Communist pressures.

I said that India, Pakistan, and Afghanistan were the only countries on the borders of the U.S.S.R. and its satellites for which we had no program of economic assistance. Experience had shown that such countries needed the stiffening and confidence provided by our assistance. In the Arab countries there were the added pressures arising out of the emergence of Israel. Economic aid, which only we were in a position to provide on the scale required, was necessary to assure increased political stability and a more Western orientation.

I pointed out that Economic Cooperation Administration (ECA) grant aid had been furnished Greece and Turkey on the west, and was now planned for the Southeast Asian countries, starting with Burma on the east. However, except for the limited Arab refugee program and small Ex-Im Bank loans to Saudi Arabia, Afghanistan, Israel, and Egypt, no direct U.S. assistance had been provided for the half billion people in the other Middle East and South Asian areas. Funds under Point Four were not adequate to make an impact on the needs of the area. Private capital had not been, nor was it likely to be available in sufficient quantities. Any loans from the World Bank and Ex-Im Bank would be helpful, but would not be adequate. They would not meet the deficiency in local currencies for development purposes and would require interest and amortization charges beyond the capacity of the countries of the area to pay. The sterling balances held by the countries were not adequate to meet their needs.

I said that I believed we should begin now to plan a new program to enable the countries of South Asia—India, Pakistan, Sri Lanka, and Afghanistan, and selected Middle Eastern states—beginning in fiscal year 1952, to carry out developmental projects which would promote long-term economic progress, particularly in agriculture. Our bureau had estimated, admittedly on the basis of inadequate information, that initially about $200 million would be required annually. Provision should be made, where absolutely necessary, for local currency requirements. Such assistance should be supplemental to that available from the country's own and Commonwealth sources. It should not be designed to meet balance-of-payments deficits.

I advised that this program should be closely related to that we had proposed for Southeast Asia, involving use of Japanese yen counterpart funds. The program might be administered by ECA, or a parallel organization, through country missions. I believed the best strategy to get approval was to lay a foundation through properly timed statements by high department officials. This new program might be considered an extension of aid to Southeast Asia, which was largely the result of congressional initiative. Our program would then cover all areas of potential instability. The Department created a working group to make recommendations for aid to areas both within and outside my jurisdiction.

On July 15, I sent a telegram to Ambassador Henry F. Grady in Teheran, who had had valuable aid experience both in Greece and Iran, asking him for his views on the general question of assistance to the area as a whole.[2] I had particular confidence in Grady's judgment in aid matters. I advised him that we were reviewing possible action in all areas threatened in the present world conflict, including grants to the Middle East and South Asia, along the lines of that extended to the Far Eastern countries. Our purpose would be to strengthen their orientation to the Western democracies and help them build economic and, indirectly, military strength, to protect them against Communism. Taking into account limitations of resources and priorities, the bureau was thinking in terms of $250 million the first year. I had already raised the ante since my original memorandum to the Secretary. I asked Grady for his views on the whole question how he thought initial contacts with recipient countries should be made.

In his reply Grady concurred in the importance of an aid program to give confidence to those countries which, despite their precarious situation, had been skipped over by American aid.[3] He considered grant aid essential in Iran to supplement Ex-Im Bank and Point Four funds in the fields of health, sanitation, and agriculture, and for general technical assistance. Projects already planned could absorb $50 million the first year. Extension of aid in this amount would help us get the Iranians to make better use of their own resources, and to make the necessary fiscal and other reforms. Grady stressed the need for continuity in programs once established, which had contributed to our success in Europe. He urged that our technicians be coordinated by the Ambassador, as he had done in Greece, rather than by an independent economic mission.

Grady also gave his views on the need for U.S. assistance in other threatened countries. He considered aid to be particularly important for Afghanistan which, like Iran, would likely be of interest to the Soviets in reaching the Persian Gulf, India, and South Asia. He thought development loans could be used effectively in Pakistan, but had serious doubts about grant aid to India, where he had served as Ambassador. The Indians already had large sums accumulated in London during the war. Grady considered overgenerous grant aid fruitless. A liberal and intelligent lending agency could put aid programs on a firmer basis.

On August 28, in response to a request by Secretary Acheson, I prepared a memorandum to the President proposing that we develop an assistance program for South Asia, the Arab states, and Iran.[4] I drew on the advice of Grady, other departmental officers, Treasury, and other agencies. The memorandum said that our prime object of policy for the next few years must be to create political and economic strength in critical areas. (It is interesting that we felt at that time that the fall of the Middle East and South Asia to Communism was possible, if the situations in those countries were not improved. We were greatly influenced by the aggressive moves the Soviets had made in Greece and Iran, also the recent fall of China to Communism, which we felt threatened all of Southeast Asia. We had not yet had enough experience with the Middle East and South Asia to have confidence in their ability to stand up to the Communists.) I advised the President that we believed the minimum requirement to be $300 million a year over a five-year period. (This figure kept going up.) The first emphasis, I continued, should be on improvement in the locally grown food supply to strengthen the morale of the people. Priority should be given to increasing economic strength, and thus to military potential. We should ensure demonstrable reciprocal benefits to the U.S. I requested authorization to discuss this proposal with congressional leaders.

Although he did not show him my memorandum, Acheson discussed the situation with the President the next day. Truman's immediate reaction was that it would be utterly impossible to get Congress—certainly in the immediate future—to consider substantial economic aid for South Asia and the Middle East.[5] On the other hand, Acheson reported, the President believed that such measures were sound and probably should go in the program for next year. They would take some time to work out. The President saw some advantage in our beginning discussion with appropriate people on the Hill, as long as they understood that we were not going to face them with a new request that fall, but were only following accepted consultation procedures. Apparently the President felt that Congress, in the face of massive outlays for the Marshall Plan and aid to Greece and Turkey, would be reluctant to initiate substantial new programs in such uncertain areas. It would take more time and a clearer realization in Congress of the weaknesses of those countries.

Since the President had authorized discussions I immediately arranged two meetings for this purpose. On September 1, I met with Representatives Francis Bolton (Ohio), Omar Burleson (Texas), A. S. J. Carnahan (Missouri), Richard Chatham (North Carolina), Robert Chiperfield (Indiana), Clement Zablocki (Wisconsin), and Jacob Javits (New York), all key members of the House Foreign Affairs Committee.[6]

I said that the Department welcomed the opportunity to consult House leaders before making any commitments on a new program which we considered of great importance. I referred to a previous meeting of the Near East and Africa Subcommitee, when I had described the serious deterioration of the economies in various South Asian and Middle Eastern countries. I referred to the shortage of four to five million tons of grain in India and the famine in West Bengal,

Madras, and Bihar. In Iran the crop failure in 1949 had resulted in grave food shortages and a generally deteriorating economic situation. In Pakistan, while grain supplies were plentiful, it was necessary to import other food, which was made difficult by the impasse in trade with India.

As further evidence of economic deterioration, I cited price rises of 3 percent monthly in India and Pakistan. India was also facing deterioration in its industrial plant through disinvestment. New investments from abroad in India since the war had amounted to only $20 million, of which only $1 millon had come from the U.S. A third adverse indicator was India's balance of payments, which had been unfavorable since April 1950. The drafts India could make on her sterling balances were insufficient. Pakistan also had an adverse balance of trade and Iran had a deficit of $30 million for 1950. Large-scale unemployment had resulted. There were, as a result of partition, 10 million refugees on the Indian subcontinent, only half of whom had been resettled. There were also 750,000 destitute Arab refugees as a result of the recent Palestinian conflict.

I then turned to the significance of the area as a whole in view of U.S. interests, and the importance of saving it from loss to anarchy or Communist aggression. The countries there, in particular India and Pakistan, represented an important nucleus of strength. They had a military tradition fostered by the British and an ardent nationalism which would help them in resisting outside aggression. I mentioned the manpower contribution of India in the last war, and cited the great value of Nehru's support of our policy in Korea. These countries had free middle-of-the-road governments which it was in our interest to support.

The question remained as to how we could best help remedy the present situation. Resources available to help bolster local economies were inadequate. On the other hand, grant aid on the scale of our European aid programs was not required. The findings of Gordon Clapp had shown that the needs of the area required more technical than financial assistance. I told the group that Clapp thought that a grant program of between $300 and $500 million annually might well suffice. This, plus administrators who would obtain the necessary leverage in local situations through their authority to allocate funds, should be able to meet the situation. In his view, direct military aid was not needed. The program would be similar to UNRWA, the UN refugee program Clapp had helped initiate. We would specify terms for use of our aid, under country programs of specific projects. I explained that the President had authorized discussion with the congressional committees, and that we sought their judgment.

The response from all present appeared to be favorable. I was requested to present the case again before a full meeting of the Foreign Affairs Committee on September 14. Francis Bolton, a key member, requested that I keep the Foreign Affairs Committee and the NEA Subcommittee informed as to our progress during the congressional recess. I came away quite encouraged. Alas, there were still many obstacles yet to be overcome.

I held a similar meeting on September 1 with Senators Pepper (Florida), Ferguson (Michigan), and Smith (New Jersey) and Representative Poage (Texas). Their reaction was less enthusiastic, more one of acquiescence.[7]

The Department, in accordance with President Truman's decision, abandoned efforts to secure a significant economic-aid program for the Middle East and South Asia in 1950. In cooperation with the Bureau of Public Affairs, I continued to draft plans on information policy in order to stimulate congressional and public interest. The following year, however, saw the fruition of these efforts in the Mutual Security Act of 1951. Transmitted by President Truman to the Congress on May 24, this act requested the first large-scale aid to the Middle East and Africa, including Greece, Turkey, Iran, Libya, Liberia, Ethiopia, and "other countries." South Asia had to wait. "The pressure against the Middle East is unremitting," said the President in this transmittal message. "It can be overcome only by a continued build-up of armed defenses and the fostering of economic development." In October Congress appropriated $396 million for military aid and $160 million for economic aid for the Middle East and Africa. The problem was no longer considered simply an economic one: the increasing Communist threat to the Middle East had finally persuaded the Congress to help the states of the area build up their security forces, as well as their economies.

The reaction from other bureaus to my proposed new large aid grants was often sharp. My friend Eddie Miller, Assistant Secretary for Latin American Affairs, called a meeting between our bureaus and attacked our proposed Indian grain grant strongly. He had been under pressure for aid by the Latin American countries, particularly Brazil. How could he explain, he asked, such large grants to a neutralist country? Our debate became heated. Unable to satisfy Eddie, I finally proposed that we agree to disagree and let Under Secretary Webb decide. India won.

In the years following World War II, Americans generally accepted without question the general proposition that democracy was every nation's ultimate goal, and that it could be achieved through economic development and mass education. Development aid, as much as military assistance, was recognized as a deterrent to the spread of Communism. With this view in mind, the U.S. had initiated vast aid programs that by 1981 had funneled almost $150 billion into foreign economic assistance, exclusive of $90 billion in military aid. Nearly $20 billion was appropriated for economic assistance during my three year tenure as Assistant Secretary. The major portion of our aid was, of course, allocated for the reconstruction of Europe under the Marshall Plan, which was highly successful. Aid to other regions, including the Middle World, did not produce such dramatic results.

Perhaps this was because we lacked the patience to sustain a commitment to long-term programs. Our efforts were often frustrated by instability, inexperience, and corruption in recipient countries. They did not produce democratic societies or economic development according to schedule. Accordingly, the level of U.S. appropriations for the Middle World under the Mutual Security Act suffered an early decline. Although greater in sheer volume, American foreign economic aid today represents a smaller share of our budget and of our national wealth than aid provided by other Western industrialized countries. Taking into consideration inflation and the expanded needs, our contribution is disappointing in comparison to our efforts under the Marshall Plan.

It is interesting to compare the most recent aid figures under the International Security and Economic Cooperation Program for fiscal year 1983.[8] Former Secretary of State Alexander Haig, in his letter to the Congress, emphasized that we must build deterrence and defense against conflict world-wide; protect our peacemaking efforts, as in Israel and Egypt; assure retention of military facilities and rights as well as markets and commercial ties; and address economic crises in the developing world which would invite exploitation by others.

Economic aid to 44 countries in Africa aggregate $516 million for fiscal year 1983. Development assistance to individual states ranges from $1 million to the Central African Republic, Equatorial Guinea, and Sierra Leone, to $25 million to the Sudan and $27 million to

Kenya. Total military assistance of all types is projected at $242 million, about one-half of economic assistance. Economic aid to 16 countries in the Near East (Middle East as used herein) and South Asia for Fiscal Year 1983 is scheduled for $2.5 billion; however, $1.8 billion is for economic support (of our large military programs) to Egypt ($1.3 billion), Israel ($1.7 billion), and Pakistan ($275 million). The major programs of economic-development assistance are to Bangladesh ($76 million), India ($87 million), Sri Lanka ($40 million), and North Yemen ($27 million). Many of the Middle Eastern countries have large oil incomes and do not require assistance.

Looking at it from the beginning, overall U.S. foreign assistance—economic and military—in current dollars, peaked in 1950 at about $8 billion and, after a decline until 1958, has risen in 1983 to an all-time high of almost $14 billion. In constant 1950 dollars, however, our overall foreign aid has remained virtually level since 1955 at around $4 billion annually. As a percentage of total expenditures of the federal government, total aid has decreased from a peak of 20 percent in 1950 to about 2 percent in 1980, and to a projected 1 percent in 1985.

These changes represent the net effect of a variety of factors: progress by some countries, which makes further aid less important; changes in the technology of aid, particularly in agriculture; increased economic aid by other industrialized countries, and by the OPEC states; and U.S. foreign-exchange and budgetary problems. There has also been a disillusionment on the part of the American people in the efficacy of foreign aid and the benefits to us. This has been accompanied by a conscious concentration of our aid on our national security needs, as represented by aid to Turkey for Middle East defense, to Pakistan as a counterpoise to the Soviet conquest of Afghanistan, and to Israel and Egypt as a means of carrying out the Camp David accords and furthering peace between Israel and the Arab world.

The economic and political benefits to be derived from development aid have, as a result, been brought into question. Economic aid to the "poorest of the poor" has, according to congressional mandate, been given a clear priority. The net result has, I believe, been a decreased emphasis on development aid as a factor in our relations with the developing countries, which has hurt our image as a disinterested donor for humanitarian reasons. These trends, I believe, must be reversed, if America is to have the positive influence in the world we once had and can, even if on a reduced scale, still have.

19

Meeting with the French Foreign Ministry

September 23–25, 1950.

Following my meetings in London with British Foreign Office officials from September 18 to 23, 1950, I went to Paris for discussions of African problems with officials from the French Foreign Ministry and the Ministry of Overseas Territories, from September 23 to 25.[1] Although not of great importance in itself, the meeting illustrates the state of our relations with the French on colonial problems. Our contacts with the French up to this point had not been on the same intimate and cooperative basis as those with the British. The lengths of time allocated to the London and Paris meetings reflected this. We had not, of course, had relations with France comparable to those developed with the U.K. during the war. There were, however, other reasons for the difference.

The French were in a difficult position at this time. They were under great pressure, particularly from the developing world, to relinquish their colonial possessions. Although we had tried to be sympathetic, there was no question that the Department, and the American public, felt that the French were moving too slowly. The French, on the other hand, considered us to have an anticolonial prejudice, and suspected that we were undermining them in their difficult task of coping with their colonial problems. From their point of view, they had reason to be wary of us. The main purpose of my visit in 1950 was to attempt to understand the French position, to explain ours, and to offer them support insofar as individual circumstances permitted. We realized, however, that some of our views were far apart.

We had several meetings during my visit, the principal one on the afternoon of September 25. The French had ten representatives, headed by Baron Guy de la Tournelle, Director General of Political Affairs for the Foreign Ministry. I was accompanied by my valued colleague Elmer Bourgerie, Director of the Office of African Affairs; by John Utter and Rupert Lloyd from our Paris Embassy; and by my old friend from Oxford days, Lincoln Gordon from the ECA Paris office. Link was later to become Ambassador to Brazil and president of Johns Hopkins University. Our discussions, reflecting the mood of the time, centered on the Communist threat to Africa.

The meeting followed an excellent luncheon, for which the Quai d'Orsay is famous, and we were in a good mood. In my opening remarks I emphasized that our interest was motivated by two considerations: our obvious strategic interest in the African continent and our desire to see the French overseas territories, by their economic development, assist in the strengthening of metropolitan France. The recent Foreign Ministers' meeting and other U.S.-French conversations had gone a long way toward dispelling suspicions of any critical attitude by the noncolonial powers toward those having African possessions. The great strides which France had made in the development of its overseas territories were fully appreciated.

I said that there were a few questions which I wanted to ask, mainly concerning Communism in Africa. I realized that this was not yet a major problem, since Africa was now one of the most stable areas of the world. The native population was, however, vulnerable to agitators offering an alternative to colonial rule. I felt, therefore, that there was a potential threat in certain strategic areas and wanted to know what plans the French had for countering this threat.

Pierre Francfort, Assistant Chief of the African Section of the Ministry, replied that the basis for a Communist movement in French West Africa was fundamentally weak, since the section of the population on which Communism usually relies most heavily for its recruits—i.e., the industrial proletariat of large cities—was of little importance in Africa. The peasantry, on the other hand, did not offer a fertile field for Communist propaganda, since it was still in a more or less primitive state and, of course, very backward from the political point of view. The Communists had, therefore, sought an outlet through nationalistic groups, a maneuver which they have used with success in other parts of the world.

Especially since 1947, the Communists had attempted to capture the Rassemblement Démocratique Africain (RDA) by their usual methods of infiltration. The RDA, an African political coalition formed by President Félix Houphouet-Boigny of the Ivory Coast, had found it advantageous to associate itself with the Communist Party, since its eleven representatives in the French National Assembly constituted too small a group to exercise much influence when acting independently. There were, nevertheless, Socialist members of the RDA who could be counted on to support the French government.

The recent evolution of the RDA and the signs that it might well proceed to clean its own house of Communist influence, had made the question of exerting pressure on the RDA an extremely delicate one. Such pressure from the French government might serve only to crystallize anti-French feeling, interrupt the progress now being made, and thus play into the hands of the Communists. The central government had, therefore, considered it preferable to leave to the governors of the various African territories the task of persuading RDA members to adopt a broader attitude toward French aims in Africa. With respect to Communist influence in the labor movement, it might be said that, although no labor union in Black Africa was entirely dominated by the Communist party, a great many of the union leaders were Communists. The situation was, therefore, potentially dangerous and should be closely watched.

According to Francfort, since the RDA was a legally constituted political party, the tactics of the French government were to attempt to win over, individually, the more influential members of the RDA rather than to attack the party itself. Whenever illegal action occurred, the French government would act promptly and with vigor. In the meantime, the government would do everything possible to throttle Communism in the overseas territories by acting through local administrations, without violating French law or France's international undertakings. Francfort pointed out that, although the RDA was the most important political outlet for the nationalist movement in all of West Africa, there were other political parties representing separate territories. These included the Progressive Party (Parti Progressiste) in the Ivory Coast, home of the RDA. Personal and sectional rivalries must also be taken into account.

All programs of agitation by the Communist Party had, Francfort said, been conducted in the name of nationalist aspirations. Thus, while all nationalists were not Communists, they could frequently be led to act along the same lines as Communists. This was the most disturbing facet of the situation. The nationalists were now convinced that the only answer to their aspirations was complete independence. It did not seem, however, that this would be an acceptable solution, since the trend internationally was now in the opposite direction, i.e., association on a regional or world-wide scale. The dependent areas, if given complete independence, would be inclined to adopt an attitude of neutrality in the present ideological conflict and thus open the way for the same type of blackmail in Africa as is today being practiced in the Far East, playing the East against the West.

Guy de la Tournelle, in turn, summed up the situation. He told us the Communist movement in Black Africa had only recently assumed any importance and was closely tied with nationalism. The African adherents to the Communist philosophy, like those in the Soviet Union, repudiated any form of cooperation with non-Communists. International Communism probably considered the African continent as its second objective, after Asia. The center for its African campaign seemed to be located in Ethiopia, and the most effective way to counter Communist tactics in French Africa was to persuade the indigenous groups that their aspirations for self-government could be realized within the framework of the French Union, and that their best interests, materially and otherwise, lay in close cooperation with France.

I asked whether the French considered the Ethiopian center more important than the RDA as a means of furthering Communist aims in Africa. Francfort replied that the activities were on different planes: the Communist sought to work through outstanding personalities in the case of the RDA, whereas the Ethiopian center handled the day-to-day business of the program. The two types of activities were designed to complement each other.

I inquired whether the Communists were organized well enough to carry out extensive sabotage in the event of hostilities and, if so, whether they were making any definite plans to follow through along these lines. There had been reports that the Communists were planning, in the event of an armed conflict, to instigate an uprising along the African fourteenth parallel, lying just south of the Sahara.

De la Tournelle did not think the Communists had worked out any definite sabotage and said that their major effort seemed rather to be concentrated on undermining French authority. Government officials were aware of rumors that the Communists were planning disturbances along the fourteenth parallel and that they probably had already attempted something in this direction. He felt that any such effort was doomed to failure. The inhabitants of the region concerned were, for the most part, fanatically devout Muslims and as such were likely to resist Communist ideas. The Communists might, however, be instrumental in inciting a holy war in this area, and this was believed to constitute the only real danger.

I asked if the French cooperated closely with the British and with Liberia in the surveillance and control of Communist activities in Africa, and learned that the cooperation with the British was very close in this respect. The French side said that it was, however, difficult to work with Liberia, because of arms smuggling into Guinea and the Ivory Coast via Liberia, which was causing the French some concern.

I brought up the question of African students in France and asked whether the Communists were active in seeking to influence them. Did the French government encourage African students to come to France? Francfort replied that while he could cite no particular cases of Communist efforts to influence the African students in France, such activity was undoubtedly going on. The French government encouraged African students to come as a means of acquainting them with French life. There were three thousand students there at that time. Naturally there was danger that those students would come under the influence of French Communists. Experience had shown, however, that relatively few became Communists and that the majority, many of whom wanted to return to occupy important administrative posts in the overseas territories, supported the French.

I asked whether the Africans could be brought to realize that Communism would impose a far worse form of imperialism than that now existing. Francfort did not believe so, as the African native was far too backward politically to grasp a concept which a great many Europeans found difficult to understand. The greatest bulwark against Communism in these territories was, in his view, the French administration. When the French felt that they had the support of other powers in their task, they would be able to act with even more confidence and vigor. In effect, Francfort was telling us that the French could succeed if we supported them. It was up to us.

I asked whether an effort was being made to offer means of expression to non-Communist nationalists. Francfort replied that the French had attempted to persuade bona fide nationalists that their aspirations could be achieved within the framework of the French Union, not through Communism. This was, of course, a long-term matter and the principal difficulty was convincing them of the necessity for a gradual evolution toward greater self-government. Jean Binoche, Director of Afrique-Levant, Foreign Office, added that France was confronted with a dilemma: the government was eager to see the native population advance as rapidly as possible toward self-government and would like to accelerate that evolution. On the other hand, the government felt that the premature relaxation of certain controls would play directly into the hands of the Communists. This situation made it difficult to persuade the peoples of Africa, and other nations as well, that France was actually moving in the right direction.

Guy Monod, Chief of the African Section, introduced the subject of social developments in the French territories of Black Africa. Reports on this matter had been submitted to the UN, but there was one aspect which he desired to stress: namely, the work of the Commission de Cooperation Technique en Afrique (CCTA). Monod reviewed the development of this organization from its beginning in 1945, outlining its organizational structure and giving a résumé of its work by listing the various conferences held. This included veterinary medicine, tsetse fly control, medicine, education, nutrition, commerce, transportation, and soil erosion.

Although I had sympathy for the French, I did not, after this meeting, have great confidence that they would be able to work out their difficult colonial problems. The dilemma they saw between development and Communism was, in fact, between development and continued French colonialism. They could not assist in the development of their colonies because of the risk of losing them. This, despite their protests to the contrary, they were not prepared to do. The French remain today the only colonial power that has not left the countries to which they granted independence. They have maintained intimate political, economic, and even military ties with their former colonies in Africa. This is, in part, the result of a colonial policy that aimed at fusing colonies with metropolitan France and training a colonial elite to think of itself as French as well as African. In 1960, all but Guinea accepted the voluntary association with France offered by de Gaulle to African colonies soon to be independent. Today the dependence of the former colonies is as great as it was then—and in some respects greater.

The francophone states in Africa range from the relatively prosperous to the wretchedly impoverished, and from committed Marxist states like Benin and the Congo, to those with conservative regimes like Senegal and the Ivory Coast. In all of them, however, French is the language of administration and education, and public institutions are patterned on the French model. The French government provides teachers and technical personnel as a part of the largest and most effective development-aid program in Black Africa—amounting to about $1.5 billion annually—which is tied to the acquisition of French goods and services. French exports to the region total $8 billion a year. Nor are France's economic relations there a one-way proposition. Trade agreements guarantee France access to strategic materials and to about 20 percent of its oil requirements. Imports from former colonies in the region were valued at more than $10 billion in 1980.

France has also concluded a series of security treaties that have kept 10,000 French troops garrisoned in Africa to bolster pro-French regimes there. Although the Mitterrand government plays down France's role as gendarme-of-Africa, the French presence, economic and political as well as military, remains a stabilizing factor in Africa's francophone community of nations.

20

The End of an Era in Tunisia and Libya

Visit to Tunis, Tunisia, and Tripoli, Libya. Bey of Tunis,
Grand Mufti of Tripoli. September 27–28, 1950.

In the fall of 1950, shortly before the U.S. North African Diplomatic
and Consular Conference held in Tangier, I made brief visits to two
of North Africa's aging leaders, the Bey of Tunis and the Grand
Mufti of Tripolitania. The visits gave me an opportunity to gauge
further the level of nationalist sentiment in the region, and to express
American interest in the future of this important area. Tunisia is both
Arab and African, and yet is located just across the Mediterranean
Sea from Europe and was formerly under European rule.

My first stop was Tunisia, one of the loveliest countries in the
world, with its Mediterranean seacoast, its mountainous northeast,
and its southern desert land that is part of the Sahara. Like so many
countries of the Middle World, Tunisia was in 1950 just emerging
from centuries of outside domination. The Arabs had conquered the
area in A.D. 647, bringing Islam to Tunisia. From their base at Qair-
wan, the Arabs had prepared for their conquest of Morocco and
Spain. Tunisia had fallen in 1500 to the Ottoman Empire, and the
Turks had ruled there for over three centuries. In 1868, the Bey of
Tunis was unable to repay his country's debts and Tunisia came under the joint fiscal control of Britain, France, and Italy. In 1878, the
Great Powers met at the Congress of Berlin, and France was ceded
power in Tunisia in return for French recognition of Britain's rights
in Cyprus. Three years later France occupied Tunisia.

Nationalist sentiment in Tunisia, which had survived the French
occupation, had begun to grow by the end of the First World War.
Tunisian nationalists, represented at the time of my visit by the Neo-
Destour (or New Constitution) Party, were led by Habib Bourguiba,
who founded the party in 1934 and worked indefatigably for Tuni-

sian independence until it was achieved in March 1956. Bourguiba subsequently became Tunisia's first President, and continues to rule as of this writing. When I visited Tunisia in 1950, Bourguiba was in self-imposed exile in Egypt, and a more radical member of the Neo-Destour Party, Salah Ben Youssef, was in command. Under Bourguiba's guidance, however, the Neo-Destour Party had for the most part taken a gradualist, rather than a revolutionary view of the struggle for independence.

But in the fall of 1950, although the hereditary Bey was the titular head of government, France still ruled Tunisia. Virtually a captive of the French, the Bey lived in a modest villa at the site of ancient Carthage. He had moved there from his former beautifully decorated palace, the Bardo, now the Aloui Museum in Tunis. Thus the situation was such that it was French, not Tunisian officials that met our party on arrival, and we stayed at the French residency, La Marsa. Traveling with me were State Department officials Elmer Bourgerie, Director of African Affairs, and Samuel Kopper, Deputy Director of Middle Eastern Affairs.

U.S. policy toward Tunisia at this time, as summarized in a memorandum of August 23 by former Consul-General at Tunis, Earl L. Packer,[1] was considered to be primarily strategic, because of its proximity to Europe. This made Tunisia of great importance in providing land for U.S. and other allied bases which would be of great importance for the control of the Mediterranean. We were at this time encouraging reform measures in Tunisia, including a timetable for independence as proposed by Jean Mons, the French Resident-General preceding Louis Périllier, with continuing close relations with France. We had pointed out tactfully in Paris the difficulty we would face, in the absence of such reforms, in opposing UN proposals for early Tunisian independence. In the meantime we thought U.S. Information Service activities in Tunisia should be extended, European Economic Administration aid reaching Tunisia should be better publicized, direct Point Four aid should begin, and our missionary efforts should be maintained. Although we hoped to expand our trade, our economic interests in Tunisia were considered slight.

The evening before my arrival, Consul-General John D. Jernegan had been approached by Hedi Nouira, Assistant Secretary General of the Neo-Destour party, requesting that I grant an inverview with Salah Ben Youssef, Minister of Justice and Secretary General of the party. The delicacy with which we viewed our relations with the

French at that time was reflected in my decision not to grant the interview, which would have upset not only Périllier but the entire French government.

Our group paid an official call on the Resident-General the morning of our arrival.[2] In my opening remarks I emphasized my belief that the forces of nationalism, which were widespread in the world, were not necessarily bad and could be constructive. Périllier agreed, saying that the French believed it was necessary to make concessions to nationalist sentiment in Tunisia in order to prevent the Tunisians from joining forces with the Communists, who were promising complete independence. However, he warned that one should not overemphasize the importance of nationalism in the Tunisian picture. Nationalist sentiment was really strong only among the relatively small group of intellectuals, while the uneducated mass of the people had little interest in anything outside of their daily survival.

The Resident-General characterized French policy in Tunisia as an experiment, an attempt to carry out an evolutionary process with the collaboration of nationalist elements. It remained to be seen whether the Tunisians had sufficient maturity and grasp of the problems of government to make this policy a success. Périllier believed their tendency was to try to go much too fast and always to push beyond the terms of reference under which the collaboration had been undertaken. In any case, France had decided its course and would put the reforms into effect even without nationalist cooperation, if that should become necessary. The task was a difficult one and the outcome was not certain, but he was hopeful of success. I expressed my appreciation of the difficulty involved. We discussed Tunisia's strategic importance and agreed that, if another outbreak of war were to occur, it would be extremely useful to have voluntary Tunisian cooperation.

My later calls on Prime Minister Mohamed Chenik and Secretary General Jacques Vimont were brief and devoted principally to an exchange of friendly remarks.[3] The Prime Minister emphasized the devotion of the Tunisian people to democracy and their determination to support the democratic principles upon which Islam was founded. Tunisia, he said, would continue to defend those principles alongside the U.S. and France. Secretary General Vimont, who seemed to me very sincere, echoed the Resident-General's definition of the present program of cooperation with the nationalists as an experiment. He said that there were many difficulties to be overcome but that the French were putting into the task all the good faith and good will that the situation required and had high hopes of a successful outcome.

The final and ultimately most interesting diplomatic exchange was with the Bey himself at his Bardo Palace.[4] The Tunisian ministers were present, as were the Chief of Protocol and the Bey's second son. The usual formula of English to French, then French to Arabic translation was followed. The portable radio I had presented to the Bey had been delivered in advance and was sitting on a table in the throne room.

The Bey greeted me in a friendly way. I expressed appreciation for his receiving me and for the hospitable reception accorded me since my arrival in Tunisia. I remarked that I was reminded daily of Tunisia, since just opposite my desk in Washington hung a portrait of His Highness Sadok Bey, then Bey of Tunis, which had been sent by the Bey to President Johnson on Johnson's inauguration in 1865. The Bey had congratulated Johnson on the end of the Civil War and expressed his condolences for the death of President Lincoln. I presented the Bey with a photograph of the portrait of his esteemed predecessor.

The Bey told me that he had a souvenir of the U.S., a signed photograph of President Franklin D. Roosevelt, which he kept in his private office. He sent for the photograph and showed it to me, and then inscribed a photograph of himself, which he presented to me with the hope that it would be a further reminder of the close ties between Tunisia and the U.S. The Bey's official message was on a more serious note. As translated by Salah Ben Youssef, it was as follows: "The Tunisian people are Muslim and share the characteristics of all Muslims. Islamic peoples have strong sentiments of dignity and pride. Such a people cannot live in servitude."

I replied that the U.S. had close relations with the Muslim nations and that we understood their sentiments. We believed that there were grounds for solidarity between the Muslims and ourselves in the present struggle between opposing forces in the world, as there had been during the past war, when we had fought together against the common enemy. The Bey's answer was again translated by Salah Ben Youssef. He agreed that there was a close relationship between the U.S. and Muslim peoples. Unfortunately, despite the wartime efforts of the Muslims, and especially the Tunisians, at the side of the Americans in the fight for liberty, six years had gone by and there had been no change, no progress, no amelioration in the situation of the Tunisians. During this exchange, while Salah Ben Youssef was speaking with marked emphasis, I noticed that the Bey was devoting most of his attention to inscribing the photograph he was presenting me. He gave me no indication of expressing in his remarks to me anything more than polite platitudes.

I replied that I understood certain progressive steps had already been undertaken, adding that I hoped the Tunisian people would continue in the path of progress in cooperation with the French. I knew that His Highness had the welfare of his people at heart and I wished him all success and prosperity. Dr. Ben Salem, Tunisian Minister of Public Health, who understood English fairly well, quickly volunteered to interpret this statement directly from English to Arabic. The Bey's reply, retransmitted directly through Dr. Ben Salem, indicated approval of my observation.

After the customary amenities our party took leave of the Bey. In the anteroom of the palace the Chief of Protocol presented me on behalf of the Bey a handsome gold cloisonné Swiss watch inscribed with the Bey's name. I still have it. During the luncheon given for us later that day (at which no Tunisians were present) by Resident-General and Madame Périllier, he remarked that the aggressive attitude demonstrated by Salah Ben Youssef was evidence of the difficulties confronting the French in trying to work out their program.[5] Ben Youssef was a man of no education, he said, but the Bey and all the Cabinet members were afraid to say or do anything to check him.

I asked Jean Darche, an Arab specialist present, whether Ben Youssef had given a correct translation of the Bey's remarks. Darche replied that the translation had been far from correct and that the Bey had, in fact, confined himself to generalities and platitudes. Darche said that he had already reported to the Resident-General that I had handled the situation extremely well and that I had said nothing that could be interpreted as being incorrect. He added that Salah Ben Youssef's deliberate mistranslation of the Bey's remarks was evidence of the bad faith of the Neo-Destour party, with which the residency had to cope at every turn.

The Bey was at this juncture obviously a figurehead with no real role to play, and I had no doubt that his long family line was about to come to an abrupt end. Only a few months after my visit, early in 1951, the Bey was permitted by the French to issue six decrees giving a greater amount of self-rule to the Tunisian government. In 1955 agreements were signed giving Tunisia self-government in internal affairs, and in 1956 came full independence.

After my departure, the *Christian Science Monitor* commented that the Neo-Destour had been uncharacteristically quiet during my visit, and concluded from this that French efforts at political power-sharing "had proved to be a sufficient concession to the Tunisians, at least for the present." But an editorial in *Petit Matin* indicated otherwise. The writer considered it an insult to Tunisians that "the generous guests" of the regency, who came to inquire about the "last fief of French colonialism," were received at the Maison de France. After enumerating all of the countries that had obtained their independence, the editorial criticized the French government which, he said, had granted to the Tunisians merely the right to set up a ministry to conduct negotiations within the framework of the treaties imposed upon His Highness the Bey. The article concluded by denouncing the arabuscades of the "selfish colonialists of Tunisia."

Apart from my discussions, I was happy to be back in Tunisia, which I had first visited while a student at Oxford. A visit to Carthage had been arranged, although this was before the more recent extensive international excavations, so there was little new to be seen. Jack Jernegan and his vivacious wife, Mary, who were old friends from Jack's Department days when he had done a fine job of handling the difficult post of Director of Greek, Turkish and Iranian Affairs, entertained our party at their pretty villa overlooking the sea.

The career of Habib Bourguiba has been synonymous with the development of modern Tunisia. In a sense shared with only a few leaders, present and historical, he is the "father" of his country, and he is one who has taken his paternal status seriously—indeed, too seriously for some Tunisians. France ended its protectorate over Tunisia in 1956. The following year Bourguiba, then Prime Minister, deposed the Bey and established a republic, of which he became President, an office that he still holds. In 1964, he reorganized the Neo-Destour as the Destourian Socialist Party, which remains the country's only legal political organization. But Bourguiba's one-party state has produced a relatively benign authoritarian government that appropriates three times as much for education as it does for defense and allocates more for public health than for internal security.

Soon after my return to Washington from North Africa, Bourguiba came to Washington on a French passport. Since we had advised the French Embassy and they had made no protest, arrangements were made for him to meet with our officials at the country level. When the French protested, I pointed out the circumstances, including the fact that they had not objected. The affair did, however, increase French suspicions of me and NEA.[6] In developing a political base for his government, Bourguiba faced a difficult problem. At different levels, Tunisia's professional elite and urban population have been more deeply influenced by European values, transmitted by France, than their counterparts in the other Muslim societies of the Maghrib (North Africa). A middle class, large by the circumstances of most Arab countries, has benefited from a mixed economy that has been receptive to foreign participation. When conservative smallholders in the countryside protested attempts to collectivize agriculture, the project was promptly abandoned. Despite the apparent success of the Bourguiba regime in bringing Tunisia political stability, a semblance of prosperity and international respectability, the country's outstanding problem for the future is Bourguiba himself—or rather the orderly transfer of power from Bourguiba, who was born in 1903, to his successor.

I kept my contacts with the Tunisian government after independence, and President Bourguiba invited me back, along with my family, in 1965 when I was Ambassador to Germany. We stayed at the government guest house by the sea at Hammamet. The President and his wife gave a delightful luncheon for us at their residence in Tunis, and arranged for me to have a discussion with a group of students about the problems facing Tunisia. The house in which we stayed, which has been described in architectural journals as "the most beautiful in the world," was built by the late George Sebastian, a Hungarian of great artistic talent, whom we later met in Washington, who was then married to an American heiress. The entire house and outbuildings are stark white, in sharp contrast to the dark green of the surrounding cypress trees and the azure blue of the bay beyond.

The day after my visit in Tunis and discussions with the Bey, Elmer Bourgerie, Sam Kopper, and I flew to Tripolitania to meet with Sheikh Mohammed Abdul As' Ad Al Alam, Grand Mufti of Tripolitania, one of the three provinces of modern Libya. We arrived early on September 28 at the U.S. air base known as Wheelus Field, at the time a key part of the U.S. postwar base system. I toured the field with Col. Fred Easley, Commanding Officer, who entertained us later at cocktails. I was able to help him, after my return to Washington, in working out some of his base-development problems with the Air Force Planning Staff. Later we were guests of the Honorable W. Travers Blackley, British Chief Administrator, at Government House, who gave a dinner in our honor and arranged for us to meet with members of the UN Council and other foreign representatives in Libya. They provided valuable background on the important steps being taken to launch Libya as an independent state.

Libya in 1950 was a country of about a million inhabitants, all living on one-half of one percent of its land in a fertile strip along its 1,300-mile coast. Libya has over the centuries been controlled in turn by the Phoenicians, the Greeks, the Ptolemies of Egypt, Rome, the Byzantine Empire, the Vandals, the Arabs, and, since the sixteenth century, by the Turks. Italy took it from the Turks in 1912 but did not fully subdue the country until 1925. It was the scene of important battles during the war and was liberated from Italy by the Allies in December 1943. In December 1951, Libya became the second independent state created under UN auspices.

When I visited Tripolitania it was still under military rule. The Grand Mufti was the spiritual ruler of this major province, whose principal city, Tripoli, had about 150,000 inhabitants. Tripoli was also the seat of the temporal ruler, Sayad Mohammed Idris el Sanusi, who became King Idris I when Libya became independent. Idris I was overthrown in 1969 by a junta headed by Colonel Muammar al-Qadhaafi, who has run Libya ever since as a military dictator with strong Soviet ties. U.S. relations with Libya since Qadhaafi came to power have been affected by the vicissitudes of the U.S. oil companies who developed Libya's extensive oilfields, and the antagonistic and aggressive attitude of its radical and anti-Zionist ruler.

My Libyan contacts in 1950 were limited to the Grand Mufti. The question of Libya's future was at this time under active discussion at the UN. The UN Commissioner for Libya, Dr. Adrian Pelt of the Netherlands, in consultation with the UN Advisory Council for Libya—of which the U.S. was a member—had submitted his report in September. Along with reports by the U.K. and France, as administering powers, Pelt's report would be considered by the Ad Hoc Political Committee in October.

Libya's future had been a hot international issue since the end of the war, when the country's three divisions had been left to military administration, Cyrenaica and Tripolitania to the British and Fezzan to the French. In 1948, when the Allies were unable to reach an agreement, Libya's fate was put in the hands of the General Assembly of the UN. On March 21, 1949, by UN resolution, it was decided that Libya should become an independent and sovereign state as soon as possible, and in no event later than January 1, 1951. In preparation, the Council of Libya had formed a twenty-one-member Preparatory Committee, with representatives from the three territories, under the presidency of the Grand Mufti of Tripolitania. This had occurred in April 1950, some five months before my visit.

In June, I had told Pelt that the U.S. was opposed to any continuing UN control after independence. This had been decreed by the UN majority, which had declared that Libya was capable of exercising its sovereignty. I defended the British subvention of Libya as being comparable to the British position in Jordan, which was accepted by the Arabs. I characterized opposition to the British position as being a straight Communist line. Libya needed help in standing on its own feet and adopting a constitution which would protect Libyan rights and interests.[7]

In my meeting with the Grand Mufti, I asked him how the U.S. government could help Libya.[8] He replied that Libya was a poor but vast territory, fit for pastures and agriculture, and that its undersoil might contain mineral resources. It would be useful, he said, to have American experts carry out surveys in Libya so the wealth of the country could be better developed. I pointed out that President Truman's Point Four Program had that very objective, and the program included Libya. The Mufti stressed that Libya was relying upon the U.S. for aid, adding that my visit was proof of U.S. concern toward the country.

I queried the Grand Mufti about other fields in which the U.S. might help. He suggested that we could send teachers and open schools as had been done elsewhere in the Middle East (Lebanon, Egypt, etc.). He observed that the U.S., which had once pursued a policy of isolation, was now concerned with helping free nations surmount their economic crises. In this connection the Grand Mufti also said that both the chief UN administrator and Mr. Scott, Director of Education, had good intentions to improve educational conditions in the territory but lacked sufficient funds.

I then asked the Grand Mufti if he was satisfied with progress made in the political field since the passage of the UN resolution. He replied that he was, but expressed fear that foreign powers with territorial objectives in the country would create obstacles. He mentioned specifically France and Italy, adding that Great Britain and the U.S. had no such aims. I assured him our desire was to see the establishment of a unified Libyan state.

The Mufti praised our representative, Lewis Clark, for his work on the UN Council for Libya. He was surprised, however, that the Fezzan, a region of only 40,000 inhabitants, could be considered by the UN to be equal to Tripolitania with its 750,000 people, and Cyrenaica with 250,000. I pointed out that the U.S. also had a federal government with some states having small populations, but that they were all represented by an equal number of senators in the American Congress. Somewhat exasperated, the Mufti emphasized that Tripolitanians had no direct contact with the people of the Fezzan, and remarked that it would be easier to cross the Iron Curtain and penetrate into Russia than to enter the Fezzan. He wondered how Tripolitania and the Fezzan would be able to live in harmony after independence.

The Grand Mufti then declared that Communism had been forced to retreat and that its policy of world domination had been defeated by the U.S. By assisting and supporting the countries of Europe and elsewhere to overcome their postwar crises, we had kept Communism and its destructive ideology away from them. I responded that I was glad to hear this from the Grand Mufti and emphasized that the U.S. was sparing no effort to save the free countries of the world from the Communist plague. The American government would continue to do its best through the UN to remove the obstacles facing Libya. My government wanted to be a friend of the Libyan people and wanted to cooperate with them.

Regarding Wheelus Field, I assured the Mufti that the U.S. government was not keeping it with the aim of interfering in the affairs of Libya. I pointed out that the money we spent on the field constituted an asset for Libya. The Grand Mufti agreed and observed that the Libyans considered themselves to be lucky that the Americans were maintaining Mellaha air base. The enemies of Libya would never dare to attack the country for fear of America, he conjectured.

The meeting, although somewhat perfunctory because of the limited power of the Mufti, was useful as background for our forthcoming conference in Tangier, where participants urged a clarification of the British role in Libya and closer cooperation between Britain and France in fulfilling the UN resolution for an independent Libya. As useful as they were in helping to prepare our group for the upcoming Tangier conference, the visits with the Bey and the Grand Mufti, as representatives of an era fast drawing to a close, gave little clue to the subsequent evolution of events and personalities in this vital part of the Middle World.

Despite their somewhat common history, the relations that Tunisia and Libya have subsequently maintained with the U.S. have been radically different. Tunisia has remained a close U.S. friend, although Bourguiba has been disappointed by our support of Israel. On most other issues, nevertheless, we have been able to count on Tunisian support, and Bourguiba has looked upon us as a friendly nation. The situation in Libya is quite another matter. Since the overthrow of King Idris by Qadhaafi and his Free Officers Movement in 1969, U.S.-Libyan relations have experienced a steady decline, which hit a new low in early 1982, when it was rumored but never proven, that Qadhaafi had organized a "hit squad" to assassinate President Ronald Reagan.

Libya has played an active role in international, and especially regional, affairs. Qadhaafi is a firm supporter of the Palestine Liberation Organization and an equally firm opponent of U.S. policy in the Middle East. In 1975 Libya's relations with the U.S. were strained when we refused to permit the export of military aircraft to Libya, owing to the belief that Qadhaafi was supporting terrorist groups. He then turned to the Soviet Union to purchase the military equipment he sought. Our relations have subsequently worsened as a result of a Libyan attack on U.S. planes over international waters, and the abortive seizure by Libya of Chad. As a fervent Muslim, Qadhaafi has not embraced Soviet-style Communism, but his rule in Libya has been typical of the phenomenon known as "Arab socialism." Libya's capacity to play its capricious role can be attributed largely to its hefty revenues from oil, which was discovered in large quantities by U.S. oil companies in the late 1950s.

21

The Embattled Sultan

Visit to Rabat, Morocco, King Mohammed V,
September 29–October 1, 1950.

My visit to the Moroccan capital of Rabat in the fall of 1950 was one of those occasions that, in hindsight, demonstrate the role of chance and luck in diplomacy. My four days there had been intended merely as a formal stopover on my way to the Tangier Conference, held October 2–7. The U.S. had in mind no particular modification of its relations with the Moroccan government, which at the time had Sultan Mohammed Ben-Youssef as its titular head, but was in fact run as a French protectorate under the governorship of General Alphonse Juin.

I personally felt that governing Morocco as a virtual colony in 1950, when the colonial era was fast drawing to a close, was a serious mistake on the part of the French. But the U.S. government position was not to interfere with French hegemony in the country, even though we wanted to let the Sultan know that we were keenly interested in the future of Morocco. My talks with both Juin and the Sultan followed these guidelines. But a mere four months later, when a crisis developed in French-Moroccan relations, the U.S. intervened on the side of the Sultan, a role that we might not have played had it not been for the personal contacts I had established with Juin and the Sultan, almost by chance, shortly before.

Morocco, a country with a present population of twenty-one million persons of Berber and Arab stock, has long been a strategic vortex. Located in the northwest corner of Africa, it is the one Arab-African nation geographically closest to Western Europe, separated from Spain only by the narrow Strait of Gibraltar. Its history as an independent political entity goes back twelve hundred years, and oddly enough the only time when Morocco was not independent was in the twentieth century, from 1912 to 1956.

Interest in Moroccan affairs heightened during the nineteenth century as the European powers went about the business of carving out their spheres of influence. France's control over Morocco's neighbor Algeria led to an informal understanding among the so-called Great Powers that French predominance in Morocco, like Britain's in Egypt, would not be questioned. In 1912, after increasing French control was met by bloody resistance from the Moroccans, a formal regime was established whereby France held total control over Morocco's finances, armed forces, and foreign policy; Spain controlled the northern coastal area that bordered on the strait; and the city of Tangier was assigned the special status of "international zone." The Sultan was to remain as spiritual leader and titular head of the government.

By the 1920s an independence movement had begun to grow, drawing on Islamic nationalism and on the sentiments of French-educated Moroccans of the upper classes, who organized a secular nationalist movement. The French refused to act on a Plan of Reform urged by the independence movement in 1934, and as tension mounted in the wake of the refusal, the French administration acted to suppress the movement.

A decade later, after Morocco had participated in the war effort in support of the Allied cause, Moroccans were disappointed to discover that France intended to rule the country as a quasi-colony. A broad-based independence movement, the Istiqlal (Independence) Party, was formed in 1944 to struggle for complete independence from France. The movement had the support not only of Morocco's Islamic leaders and its middle class, but also of the Sultan, Mohammed V. Following a violent incident in which French police killed several hundred Moroccan nationalists in Casablanca, the Sultan delivered a speech in Tangier in April 1947 calling for self-government.

The French were incensed, and responded by sending the hard-line, hawkish General Juin to be the new Resident-General. An impasse quickly developed: Juin refused to accede to any nationalist demands for reform, and Sultan Mohammed V declined to sign most of the decrees presented to him by Juin. It was into this tense and potentially explosive situation that I stepped on September 29, 1950, although this was not my first experience in Morocco.

As a student at Oxford, I had in 1934 visited Tangier and the adjacent mountainous area known to Moroccans as the Riff, which is unforgettably picturesque. We entered the Spanish zone of Morocco to see the old Portuguese stronghold of Ceuta and Chechaouen, a romantic village high in the Riff. Perched under the crest of a hill overlooking a deep valley, Chechaouen has been called the most extravagantly picturesque town in Morocco. In moonlight, its Spanish-Moroccan architecture of glistening white walls, capped by red and blue tiles, its gushing fountains, and brilliantly flowered lush vegetation, provided an unforgettable setting—almost like a stage setting. Morocco had cast a spell over me which still exists.

This was the country of the legendary Abd el Krim, who in the early 1920s conducted one of the most remarkable anticolonial campaigns in modern history. Leading a force of Berber tribesmen, Krim, an educated man who had held posts in the colonial government before joining the rebels, founded a Riff Republic in 1923. It took the combined forces of 400,000 French and Spanish troops finally to force Krim into exile and put down the rebellion in 1926. His story served as an inspiration to the generation of Moroccan nationalists who finally liberated Morocco in 1956.

Years later, while attending an Arab League reception in Cairo in 1948, this story came to life for me when I met Krim himself, a short, stout man with a ruddy complexion and little trace of age, and heard from him some of his recollections of the five years he ruled the Riff as sovereign (and outlaw).

Fascinated by my first trip to Morocco, I had returned in 1935 to spend six months working as a geophysicist for the French firm Compagnie Générale de Géophysique, advising their local manager, M. Jabiol, on American seismic prospecting techniques. With Jabiol I visited the homes of some of the French settlers, the *colons,* who numbered 300,000 in a country of 8 million, and learned about their attitude toward the Arabs and their way of life. On hot afternoons I would sit with the planters at siesta time in their thick-walled farm homes, curtains drawn, and sip white port and water.

In the field I had working contact with the local Berbers, who were an easygoing, fatalistic lot. The answer to most problems was a shrug of the shoulders and the Arab equivalent of "So what?" translated as "It's all the same thing, nothing at all." In the field one day in a veritable treeless desert at the foot of the Moyen Atlas Mountains, with the temperature at 120 degrees, my friend, the Arab foreman, asked me what I thought of the area we were working in. Not wishing to offend, I replied equivocally that it seemed fine. He added in complete sincerity that, although he had never been anywhere else, he thought it must certainly be the best land in the world. I have often thought how fortunate he was to have felt so.

I recalled my previous visits as I landed in 1950 at the Rabat airport, which was still in disarray from the wartime activities there.[1] We were flown on a navy plane from Port Lyautey (now Kenitra) where we had been guests for lunch with Captain Thurston Clark, commanding officer of our base there. I was accompanied by Elmer Bourgerie and by Sam Kopper. Also with me was Edwin Plitt, who had served as American diplomatic agent and Consul-General in Tangier since 1947. Plitt was a colorful career officer from Baltimore, who had started out as an army engineer and had served in a series of posts in Eastern Europe. He was in full control of his interesting assignment in Tangier. We were met by John Madonne, the French-speaking U.S. Consul-General in Casablanca, and spent the evening in his villa at nearby Anfa.

After dinner we discussed U.S. objectives in Morocco. We considered Morocco of major importance because of its strategic location; its phosphate, manganese, and other mineral resources; and its historic ties with our country. Our long-range goal was the maintenance of a peaceful and stable Morocco under a regime friendly to us. We recognized that there was considerable tension and lack of understanding between the French, as protecting power, and the Moroccans, which might lead to serious unrest. The French were trying to make their zone a part of the French Union. The Sultan and the nationalist Moroccans sought an autonomous Moroccan state, independent of France, that would enjoy a greater share of Moroccan national wealth and preserve their Muslim culture. The Moroccan Communist party had not been successful in establishing any real influence.

U.S. policy was to encourage the French to proceed with political, economic, and social reforms in order to improve their relations with the Moroccans, and to help the Moroccans in their gradual evolution toward self-government. We wanted the French in the meantime to continue their responsibilities toward Morocco, and we avoided putting pressures on the French through the Moroccans. But we also maintained friendly contact with the Moroccans and sought to play a direct role in their economic development through the Marshall Plan.

In preparation for the Tangier meeting I had, in company with Elmer Bourgerie, John Utter of the Paris Embassy, and Lincoln Gordon of the ECA office in Paris, visited representatives of the French Foreign Office at the Quai d'Orsay on September 25 and 26. At the

Tangier meeting I reported that, insofar as they concerned Morocco and other French territories in North Africa, these talks had been less than satisfactory. The French appeared to be on the defensive: they were not frank and gave no evidence of a liberal policy. Although we had attempted to allay their fears concerning our own intentions, there had been no real meeting of minds.

At the conference which took place immediately after my visit to Rabat, we agreed that nationalism, although it had at times been exploited, constituted a strong force of the future in North Africa. Most American diplomats in the region thought that U.S. relations with Morocco suffered from our close association with the French. Although the strength of Communism was considered negligible, the apparent stability of the area derived mostly from repression by the conservative, uneasy French *colon* and regimes such as that of General Juin in Morocco. He considered reforms meaningless and believed that his sole function was to impose a military rule. In view of the importance of stability in the area because of possible military requirements, the Tangier meeting concluded that we should not press the French to grant more self-government lest the situation get out of hand. In the meantime, it was decided, we should reassure the French of our continued support for their predominant position in North Africa while encouraging them to carry out needed political reforms.

Although it was clear that the thrust of U.S. policy was to encourage more rapid progress toward Moroccan independence, we were not very sure about when Morocco would be ready. We did not want to expose ourselves to an open-ended commitment of assistance. France was a wartime ally and fellow member of NATO, whose cooperation was needed in Europe and in French areas of influence around the world. France was, moreover, willing and able to continue her contribution toward Moroccan development, and not just for the benefit of the resident *colons* or national gain. It was also a matter of French national pride. We did not want to disturb the French.

It was with these guidelines in mind that I paid a call, the day after my arrival, on Juin, who had invited me and three embassy and consular officials to lunch at his residence. Born in Algeria, son of a French gendarme and a Corsican mother, Juin was a career officer, a graduate of St. Cyr, a classmate of de Gaulle, and stood at the head of his class list. As commander-in-chief of Vichy French forces in North Africa he had deserted the pro-German Marshal Pétain, joined the

Allies, and proven himself a brilliant commander. A tough, hard soldier, he was at a later time suspected of planning a coup in France which would have made him dictator. He had been sent to Morocco to get things in hand after the famous Moroccan uprising called the "Casablanca Affair."

Juin's conversation was terse and to the point. He displayed the characteristic French-Algerian feeling of condescension toward the Moroccans. He is reported to have described himself as "the last uncrowned King in the world." His whole outlook was in sharp contrast to that of Marshal Louis Lyautey, who had established the French protectorate in 1912 and who had endeared himself to the Moroccans while making a remarkable record as High Commissioner. Lyautey had expounded his philosophy in an eloquent treatise on "The Social Role of the Officer." His aim had been to pacify and modernize Morocco without destroying Moroccan culture. French cities had been placed at a suitable distance from the Moroccan population centers, leaving the Moroccans free to continue their traditional culture.

Juin obviously considered my visit an unwanted intrusion, a bother, and wanted to finish our official meeting as quickly as possible and get on to lunch. He exuded confidence. When I asked him about progress in developing the economy and furthering mass education, he evinced no real knowledge or interest. He rather abruptly asked an assistant to bring the statistics on schoolrooms added during the past year, which seemed to me a pitifully small number.

I assured Juin that we had no desire to encroach upon French responsibilities under their protectorate. We understood that Morocco posed many problems for France. On the other hand, it was agreed by all that France's duty was to lead the Moroccan people into eventual self-government and independence. This, I suggested, could not be done without a great increase in educational opportunities. I also remarked that the standard of living, particularly among the nomadic and agricultural population, remained appallingly low. It was not a very pleasant meeting. Juin was not used to receiving visitors who questioned French policy.

Later we lunched on the terrace of his villa looking through white Moorish arches to the sea. The menu, in best tradition, was impeccable: Oeufs Mollet à la Russe, Chateaubriand, Pommes Paille, Terrine de Perdrix, salad, and Glace Plombière. I attempted to probe in a tactful way what more the French could do to speed up the timetable for Moroccan independence. I made it clear that we welcomed the contribution that France was making, indeed, that only France could make. We parted on more friendly terms.

In preparing for my meeting with the Sultan I had reviewed Moroccan history. Islam had been brought to the Berbers of the Maghrib, as North Africa is called, by Ugba Ibn Nafi in 683, fifty-one years after the death of the Prophet Mohammed. Berbers and Arabs have lived together since, under six dynasties, the last being the Alawites, who assumed power in 1666. Mohammed V, or Sidi Mohammed Ben Youssef (meaning the son of Sultan Youssef), was the fifteenth of the Alawites Dynasty. Although he was the youngest son of the pro-French Sultan Mulai Youssef Ben Hassan, he had been chosen to succeed to the throne at the tender age of sixteen by the *ulama*, the doctors of Islamic law, on the death of his father in 1927.

Juin, who was in effect Foreign Minister to the Sultan, normally did not permit him to receive foreign visitors. My audience was a concession, made more difficult by the French suspicion of U.S. motives in Morocco which had been aroused by President Franklin D. Roosevelt's private meeting with the Sultan during the Casablanca Conference of January 1943. The Sultan had already made clear his pro-Americanism after the American landings in Casablanca in November 1942. Urged to take flight, he replied, "The Americans are my friends. I will meet them here." At Casablanca, Roosevelt, who had presented the Sultan a high-powered automobile, had made clear America's keen interest in the future of Morocco and had given the Sultan the impression that we would support Moroccan independence. Roosevelt followed this with two letters along the same lines before his untimely death in April 1945.

Mohammed V had become increasingly unhappy about Juin's reluctance to proceed with the granting of his promised "full rights" and "eventual freedom." On several occasions the Sultan, emboldened by the rapid growth of the Istiqlal party, had withheld his signature from Juin's decrees. The Sultan opened free schools at his own expense and took what limited measures he could to prepare Morocco for statehood. Following the signing of the North Atlantic Treaty in 1950, the French had granted the Sultan the right to a personal cabinet, as a contribution toward stabilizing Morocco in anticipation of prospective U.S. air bases there.

Our visit was set for 5:30 P.M. The royal palace is located on the south side of Rabat near the Babaer, a gate with rooms above restored in the eighteenth century. The palace, although begun at the same time, was built largely after the French occupation. In addition to the Sultan's quarters, it housed the Supreme Court, offices of the President of the Council, a mosque, and an oratory, all surrounded by extensive gardens. We went through a high alabaster entrance hall and were received in the throne room. The Sultan sat on a low gilded chaise in a tiled recess. Jacques de Blesson, Secretary General to Juin, presented us, otherwise was merely an observer. M. Marchant, diplomatic counselor to the Resident General, and other French officials, also attended.

I was deeply impressed by Mohammed V, who has subsequently been recognized as the father of modern Morocco and is remembered with a magnificent mausoleum in Rabat near the famous twelfth-century Hassan Tower. Dressed in a long white robe and a white hood, he had a handsome, gentle face with an aura of intense sincerity. He was careful in the formulation of his words, and despite his natural dignity, there was no trace of condescension in his manner; there was, indeed, a touch of humility. Speaking in Arabic, which was translated into French and then English, as my remarks were also first translated into French and then Arabic, Mohammed V welcomed me to Morocco and expressed appreciation for the visit of a high American official to his country.[2]

Although I had no specific instructions from my government, my purpose, seven years after the Roosevelt visit, was to make clear our continuing interest in Morocco and give the Sultan new hope for our support in the future. I wanted to avoid, however, creating a problem with the French, whose representative was present and listening carefully. Under the circumstances, there was not much of a specific nature that either I or the Sultan could say. I attempted to convey my message more by empathy, through a friendly manner. The Sultan, for his part, without violating the rules under which he reigned, sought to express clearly to me the importance he attached to American interest in his country, and what it could mean for the future. I expressed pleasure at being in Morocco again and emphasized how much we valued our friendship with His Majesty and his people. The U.S., I said, attached increasing importance to our relationships with Morocco. We were fully aware of its strategic significance. We appreciated the Moroccan contribution during the recent war. I was sure the Moroccans could be counted on if there was another aggression.

The Sultan recalled the bond which had developed between the Moroccans and the American soldiers following the American landings in 1942. He had greatly enjoyed his visit with President Roosevelt, who had subsequently become a person of historic stature. He asked me to convey his best wishes to Mr. Truman, as President of a great nation which played an important role in world affairs. The Sultan said that we could rely on the friendship of the Moroccan people; that it dated back a long time; indeed, the Moroccan government had been the first to recognize the U.S. as an independent country.

In order to placate the French representatives present and put in perspective our position in the triangular relationship represented by our meeting, I also referred to our traditional friendship with France. I noted that France had assisted us in obtaining our independence. The Sultan responded that his country also owed a debt to France, which had greatly helped its economic development.

There followed a discussion of the Communist threat, not only to Morocco but to the peace of the world. I observed that we considered Islam an important barrier against the spread of Communism. We felt that the Muslim religion was by its nature antipathetic to Communism. The Sultan agreed that the tenets of Islam were fundamentally opposed to the Communist philosophy. God-worshiping people could never have anything in common with the godless. I emphasized our world-wide commitments in the struggle against Communism, which made it impossible to concentrate on any one region. The Sultan replied that he was fully aware of our widespread efforts. He congratulated us on the success of our troops in Korea.

I complimented the Sultan on the great progress made in Morocco since my last visit there fifteen years ago. Much development had taken place. Excellent roads had been built and better housing for city residents had been created. The adverse effects of the war on Morocco had been overcome and the lot of the average Moroccan had improved. I commented on Morocco's rich cultural background, adding that there was much we could learn from the art of Islam. I referred to the beauty of the Sultan's palace and the magnificent early mosques and schools of Fez and Marrakech.

The Sultan then told me about his projected trip to France. He expected much good to come of it, particularly from the opportunity to exchange views with the President of France. He hoped that the visit would result in better French-Moroccan understanding. (Neither of us realized at the time that this visit would end in failure, and the importance of ensuing events.)

In closing I asked if there was any specific way in which we could be helpful to Morocco. We stood ready to assist in any way we could. Mindful, I was sure, of the presence of de Blesson, he replied that we had been informed of the needs of Morocco. He left it to us.

The Sultan then presented me with a signed photograph. I had sent him, in advance, one of the early tape-recording machines; however, in accordance with Islamic custom regarding gifts, neither of us referred to it. He said that he would like to present me with his highest award, the Order of Ouissam Alaouite, in the grade of grand officer. However, he understood that our government regulations forbade my accepting it. He then rose from his throne and terminated the meeting with the exchange of the usual courtesies.

Later, on March 21, 1951, through the U.S. Legation in Tangier, the Sultan sent me a certificate of the award he had referred to in our meeting to use when I was free to accept it.[3] The certificate and citation read as follows:

> The badge of glory is a precious lustre which causes man to shine with a dazzling light here below.
>
> If you wish to be honored by your fellow-men proudly wear the insignia of our Dynasty.
>
> Praises to God alone! Nothing else is lasting except His authority!
>
> (Stamp of the Great Seal of the Sultan of Morrocco bearing the following inscription:)
>
> "Mohammed Ben Youssef Ben El-Hassen; God is his Protector; He who asks the assistance of him who is the Messenger of God—would awe the lions in their own dens; He who seeks refuge in you, on the most noble of creatures, God will protect him against all perils."
>
> By the Grace of God and His power, we bestow to the friend of our Majesty.
>
> Mr. George McGhee
> Assistant Secretary of State of the United States
>
> the second rank (Grand Officer) of the Order of Ouissam Alaouite Sherifian, in recognition of his merits. That he wear it proudly and that he look upon it as a

token of the respect and esteem in which he is held by
Our Majesty.

Done in our Capital of Rabat, February 7, 1950

Our consulate in Tangier made the following comments on the
meeting to the department:[4]

The meeting between Assistant Secretary of State McGhee and the
Sultan exceeded the customary 30 or 40 minutes usually allotted by
palace protocol to such courtesy visits by more than a half hour, but
the Sultan seemed quite content and anxious to have the meeting continue for a longer period of time. Throughout the meeting it was evident that the Sultan was somewhat inhibited by the presence of French
officials, but as it progressed he seemed to relax considerably and shed
some of the imperial restraint and formality that was evident in the
early part of the interview.

Some of the Sultan's remarks were somewhat complimentary to the
French, but at the same time he lost no opportunity to extol the merits
of the United States Government and its people. It was also evident
that the visit would be interpreted broadly by Moroccans as a means of
lending emphasis to the view that Morocco is still considered as a
sovereign state even though for the present, it is under French and
Spanish protection in two zones, and under an international administration at Tangier.

The U.S. Vice-Counsel in Rabat reported:[5]

Although the meeting took place under terms of strict protocol, it
was nevertheless extremely useful for U.S. relations in Morocco. It can
only be concluded that the net result of the Secretary's remarks will be
to improve relations with both the French and Moroccan elements in
this country. Moroccans should take comfort from the extraordinarily
friendly remarks which the Secretary made regarding the feeling of
the U.S. for the people of this nation, while the French should be
likewise gratified by his very friendly references to present and past
relations between France and the United States.

My visit occurred at a critical juncture in Moroccan history, in
which I was, as a result, able to play a role. The Sultan had referred
in our meeting to his visit to France eleven days thence at the invitation of Vincent Auriol, the French President. The visit was much
criticized in Morocco, but on his arrival in Paris on October 11, the

Sultan received a tremendous ovation from the French populace. He was fêted and accorded every honor. Nevertheless, he took advantage of his freedom from Juin to present to the French government a note of his grievances, which he followed up in words.

A Moroccan spokesman told the press: "In forty years the world has changed. The Moroccan people cannot remain indifferent to the examples of India and Egypt." Although he received in reply written assurances of minor reform, no reference was made to progress toward Moroccan sovereignty, the need for which he emphasized in a second note. When he received no further reply, he returned abruptly to Morocco on November 5, to a warm welcome from his people but concern on the part of Juin and the *colons*.

The *New York Times* reported on October 12 from Paris that the Sultan had, in his conversation with President Auriol on the preceding day, asked for more personal power, including full power over the central government to appoint all pashas, caids (tribal chieftains), and cadis (magistrates), and had requested that his personal cabinet receive powers hitherto exercised by the central government. General Juin, it was reported, strongly opposed these demands. The article reported further that "Despite denials emanating from the French Foreign Office, divergences have characterized French relations not only with the Sultan and his entourage but also with diplomatic representatives of the United States." These have resulted from the "frequent contention that the best way to block the expansion of Communism in North Africa is to encourage Arab nationalism, a view that the French attribute to George C. McGhee, Assistant Secretary of State, who visited Morocco late in September, and to Edwin A. Plitt, U.S. Minister in Tangier."

Upon my return to Washington, I met with French Ambassador Henri Bonnet and described to him in very frank terms the bad impression I had received from Juin during my visit to Morocco. I advised Under Secretary David Bruce that I thought there would be real trouble if Juin continued to quarrel with the Sultan.[6]

During the last week of January, three months later, Juin was required to accompany the French Premier on an official visit to Washington. On January 26, just before his departure, he called on the Sultan and, after a stormy meeting, declared—apparently on his own initiative since he had been given carte blanche in dealing with the Sultan—that the Sultan must either denounce the nationalist Istiqlal party or abdicate. He gave the Sultan until his return from Washington to decide.

The ultimatum shocked not only Morocco but the entire Arab world. Taking advantage of my recent visit, I obtained approval from the Department and President Truman to meet with Juin and tell him we supported the Sultan. French and State Department representatives were present when he called on me on March 31.[7] I referred to his ultimatum and told him clearly that the U.S. opposed any French move to depose the Sultan. I added that Juin's demands that the Sultan denounce the Istiqlal party had put the Sultan in an untenable position. Moreover, in view of Mohammed V's popularity, his departure would result in a severe setback in French relations with Morocco and French efforts to prepare Morocco for independence. Although we would be reluctant because of our close ties with France, we would, if Juin persisted, be forced to denounce the threatened action publicly and declare our support for the Sultan. With much bluster Juin attempted to minimize the affair. "I know how to handle the Sultan. You will see." After making a strong defense of French policy in Morocco Juin concluded, "The Sultan must condemn the Istiqlal party or the people will throw him out."

I again expressed U.S. opposition to any French move to depose the Sultan. The U.S. would be severely embarrassed if Arab League members raised this matter in the U.N., and we could not assure the French of our support there if France took arbitrary action against the Sultan. Juin gave the impression that he was absolutely uncompromising on this issue. The meeting was friendly; I attempted to convey our position as tactfully as possible. However, Juin showed his resentment at what he considered our interference with French responsibility in Morocco.

To make our position very clear we advised our Embassy in Paris, for their discussions with the French Foreign Office, as follows:[8]

> France does not have unqualified US support in their confrontation with the Sultan and we will say this publicly if our position is misrepresented. We are concerned over the effect on the stability of Morocco of the French threat to remove the Sultan. If the French take such action the US will publicly oppose it. If the question is raised in the UN we will not support France. We are not advocating immediate independence for Morocco, only an evolution of the present situation.

Juin was still in Washington when he received a report of our Embassy's follow-up démarche with comment by the Quai d'Orsay. He was furious. By the time he returned to Rabat, however, he is reported to have been in a chastened mood. There was no more talk of forcing the Sultan to abdicate. That was to come two years later, after the French government, following much criticism of Juin in France, replaced him with General Augustin Guillaume. After a meeting in August 1953, in which he attempted but failed to persuade the Sultan to abdicate, Guillaume had his security chief escort the Sultan at gunpoint to an ignominious exile, first in Corsica and then in Madagascar.

The exile turned out to be a catalyst for Moroccan independence. Moroccans were furious at this action and the nationalist movement became stronger than ever. Finally Mohammed V returned in triumph from exile in November of 1955, and independence was declared on March 2, 1956. When I later recounted my intercession with Juin in 1950 to the first Moroccan Ambassador to the U.S., he smiled wryly and told me that, by delaying the King's exile, "you merely delayed our independence by two years."

In his memoirs Acheson describes the difficult position he was put in during this period with his French opposite number, Robert Schuman, who considered the U.S. uncooperative with France's North African policy even though they had granted us vital Moroccan air bases and were trying to make Morocco a modern democratic state within the French Union.[9] Acheson wrote:

> It was all so reasonable and so utterly hopeless. Opinion in the Department was united on the continued need for French influence and guidance in Morocco and in nearby Tunisia and on the ineffectiveness of current French policy in accomplishing that result. The European and Near Eastern divisions differed on the practicality and wisdom of pressing the French Government to the extent necessary to adoption of the extreme measures the situation demanded. The European Division believed—probably correctly—that the Government would see such a decision as its own death warrant; the Near Eastern Division [meaning me] believed—less demonstrably—that anything short of it would mean the end of French influence in Morocco. I made an understandable, but possibly the worst, decision—to push Schuman hard enough to annoy but not hard enough to succeed. To both our short- and long-term interest there did not seem to be much difference between success and failure.

My visit to Morocco was, I believe, a typical example of U.S. policy dilemmas in the immediate postwar period. It reflected overconfidence in our ability to solve the manifold problems emerging from the war, many with origins going back further than our national existence. My own experience as Coordinator of Greek-Turkish Aid, by which we succeeded in helping the Greeks overcome the Communist guerrilla threat, had undoubtedly contributed to my own personal overconfidence. We were first and foremost worried about stopping the spread of Communism. The deep American prejudice against colonialism was also always clearly in evidence, whether spoken or not. We considered education and economic development the key to the solution of all problems. Democracy was accepted without question as everyone's final goal.

My visit undoubtedly gave the French an unwanted nudge toward liberalizing their Moroccan regime. On the other hand it is ironical that, by intervening directly in their crisis with the Sultan, I relieved them of facing the consequences of their intended actions, thereby delaying the day when they would be forced to account for them. The ways of history are often obscure.

Mohammed V was to rule for a decade after my visit, until 1961, when he died of natural causes and his thirty-two-year-old son Hassan II succeeded to the throne. Hassan survived two major coup attempts, in 1971 and 1972, and attempted to introduce a form of parliamentary democracy to Morocco, although he reverted to ruling by fiat between 1965 and 1970.

Hassan has played a moderating influence in Arab-Israeli relations, by on the one hand supporting Arab states threatened by Israeli aggression, and on the other backing Egypt's Anwar Sadat in his 1977 peace negotiations with Israel. Hassan's regime is nonaligned, but Morocco's longstanding ties with France, its proximity to Western Europe, and the large amounts of aid it has received from Western countries have meant closer ties with the West than with Eastern-bloc countries.

Since 1976 Morocco has been embroiled in a bitter dispute over a formerly Spanish-controlled territory known as the Western Sahara, where large phosphate deposits were discovered in 1963. Along with Morocco, neighboring Algeria and Mauritania began to push for an end to Spanish colonial control in the region during the mid-1960s. But Morocco and Mauritania both wanted the region for themselves, claiming historical possession, while Algeria supported the indigenous independence movement, the Polisario Front. Despite attempts to intercede, over the past fifteen years, by the UN, the Arab League, the Organization of African Unity, and several individual nations, Morocco continued to fight a war of attrition with the Polisario forces, and its relations with Algeria deteriorated as a result. Attempts to bring the Polisario Front into the OAU have caused Morocco to threaten withdrawal from the regional organization, thus imperiling its unity.

Morocco's relations with the U.S., however, have continued to be quite good. A considerable amount of U.S. assistance funds have gone into agricultural and industrial development programs, and the U.S. has supported loans to Morocco by multilateral agencies. I cannot help but look back to the period of our intercession on behalf of Mohammed V as a key moment in the history of relations between our two countries.

22

Conference on North Africa

Tangier, Morocco, October 2–7, 1950.

Following my visit to Morocco September 29–October 1, I presided over a conference of our diplomatic and consular representatives in North Africa from October 2 to 7 in the picturesque old city of Tangier.[1] Our meetings were held in the historic buildings which had for many years served as the offices of our diplomatic agent. These have now been made into a museum, whose board includes a number of former American diplomats stationed in Morocco and interested in Morocco, like myself.

Although legally accepted as part of Morocco's Sherifian Empire, the city of Tangier, with its long turbulent history, had for centuries been dominated by foreign governments and carried overtones of intrigue and mystery. The narrow streets of the Kasbah, filled with Arab men dressed in white robes and veiled women, lent enchantment. The ancient Roman city of Tingis was located near the present site of Tangier on the Strait of Gibraltar, seven miles east of the beautiful pine-covered Caps Spartel. Tingis had become a free city under Augustus, and was held in succession by the Vandals, Byzantine Greeks, and Arabs. The city fell to the Portuguese in 1471, and was later presented to England in 1662 as part of the dowry for Catherine of Braganza's marriage to Charles II. But the English in 1684 abandoned Tangier to the Moors.

To control local terrorists, the Conference of Algeciras in 1906 placed it and its police force under the control of Europeans. In 1913, Great Britain, France, and Spain, all interested in Tangier's potential role in the defense of Gibraltar, drew up a convention creating an international regime in the city. The agreement survived, in various forms, until Tangier was incorporated into newly independent Morocco in 1956. During our visit in 1950, Tangier was, insofar as the residual rights of the Sultan were concerned, under the control of the pleasant, rotund Mendoub of Tangier, acting as the Sultan's local viceroy.

I stayed in the charming El Minzah Hotel, along with the other delegates. It was built in the Spanish style around a courtyard surrounded by an arcade. We spent happy respites from our work on the hotel's vine-covered terraces. On the first evening of the conference we were entertained by two legation couples at a residence on New Mountain Road, which had a fine view of the Atlantic. There was present a congenial group of new arrivals for the conference, and representatives of the legation and the Tangier international community.

The meetings started promptly at nine each morning and continued until seven in the evening, with two hours out for lunch, for six days. The junior officers of the legation and their wives gave a cocktail party for the group on October 4; the French Minister and Madame de Panaflou and Ed Plitt gave dinners for separate groups on October 5. On October 3, Plitt gave a small midday reception to introduce us to members of the Committee of Control, leading officials of the International Administration and local consular representatives. On the morning of the 2nd I was received at his residence by the Mendoub, His Excellency Ahmed Tazi, who invited me to a *diffa*, or Moroccan luncheon, on the 4th. The Mendoub, although somewhat of a figurehead, was a charming and friendly host. His villa, which has since been acquired by Malcolm Forbes, publisher of *Forbes Magazine,* was of striking and authentic Moorish architecture with a magnificent view of the Atlantic.

But it was the luncheon that I will always remember. It was by all odds the most delicious Moroccan meal, perhaps any meal, I have ever enjoyed. I was told that its preparation took a week. We sat on cushions while at least seven delicate dishes were brought, one by one, by a large staff of servants. I remember particularly a delicious dish of rice with almonds and slices of orange. I was to have many excellent Moroccan meals but none that equaled this luncheon.

On the sixth, Ed and Jeanne Plitt reciprocated with a dinner for nearly seventy-five people at the El Minzah in honor of the Mendoub; it was attended by the members of the conference as well as by the French and British Ministers. The menu of Filet de Sole au Fours, Tournedos Grillé Henry IV, and Omelette Norvégienne was a worthy response. The Portuguese minister invited our group to his National Day reception. One afternoon several of us visited the American

School, which a number of enterprising American businessmen and other residents had opened for children at the primary level. I was so impressed by their efforts I contributed to their fund. I also inspected the important Voice of America relay station located twenty-one miles southwest of Tangier.

During the conference we worked very hard, but brief occasions were afforded for sightseeing. I spent what time I had exploring the narrow streets of the old city, ducking into small shops and cafés. I was able to purchase a number of Moroccan objects, which would later form the nucleus of a Moroccan collection that has grown over the years. My purchases included a fine gold-and-silver-brocaded robe and several examples of "Fezware" ceramics, including some of the blue variety. Often I would sit alone among Moors who were smoking themselves into relaxation with their water pipes. The atmosphere imparted by a Moorish city has never ceased to fascinate me.

The day after my arrival I gave a press conference. Although it was too early to say anything concrete, I did want to respond to the representatives of the press, given the great interest they had shown in the conference, and try to cool down speculation on its purposes. I characterized the conference as a means of making contacts, exchanging views, and transmitting recommendations, not to make decisions.

The conference itself comprised some sixty representatives, including the Honorable Richard Butrick, Director General of the Foreign Service, and Elmer Bourgerie, Samuel Kopper, Norman Burns, Ruth Sloan, and Vernon McKay from the Bureau of Near Eastern, South Asian, and African Affairs in Washington. Foreign Service officers present, in addition to Plitt, were Lewis Clark, U.S. Representative, UN Advisory Council for Libya; Thomas Lockett, Consul-General in Algiers; John Madonne, Consul-General, Morocco; and Jack Jernegan, Consul-General in Tunis.

Admiral Richard Conolly, Commander of the American Mediterranean Fleet, joined the conference for the afternoon of October 6. Particularly in light of his responsibility for strategic planning for the Middle East, Conolly made a valuable contribution. Our naval attaché in Tangier honored Conolly and me with a pleasant luncheon that day.

After Plitt's welcoming remarks, I presented a general statement to open the conference. I began by reminding the participants of our main purpose: to discuss the broad range of U.S. interests in North Africa and to reach some conclusions as to how we should handle them. Our interests in the region were both strategic and economic. The significance of North Africa's proximity to Western Europe had become clear during World War II, when it was a key base for the Allies. In addition, North Africa was a stepping stone to the Middle East and to Africa south of the Sahara. Because of North Africa's geopolitical importance, and because events surrounding the Korean War indicated that the Soviet Union was willing to take the risk of precipitating a new war, it was time to review our policies in North Africa in this light.

The situation that confronted us throughout most of North Africa was that of a decaying colonial system in confrontation with the forces of nationalism. There was no Communist menace per se, although some nationalists had been willing to flirt with Moscow in the hopes of realizing their objectives. Our problem was to prevent the Communists from capturing the nationalist movements for their own ends. The diversity of levels of political and economic development among the North African countries made this task all the more difficult. Some countries, like Libya, were moving toward independence; others, like Morocco, were in the firm grip of a colonial power; others still, such as Somaliland, were quite backward. Our goal, I suggested, should be to assist each country in gaining the capability for exercising self-government, while at the same time not offending unnecessarily the colonial powers, who were our allies.

France, in particular, was both the principal colonial power in North Africa and the key to our strategy for the defense of Western Europe. The French had taken on certain responsibilities in North Africa that the U.S., already overextended, was not willing to assume, and North Africa was very important to France. So as a broad policy the U.S. should not take actions that might weaken the French position, and give the French the benefit of the doubt in their dealings with North African territories. On the other hand, U.S. commercial interests in North Africa would best be served by assuring an open door in the region for American trade and investment. Stability was a vital factor, I pointed out. It would be short-sighted to believe that long-range stability could be achieved through repressive measures. Thus our ultimate goal was to encourage the colonial powers to be more responsive to the needs and demands for progress of the Arab and African populations.

Both our strategic and commercial interests dictated that we bear in mind the attitude that North Africans would have toward the U.S. ten years down the road. So, under all circumstances, it was important for us to promote tolerance and respect for the human rights of the indigenous populations, and to make clear the underlying American sympathy for the aspirations of colonized peoples for independence. During the course of the conference several committees were formed to appraise the political situation in key North African countries. The results of the committees' findings were as follows.

They found that the French had taken an extremely hard line in Morocco, rebuffing the country's evident desire for independence as well as U.S. suggestions for political reform. The main goal of the French appeared to be the rapid extension of French political power and the development of the French zone, with the needs of the Moroccan people left to a secondary plane.

Under the guise of benevolent protection, the French had done everything possible to keep the Sultan in check. Moreover, they seemed to view the nationalists as a greater threat than the Communists, frequently resorting to physical repression against the nationalist movement. The nationalists themselves, however, had not shown any interest in cooperating with the Communists. Despite our efforts to convince the French that we were not working against them, they continued to be suspicious of our interest in Morocco. Although the U.S. had argued that stability might best be achieved through some concessions, the French were convinced that the Moroccan elite was not yet ready to assume power, and had given little thought to early autonomy.

French policy in Tunisia, the Committee concluded, differed markedly from that in Morocco in that there was an active reform program to promote Tunisian self-government at the national and local levels, including the formation of a cabinet with nationalist participation. Conference committee members felt that if the French were willing to follow through rapidly with the reform program, Franco-Tunisian relations would experience a meaningful détente. But if the Resident-General were to slow down the pace of reform as a concession to the French colonists, it was believed that the nationalists would probably withdraw from the cabinet and cease to cooperate.

Despite these uncertainties, committee members reported that Tunisia's overall situation was positive: economic conditions, favored by two successive years of good crops, were better than they had been before the war, and Habib Bourguiba, leader of the nationalist

Neo-Destour Party, had returned from Cairo. Communist strength was at a low ebb, and it was hoped that the flexible attitudes of Bourguiba and the French Resident-General, could serve as an example in other French-dominated Arab territories. The committee felt that problems of Franco-Algerian relations presented yet another variation on the colonial theme. Unlike Tunisia and Morocco, Algeria had been integrated into France by law, and every indication was that French officials, legislators, and residents in Algeria had no intention of considering future autonomy, much less independence, for the territory. Instead, they seemed determined to govern Algeria for the benefit of themselves and France, paying little heed to Algerian needs and brutally suppressing all nationalist activities.

French colonists were the group pressing hardest for a policy of control. They owned the best land in the country and insisted on protecting it and their dominant position, at all costs. The colonists had put aside their separatist tendencies to gain the protection of the French military. Committee members feared that France's anxiety to control nationalist forces might lead them to underestimate the potential of Communist influence and ignore the possibility that the nationalists might collaborate with Communists as a last resort. The French were sure that Muslims were so opposed to Communism that such a turn of events would be impossible.

The committee recommended that the U.S. steer a middle-of-the-road course. Although we sympathized with the Algerians' desire for political and economic advancement, we also had to continue to bolster France because of our global anti-Communist commitment. Yet the Committee pointed out that if the French remained unresponsive to the Algerians' demands for education and a higher standard of living, as well as for independence, the situation would become explosive. If the Algerians broke with the French, stability in Algeria and U.S. hopes for friendly relations with its people would be set back.

Following reports of the committees, conference participants set about the task of reaching some final conclusions and making recommendations for U.S. policy in North Africa. It was concluded that, despite the existence of a reservoir of goodwill toward the U.S. among both the Arabs and the French, our middle-of-the-road policy had not particularly endeared us to either side. The Arabs were impatient with our apparent reluctance to side with their nationalist aspirations and our willingness to support France to buy temporary security against the Soviet menace. The French, on the other hand, found our relative openness to the nationalists suspect, and viewed our encouragement of Libyan independence as a threat to their hold on Algeria, Tunisia, and Morocco. Among the Arabs, however, our prestige was probably highest in Libya, precisely because of this policy.

While the French welcomed U.S. Marshall Plan and NATO assistance to North Africa, Arab leaders viewed it as a factor helping to strengthen France's hand in the region. Opinion differed sharply over the role of the UN as well. Arab nationalists tended to look at the UN as the best forum for bringing their cause to the forefront of world opinion; the French were even more sensitive to UN criticisms of their colonial administration and resisted attempts to discuss North Africa at UN meetings. French authorities were also concerned that the Arab League might take action on the North African question. Conference participants felt that unless France showed a good-faith effort to undertake reforms, the U.S. would have little leverage with which to play a moderating role in world forums or with Arab leaders.

Although Arab nationalist forces were not in a position forcefully to threaten French domination, the conference members concluded that a continuation of repressive policies could drive them into the arms of the Communists, thus strengthening their military capability. Communism was already fairly well entrenched in North Africa and would attempt to take advantage of any crisis to embarrass the French and their allies. Despite what the French believed, and despite the uniform opposition to Communism by local leaders throughout North Africa, the conference concluded that Islam was by no means an insurmountable barrier against Communism. It was recommended that the U.S. take more positive measures to combat Communism in the region.

The conference, according to Plitt's report, aroused great interest among local diplomats, journalists, and nationalists. Although the Spanish press was not unfavorable, there was an indication that General Varella, High Commissioner of the Spanish Zone, was piqued because I had not called on him during my visit on October 8. (I had not done so because the U.S. had not established relations with the zone.) French reactions also were not unfavorable, although the French Minister in Tangier was reported to have criticized our receiving nationalist visitors at the legation. *Le Monde* of October 10 referred to the "present disquieting activity" in Morocco.

North African nationalists had placed exaggerated hopes on the conference. Manifestos had been received from the Islah, Istiqlal (Independence), and Algerian MTLD parties, and from Abd el-Krim's Committee for North African Liberation, as well as from the pro-French Moroccan Democratic Party of Sharif el Drissi. Disappointment was expressed by the nationalists because I had declined to interview them during the conference. However, they seemed to be satisfied that we held the conference in Tangier and with the results of my call on the Sultan in Rabat. All in all, Plitt, too, was satisfied, since the conference had created no demonstrations, adverse criticism, or offense to any of the political groups represented in the Tangier complex. The Acting Administrator and police of the zone must have breathed a sigh of relief when I departed for Madrid on the morning of June 9, en route to Washington.

The conference had, of course, been about the French and their relations with the Arab peoples of North Africa. Although held in Tangier, which was governed by an international regime, for the French our meeting must have been comparable to their holding a meeting in Mobile, Alabama, to examine the status of black American citizens in the South. Naturally they were highly suspicious of our motives. I came away from the meeting with deep foreboding. The French, particularly the North African *colons*, considered their colonies as properties, which they intended to hold on to and use to every possible advantage. Although Tunisia was beyond the point of no return toward independence, I could see no solution in Algeria and Morocco short of a bloody colonial war.

As I visualized the situation then, Morocco seemed to pose the greatest threat. In fact, of course, the long bloody war took place in Algeria, where because of the prestige and courage of General Charles De Gaulle, a settlement was finally reached in 1962. Algeria, however, has held itself aloof from the West ever since. Surprisingly, Moroccan independence came easily in 1956, in the aftermath of French removal of Mohammed V. Today, as a result of the statesmanship of French leadership at that time, Morocco and France enjoy a very healthy relationship to their mutual benefit. French business interests, French tourists, and French culture play an indispensable role in Morocco today.

The post-1950 history of the other North African countries have been dealt with separately in connection with my visits there. It might, however, be of interest to review in more detail what happened in Algeria. Algeria was in 1950 formally attached to metropolitan France, although the vast majority of its Muslim inhabitants were not full-fledged French citizens and did not participate in the country's political life. Therefore, it fell outside the jurisdiction of my office. Its future, vital to the stability of the region, was, however, a matter of concern to our bureau. In 1954, the National Liberation Front (FLN) opened its armed struggle to force the French out of Algeria. The brutal war that ensued was a civil war as much as it was a war of liberation, leaving an estimated one million dead in the course of eight years of gradually escalating fighting. The French army was capable of preventing an FLN victory but it could not bring the war to a successful conclusion. France itself was also sharply divided on the issue of the Algerian war, which involved the fate of nearly a million French settlers.

De Gaulle, who had been returned to power to keep Algeria French, wisely determined to cut France's losses by disengaging from a situation that defied an acceptable solution. In 1962, Algeria received its independence, setting off an exodus of 1.5 million people. These included most of the Europeans and virtually the entire Jewish community, as well as those Muslims whose support for France during the war had made continued life in Algeria untenable. A new government was formed by Ahmed Ben Bella, the political leader of the FLN, but rivalries within the nationalist organization that had surfaced even during the war brought challenges to his authority from the start. In 1965, Ben Bella was overthrown by an army officer, Colonel Houari Boumedienne, who established a military-backed regime. Boumedienne imprisoned most of the early nationalist political leaders who survived, or forced them into exile or obscurity.

Boumedienne's aims, like those of his predecessor, continued to be the maintenance of a one-party, socialist-oriented Islamic state, officially part of the non-aligned bloc but cultivating amicable relations with the Soviet Union. Over the years, Algeria has built a reputation as a leader and spokesman for the non-aligned countries. Algeria is today an important petrochemical producer and a major supplier of natural gas to the U.S. Despite the war of liberation and subsequent nationalization of French property, including French-owned petroleum interests, Algeria and France retain close ties.

Boumedienne died in 1978 and was replaced by Colonel Bejedid Chadli. The military remains the most important element in the political structure of the country, but Chadli has undertaken to moderate the authoritarian nature of the government. Although much of the old revolutionary and Marxist rhetoric remains in vogue, Algeria has also made efforts to improve its relations with the U.S., and its government acted as a valuable go-between during negotiations between the U.S. and Iran over the release of American hostages held in Teheran.

23

Greek-Turkish Entry to NATO

Middle East Chiefs of Mission Conference, Istanbul, Turkey,
February 14–21, 1951.

The second Istanbul Chiefs of Mission Conference during my tour as
Assistant Secretary took place February 14–21, 1951.[1] It was held
under quite different circumstances from that in 1949. The Middle
East had become even more critical to our security. Whereas in 1949
it had been concluded that we should not attempt to negotiate security pacts with the Middle Eastern states, by 1951 active consideration
had been given to the possible inclusion of Greece and Turkey in
NATO.

The Joint Chiefs of Staff, under the able direction of General
Omar Bradley and with the sound advice of General Joseph Collins,
Army Chief of Staff, had, however, been reluctant to extend a military guarantee to the Middle East until we had made more progress
in fulfilling our undertakings toward building up the military
strength of NATO. Denmark and Norway had been cool to the expansion of their security commitment to the volatile Middle East, but
there had been movement. Both public and intelligence sources indicated that Greece and Turkey were ripe for the acceptance of a
NATO invitation. Whereas in 1949 I had been unable to get the
Department to permit me to invite Admiral Conolly to attend our
meeting, both Admiral R. B. (Mick) Carney, Commander in Chief,
U.S. Naval Forces, Eastern Atlantic and Mediterranean, and my old
friend Secretary of the Air Force Thomas Finletter, were with us this
time.

Before leaving for Istanbul I asked for a meeting with the Joint
Chiefs of Staff.[2] They received me on February 6. Present from State
were Dean Rusk, Paul Nitze, and others. I had distributed a paper
which the Chiefs had not had a chance to study fully. My purpose

was to see how far they would let me go, in the forthcoming Istanbul meeting, in discussing an increased U.S. contribution to Middle East defense, which the Chiefs had, up to then, opposed. I pointed out the Department's growing concern over the deteriorating political situation in the Middle East. There was a threat that the smaller states in the area, increasingly concerned over their future, might defect, even in peace, if we could not provide the security assurances they wanted.

I made it clear that I did not suggest a U.S. military guarantee nor relieving the British of their primary responsibility for the area, but an insurance to protect our large military investments in Greece and Turkey by providing political stability in depth through a regional approach. Specifically, I asked for limited material assistance, five to ten million dollars, and small military missions to Syria, Lebanon, and Israel to create at least internal stability, leaving Egypt, Jordan, and Iran to the British, who had treaties with them. I proposed creating a U.S.-U.K. coordinating mechanism for the Middle East as a whole.

In the course of an extended discussion Admiral Forrest Sherman, representing the Navy, and General Collins, for the Army, argued against extending our limited U.S. military strength further in the Middle East at that time. Sherman wanted to keep the defense of Greece and Turkey separate from the rest of the Middle East. Collins wanted us to concentrate first on the defense of Western Europe and not relieve the British of their overall responsibility for the Middle East. General Bradley, however, tended toward the position that, since we were already in Greece, Turkey, and Iran on a large scale, a small diversion to other Middle Eastern countries was justified. He saw it as strictly a Cold War problem. He said, "The more solid we can keep an area the better off we are. I can see great advantages in this." It "would tend to increase our influence in depth."

In the end, however, the Chiefs would only agree to an NSC paper to study the problem from the Cold War viewpoint. All agreed, however, that the British should not be involved in coordination with us in Greece and Turkey, and that although nominally responsible, the British capability for defending the rest of the Middle East was very limited. I had pointed out that this involved only 11,000 men concentrated on defending the Suez. It was on this note that I left, soon after, for our conference in Istanbul.

Following this meeting I sought to clarify the situation by directing an NEA paper to the National Security Council on "U.S. policy toward the Arab States and Israel."[3] It recommended that the U.K. and the U.S. should, on a coordinated basis, seek the right to operate forces in the states involved upon the threat or initiation of hostilities, help the states develop suitable fighting techniques, initiate limited arms supplies to selected countries, and on request send small military advisory and training groups. The U.S. should, at the same time, accelerate economic and technical assistance to improve the morale of the people.

Officials accredited to individual countries and organizations attending the conference included U.S. representative on the UN Relief and Works Agency, Ambassador John B. Blandford; Ambassador to Syria, Cavendish Cannon; Ambassador to Iraq, Edward S. Crocker; Ambassador to Israel, Monnet T. Davis; Chargé d'Affaires to Jordan, David A. Fritzlan; Ambassador to Iran, Henry F. Grady; Ambassador to Saudi Arabia, Raymond A. Hare; Counselor of Embassy, Cairo, Gordon Mattison; Ambassador to the UN Palestine Conciliation Commission, Ely E. Palmer; Minister to Syria, Lowell C. Pinkerton; Ambassador to Greece, John E. Peurifoy; Ambassador to Pakistan, Avra M. Warren; and Ambassador to Turkey, George Wadsworth, our host. Of this group only Wadsworth, Grady (then in Greece), and I had attended the Istanbul Conference of 1949.

The conference was also joined by the First Secretary from the London Embassy, Joseph Palmer, and a large delegation from the Department of State, including Lewis Jones, Director of Middle Eastern Affairs; William Rountree, Director of Greek, Turkish and Iranian Affairs; and Mary E. Hope, Policy Information Officer.

Although the conference was a hard-working one, some time was available for diversions and sightseeing. As during the 1949 conference, I made my usual calls on the Governor and Mayor of Istanbul, Professor Fahrettin Kerim Gokay, and the Patriarch Athenagoras in the Phanar, both of whom returned the calls with great fanfare. George Wadsworth provided an excellent buffet luncheon every day for the conference delegates, who were free to attend or not as they chose. These were most congenial affairs, since the group consisted mostly of friends of long standing, who used the opportunity to exchange Foreign Service gossip.

Side trips were also provided for those with the time and inclination. One was to the Sultan's palace, with a visit to the treasury and to the Chinese porcelain collection comprising some ten thousand outstanding pieces of Ming Blue and Celadon pieces. Another was to the Hagia Sophia, now a museum, and the nearby Sultan Ahmed Sulaimaniye and Rustem Pasha mosques. On another day visits were paid to the Dolma Bahce and Yildiz palaces on the Bosphorus via the faithful consulate launch, the *Hiawatha,* which was to serve me well later when I was Ambassador. Admiral Carney gave us a boat trip up the Bosphorus and a fine Navy lunch aboard his flagship, the U.S.S. *Columbus.* Visits were paid to the underground Byzantine cisterns. There were miscellaneous cocktail parties and receptions and, on the final evening, Cecilia and I gave our traditional humorous farewell dinner. Nothing serious could be said. The ambassadors all responded this year to the theme, "The Flight of the Ambassadors," comparing their flights in their planes to the flights of birds.

In my opening remarks to the conference I attempted to summarize the world background of the meeting and what we should seek to achieve. I said that our general purpose was not to stimulate a detailed review of country problems but to re-examine the broad area problems which confronted us. We must gain the cooperation of the states of the area to prevent a world conflict or, if war came, to win it. In the case of countries like Greece and Turkey, already cooperating with us, we must keep them on our side. We must also create increased strength and stability in depth in the Middle East behind the Greek-Turkish barrier. To these ends we must induce all of the countries of the area to utilize their resources and manpower to the utmost.

I noted that the apparent absence of a positive U.S. security policy for the Middle East had led to an increasing fear of its peoples that we would abandon them in the event of war. This had already created political disaffection. Our failure to halt this trend could well result in the loss of the Middle East, even without open Soviet intervention. I said that the Kremlin was fully aware that denial of Middle Eastern oil would profoundly affect the economic and strategic power of the West. Conversely, Soviet control of the Middle East and its oil would enormously enhance Soviet power and the Soviet military threat against Western Europe. This was only the beginning of our concern over Middle Eastern oil, which has assumed much greater importance over the years.

I advised the conference of the recommendations the Department had made to the National Security Council following my discussions with the Joint Chiefs, directed at strengthening the U.S. contribution to Middle East defense. This would include a substantial increase in Turkey's armed forces; efforts to achieve greater political stability in the Arab states and Israel; and the improvement of local area defense through combined U.S.-U.K. leadership. Military and economic aid to Greece and Iran would be moderately expanded, and Turkish participation in the defense of Iran would be explored. We proposed that the U.S. declare to the world that, because of vital U.S. security interests in the Middle East, we were prepared to assist these states in their defense against aggression.

We further proposed that the U.S. and U.K. strengthen the forces of both the Arab states and Israel on an equal-to-equal basis, to promote their stability and pro-Western orientation. We also recommended that we join the U.K. in establishing a combined military mission in the Middle East to develop plans for area-wide defense in cooperation with local states. Such a mission, a kind of Middle East security center, would maintain primary U.K.-Commonwealth responsibility. I made it clear however, that the Joint Chiefs and the NSC had not yet approved our recommendations. I sought the views of the group on those proposals.

With that I opened the meeting for a discussion which would go on for three days. The group included strong-minded and articulate men who expressed themselves forcefully. Admiral Carney, who was later to become chairman of the Joint Chiefs of Staff, briefed us as regional commander of U.S. Naval Forces. Jack Peurifoy, a charming Southerner and an old friend who had served with distinction as chief administrative officer of the Department, had strong views on the role of Greece in area defense and on why Greece should be admitted to NATO. Jack died tragically in an automobile accident while serving as Ambassador to Thailand not long after our meeting. Henry Grady, a distinguished economist, who had had experience as director of aid to Greece, took an equally strong position for increased U.S. military assistance for Iran. The question of Greek and Turkish entry to NATO, because of its extreme sensitivity with the countries themselves, the U.S. Congress, and our NATO allies, was handled with great secrecy as a separate matter.

After three days of discussion and debate the conference agreed that our basic objectives in the Middle East must be the maintenance of peace and the development of area stability and security, the enhancement of U.S. prestige, and the orientation of the area to the U.S. and the Western powers and away from the U.S.S.R. Our main goal during the Cold War period was to prevent the U.S.S.R. from gaining control of any of the Middle East countries by subversion or by other means short of actual war.

In the case of states bordering on the U.S.S.R. we should continue large-scale military aid and, where necessary, economic aid, and encourage strong popular resistance to Communist aims. In the case of countries not contiguous to the U.S.S.R., military preparedness, except that required for internal stability, was not yet considered an important factor in the Cold War. These countries should for the time being be given only technical and financial assistance required to achieve political and economic stability. The U.S. should not attempt to negotiate security pacts with the Middle Eastern states. New arms assistance should, for the time being, only be given to Saudi Arabia, and that on a reimbursable basis. We must maintain a policy of active interest within a framework of strict impartiality between the Arab states and Israel. We should encourage direct negotiations between Israel and the Arab states on the Palestine problem, but should ourselves refrain from putting forward any specific proposals for settlement, leaving this to be determined by the relative bargaining positions of the parties.

The conference endorsed in general the recommendations made by the Department to the NSC on February 10, including the initiation of limited arms supplies and military missions on the basis of a coordinated U.S.-U.K. effort. The conference recommended clarification of U.S. and U.K. military responsibilities for the Middle East as a whole, while retaining the leading role in Greece and Turkey and a special position in Saudi Arabia. It was also agreed that we issue a unilateral statement that we would, in coordination with the U.K., help strengthen the Middle East states against aggression. The conference recommended that an effort be made with the U.K. to bring the policy of the Anglo-Iranian Oil Company into conformity with our foreign policy objectives in the Middle East. Most important of all, however, was the conference's recommendation that we enter into reciprocal security arrangements with Greece and Turkey, preferably through their direct adherence to NATO.

On the evening of February 21, when the conference was over, I held a press conference at which I issued an official statement. I noted that in light of the changed international situation the conference had focused on the security of the countries of the area. We were satisfied with progress made by Greece, Turkey, and Iran in building up their security forces and with the contribution of Greece and Turkey to the UN collective security action in Korea. In the conference held in November 1949, emphasis had been placed on economic and social development. These were still of great importance. I saw no definite indication of war in the Middle East, and refused to be drawn into any discussion of Middle Eastern pacts.

(Although the conference had reached its conclusions on this issue, our government had not.)

There was considerable comment about the meeting in the world press. The *New York Times* of February 14 emphasized the secrecy surrounding the conference and the presence of Admiral Carney, a recognized expert on Middle Eastern military strategy. It said, "The presence of nearly 20 important diplomats in a secluded huddle in this ancient city has aroused the keenest interest here. The local press stress one thing—that Turkey be admitted to the North Atlantic Pact." The Washington *Post* of the same date said the conference agreed that the U.S. should "consider ways to increase U.S. influence in this region, and if necessary, help defend it against aggression . . . Special attention was certain to be given to the Cominform threat against Yugoslavia, Soviet designs on Iran, Middle East oil in general, the possibility of a Mediterranean Pact and Arab-Jewish enmity."

The Dallas *Morning News*, after referring to the fact that a hometown boy had been chairman of the conference, cited the meeting as further evidence that we were prepared to use U.S. naval and air forces stationed in Europe and the Mediterranean in the defense of the Middle East. "We believe Messrs. Hoover, Truman, Taft and Dewey see eye to eye on what our representatives may be discussing."

From Moscow, the Soviet Middle Eastern News Service reported in Farsi that the nations of the Middle Eastern countries should know a few facts about the chairman of the conference now in progress in Istanbul. "McGhee is a very dangerous person. When one says McGhee, one means oil, one means dollars. And when one says oil or dollars, it means war." I was described as "one of the greatest owners of oil industries," a designation I only wished I had deserved. I was described as working for companies owned by Rockefeller and Morgan. "Thousands of workers are being exploited in his oilfields.—For having worked for Will Clayton (of Anderson Clayton Co., cotton traders) when he was Under Secretary—Clayton, the cotton king, became the master of McGhee, the owner of oil interests." It was pointed out that I had not divested myself of my oil interests, having retained my membership in the Dallas Petroleum Club. "The American monopolies have requested McGhee to bring into their possession all the oil deposits of the East."

On February 13, A. E. Yalman, publisher of the Istanbul paper *Vatan,* who was later to become a close friend, wrote a very perceptive editorial addressed to me and my collaborators. He described the atmosphere of confidence between Turkey and the U.S. as "one of the fundamental factors of stability in the midst of the present confused situation." Turkey was blessed to "win such a powerful fellow-companion." He pointed out, however, that there resulted a heavy burden for Turkey, which Turkey would bear not in return for aid or to please us but to fulfill its historic role in the defense of the Middle East. Yalman described this as a national policy. He also assured us that "Democracy and freedom have taken roots in Turkey in a manner never to be shaken again."

One of the principal topics of discussion during the conference had, of course, been Greek-Turkish admission to NATO. I was thoroughly convinced that this was a vitally needed step to bring the very considerable Greek and Turkish forces, particularly the Turkish army, into the NATO defensive line. Only in this way could the Soviets be prevented from making a military "end run" around NATO. Turkey would be the NATO eastern anchor. No longer would the other weak Middle Eastern states be such easy targets for Communist subversion or military attack. Their morale, as well as that of Greece and Turkey, would be given a great boost. Both countries ardently desired to become full-fledged allies with us in NATO and to gain a guarantee of collective defense and access to more arms. Acheson and Bevin had been giving both countries oral assurances. Their full admission had, however, been delayed by NATO in September 1950. They had been temporarily appeased by an invitation to become associated with NATO planning.

During the Istanbul meeting, after discussion with the other participants, Admiral Carney and I sent, in the name of the conference, a top-secret telegram to the State Department urging that the departments of State and Defense give renewed attention to Greek-Turkish entry into NATO. We cited not only the well-known arguments but also intelligence that we had received during the meeting to the effect that the Turks, although they sought strongly to join NATO, were getting discouraged and considering alternative courses of action if their entry was further delayed. We argued that we could make a better agreement with the Turks when they were eager to join than when their interest might be declining, and pointed out that the Turkish army was larger than that of any current NATO member.

This telegram and the participation of Carney and Finletter in our Istanbul conference gave a powerful impetus to Greek-Turkish membership in NATO. Both countries were pressing for entry publicly. Upon my return to Washington I lobbied strongly for a favorable decision, particularly with General Collins and the other Joint Chiefs. On May 15, the U.S. made a formal proposal to the U.K. and France. Although the Norwegians, on June 29, questioned this solution to the Greek-Turkish problem, the U.K. gradually changed its position in favor of admission. On July 18 the new British Foreign Secretary, Herbert Morrison, publicly announced support and so advised the Greek and Turkish governments.

The question was placed on the agenda for the meeting of the North Atlantic Council to be held in Ottawa in July. George Perkins, Assistant Secretary for European Affairs, was in charge of the conference as a whole for Secretary Acheson. I was named one of the senior advisers on the delegation to handle the Greek-Turkish question. It was a hard-working meeting but there were pleasant interludes. Cecilia accompanied me, and several other spouses participated, including Alice Acheson. The Canadian government provided a splendid dinner and other entertainment.

But getting Greece and Turkey into NATO proved to be more of a problem than we had anticipated, even with U.S., British, and French agreement in advance. We had prepared arguments to meet the expected opposition of the Nordic members. Having joined NATO to assure protection of the North Atlantic area where they lived, they did not want to be drawn into a war in the perilous Middle East. There was much discussion. Denmark was the last to withdraw opposition. But just at this juncture, with the other nine members waiting in the conference chamber to vote in favor, the U.K. and France decided to try to wring national advantage from the decision they were already committed to.

France sought to use its approval as leverage to place a French admiral as chief of a new Mediterranean naval command; the U.K. sought to get Turkey, as the price of entry, to agree to place Turkish troops, in time of war, under a British-led Middle East Command. The latter proposal, coming when it did, was the dying gasp of an old British proposal we had at one time espoused. It had, however, been sharply rejected both by the Arabs and Turkey. We told the British that if Turkey would accept willingly we would raise no objection, but that we would not join in any attempt to coerce Turkey to accept wartime British command. I was in touch with the Turks through their representative in Ottawa and, predictably, they held firm against the British proposal.

There remained many hours of thrashing about between the three powers on these two issues, which became increasingly embarrassing vis-a-vis the other NATO members, several of whom we had persuaded to support Greek-Turkish entry against their better judgment. Morrison, in a clumsy way, attempted to carry out his bluff. He lectured me and other American delegates as though we were members of his Foreign Office. Although the U.S. side attempted to be patient, we stood firm and in the end reason prevailed. Secretary Acheson and the British and French Foreign Ministers went back into the council meeting and the invitation to Greece and Turkey was passed unanimously. I breathed a sigh of relief. The long battle was over.

A protocol admitting Greece and Turkey to NATO was signed by the Council of Deputies during mid-October. Denmark was the last country to sign final acceptance, and the protocol went into effect finally on February 15, 1952. The area of the treaty was extended to include Greece and Turkey. There could no longer be any Soviet "end run" around NATO. The defense of the Middle East was assured.

There is a sequel. I relinquished my post as Assistant Secretary and arrived in Turkey on December 1, 1951, as U.S. Ambassador (actually, as a recess appointee not yet approved by Congress, which would do so later). Soon after my arrival I was present in the visitors' balcony of the old Turkish parliament building when the Majlis voted unanimously, with one abstention, to accept the invitation to join NATO. I often wondered what happened to the member who abstained. This vote is more remarkable in light of the fact that eighteen U.S. senators opposed our entry into NATO. I was, of course, jubilant. My tour as Ambassador had been given a good start. The Turks were very much aware of my efforts as Assistant Secretary to help them gain entry into the select organization which they had coveted so ardently.

Because of Turkey's importance to NATO, I will summarize briefly recent Turkish history leading up to her admission. Kemal Atatürk, the "Father-Turk," laid down six "fundamental and unchangeable principles" to guide the development of the modern Turkish state that he founded after World War I. Called the Six Arrows—secularism, republicanism, economic statism, populism, nationalism, and reformism—they were intended not only to break the country free from the orientalism of the old Ottoman Empire but to promote the westernization of the new Turkey. Turkey's membership in NATO in 1952 was, of course, a recognition of its strategic position, but, for the Turks, it was also a verification that they had become European.

Over the years since Atatürk's death in 1938, his Six Arrows have been accepted as articles of faith—at least officially—by the major political parties, the modernizing elite, the bureaucracy, and, most importantly, by the armed forces, to which Atatürk bequeathed responsibility for guaranteeing the gains made by his revolution. Events would prove, however, that Atatürk's secularism was not easy to accomplish. Correspondingly, insistence on economic statism led to public investment in uneconomic enterprise that impeded private initiative and had a long-range negative impact on Turkey's economic development. In 1960, a military coup instigated by junior officers who felt that Adnan Menderes, the Democratic party Prime Minister, was using authoritarian methods, supplanted the parliamentary regime with an interim military government under General Cemal Gürsel and suspended all political activities. In September 1961, Menderes was brought to trial, charged with abuse of power, and executed.

The military government supervised the rewriting of the constitution and promptly turned over control of the country to the Republican (RPP) leader Ismet Inönü, Atatürk's chief lieutenant in war and his successor as President, who came out of retirement to head a new civilian government. But in the 1965 election, the first held since the coup, the Turkish electorate gave an overwhelming majority to the Justice Party, which had been formed from the banned Democratic Party. The government of Prime Minister Süleyman Demirel was unable to cope with renewed political and sectarian violence or to deal with strikes. In 1971, the armed forces acted again, demanded the resignation of Demirel's government, and instituted a period of "guided democracy" under a civilian government of technocrats deemed "above party."

In the meantime, the scholarly Bülent Ecevit had become leader of the RPP and had set the party on a leftward course. He aligned it with European social democratic parties while calling for a more independent foreign policy that emphasized improved relations with other Muslim countries of the Middle East. The RPP emerged from the 1973 election as the largest party in a crowded field but short of a parliamentary majority. The government, which depended on an uneasy coalition with the Islamic National Salvation Party, was short-lived, resigning early in 1975 as a result of loss of confidence by the public in its handling of the Cyprus crisis.

In July 1974, Turkish forces, acting on Turkey's rights under the treaties of Zurich and London to protect its minority in Cyprus following the overthrow of the Makarios government by a Greek-instigated military coup, had invaded Cyprus. The U.S. government, strongly influenced by the Greek-American lobby, retaliated by imposing an embargo of military supplies against Turkey that remained in effect until 1978. The Turkish government, in return, restricted American bases on its territory, and the good relations which had existed between the two countries since 1951 deteriorated badly.

Demirel, who had taken a hard line on Cyprus, replaced Ecevit as Prime Minister, but neither he nor the RPP leader, who was returned to power for a short time in 1978, was able to deal with the escalating violence between political extremists, in which thousands were killed annually. Nor could they come up with a convincing prescription for treating Turkey's severe economic ills. To save the situation, the armed forces intervened once again in September 1980. General Kenan Evren deposed the civilian government, took political leaders into custody, and established a military council to govern the country. Evren pledged to restore democracy to Turkey according to a timetable that would allow for an election in 1984. In the meantime, a constituent assembly, whose members represented interests identified with the military, was named to draw up a constitution which was approved in a referendum in November 1982.

While the European Economic Community to which Turkey aspires has condemned the military government, the OECD has praised the austerity measures that it imposed as part of an economic stabilization program which has drastically reduced inflation. The program emphasizes reliance on a market economy and agricultural development. In the meantime, U.S.-Turkish relations have greatly improved. U.S. military assistance in meeting Turkish NATO commitments, and economic aid, have risen on an annual basis over $800 million.

24

South Asia Evaluated

Visit to Colombo, Sri Lanka, Prime Minister
Senanayake. South Asia Regional Conference
of U.S. Diplomatic and Consular Officers,
February 24–March 6, 1951.

As a part of department policy to hold regular regional conferences, we had planned a South Asian Conference in 1951, the last having taken place in 1949 before I assumed my new position. This was particularly important in view of the trend toward neutralism in South Asia led by Prime Minister Nehru, and the threat to the area which we perceived following the Communist invasion of South Korea. The conference was scheduled to take place in the delightful highland resort of Nuwara Eliya in Sri Lanka (then Ceylon), immediately following the Istanbul conference. I looked forward eagerly to hearing the views of our able ambassadors in South Asia and attempting, with them, to reach some conclusions as to the mood of the states of this area and the consequences for U.S. policy.

Both before and after the conference, which was held February 26–March 3, 1951, Cecilia and I made another official visit to Colombo, just a little over a year after our first visit. We were met on arrival by our good friends from Washington days, Joe and Leyla Satterthwaite, who took us to the Embassy where we had an opportunity to chat about old times before dinner. Prime Minister Senanayake was absent from the city, but there were present Sir Kanthiah Vaithianathan, Permanent Secretary of the Ministry of Defense and External Affairs; Dr. John W. Burton, High Commissioner of Australia; Baron Pinofeau, Minister of France; and U Tint, Minister of Burma. We had a lively discussion of the general political situation in South Asia in the aftermath of the Communist invasion of South Korea.

The following morning Cecilia and I departed by car for Nuwara

Eliya, where our conference was to be held, driving through the many tea plantations which looked like vast, perfectly manicured parks. The air, as we ascended into the hill country, was crisp and clear. Our conference had been described in *New York Times* articles as being held to improve coordination in the field and "to take up the threat of Communist China in Southeast Asia and discuss means of combating Communism through economic aid."

There were fifty-seven officers present at the conference.[1] The meetings took place in the ballroom of the attractive Grand Hotel, which had wide verandas and large rooms with high ceilings reminiscent of the colonial era, when the prosperous tea planters would gather here with their families to escape the heat of the plains. A room with meals cost in 1951 $6 per day per person. The surrounding grove was a veritable arboretum. There was an eighteen-hole golf course. Our wives took the tour to Kandy, where one could see the Peradeniya Botanical Gardens and the Temple of the Tooth or watch the elephants bathe.

From the State Department came Donald D. Kennedy, Deputy Director, Office of South Asian Affairs, with the heads of the Economic and Labor Offices. There were also representatives from Defense, Agriculture, Commerce, and other agencies. The stars, however, were our ambassadors: Loy W. Henderson from India; Joseph C. Satterthwaite from Ceylon; Avra Warren from Pakistan; and George Merrill, Ambassador-designate to Pakistan; also our First Secretary in Kabul, Fred Jandrey. There were also five consuls general. It was a congenial and hard-working group.

In my opening remarks to the conference I attempted to set the keynote. I said that although some might think that the Korean War should have led to a cancellation of the conference, I believed it was now more essential than ever. We needed as never before the pooling of our knowledge so we could better judge where we were going. Our central goal was the security of the U.S. and the maintenance of our free institutions. The world was quite different from what it had been two years earlier, when our last South Asia conference had been held. Communist aggression in Korea had demonstrated that the Soviets were willing to take greater risks. The UN had taken prompt military measures against the North Koreans, and we had sought further UN action against Chinese Communist aggression which had created difficulties for us with certain South Asian countries. There was, for example, a growing tendency toward neutralism, particularly in India.

I recalled our increasing military assistance to the North Atlantic Pact countries. We had also initiated economic aid to Southeast Asia and military aid in the form of equipment, from funds provided "for the general area of China" under the Mutual Defense Assistance Act. This had already yielded positive results. We had embarked at home on a general mobilization supported by economic controls. Events had forced us to give overriding weight to our security needs. As a result of the Mutual Security Program we had for the first time real weapons, economic and military, at hand. We must ask, "Who are our friends? On whom can we rely in a crisis?" There was now a sense of urgency and a need for a new assessment of our world position. This was the time for a serious examination of where we stood in South Asia.

I emphasized the importance to us of South Asia itself. The loss of China, the immediate threat to Indochina and the rest of Southeast Asia, the invasion of Tibet, and the recent reversals in Korea had greatly increased the importance of the resources of this region. India and Pakistan had leaders of international prestige. The future of these countries would have world significance. India also had certain strategic materials necessary to our national defense. These considerations underscored the necessity for maintaining non-Communist governments in South Asia and improving stability in the area.

I pointed out, however, that South Asia still had a low priority among the areas where we could make an impact. Our present resources were limited and we had to direct our aid toward top-priority goals. I pointed out that this posed a serious dilemma. The loss of India and Pakistan to Communism would mean for all practical purposes the loss of the whole of Asia, a most serious blow to our security. I pointed out the many difficulties we faced: the worsening of Indo-Pakistan relations and lack of progress on Kashmir; lack of understanding, especially by India, of the aggressive intentions of the Communists, both Chinese and Russian; failure of the South Asian countries to make economic progress; a growing anti-Western attitude, particularly the emotional anti-U.S. attitude of Nehru; limited U.S. resources available for South Asia in light of our own defense needs; and the growing unfavorable reaction of Congress as a result of the failure of India to cooperate in opposing Communism.

Later, each ambassador summarized the situation in the country to which he was accredited. According to Henderson, Nehru had for the past year based India's foreign policy on the thesis that the world was divided into the Western bloc led by us and the Communist bloc dominated by the Soviets. Each of these blocs he said was playing power politics and was approaching international problems in the light of its own selfish interests. India and a few other nations were refusing to participate in either bloc and were endeavoring to base their decisions on what they considered to be high moral principles. India sought to lessen the possibility of a world conflict by persuading neutral countries not to join either bloc; by urging the U.K., the Commonwealth countries, and the Europeans to break with us; and by attempting to get Communist China to sever relations with the Soviets. In addition to weakening our international influence and that of the Soviet Union, India was trying to strengthen its own by acting as spokesman for the colored peoples of the world and to gain acceptance as the chief opponent of colonialism and imperialism. India's definition of colonialism was the political control by white peoples of colored peoples; its definition of imperialism was the economic exploitation by white peoples of colored peoples.

It would, in Henderson's judgment, be a grave blunder for us to consider that genuine friendship with India was out of the question. We should not give up hope for the cooperation of India in case the Cold War should continue indefinitely or develop into a fighting war. He was convinced that underneath India's critical front there lay a core of friendship and confidence in our motives. We must continue patiently to improve relations with the Indian leaders and people, he said. We should not, however, assume a cringing or flattering attitude toward Nehru, which would give him the impression that he had the whip hand over us. Nor, on the other hand, should we take an attitude of truculence or hostility, which would strengthen the influence of our enemies in India. We should always bear in mind that Nehru was not India; and that he could not ignore Indian public opinion. Events beyond his control might force him to decide to change his present tactics and methods.

Henderson advised that we prove quietly by our actions that we were friends of India and would like to assist India should she desire economic and cultural assistance. He recommended that we consult with India on international problems in which India might have a special interest, and explain the reasons for our actions when we could not follow India's advice. We should not apologize to India for our policies or attribute them to American public opinion, nor show hesitation or vacillation even on policies, such as those concerning Korea, which India opposed. Henderson suggested that we act as though we considered India basically a moral country and on the side of forces opposed to aggression. On these grounds we could take an interest in Indian defense efforts without appearing to side with India against Pakistan. We should explain our world-wide objectives to Indian leaders to offset charges that we were more interested in combatting Communism than in the welfare of the peoples of Asia. And finally he advised us to avoid giving the impression that we thought "we know better than you what is for your good."

Avra Warren, Ambassador to Pakistan, gave a most interesting report on that country. He said that the most significant factor in the political life of Pakistan was its obsession with India, coupled with the conviction that India's foreign policy was an expression of the opinions and ambitions of one man. The Pakistanis felt Nehru to be more preoccupied with aspirations for world leadership than with the security of his neighbors. He neglected no chance to weaken Pakistan and embitter its relations with other powers, especially Afghanistan. Pakistan believed its own security could best be advanced by building friendships in the West, beginning with the Arab states. It would like to be considered the flank of the Middle East and, in exchange for a guarantee against aggression from India, would be willing to contribute its forces for the defense of the Middle East. It would give all possible armed support to Iran in event of an attack on that country. Pakistan also would offer significant military assistance to us in the event of a war with the Soviet Union and would furnish bases, provided we guaranteed Pakistan against aggression from India.

While Pakistan was smarting under a sense of neglect because the post of Ambassador in Karachi had before his arrival been vacant some time, Warren said that my visit to Karachi in November 1949 and the invitation to the Prime Minister to visit the U.S. had been well received throughout Pakistan. Pakistan's strong pro-American attitude was illustrated most dramatically by its support of the UN action in Korea and Pakistan's successful efforts to influence Arab, particularly Egyptian, opinion. This helped counteract Indian maneuvers directed against the UN action in Korea. Warren felt this favorable attitude could be short-lived. The failure of the Dixon Mission to resolve the Kashmir dispute was considered by many Pakistanis, in and out of government, as evidence of an American and British desire to balance their interests as between Pakistan and India.

Joseph Satterthwaite filled us in on the situation in Ceylon, whose foreign relations were dominated by the U.K. and India. Ceylon had always been the favorite colony of the U.K., which had recognized

Ceylon's money-earning ability and had dealt with its people fairly. When Ceylon had achieved independence three years earlier, she had signed a mutual defense pact with the U.K. In 1951, British troops stationed there had been recalled, and Ceylon had formed its own army of almost a thousand men, three Chipmunk trainer planes for its air force, and a minesweeper for its navy. The British naval base at Trincomalee and the Royal Air Force base at Negombo, though now occupied by skeleton forces, could be put at full strength quickly.

Ceylon held the place of favor among the Asian Commonwealth dominions. Within the country great stress was placed on the Commonwealth connection. Attitudes were for the most part pro-British. Ceylon had several problems arising out of the present world crisis. Her leaders feared India. There was concern that American interests would take over the influence once held by the British. The fact that Ceylon was not a member of the UN created emotional as well as practical reactions. The people blamed the Soviet Union's veto, but they felt keenly that this meant they were still regarded as a British colonial dominion.

Fred Jandrey, First Secretary of the American Embassy in Kabul, described the situation in Afghanistan. In light of the current Soviet occupation of Afghanistan, his report is particularly interesting. Jandrey said that Afghanistan's position on the borders of both Soviet Russia and Communist China gave us a strong interest in its future stability. But there were internal elements in the country working against stability. Afghanistan was ruled by an autocratic regime which was losing its prestige because of a growing feeling in the world that the royal family was not ruling well and was acting in its own self-interest.

The opposition in Afghanistan, though, was small and disorganized, and had made little progress toward achieving a more democratic government. Jandrey said that we should try to persuade the ruling family that a systematic move toward democracy was inevitable, and would contribute to the future stability of Afghanistan. Jandrey added that Afghan support of a Pushtunistan state had further contributed to instability. On November 6, we had urged the Afghan and Pakistan governments to talk, in an effort to resolve their differences over this issue. But it seemed unlikely that Pakistan would agree. What was the next step? On the economic side the U.S. had tried to promote stability in Afghanistan through several programs: a $21 million loan for the Helmand River Valley Development Plan;

technical assistance in mining; and the institution of a small Point Four Program. We had also urged the UN to increase activities by the UN Technical Assistance Mission. Although Afghanistan was weak militarily, Jandrey felt we should consider only aid for internal security.

After these reports, there followed a lively discussion focused principally on the possibility of defending South Asia from Communism and on the dangers of neutralism. The final conclusions of the conference were decided on as follows and transmitted to the Secretary of State. The conference agreed that effective defense of South Asia would require strong flanks, and that we should therefore help build up military strength in Pakistan, Iran, and Turkey on the west and in Indochina on the east. We recognized the importance of Pakistan's potential contribution to the defense of the Middle East. We also agreed that India, even though it now had little interest in collective security, should be considered as a worthwhile long-term military risk and that we should try through nonpressure methods to ensure India's friendship and ultimate support. It was acknowledged that India's foreign policy dominated the area. Thus, our policy toward India should show patience built on firmness. Whenever Indian policy undermined collective security, we should challenge it vigorously, both at home and abroad, through all media.

We noted that South Asian countries generally concentrated upon regional tensions to the exclusion of what we considered the greater danger, the world Communist threat. Kashmir remained the central and most acute issue, affecting relations between Pakistan and Afghanistan as well as Pakistan and India. Stronger efforts should be made to minimize these regional differences by stressing the Soviet threat. The U.K. should continue to take the lead in pressing for a Kashmir settlement. Every effort should be made to avoid division of the UN into opposing Asian and Western blocs, and we should oppose Nehru's efforts to create a neutral bloc among Asian and Arab states. Grant aid programs, combined with technical assistance and loans, would be of great benefit in South Asia for political purposes. Existing resentment would be reduced, and the economies of the South Asian countries improved. The proposed food-grain program for India would be of particular value in convincing South Asia that we were genuinely interested in their welfare, bringing them closer to the West and away from Communism.

The final evening, in accordance with our custom, Cecilia and I gave a formal dinner for the delegates. By prior arrangement each chief of mission made a speech as if he were the representative of the country to which he was accredited, and in a purely farcical vein. The assigned subject was "The Americans, Why Do They Bother Us?" Nothing serious could be said. The following summaries of the speeches do not quite catch the humor of the actual occasion.

The Delegate from Afghanistan: Until Americans became interested in us, we never had any problems and could devote ourselves to fighting wars with the British Raj. We fought the First Afghan War, the Second Afghan War, and the Third Afghan War. Things have been shaping up nicely for a Fourth Afghan War but now the U.S. has stepped in and tried to prevent a renewal of the series. The Americans are ruining our national pastime, which reached its highest peak with the development of the Khyber Pass as a means of carrying the ball beyond the Durand line. Of, for a good old Afghan War again!

The Delegate from Ceylon: I am glad you asked me this question and I will give you a straight answer. America wants to subvert us from tea. Back in the days when the British were here, they propagandized the world for our main product. They made it almost compulsory for every British man, woman, and child to drink six cups a day. Trade boomed. We got rich. But now the Americans are assiduously trying to undo all that. How? By icing the drink and making it less attractive. Already our market with the Eskimos has gone. Patagonia will be next, and soon our market will be confined to a small tea-drinking belt bounded by the Irish Sea and the English Channel.

The Delegate from Pakistan: You will never believe it when I tell you the enormity of the crime which America is about to perpetrate in Pakistan. It has come to me in a very top-secret report from the Minister of War but I feel it my patriotic duty to expose it. America's aim in Pakistan is no less than to assure to herself the entire known resources of sand in Baluchistan. We have incontrovertible proof that the spinach growers of America are behind this bold move and that already Point Four experts are in Baluchistan studying the possibility of erecting a branch factory of the Hour Glass Corporation of America.

The Delegate from India: We are highly grateful for two recently approved technical assistance programs which the U.S. has set for India. Under the first program, a mission headed by a distinguished former governor of Kansas and containing a number of experts from the World Christian Temperance Union will advise the government on ways and means of making prohibition more effective. This program is to be paralleled by work in another field by a mission of distinguished experts from Chicago, who will set up demonstration projects on bathtub-gin production, speakeasy operation, and other related matters. We are grateful to America for this assistance and we should not criticize her.

The Delegate from Ethiopia: I have come to this conference to complain about the American proposal to use Ethiopia as a mobile buffer state in South Asia. As is well known, the American plan is to secure a number of barrage balloons around Ethiopia's boundaries, inflate them, pull us loose from our African moorings and deposit us in the sensitive area of the moment in South Asia. To assist us in resisting aggression in our new location, we shall be well-manned by "gorilla" forces recruited in the Belgian Congo! We protest at being used as a Trojan horse.

It was, all in all, a very worthwhile conference.

I held a press conference on March 4 in Colombo.[2] The Reuter's dispatch of that day stressed my comment that the U.S. planned more help for countries in South Asia. I expressed gratification at the trade agreement just signed between India and Pakistan and hoped Afghanistan and Pakistan would settle their differences over Pushtunistan. I pledged U.S. support for the recently-announced Commonwealth Colombo Plan for mutual assistance. If pending legislation giving India two million tons of grain was approved, it would constitute a significant contribution to the plan.

On Sunday, March 4, Ambassador Satterthwaite took me to see the Right Honorable D. S. Senanayake, Prime Minister and Minister of Foreign Affairs. I had met the Prime Minister on my visit to Ceylon in December 1949. Senanayake, who had been a leader in his country's independence movement, not only held the most important posts in the government; in fact, he *was* the government. During our meeting, which lasted an hour, I reported the results of our conference just completed. I stressed the dangers of neutralism and the necessity of combatting it. I stressed how much Ceylon needed Great Britain. We hoped that the ties between Ceylon and the Commonwealth as a whole would be strengthened.

That evening I saw the Prime Minister again at a reception given at his residence, Temple Trees, to which were also invited some of the members of our conference, also members of the cabinet and diplomatic corps. I was happy to meet my old friend Sir John

Kotowalawa, former Minister of Finance and later Prime Minister, who had been a frequent visitor to Washington. He wanted to take Cecilia and me to watch the elephants bathe; however, we were scheduled to return to the Embassy with the Satterthwaites for a buffet supper. We enjoyed meeting the Ceylonese with their charming, open, smiling manner. I liked the attractive wrap-around dresses the ladies wore. I have always thought the sari does something for a woman that Western women's clothing can't match. There was among the Ceylonese official group an air of innocence and credulity, with a shyness and apprehension resulting from their newly-attained independence. They did not ever want to be controlled by outsiders again.

At dinner the Satterthwaites assembled a congenial group, including Sir Walter Hankinson, U.K. High Commissioner; his deputy M. R. Metcalf; Air Commodore F. L. Pearce, commander of the RAF forces in Ceylon; and Armand Gandon, Counselor of the French Legation. The following morning, accompanied by Satterthwaite and Kennedy, I visited E. C. Ponnambalam, Minister of Industries, Industrial Research, and Fisheries; J. R. Jayewardene, Minister of Finance; Sir Oliver Goonetilleke, Minister of Home Affairs and Rural Development; and Sir Kanthiah Vaithianathan. I covered in these meetings the same ground I had gone over with the Prime Minister.

At the request of S. Shepard Jones, an old friend and Oxford classmate who was in charge of public affairs for our NEA Bureau in the Department, and A. J. Tressidder from the Embassy, I was a guest at a luncheon given by L. M. D. de Silva and C. E. L. Wickremesinghe, whose firm, Lake House Press, published the influential *Observer* and several other local journals.[3] When, as guest of honor, I was called on to speak, I dwelt mainly on neutralism in Ceylon and India. However small and weak Ceylon might be, I said, it should let the U.S.S.R. and the world know its opposition to Soviet Communist expansionism. I described what I thought would happen to Ceylon if the Communists gained control. Communist imperialism would be worse than anything Ceylon had hitherto experienced under colonial rule. Freedom would perish. I emphasized the lack of freedom in the U.S.S.R. I took a strong line and should have anticipated the rebuttal I received.

De Silva responded that, while in the main he agreed with me, he did not believe I understood public opinion in Ceylon and India. There was a great desire on the part of a majority of the population in Ceylon and throughout South and Southeast Asia to remain aloof from either side of the Cold War if that was at all possible, call it neutralism if you like. He said that this was probably not realistic, but many Asians felt that the democracies might not be strong enough to maintain two fronts against the Communists, in Europe and Asia. If the West was forced to make a choice as to which to abandon, Asians feared that they would be sacrificed. De Silva felt that there was a considerable body of public opinion in the U.S. and U.K. who shared this view. He considered public opinion in the U.S. to be more volatile, changeable, and subject to pressures than in the U.K.

With reference to U.S. aid and the Colombo Plan we should, if eliminating Communism was our objective, tell Ceylon whether we felt it was doing enough. If its effort was to be successful, a great deal more must be done to raise the standard of living of the Asian masses. The Colombo Plan was not broad enough to attack the problem, which would require experts from abroad and substantial U.S. financial assistance. He did not know whether the U.S. had the resources to do the job. The numerous requests being made by his government from the U.S. had, for example, not been properly coordinated. A team of outside experts should spend at least six months making a thorough survey of the island to see what should be done to improve the economy. De Silva thought there was a very real danger of the Communists' coming to power in Ceylon. The governing United National party was too complacent. In a sense, he was asking us to put our aid where our mouth was. I listened attentively and assured de Silva that I would consider carefully what he had told me and see what could be done. I had been impressed with the sincerity of his expression.

That evening, accompanied by Satterthwaite and Henderson, Cecilia and I paid a call on the Governor-General of Ceylon, Lord Soulbury, and his wife, whom we had met during our 1949 visit. We had a pleasant conversation catching up on what had happened in South Asia in the intervening period. The next day I attended an Embassy staff meeting and, as a former member of the International Committee of the YMCA, visited the local Y. Later, Cecilia and I were to be entertained at dinner by Sir Kanthiah Vaithianathan. Several other ministers I had seen during the day were there also. It was apparent that Sir Goonetilleke, who had only recently returned from serving as the first Ceylonese High Commissioner in London, was destined to play a more important government role in Ceylon. Our discussions mainly concerned the future of Ceylon's rubber production.

Early the next morning, Cecilia, Ambassador Henderson, and I departed in his air attaché plane for an official visit to New Delhi. The series of visits which followed were intended to take advantage of my return from Ceylon to discuss current matters with the leaders of the countries along my route. In particular I wished to discuss with Nehru our concern over his increasing trend toward neutralism. I wanted to take up with the Afghans and Pakistanis the Pushtunistan problem we were attempting to resolve. My visit to Teheran was precipitated by the Anglo-Iranian oil nationalization threat following the assassination of General Razmara. My stops in Iraq and Lebanon were too brief for me to expect to go deeply into policy matters; however, I hoped that my visits to Syria, Jordan, and Egypt would yield interesting insights into these troubled countries. Egypt was at a critical point in its confrontation with the U.K. over the Suez base issue.

Ceylon, I had found, was not prepared to renounce neutralism and join our crusade against Communism. It is interesting to trace the subsequent history of Ceylon, after 1972 Sri Lanka, through the intervening years. The basic political cleavage in Sri Lanka derives from the ancient conflict between the country's two ethnic communities, the Buddhist Sinhalese and the Tamil-speaking Hindus, which overrides the more modern ideological divisions in relative significance. The Sinhalese majority are intent on maintaining their political and social predominance and preserving the distinct Sinhalese character of the country by giving official status to the Sinhala language and to Buddhism. The Tamils, related to the population in nearby southern India, want equal recognition in a bicultural country, and more extreme groups among them have called for a separate Tamil state on the island. Despite the often violent conflict there, Sri Lanka has managed to keep its vigorous democratic institutions in an ethnically-based, multiparty system that has allowed for the orderly transfer of power.

Ceylon achieved independence in 1948 under the moderate social democratic United National party (UNP), which although Sinhalese-based sought to provide for the interests of the Tamil minority. Its principal opposition in the years since has come from the leftist Sri Lanka Freedom party (SLFP), which formed the government for the first time in 1956 under Solomon Bandaranaike. Following his assassination in 1959, Bandaranaike's widow, Sirimavo, formed a coalition with Trotskyite and Communist factions that survived in and out of office until 1977. In the general election held that year, the UNP won an overwhelming parliamentary majority, and its leader, J. R. Jayewardene, formed a new government that dealt in a determined fashion with strikes, left-wing terrorism, and renewed ethnic violence. The following year, a constitutional amendment gave Sri Lanka a presidential form of government, with Jayewardene assuming the presidency.

25

Nehru Revisited

Visit to New Delhi, India, Prime Minister Nehru,
March 6–8, 1951.

Cecilia and Loy Henderson and I arrived in New Delhi on March 6 by Air Force plane at Palma Field.[1] We were met by Elise Henderson, Shri I. S. Chopra, Indian Chief of Protocol, and Major Yunus Khan, Deputy Military Secretary to the President of India. Although we had, during our previous visit, stayed at the Embassy residence, we were on this occasion guests of the Indian government at Government House.

Our quarters, described in the printed schedule for Government House as the Irwin Bed Room and Sitting Room, were several times the size of a normal hotel suite and elaborately furnished. Servants were available at all times for tea or other services. The ground floor of Government House was occupied by five officers, including Major and Shirmiarti Khan. We shared the first floor, in the English terminology, with the President of India and his family, who occupied the Rajaja, Edwina Mountbatten, and Chelmsford rooms. Also on this floor were the Honorable and Mrs. C. E. Martin in the Birdwood rooms. On the second floor were the Maharajkumar and Kumerani of Sikkim in the Olive, Wellesley, Roberts, Lytton, Stanley, Goschen, Napier, and Canning rooms. Empire still lived.

Guests of Government House were advised of the rules in "Notes for Guests," a printed form issued by B. Chatterjee, Colonel, Military Secretary to the President. Breakfast could be ordered up to 9:30 A.M., luncheon was at 1 P.M. and dinner was served at 8:30 P.M. Those who wished to be out for luncheon or dinner should indicate "out" in the meal book or advise the A.D.C., who also provided cars, postal services, and police passes, and handled gratuities. The only meal we had was breakfast, which was served with great ceremony by a number of servants and a marked division of labor, some carrying juice, some coffee, some eggs.

On the evening of our arrival, Loy and Elise gave us a family reception at their residence. Most of the Embassy staff were present. The following morning I had scheduled meetings starting at 9:30 with Chakravarti Rajagopalachari, Minister for Home Affairs; N. G. Ayyanger, Minister for States; and my old friend Sir Girja Shankar Bajpai, Secretary General, Ministry for External Affairs. Sir Girja, always a favorite of Americans, was a graduate of Oxford and was, with his characteristic rapid speech and quick mind, recognized by all as a master of statecraft. Although overshadowed by Nehru, he was, by those who knew, given great credit for the remarkable accomplishment of launching India as an independent state.

Later, at a luncheon for us at the residence of K. M. Munchi, Minister for Food and Agriculture, I was to see Mr. D. C. Deshmukh, Minister for Finance, a charming and talented official with whom I maintained contact for many years when he headed the UN Food and Agriculture Organization. In the afternoon, I met with M. S. Gore, acting principal, Delhi School of Social Services, who took Cecilia and me to an Indian village. It was not, of course, a typical village but somewhat of a showplace. Nevertheless, it demonstrated the great effort the government was making to improve the half million villages of India. Those I had seen in the early days of independence were most depressing. One could only remember the crumbling earth houses and muddy roads, and the multiple-use water ponds, where cattle wallowed, clothes were washed, waste dispensed, and drinking water drawn.

In the evening the Hendersons gave an elaborate dinner for thirty-four guests. In addition to the embassy staff and those I had seen earlier in the day, there were Sir Harilal J. Kania, Chief Justice of India, and the unforgettable Raj-kumari Amrit Kaur, with haunting dark eyes and long dark hair, who had dedicated her life to helping the Indian masses. Also there were Nepalese Ambassador General Shingha Jang Bahadur Rana and the Princess Rana. Embassy dinners like this one are very difficult to prepare. Some guests don't eat meat. Some don't eat butter or eggs. Some don't eat spices. Almost none drink alcohol. Some won't eat at all in a foreign house.

The following morning, Cecilia and I breakfasted with General Cariappa, Commander-in-Chief of the Indian army, with whom we had lunched during our visit in 1949. The General, as before, was a delightful host, still a caricature of a British Sandhurst graduate. After a staff meeting at the chancery and a call on K. P. S. Menon, Foreign Secretary for Commonwealth Affairs, we prepared for the highlights of our visit, my meeting with Prime Minister Nehru and our luncheon with him at his residence. The meetings with the various ministers had been more or less routine. Most I had known before. I went over with them the state of our efforts at cooperation in their particular fields. I admired the way they were attempting to adapt their English education and English colonial precedents to the task of launching a democracy of 400 million people, in the face of almost overwhelming difficulties.

The background of my discussion with the Prime Minister was dominated by the Korean War, in which we had suffered severe casualties, and by the pending Indian request for food grains then before the Congress. Nehru's attitude toward the Soviet Union and Communist China's entry into the Korean War had been explored in depth by Henderson in a meeting at his request on February 20, in preparation for the Nuwara Eliya conference.[2] In response to Henderson's expression of U.S. regret at the recent attack by Stalin against the UN, and the Soviets' continued efforts through international Communism to overthrow non-Communist governments, Nehru had replied in his usual equivocal way.

He had acknowledged that there was truth in much of what Henderson had said; he had cautioned, however, against merely accepting the available evidence of aggressive intent by the Soviets and other Communist countries. What he felt was needed was an analysis of the world situation in its entirety, to avoid a world war. After explaining the futility of a war from the standpoint of both sides, he had defined the immediate task as convincing each world that the other did not really desire a war, avoiding suspicions which might cause an unwanted war, and not pursuing developments which might lead to war.

India's efforts, Nehru had said to Henderson, were directed toward this end. This had been made clear by the position India had taken toward China, which Nehru did not consider to have an aggressive intent in Asia beyond retaking Formosa and Tibet. He was obviously referring to his own message, which had come across my desk in the Department, conveying the warning by Indian Ambassador Panikkar in Peking that China would enter the war if U.S. forces went into North Korea. Nehru had sent a similar personal message to Secretary Acheson through Madame Pandit in January. Nehru believed that there could be no Far Eastern solution without a settlement of the Japanese problem. In the peace treaty, he said, Japan should be permitted only limited forces, with its security guaranteed by the UN. At the end of Nehru's statements, Henderson had advised Nehru that he was forced to conclude that there remained a fundamental difference between us about the aggressive intent of international Communism.

I met with Nehru on March 8.[3] I opened the conversation by explaining that Secretary Acheson wanted to make it clear that we did not wish whatever differences of view might exist between India and the U.S., centering around Communist China, to affect our basic understanding or impede full consultation with each other on matters of common interest. I asked the Prime Minister how he assessed the present intentions of the two Communist states. I made it clear that it was their apparent aggressive intent, more than their Communist ideology, which gave us concern.

The Prime Minister then embarked on a long and boring historical discussion in which he sought to prove that wars do not achieve their objectives but merely lead to new wars. The First World War had resulted in the Second World War, which in turn raised the problem of Soviet Communism. Russia, he said, was what she was largely because of the way the nations had isolated her when she was young. Nehru expressed his belief that the same mistake was being made with respect to China. He went on to prove the undesirability of war in terms of the social and economic chaos created. Even if the Soviets were defeated, the world would be left as easy prey for Communism. We could not occupy and impose our will on Russia.

I replied that we were as thoroughly convinced as anyone of the undesirability of war. However, we would rather face war than fall under Soviet domination. Although a possibility existed that the world would still face a Communist threat after a destructive war, domination would appear a certainty if we did not prepare to stop the Russians in their immediate objective of world conquest. I pointed out the great disappointment of Americans over India's present policies, which appeared to us to run counter, even to undermine efforts to develop effective collective security against aggression. I said that this threat constituted the greatest present danger to world peace. Although as a democracy it had unfortunately taken us a long time to become convinced of these threats, we were now firmly determined to meet any further aggression by force. We had therefore decided to rearm on a large scale, even though this entailed great sacrifices for our citizens through increased taxes. We had begun to

build up our military forces. Many normal citizens who had fought in
the last war were going back into uniform. In response to the UN call
we had suffered 50,000 casualties in Korea. We were helping arm
and train other nations threatened.

It was, therefore, I continued, a great disappointment to us that
India had voted against the Security Council resolution condemning
China's aggression, and appeared actively to be seeking to influence
other states toward neutralism. This constituted a great danger. It
detracted from the strength of the free world, which could only come
from unity. It provided encouragement to the aggressor states by
raising doubt as to whether the neutral states would be willing or able
to defend themselves.

The Prime Minister agreed that the Russians had aggressive and
expansionistic designs. He did not feel, however, that China now had
such intentions. It would take China a long time, perhaps a decade or
so, to consolidate its newly-won independence. He did not agree that
Chinese actions, either in Korea or Indochina, were clear evidence of
aggressiveness. China's support of Ho Chi Minh had not involved
actual Chinese forces, although, since China had already been branded as an aggressor in Korea, it had little further to lose. Nehru refused
to accept our view that the Chinese posed a present threat to Burma,
even though I told him of evidence we had to this effect and that it
was considered a possibility by members of his own government.

Nehru denied that there was any essential difference between his
approach and that of other free nations, except as to method. In the
last Commonwealth meeting in London he had found his objectives
and those of the other Commonwealth countries to be the same.
When I pointed out that the U.K. and most other Commonwealth
countries had since branded China as an aggressor and were rearming, he observed that each country must pursue policies in conso-
nance with its own traditions. It was in the Indian tradition to make
every effort to explore possibilities for a peaceful settlement before
resorting to war, which was repugnant to Indians. Nehru continued
that he felt those who had reacted to the Communist threat by arm-
ing themselves would provoke war. The existence of opposing forces
would make war inevitable. Someone would start it off through
accident.

I replied that although we were rearming ourselves, since in the
face of the Soviet threat we had no alternative, we would never start
a war unprovoked. In our nation public opinion prevailed, as indeed
it must in any democracy, and public opinion was too much against

war. When I asked whether he thought his method of negotiating with Communist China had produced results, he said it had. It had stopped them from taking all of Tibet and had produced a reply to ceasefire proposals which, although crudely stated, was close to being satisfactory.

Pressing my basic point, I asked Nehru how any responsible government could fail to take steps to protect its people against a threat which had at least some degree of possibility, if not probability. The possible consequences of miscalculation were so great as to impose a grave responsibility on any government. Nehru did not yield, refusing to respond to the suggestion that there was any such threat to India. I expressed admiration for the strong leadership qualities he had displayed, both in India and other countries. His greatest possible contribution to world peace, and probably the only way to assure that there would not be another war, would be to lead the wavering states into a support for the principle of collective security against aggression. Surely this did not mean the creation of any bloc, a term which we knew he disliked. We were convinced that this was the only sure way to deter aggression or, if it came, to assure victory.

Nehru gave no particular reaction to this suggestion. He appeared to respond by proposing that the U.S. and India seek more complete consultation on matters of common interest, using the pattern of Anglo-American consultation as an illustration. He agreed that it was better to discuss controversial matters among ourselves privately, rather than publicly and in the press. It was, of course, presumptuous of me to press Nehru, the acknowledged leader of world neutralism, to abandon the fundamental point of his political philosophy. For him neutralism was deeply rooted in India's long struggle for independence and the use of nonviolence as the basic tool toward this end. It reflected also the weakness of India militarily even to defend itself—as was demonstrated in 1962 by the virtually unopposed Chinese invasion of the north Indian border. India was preoccupied with the staggering problem of feeding its people and the survival of the central Indian government against the forces of separatism.

Nehru, of course, could not yet yield on this point, illogical as it might seem to those of us who were convinced that the Communist threat was the greatest danger to all free nations. To me Nehru seemed to be hiding his head in the sand. The proposition that a state should not arm to defend itself against a potential aggressor was to me incomprehensible. In fact, however, there was really little Nehru could do. He had not much choice, even assuming he did understand the threat, but to rely on us and other nations to build a defense against Soviet expansion. In the meantime, Nehru obviously considered his stance valuable in holding his sway over the Indian people, and in maintaining his mystical role as leader of the ex-colonial developing nations. In the end Nehru did not really respond to my appeal. He tactfully ignored it and reverted to the proposal I had conveyed to him by Secretary Acheson, that we not let the differences in our views on Communism affect our understanding and consultation on other basic issues.

Following my meeting with Nehru, I called on the U.K. High Commissioner, Sir Archibald Nye. I told him the substance of my various conversations with Indian officials, including Nehru. The British, I thought, bore their changed position very gracefully. As long as they were advised, and not subjected to surprises, they did not contest our new role with India. I tried to make it clear that we had no desire to replace them, or assume any responsibilities that they were willing and able to fulfill. Indeed we were happy that we were shielded from so many of India's needs and growing pains. I often shuddered at the thought that Nehru might someday seek large-scale military and economic aid from us. The grain bill was proving enough of a headache.

Nehru gave a small luncheon for Cecilia and me on March 8 at his residence. His daughter, Shrimati Indira Gandhi, who in 1966 became Prime Minister herself, was his hostess. Present, in addition to the Hendersons, were the Bajpais and Menons. It was a pleasant occasion, undisturbed by any political disagreements. Conversation was in a light, sophisticated vein in the upper-class English manner. It centered on Nehru's great friend Lady Mountbatten, who had recently been visiting him.

At 4 P.M. I held a press conference at the chancery.[4] I met with the American press at 5 at the residence. In a lead editorial on March 7, the day following my arrival, the *Hindustan Times* had said:

> To American eyes, the expansionist threat of Communism and the efforts to contain it may appear to be the major factor in Asian affairs in the postwar era. But to most people in Asia the major threat is not Communism from outside but the poverty of their own people which allows a good breeding ground for the development of noxious creeds.
>
> We trust that Mr. George McGhee during his two day stay in this country will have some opportunity to study the truth of this.

The lead paragraph in the *Hindustan Times* March 9 article on my press conference quoted me as expressing hope that there would be increased "unity of view" among the nations of the free world. I was quoted as saying, "We are determined to resist Communist aggression." I had reassured India that the U.S. had a very real interest in the economic improvement of the underdeveloped areas. Although our own foreign-policy objectives had to be taken into account, our food offer to India was basically on humanitarian grounds. The lead to the article in the *Indian News Chronicle* of March 9, also based on my press conference, stated that it was not the aim of American foreign policy to fight Communism, but Communist expansion by force. I added that we did not seek to impose our political or economic system on anyone. I said that we accepted the proposition that Yugoslavia was a part of the free world.

A final dinner given for us that evening by Sir Girja Bajpai was pure pleasure. It was evidence that India and the U.S. could agree to disagree on the threat of Communism without destroying our new-found friendship. The following morning, we breakfasted early and boarded an Air Force plane for our first visit to Kabul. Staff instructions at Government House included not only early breakfast but refreshments for the journey.

My disappointment over Nehru's attitude toward Cold War issues did not alter my evaluation of his importance and that of India in the world scene, and the necessity for us to continue to try to help India with her immediate problem of a threatened famine. Later, on my way home, I became concerned about lack of progress in Congress in approving India's $750 million grain request, which had been dragging on for some eighteen months and in which I had taken the lead for the government. The submission of the Indian grain bill to the House of Representatives was delayed by a statement made in Texas by the Indian representative on the UN Social Commission that "our chief enemy in the Far East is not Communism but Western imperialism." As usual the Indians were making it difficult for their friends to help them.

Because it represented a new type of aid, and for a large amount that might set a dangerous precedent, President Truman had been reluctant to make a clear request to Congress but had given the Department only a sort of "hunting license" to see if support could be aroused in Congress. In view of Nehru's neutralist position and the adverse reaction he had created during his U.S. visit of October 1949, we concluded that success depended on a genuine upswelling of sympathy for the Indian people in the face of impending large-scale famine.

I stalked the halls of Congress and found strong support in the senate, particularly by Senators Alexander Smith of New Jersey, Jacob Javits of New York, and Hubert Humphrey of Minnesota on the Foreign Relations Committee. President Truman invited to a meeting at the White House former President Herbert Hoover, who had a particular sympathy for starving people and strongly supported the Indian request. Soon a torrent of mail and favorable editorial comment convinced the Congress that the American people wanted to help the Indian people, Nehru or no. It was a heartening example of the generous instincts of Americans and the functioning of our democracy. But the final bill had still not passed.

I sent a strong message to the Department on March 26 from Amman, pointing out the importance of an early response by Congress on grain, if we were to receive the benefits expected in our relations with India.[5] Otherwise the strong initial impetus for private and congressional support would be lost and the views of many Indians, that we claimed to want to help them but did not follow through, would be confirmed. Fortunately, the grain bill, after many difficult negotiations both in New Delhi and Washington, was finally approved in May, and U.S.-Indian relations were given a new lease on life.

After my return, I received an interesting letter from Amrit Kaur, for whom, during two visits to India, I had developed a great admiration.[6] She said in part:

> I do hope your visit here again will convince you that whatever India does is done with the purest of motives and with only one desire, that of promoting friendship and peace between the nations of the world. I realize how difficult it is for you (Not you personally but the Western people in general) to understand that *because* we do not throw ourselves into "your bloc" we are *not* pro-Communism. We could really *never* be for violence that seeks to crush the human spirit. But I believe that it would be wise to try to be friends with China—a new China via new force that has come into being and which we must try to win over to our side in the cause of peace. Even the wrong doer has to be won over by love. War cannot solve any problem but friendship can. Communism can only live on hate and where there is discontent and where the common man—as in our land today—is without the bare necessities of life. Help us to feed, clothe and give shelter to

our people. Then you and we will *not* need armies for our Defense.

It was good to have had a talk with you even though we could not agree on some vital matters. Come again and in any case I am sure you will always have a soft spot in your heart for India. We have a man of the highest integrity at the helm of our affairs. You can trust him and those of us who believe in what our beloved Gandhi taught us. Kindest wishes from

Yours v. sincerely,
Amrit Kaur.

Thirty-five years after independence, India, with an estimated population of 700 million, remains the world's largest democracy, an experiment that has worked beyond the expectations of many early observers. Nehru's Congress Party captured a clear majority in India's first general election in 1951 and held it without interruption for more than twenty-five years. At his death in office in 1964, he was succeeded by Lal Bahadur Shastri, a colorless politician under whom the party's strength at the state level was eroded.

When Shastri died in 1966, the day after he had concluded a peace agreement with Pakistan, Indira Gandhi assumed the office of Prime Minister that had been occupied by her father. She proved to be a skillful and cunning politician, with great influence in the rural areas, and was able to restore Congress's position in the 1967 election. But she was less effective in dealing with rivals within her own party, and in 1969 the Congress split over the selection of a presidential candidate, with Morarji Desai taking a number of members into opposition.

Following the hotly contested 1971 election, Mrs. Gandhi was accused of sanctioning vote fraud. After four years of politically charged litigation, she was found guilty of the charges and was barred from holding office for six months. The Prime Minister defied the authority of the court and declared a state of emergency, granting her government extraordinary powers, which she used to detain members of the opposition and to postpone scheduled elections. When the next general election was held in 1977, voters toppled the Congress from power, and a right-wing coalition government was formed by Desai.

The new government pressed charges of corruption against Mrs. Gandhi, who was convicted and briefly imprisoned. Out of office, she set about rebuilding a political base in a fraction reconstituted from the original party, Congress Party (I), and after an internal struggle for party leadership captured the old Congress. Returned to power in a lopsided victory in 1980, Gandhi proceeded to suspend opposition-controlled state legislatures and put restraints on the judicial system.

Congress (I), which holds two-thirds of the seats in the lower house of the current parliament and eighteen out of twenty-two state governments, has a national constituency, but Mrs. Gandhi's critics see the party as a personalist organization lacking the coherent ideological program of the old party. It is obvious that she intends to create a political dynasty. Since the death of her son and designated political heir, Sanjay, in 1980, she appears to have fixed the succession on another son, Rajiv. Opponents argue that her overbearing style threatens to undermine parliamentary institutions in India.

Although India has made considerable economic progress, particularly toward self-sufficiency in foodstuffs and significant oil production, the living standards of the masses remain desperately low. It has just not proven possible, with the limited arable land and other natural resources available, and her limited capital, for India to lift her 700 million people out of poverty. The streets of Bombay, and of Calcutta, which has seen a massive influx of refugees from Bangladesh, are filled with indigent beggars, sleeping in the streets.

26

The Pushtunistan Issue

Visit to Kabul, Afghanistan, King Mohammed Zahir Shah Khan, March 9–14, 1951. Visit to Karachi, Pakistan, Prime Minister Liaquat Ali Khan, March 14–16, 1951.

Cecilia and I left the residence of the Governor of the North-West Frontier Province of Pakistan for our visit to Afghanistan early on the morning of March 9, having arrived the evening before after a flight from New Delhi. The dim light added to our excitement at the prospect of going through the fabulous Khyber Pass to the mysterious ancient land-locked kingdom it guarded. Awaiting us for our drive through the Khyber Pass to the capital city of Kabul was a disheveled young Afghan in a large and ancient American Packard limousine. He seemed ill at ease in this (to him) strange and hostile land. He was treated coolly by the Pakistanis.

At the border, marked by a stream that had to be forded, at the station of Torkham only twenty miles distant, the Packard broke down in the middle of the stream, to the great glee of the Pakistan border guards. Our driver worked desperately to get it started, obviously very embarrassed. Eventually he succeeded. We tried to reassure him that he shouldn't worry. There was no rush. There followed a long and at times difficult drive over mountainous territory and through dense forests. The road was unpaved, and in some places almost impassable. The occasional caravans we met—their loads carried by mules, donkeys, camels, and, I'm sorry to say, women—were able to pass only when our automobile was pulled over as far as possible and stopped, while the groups of two- and four-legged travelers filed by, singly and with great care.

There was a sheer cliff on one side (the side, fortunately, where we waited) and an almost equally precipitous drop to the river on the other. My wife was diverted by the sight of a baby camel wearing a "sweater," a large woolen square with a round hole to accommodate its hump. We followed generally the valley of the Kabul River. We lunched from a picnic hamper which the driver had brought, and arrived before dusk at Jalalabad, where we were to spend the night at an attractive rustic government guest house.

It was obvious that there were many other guests there and that something important was going on. We were, however, introduced to no one, given no explanation, and dined alone. We retired early in preparation for the journey to Kabul the next day, but were aware of much conversation and speechmaking in another part of the house. Later we found that the meeting was in honor of the Mufti of Jerusalem, who was visiting Afghanistan at the time. He had come to thank the Afghan government for their support of the Arab cause in Palestine and to help resolve Afghan-Pakistan difficulties.[1] All of the local tribal chiefs had been brought in for an Islamic palaver. I speculated on what the world press might have said if they had construed that I had had a secret rendezvous with the Mufti, who was at the time an extremely controversial figure in the Arab-Israeli scene.

The next day we had a leisurely drive to Kabul, where we were taken upon arrival to a charming old palace in the environs of the city; it belonged to the royal family and was set high on a hill in a spacious park overlooking the Kabul River. There were magnificent views of pine trees and distant mountains. The palace seemed immense: it must have had fifty rooms and more servants. Two two-story wings were connected by a large single-story building of stone and red stucco. The palace, called Chil-Setoon Pillars, had been built by Amir Abdul-Rahman as a summer residence. A terrace surrounded the palace. One entered by a stairway at the second-story level. My principal recollection is of the open fires, which were kept burning at all times in each room. The attendants were constantly adding small pine sticks to the flames. The smell of the burning pine was fragrant and refreshing.

Afghanistan, which currently has a population of 15 million, has existed as a state only since 1747, when it was carved by Ahmad Shah out of the conquests of Nadir Shah. The term Afghan applies only to one ethnic group, the dominant tribe known as the Durani. The remainder are a mixture of various subject tribes including Turks, Tajiks, Hazars, Uzbeks, Kafirs, and the Pathans or Pushtu-speaking tribes who inhabit what was once the border area of British India. These various tribes have traditionally lived independent lives under their own tribal codes. Typically, they all are warlike, hardy, sober, stern, and often cruel people. Traditionally they have prized their freedom and resisted taxation and incorporation into a modern state. Fiercely religious, their determined resistance to Soviet conquest could have been anticipated.

The history of the peoples of Afghanistan has been dominated by a long sequence of conquests by the various South Asian empires. Geographically the country is divided by the northeast-southeast-trending massive Hindu Kush Mountains, to the north of which lies the plain of the Amu Darya (Oxus) River, the only natural barrier between Afghanistan and the Soviet Union. British influence began in 1809 with a mission by the East India Company. Russian influence came early in the nineteenth century. After a brief British occupation, a virtual standoff between Great Britain and Russia, formalized by the Anglo-Russian Convention of 1907, permitted Afghanistan to remain relatively free of foreign influence. Afghanistan was opened to Western influence following World War I by Amanullah, who seized power in 1919. Nadir Shah came to power in 1929, after a brief interregnum following Amanullah's abdication. When Nadir Shah was assassinated in 1933, he was succeeded by his son, Mohammed Zahir Shah Khan.

U.S. prestige in Afghanistan had deteriorated in the late 1940s. In early 1950, however, because of Afghan desire to cultivate U.S. friendship to balance the Soviet threat, this trend appears to have been reversed. Careful attention was also paid by Afghanistan to advantages offered by other Muslim and European countries. Turkey sent a military mission to Afghanistan. U.S. policy toward Afghanistan in 1951 had multifold objectives. We wanted to ensure the continued existence of Afghanistan as an independent state, further integration of its diverse peoples, help maintain a stable government, improve Afghan relations with Pakistan and Iran, and encourage political and economic progress to further strengthen Afghan orientation toward the Western democracies and away from the U.S.S.R.

The autocratic ruling oligarchy in Afghanistan in 1951 under Zahir Shah had maintained a stable government for twenty years and was permitting increasing diversity of political expression. The Afghan government had up to this point expressed no interest in U.S. military equipment. So far as we knew at the time there was no significant Communist organization in Afghanistan, because of the vigilance of the government and the natural antipathy of the Afghans to Russia as a nation and Communism as an ideology. The U.S., with its limited aid funds, made every effort to help Afghanistan minimize import needs and develop economically. Our proposal in 1948 for a Treaty of Friendship and Commerce had, however, not been accepted, since the Afghans thought it too comprehensive. They feared that it might provide a basis for the U.S.S.R. to demand similar privileges.

As a small, landlocked, and undeveloped country, Afghanistan was heavily dependent on its neighbors and had learned to play off rival states against each other, at the same time enlisting the support of remote powers. It had traditionally relied on the British as an offset to Soviet encroachment, even though it mistrusted the British. Since the partition of India, Afghanistan had strongly objected to the integration into Pakistan of the Pushtu-speaking tribes west and south of the Durand line, the old division between British India and Afghanistan.

U.S. interest was to resolve or minimize this Pushtunistan issue. Afghanistan had maintained toward the U.S.S.R. an attitude of cautious correctness combined with firm resistance to Soviet penetration, particularly among the tribes north of the Hindu Kush barrier, who were close to ethnic groups in the U.S.S.R. Afghanistan activity in the Pathan tribal area on the Pakistan border had, however, given the U.S.S.R. a possible opportunity 'to intervene to stop the occasional fighting which occurred. Afghans were aware of the danger in setting a precedent with other states that the U.S.S.R. could take advantage of. Because of this we had not encouraged Afghanistan to ask for U.S. military aid.

An interesting detail had arisen before our Kabul visit when my good friend Afghan Ambassador Prince Mohammed Naim had called on me at the State Department. He said that he had come to discuss U.S. military aid and hinted that if it were not forthcoming the Afghans might have to talk to the Russians. Sensing that he was bluffing, from the obvious futility of the Afghan government's relying on Russian military aid, I picked up the phone and asked my secretary to get me the telephone number of the Russian Embassy. I wrote it on a piece of paper and handed it to the Prince, whereupon we both laughed.

It was our expectation that if there was a deterioration in the world situation or increased Soviet threat, Afghanistan could be expected to move toward neutrality. After a period of watchfulness, Afghanistan would find a suitable opportunity to align itself with the winning side. It was our hope, too, that we could, through economic and social development, increase Afghanistan confidence and reliance on the U.S. and overcome the adverse effect of a reactionary ruling group and the lack of educated manpower. We wanted to avoid the implication of support for the regime; however, in practice this is usually impossible. The Afghan people undoubtedly assumed that we backed the ruling family.

The U.S. had, on November 6, 1950, made an important intervention in the Afghan-Pakistan dispute over Pushtunistan. We had expressed concern over the rising tension between the two countries on this issue, which was impeding their economic and social progress and inviting Soviet intrigue. We offered to be a go-between, but not a mediator, by seeking agreement on the following points: both parties would cease official attacks on the other and seek to eliminate private attacks; they would make their best efforts to eliminate incidents causing trouble between them and any public statements regarding incidents that did occur; the parties would exchange ambassadors within two months; and both would designate representatives who would meet within three months for exploratory discussions without preconditions or publicity. Although the Afghan government had accepted our proposals, the Pakistanis had not done so at the time of my Kabul visit. I hoped to use the results of my visit to obtain acceptance by Liaquat, the Pakistan Prime Minister, whom I would visit in Karachi after leaving Kabul.

Soon after our arrival in Kabul, Prince Naim came to greet us. Naim had only recently retired from his position as Ambassador to the U.S. My wife and I had known the Prince and Princess quite well there (he was not only a relative of the king but also married to the King's sister, Princess Zora). In addition to our official relations, they were our neighbors in the Kalorama Road area of Washington, and we had often been guests in their Embassy. Although she had enjoyed complete freedom in Washington, Princess Zora was not with the Prince when he visited us in Kabul. Only my wife was to see her and then only at tea in the privacy of her residence. Although we did not have an ambassador in Kabul at that time, we were well looked after by our chargé, Fritz Jandrey, and his wife, who had been with us at Nuwara Eliya. They were an attractive couple who had taken a strong liking to Afghanistan. Fritz, a native of Wisconsin and a graduate of the State University, had served a typical Foreign Service career. His final post was to be Deputy Assistant Secretary for European Affairs.

On our first evening Prince Naim gave a small dinner in our honor in his home. The invitation read, "Dress, smoking [black tie], time 8:00." It was, of course, a Muslim home and reflected Muslim

customs. Cecilia was the only lady present and was completely ignored by the men. Princess Zora did not make an appearance. Naim's
home was a large bungalow done in an attractive European style.
The conversation was dominated by Prince Mohammed Daoud, who
was Naim's brother and, like Naim, a brother-in-law of the King. I
had a queer feeling about Daoud even then: he seemed evasive and
my instinct was not to trust him. In 1973 my suspicion was proven
right: he seized power in a coup that overthrew the monarchy and
replaced it with a military government, with himself as President.
Both he and Naim were to meet tragic deaths at the hands of the
Communist revolutionary forces in 1978. Surrounded by their families, they were machine-gunned down by the rebels in the royal
palace where they had taken refuge, the king being in exile. Daoud
was brave to the end, replying, "Never" to the demand to surrender.
Princess Zora, who was not killed, later resided in London.

Cecilia was offended by the smooth but complete way she was
isolated at dinner. This was much more studied and thorough than
her treatment as a woman in Pakistan and other Islamic countries.
No remarks were addressed to her until the group arose to leave and
Naim leaned toward her ear and conspiratorily whispered that Princess Zora would like to have her come to tea the following day. She
accepted quickly to save him the embarrassment of being seen talking to her. The Prince and I made the necessary arrangements.

When Cecilia called the next day at the appointed hour she was
ushered into Zora's sitting room, where the Princess greeted her
warmly, since they had had a natural, friendly relationship in Washington. Cecilia had recalled her as a pleasant, smiling woman, Paris
dressed, and she had the same manner in her own setting. Her
daughter, however, was another matter. As they drank from tiny
cups filled with sweetened green tea flavored with cardamom, Zora
spoke of the difference in the way she and her fifteen-year-old
daughter, sitting beside her, lived in Washington and at home.

"It's not so hard for me," said Zora. "When I am abroad I enjoy
wearing European clothes and walking freely in Paris or Washington,
but I always know that when I come back I must go into purdah. But
how do you explain that to a child? We were away from here for so
many years! She was so young and in Washington she ran and played
like an American child."

"I love tennis," said the girl, wistfully. "Of course, I can't play it
here. The only exercise I can get without having to wear those awful
old things is to walk around." Cecilia considered the "protective"

garments worn by Afghan women the heaviest she had ever seen anywhere. She has still not seen their equal. From head to toe fell untold yards of some thick material, of such weight that it was obviously burdensome, literally as well as figuratively. The netting through which Afghan women had to strain their eyes to see where they were going permitted vision through only a tiny hole in the finely woven mesh. Apart from the other disadvantages their garments posed, Cecilia was worried about the danger of Afghan women being hit by automobiles they couldn't see.

My meeting with the King was, of course, the highlight of my visit. Although we did not know it at the time, Mohammed Zahir Shah was to end his life in exile as the last of his line. The meeting was largely perfunctory. The King received me in his brightly-lighted, bejeweled throne room. He was a tall, dignified, imposing figure with short hair, a receding hairline, and a neat mustache. He had a lean, ascetic face. We discussed in general terms the overall relations between our two countries. I emphasized our desire to strengthen our ties and our willingness to help resolve the issues between his country and Pakistan. I emphasized the importance to both countries of improving their relations. Only the Soviets would profit from the present discord.

The King welcomed me and made the usual Afghan pitch for Pushtunistan, which was to dominate all of my discussions in Kabul. He suggested that I discuss this with Ali Mohammed Khan, the Acting Prime Minister and Foreign Minister. He professed a desire to improve relations with Pakistan but emphasized that this depended on their attitude toward the Pushtu. The King gave the appearance of being a cold man, difficult to approach. Little of his personality came through. He tried, however, to be agreeable. He presented me with a photograph of himself in a splendid silver frame and sent my wife a fine Afghan rug. I expressed our appreciation for being given one of the royal residences for our stay. Later the King and his wife, whom we did not meet, had quite a successful visit to the U.S. The Queen took great interest in inspecting American homes, particularly kitchens.

After my meeting with the King my main discussions were with Foreign Minister Ali Mohammed Khan, who was also Acting Prime Minister.[2] The Prime Minister, Sardur Shah Mohammed Khan, uncle of the King, was absent from the country. Ali entertained my wife and me at luncheon, and at a state dinner which included most of the top officials of the government. Both affairs were held in the palace of the Prime Minister. Dinner dress was "smoking." The invitations to both were translated as saying that we were asked "to accept the trouble of attending." I remember, in particular, as an engaging personality, Abdul Hamid Khan, president of the Bank Mille. The group, which included both Naim and Daoud, were all more or less related. Few individuals outside the royal family had been given foreign educations and high positions in government. One who had was Mohammed Ludin of the Foreign Office, an able man whom I would see more of later in Washington.

In my meeting with him on March 12, the Foreign Minister began as expected with a statement on the Pushtu issue. Afghanistan had always been interested in their tribal peoples and had sought a peaceful solution to their problems. He told me he had raised the question with the British Ambassador at Kabul, Sir Francis Wylie, in 1942, who had told him that the time was not then ripe to seek a solution. The issue was raised a second time in 1942 with Sir Stafford Cripps, the Lord Privy Seal, who had headed a mission to India. Again the same answer was given. When the partition of India took place, Afghanistan had expected to be consulted about the tribal area, but was not.

When, subsequently, a referendum was held in the North-West Frontier Province, the Afghan government advised Pakistan that under no circumstances would it accept the outcome as a fair means of resolving the tribal problem. Later, the Afghans agreed to send a special envoy to Karachi on condition that the status of the tribal area would be discussed. It was not. Still later, when the exchange of ambassadors had been agreed on, the Afghans once more had made an offer to the Pakistan Ambassador to discuss a negotiation of differences over the Pathan tribes, but no reply was ever received.

The Foreign Minister said that Afghanistan was therefore pleased to accept our proposal of November 6, 1950, for the initiation of bilateral talks with Pakistan. If something was not done serious trouble might result and the beneficiary would be Soviet Russia. It was in the interest of both Afghanistan and Pakistan, who needed each other, to reach a final agreement. The Foreign Minister did not, however, envision negotiations which would solve all problems at one time.

I replied that I understood the interest of Afghanistan in the Pathan tribes but this problem, as all others, had to be considered in the light of the expansionist policy of Soviet Russia, which would have no hesitancy in taking advantage of the power vacuums in Asia as well as Europe. There was no question about Soviet aggressive intentions, of which we had recently had several clear examples. The United States wished to help all countries protect themselves from Communism and we had already given evidence of willingness to help Afghanistan. I assured the Foreign Minister that our objective in the Pushtunistan issue was simply to help solve the matter by bringing the two parties together. We believed that this was the only way of settling an issue of this kind. We did not wish to antagonize either Pakistan or Afghanistan, both of whom we considered friends, by taking a definite side.

I then explained that I wanted to make several personal observations based on world-wide strategic factors. Did the Foreign Minister consider that the Afghan approach to Pushtunistan was based on legal arguments or on the principle of self-determination? He replied categorically that it was based on the right of self-determination. I then pointed out that although self-determination had been espoused by our President Wilson after World War I, it was not considered generally applicable in the present world. There was, in fact, ample evidence that the trend today was the other way, one example being the unification of Europe, where ancient nations were yielding elements of sovereignty in the interest of collective security. The United States was in full accord with this. I mentioned that the Arab states were also seeking some basis for united action.

I then made the following points. In our judgment the area called Pushtunistan was not economically or politically viable. An independent Pushtunistan would have no experienced leaders to handle its relations with its neighbors. The internal political situation in Pakistan was such that Liaquat Ali Khan could not maintain his position were he to make any considerable concessions on the tribal area. The timing of Afghan sponsorship of Pushtunistan was very important. We were trying now to prepare as rapidly as possible for a united effort in containing Soviet aggression. Keeping the Pushtunistan issue alive could harm Afghanistan by creating conditions that could lead to Soviet intervention. Without foreclosing action in the future, it would be better now for Afghanistan to seek a modus vivendi with Pakistan on Pushtunistan.

Reverting to our proposal for negotiations, I said that although Pakistan had not reached a decision, we felt they were on the point of doing so. The point which bothered Pakistan was that of sovereignty over the tribal area. I suggested that if agreement on this issue could not be reached at the first meeting, some good might still come from discussions on other points of difference, which could eventually lead back to the primary issue. Economic problems could not be separated from political problems. Efforts to improve the welfare of the tribes, which was certainly Afghanistan's major interest, could affect progress on the central issue.

When I asked the Foreign Minister whether he thought any good would come from continuing to explore solutions to the Pushtu problem short of the sovereignty issue, he replied that he could not say but he hoped so. Finally, at my urging, he said he saw no reason why I should not mention to Liaquat that Afghanistan was hopeful that good would come out of the meeting even if agreement was not immediately reached on sovereignty. The Foreign Minister also said that he could give the British Ambassador assurance (which would undoubtedly be passed on to the government of Pakistan) that Pakistan's willingness to negotiate would never be raised to the disadvantage of Pakistan in the context of efforts for settlement by some other means. I might also pass this on to Liaquat Ali Khan.

Ludin of the Afghan Foreign Office then reviewed some of the historical aspects of the Pushtunistan issue, stressing that the area occupied by the Pathans had been severed from Afghanistan. His point seemed to be a justification for the existence of a Pushtunistan issue and the desirability of Pakistan's recognizing that a problem in fact did exist. Toward the end of the conversation I became convinced that the Afghans desired to see this problem solved, and that they would during the course of negotiation be willing to listen to Pakistan's suggestions and attempt to arrive at some compromise.

In closing I assured the Foreign Minister that I would, in my forthcoming meeting with Liaquat in Karachi, make every effort to obtain agreement on the terms of our proposal of the previous November. As advised by the department in a telegram awaiting me in Kabul, I sought to prevent the Afghans from believing we favored their position or would act as mediator, and avoid positions on legal questions such as that of a plebiscite, more suitable for decision by international bodies. Although we had assured Pakistan that our recognition of their country after partition gave implicit approval of their Durand line border, we refused to be drawn into any new affirmation of such a position.

Cecilia and I departed from Afghanistan with lasting impressions of this interesting country, which had not yet joined the modern era. The problems it faced, particularly in light of the nonprogressive attitude of the royal family, who were holding on tenaciously to an untenable position, were indeed formidable. I was elated at the prospect of my meeting with the Pakistan Prime Minister. I thought I had enough ammunition from my visit in Kabul to obtain agreement on our initiative on the Pushtu issue. I was to be disappointed.

Afghanistan has recently been catapulted into world prominence by its conquest by Soviet forces. This really began with the overthrow of President Mohammed Daoud's government, in April 1978, by a Communist-led coup. After an intermediate coup by the Communist leader Hafizullah Amin, Afghanistan was invaded and occupied by Soviet forces in December 1979. Then Amin, an unpopular hardliner, was eliminated to make way for the more pliable Babrak Karmal, as head of the revolutionary council. Despite valiant resistance by the Afghan tribesmen, the hundred thousand Soviet occupation forces are strongly entrenched and the Soviets show no intention of withdrawing them despite strong pressure from the entire non-Communist world.

Cecilia and I flew from Kabul to Karachi on a U.S. Air Force plane on March 14. We arrived at Maripar Airfield, where we were met by Ambassador Avra Warren, his wife, and members of the Embassy staff. Since we were to be guests of the state, we were also met by A. M. Mustafa, Chief of Protocol, for the government of Pakistan; the military secretary, Colonel Knowles; and Flight Lieutenant M. Y. Butt, who escorted us to the residence of the Governor-General.[3] Here we were put up in a large, luxurious apartment, a relic of colonial days. We had lunch with the Governor-General, Khwaja Nazzimuddin, a kindly elder statesman, along with Ambassador and Mrs. Warren. In the evening we were given a dinner by Syed Amjad Ali, a prominent Pakistan businessman and one-time government official whom I had known through his frequent visits to Washington, at his elegant home on 18 Victoria Road.

I held a press conference the following morning at the Embassy residence at No. 2 Bonus Road.[4] The Pakistan press highlighted my remarks on Kashmir, the troubled province whose disposition remained an explosive point of contention between Pakistan and India. The *Civil and Military Gazette* of March 16 quoted me as saying that the "Kashmir issue, which had long been a threat to the peace in South Asia, would result in a catastrophe if allowed to remain unsettled." I pledged U.S. support for the Kashmir resolution before the Security Council, as modified by the debate in the Council, looking toward an early resolution of this issue.

After the press conference, I met with the Secretary-General of the Foreign Office, Mr. Ikramullah, whom I had known before. Ambassador Warren was also present. I went over with Ikramullah my conversations with the Afghan government on the Pushtunistan issue during my visit in Kabul. I said that I looked forward to my meeting with the Prime Minister scheduled for the day following and hoped he would give an affirmative reply to our proposals. The Secretary-General seemed hopeful.

Our old friend Ghulam Mohammed, Minister of Finance, who had entertained us during our first visit to Karachi, gave a luncheon for us at Bawalpur House. It was good to renew old times with this extraordinary man, who was later to play a critical role as Acting Prime Minister. The guests included, in addition to the Warrens and other friends, the former Pakistan Ambassador to Washington, Mr. M. S. H. Ispahani. Late in the afternoon, I met with the Commonwealth High Commissioners in Karachi: Mr. Johnson of Canada, Mr. Arnott of Australia, and Mr. Burnett of the U.K. Such meetings were a must in any visit to a Commonwealth member.

The Iranian Ambassador, Mr. Masoed Moazed, called on me in the evening of my first day to give me a report on the delicate situation in his country following the assassination of Prime Minister Ali Razmara on March 7. This had led to a decision in Washington that I should change my return plans and go first to Teheran to talk with the Shah and Acting Prime Minister Hussein Ala, former Iranian Ambassador in Washington. The National Front party, supported by the Communist Tudeh party and the Fidaiyan-i Islam, a religious-political sect, one of whose members had assassinated Razmara, was demanding nationalization of the properties of the Anglo-Iranian Oil Company.

Ambassador and Mrs. Warren gave a large reception at their residence that evening for us and an Embassy couple who had married that afternoon. Later we attended a dinner given in our honor by the Prime Minister and Begum Liaquat Ali Khan, whom we had first met in Peshawar in December 1949, when we invited them to visit our country. It was a happy reunion. We reminisced about their successful visit, in which Cecilia and I had participated. Among the twenty-two guests were General Sir Douglas Gracey and Lady Gracey, and Air Vice Marshal Richard Atcherly. The Pakistan military forces, like the Indian forces, were still commanded by British officers. It was a convivial evening. My discussions with the Prime Minister about Pushtunistan and Pakistan-Afghan relations would come the following morning.

On the morning of March 16, in company with Ambassador Warren, I called on the Prime Minister in his office with great hopes for a breakthrough on Pushtunistan.[5] I outlined my conversation the previous day with Ikramullah and repeated the key points made to me by the Foreign Minister in Kabul, who, I said, was hopeful for a meeting between the two countries even if the sovereignty issue was not resolved. The Foreign Minister had promised that Pakistan's willingness to negotiate would never be raised by Afghanistan to the disadvantage of Pakistan.

The Prime Minister was agreeable to calling off immediately the propaganda campaign against Afghanistan, provided the Afghans would take the same action. He was agreeable also to naming an ambassador to Afghanistan and expected the Afghans on their part to send an ambassador to Karachi. After the accreditation of the ambassadors in their respective capitals, he was prepared to receive in Karachi any representations on differences between the two countries as part of the normal discussion between countries on the ambassadorial level. In the event that problems arose that could not be settled in this manner, he was prepared to work out with the Afghan government, through the two ambassadors, the organization of a special joint conference that could take up outstanding tensions and frictions.

Very encouraged, I immediately said that I understood the Prime Minister in substance to have accepted the points in the American offer of good offices, to which he agreed. It was also agreed that at the beginning of the week Ambassador Warren would work out mutually satisfactory language with Ikramullah and inform Washington officially of the results of the conversation. Although I left Pakistan still very hopeful that our proposals had been accepted, new difficulties were soon to be put in the way by Pakistan, and hard negotiations lay ahead.

Cecilia returned directly to the States on the morning of March 16. She had been away from our children too long to accompany me on my emergency mission to Teheran. I lunched with the Iranian Ambassador, Ambassador and Mrs. Warren, and Counsellor of Embassy and Mrs. Warwick Perkins at the Metropole Hotel. Later that day I laid a wreath on the tomb of the Pakistan national hero, Quaid-i-Azum Mohammad Ali Jinnah, who, as president of the Muslim League, had led in the creation of Pakistan as a Muslim state and served as its first Governor-General. Liaquat had been his chief assistant. I toured the port and industrial areas of the city with Acting U.S. Cultural Officer John Bowling. The tenements housing the millions of Pakistanis and refugees from India who had crowded into the capital city were appalling. Disorder prevailed, and it was obvious that the problems of the new state were very great.

In the evening I paid an unexpected visit to the Indian Coffee House, a popular Karachi haunt of journalists, students, and intellectuals. Joining a table of journalists, I had a most interesting exchange with them on the current Pakistan scene. The keen minds of these young men were full of suspicion of the U.S. and probed every possible ulterior motive we might have. I attempted to assuage them. My visit was widely reported in the press. As a long-time member of the International Committee of the YMCA, I visted the Karachi branch and talked with the officers, who were, against insuperable odds, extending invaluable assistance to the young men off the streets. That evening Ambassador Warren gave a dinner, inviting the Prime Minister and the ministers I had met with during my visit. The next morning I departed in an Air Force plane for Teheran. Although buoyed up by apparent progress in getting the Afghans and Pakistanis together over Pushtunistan, I could envision the ominous pall I would find in Teheran in the wake of Prime Minister Razmara's assassination.

Later, after my return to the U.S., Secretary Acheson and I met on April 13 with Afghan Prime Minister Sardur Shah Mohammed Khan, uncle of the King, who had been absent from Afghanistan during my visit there in March. I had known him before, and found him a most attractive man, handsome and dignified, friendly to all Americans including officials of all ranks. He was often in America, trying to overcome a serious illness, and the Department assisted in every way to assure him the best medical care. On this visit he was in fine fettle and came out, with some of his aides, to spend the evening with Cecilia and me on our farm at Middleburg. He was particularly interested in fishing, which we arranged on our lake. Unfortunately the bass, the larger and more interesting catch, were not biting, so the Prime Minister had to make do with a number of sun perch, which we were able to convince him were, despite their small size, considered much more sporting. He was quite happy with those he caught.

That evening late, after a pleasant dinner and conversation, I pushed the Prime Minister hard, under the informal circumstances— harder than I had ever pushed any Afghan official. I asked him to tell me in effect whether the Pushtunistan issue was one deeply felt by Afghans, including himself, or was really intended to bolster the regime in the eyes of the people. It was perhaps an impossible, even an improper question to ask of a member of the royal family. The response of the Prime Minister appeared very sincere. Tears came to his eyes as he recounted what he considered to be the sad plight of the Pathan tribesmen under Pakistan rule. Traditionally freedom-loving nomadic peoples, they had been forced into an impossible dependent situation, which separated them from their fellow tribesmen in Afghanistan, and took away their freedom. I was so moved by his response that I never raised the question with him again.

In his meeting with Secretary Acheson and me, the Prime Minister expressed appreciation for our good offices to help his country reach agreement with Pakistan over the Pushtunistan issue.[6] Despite the encouragement given by Liaquat in Karachi, no reply had ever been received from the Pakistanis. We were able to tell him that the Pakistani government had just advised us of acceptance of three of our four points: prevention of propaganda and incidents and exchange of ambassadors. The fourth item, an Afghan-Pakistan meeting without restrictions, would be accepted if discussions after the exchange of ambassadors indicated that such a meeting might be fruitful. The Prime Minister was skeptical. In any event, he could not give us a final answer to the proposed compromise. He doubted that Pakistan would agree to the meeting and ambassadors would then have to be recalled as before. With emotion he argued that the more than four million Pathans, his brethren, should have the right to determine their own future. Only a free Pushtunistan could be a barrier to the threat from the north.

This was but one of a series of disappointments over our good-offices proposal. On October 10, almost a year after it was offered the two parties, we reluctantly advised both that we considered it at an end. The government of Afghanistan expressed regrets. Pakistan's attention was diverted by Prime Minister Liaquat's tragic assassination on October 16. The opportunities presented during my visits to Kabul and Karachi in March were not to be realized. Such is often the result of gratuitous offers by sincere and disinterested friends in helping rivals of long standing in the solution of their problems.

Since 1951 Pakistan and its offspring Bangladesh have undergone tremendous changes. From its inception Pakistan, its two sections separated by a thousand miles of a usually hostile India, lacked geographical, ethnic, and economic coherence. Islam was its only unifying feature. The parliamentary form of government established at independence proved increasingly unworkable, and in 1958 it was replaced by Pakistan's first military regime in a coup carried out by

General Mohammed Ayub Khan. Elected President of a new civilian government in 1960, Ayub introduced a system of "basic democracy" which in effect was to allow for popular participation at a lower level while leaving the executive in unfettered command at the national level.

Disturbances in East Pakistan forced Ayub's resignation in 1969 and the resumption of military rule under General Yahya Khan. In the 1970 elections prepared by the military government, the Awami League, committed to autonomy for East Pakistan, won the largest number of seats in the national legislature, where representation was divided equally between the two sections of the country. Its leader, Sheikh Mujibur Rahman, was unwilling, however, to form a coalition with Zulfiquar Ali Bhutto's left-wing Pakistan People's Party, which had emerged as West Pakistan's leading party in parliament. When the army threatened to reenter the political arena and nullify the results of the election, East Pakistan declared its independence as Bangladesh. The secession was accorded international recognition after India intervened late in 1971 and defeated Pakistani forces in the east.

Bhutto, who had come to office as Prime Minister of Pakistan at the head of a civilian government, sought to initiate thoroughgoing economic and social reforms that incorporated both the socialist and the Islamic elements of his party's program. Encouraged by the experience of Bangladesh, however, regional separatists threatened to tear apart the remainder of the truncated country and, once again, the armed forces, to which Bhutto had always appeared a dangerous radical, stepped in to restore order. Bhutto was put on trial and eventually executed, despite protests from the international community. The head of the military government, General Mohammed Zia ul-Huq, assumed the presidency in 1978, proclaiming establishment of an Islamic state. Political parties were banned, elections canceled, and civil liberties severely curtailed.

Pakistan was a charter member of the Southeast Asia Treaty Organization (SEATO) and the Central Treaty Organization (CENTO), and, considering itself a member of the Western bloc, was continually disappointed that the U.S. was reluctant to favor Pakistan over a neutralist India. To counterbalance Soviet influence in India, China offered assistance to Pakistan, relations between the two countries growing particularly warm during the Bhutto years. In the 1970s, Pakistan also drew closer to other Muslim countries in the Middle East. Relations with the U.S. were strained when we refused to aid the Pakistani nuclear program. The Soviet invasion of Afghanistan in 1980, however, has caused both Pakistan and the U.S. to seek improved relations, involving increased American military support.

With the Pakistani withdrawal from Bangladesh in 1971, Sheikh Mujibur was allowed by Bhutto to return to Dacca, where as Prime Minister he formed the new nation's first government. War-related economic dislocation, famine, and terrorism prompted Mujibur to replace parliamentary government in January 1975 with a presidential system giving him dictatorial powers within a one-party state. He was, however, killed the following August in a military coup, the first of sixteen successful or attempted coups in Bangladesh to date.

The return to civilian rule promised by army chief Major General Zia Rahman was repeatedly postponed and opponents of continued military rule arrested. In 1977, the constitution was amended to create an Islamic state in Bangladesh, and Zia Rahman was formally elected its President. The return to civilian rule was completed after parliamentary elections in which a large number of parties participated, but less than 40 percent of eligible voters went to the polls. Zia Rahman was assassinated in 1981 during an unsuccessful military coup attempt. There have been a succession of short-lived governments since.

Bangladesh, the world's eighth most populous country and its poorest in terms of per capita income, presents an almost hopeless case. The country is dependent on two crops: rice for subsistence and jute for income. Shortfalls in rice production, to which 80 percent of Bangladesh's farmland is devoted, inevitably leads to famine and deaths from starvation, reaching the tens of thousands each year. The price of jute, the country's only source of foreign exchange, fluctuates on an unsteady world market. Cash reserves in 1982 equaled only slightly more than one dollar per person in Bangladesh's population. The prospects for a stable government in Bangladesh, and any relief from grinding poverty seem remote.

27

Anglo-Iranian Oil Company Nationalized

Visit to Teheran, Iran, the Shah, March 17–20, 1951. Visit to Baghdad, Iraq, Prime Minister Nuri Said, Prince Abd al-Illah, March 20–22, 1951.

This visit to Teheran had not been planned. Following the assassination of Iranian Prime Minister Razmara on March 7, while I was in the middle of my visit to Pakistan, the Department had, as I have reported, cabled me to proceed to Iran to appraise the situation created by Razmara's death, particularly the threat by the National Front to nationalize the Anglo-Iranian Oil Company (AIOC) oil concession.

The world press had highly dramatized the situation in Iran, particularly the press in Britain, the country with so much at stake. The *Daily Mail* of March 17 had as its lead headline US OIL ENVOY SENT TO PERSIA. KEEP THE SUPPLIES FLOWING, SAYS ACHESON. BRITISH 50/50 PROFIT PLAN NATIONALIZATION MAY UPSET SOVIET IDEAS. The article, datelined Washington, March 16, said that I was being sent to Iran first to urge the Iranian government to accept the fifty-fifty profit-sharing arrangement offered by the AIOC through the British government, or second, failing that, to attempt to get positive assurances that Iranian oil would continue to be available to Western customers.

Secretary Acheson was quoted as saying: "We very much hope and believe that Britain and Persia can work out a solution which would protect the interests of all countries and keep the important flow of oil moving from Persia to those markets to which it has gone in the past." The fear that the oil might find its way to Russia was underlined. This would be a great blow to allied Middle East strategy and to the British and U.S. fleets in the Mediterranean which needed Iranian oil. The *Daily Mail* reported from Teheran the same day a demonstration by three thousand former members of the outlawed

318

Tudeh party. This was not against nationalization of all Iranian oil, since Russia still had hopes for a concession in the north, but only against the British concession.

The *New York Times* of March 17 reported my arrival and the demand of the National Front that the Iranian government seize U.S.-operated oil concessions on Bahrain Island, an independent Arab state. The Iranian Senate had just voted 41 to 1 to refer to a committee, which would report on March 19 or 20, the nationalization bill which had been voted unanimously by the Majlis, or lower house, on March 15. Senate approval was expected. Since the assassination of Razmara, National Front extremists had threatened further assassinations and had created a feeling of tension that must have influenced the parliamentary votes. The Shah was not expected to veto the bill. However, there could be a two-month delay in taking over the properties, pending study by unspecified foreign experts of methods to be used in making the transfer.

Elsewhere in the world, as reported in the *New York Times* of March 19, *Pravda* charged that the U.S. was responsible for the assassination of Razmara, ignoring the fact that we had supported him for Prime Minister. Since he was a moderate, there was no reason for us to welcome his removal. American agents in Iran, according to *Pravda*, hoped "to be complete bosses" in that country. Also, according to *Pravda*, Razmara's tenure in office had resulted in improvement in Soviet relations with Iran, and U.S. setbacks. This was in part true, since Razmara had been forced to show he was not a U.S. puppet as charged. The *Times* reported from London astonishment and dismay at the Iranian swing away from the West. Although there had been a two-year dispute between Iran and the AIOC over royalties, the move for nationalization came as a surprise. Both Britain and Iran could be heavy losers. Other Middle Eastern oil concessions might be threatened. It was reported from Cairo that a bill would be introduced in Parliament nationalizing the Suez Canal Company. My visit to get a first-hand view of the situation was reported from Teheran. The U.S. was credited with a hands-off position in the dispute.

As I read these reports in 1951, my mind went back to my earlier unsuccessful efforts to convince the AIOC that they must make meaningful concessions to Iran if they hoped to forestall just such a nationalization attempt. My first contact with AIOC dated back fifteen years to the mid-1930s. As a student at Oxford I had met the attractive daughters of Sir John Cadman, Chairman of the Board of AIOC, and had visited the family in their country home nearby. One day, during a Sunday luncheon party, Cadman explained why the AIOC, even though a majority of its stock was owned by the British government, had refused to comply with the League of Nations sanctions against Italy for its aggression against Ethiopia.

"When this thing came up," said Cadman, "I called my friend Walter Teagle [chairman of the board of Standard Oil Company of New Jersey, now Exxon] in New York. 'Walter,' I said, 'What are you going to do about Italy?' 'John,' he replied, 'We've been selling oil to Italy for seventy years. I'm going to keep on selling oil to Italy.' What else could I do," said Cadman. The events of 1950-51 did not represent the first time that AIOC had acted independently of British government policy.

When I left Oxford in 1937, AIOC, with whom I had shared the results of my seismic research in an area they planned to drill in Hampshire, offered me a position as geophysicist, in Iran. I declined because, after three years abroad I wanted to return to the U.S. I had, however, a kindly feeling toward AIOC at that time.

My first encounter with AIOC as assistant secretary came on January 24, 1950, when I met in the Department with Richard Seddon, newly appointed AIOC manager in Teheran, together with Heath-Ives of the New York office.[1] I observed that during my recent visit to Iran there appeared to be only a small difference in view, concerning the amount of reserves allocated in the company's books before profits, that was blocking Iranian ratification of the Supplemental Agreement. This had been agreed to in July 1949, but never formally ratified by the Iranians.

Heath-Ives replied that if the company continued to give more, there would soon be "nothing in the till" for AIOC. I commented that the recent AIOC annual report I had just read indicated that the company had that year made a considerable profit. The situation in the Middle East had changed since the last negotiations. Better terms had been offered in the Western hemisphere and even in the Persian Gulf. In my view the oil companies must deal with this new situation realistically, recognizing the legitimate demands of the oil producing states. The AIOC officials expressed appreciation for my views.

On August 31, the Department advised our Embassy in London for their information that the ARAMCO Board had authorized renegotiation of their 1933 concession as demanded by the Saudis.[2] As soon as it became clear that ARAMCO was going to make substantial concessions to Saudi Arabia going beyond the Supplemental Agreement, I knew we must warn the British so the AIOC would have an opportunity to improve their offer to Iran. In preparation for a meeting I had scheduled with the British Foreign Office in London on September 21, I invited key officers of ARAMCO and its parent companies, and E.L. DeGolyer, leading oil consultant, to meet with me and other Department officers.[3] These included John A. Loftus, Edward G. Moline, C. Vaughn Ferguson, and Richard Funkhouser. Dick prepared an excellent background paper for the meeting.

After considering a variety of problems affecting Middle East oil as a whole, the discussion turned to Iran. It was reported to the group that Ambassador Grady felt that continued delay in getting Iranian approval of the Supplemental Agreement could result in the collapse of Iran or confiscation of the AIOC concession. Prime Minister Razmara had demanded four points to sweeten the agreement in order to obtain Majlis ratification: a ten-year Iranianization program, the right of Iran to examine the AIOC books to determine their share of the profits, oil prices in Iran equal to the lowest given to others, and full information as to destination of oil exported. Razmara also wanted installment payments against the new agreement so a start could be made on Iran's Seven-Year Plan. Although the British government was seriously concerned, AIOC was reported as feeling that giving in to Razmara would only result in new demands and that it would be better tactically to pressure the Iranians into ratification.

I then asked the oil company representatives, assuming they faced the same problem, what concessions they thought AIOC could make without endangering its position. Charles Harding of Socony-Vacuum said that it was inconceivable that AIOC could not accept Razmara's sweetening demands. DeGolyer and the other company representatives considered the Iranian demands reasonable and compliance with it a sound commercial proposition. They also agreed that Sir William Fraser of AIOC would resent any discussion of this question with U.S. officials, even with Foreign Office approval. All present gave AIOC good marks for its labor policy and employee housing. They considered, however, that the British government was not exerting strong enough pressure on AIOC to effect a settlement on reasonable terms. The meeting concluded that this was the most important point for me to have in mind when I met with the British officials in London on September 21.

It is interesting to read a Private and Confidential Memorandum from the Foreign Office to their Embassy in Washington, now available in the British archives, seeking advice regarding my visit, which they wished to confine to Persia and oil. The Foreign Office reported that:[4]

> The view has been expressed that the Americans have been rather overdoing their pressure on us in regard to the IPC [Iraq Petroleum Company] and the AIOC. The view has been expressed, though I [undesignated, succeeding pages having been removed from the record] do not myself subscribe to it, that the State Department may have been over much influenced by the American oil companies, who wish to see our companies driven into an uncompetitive position by constant pressure to raise their royalties and labor conditions. It has been further suggested that McGhee himself, as a former oil man, is not wholly immune from this feeling.

Although it is undoubtedly self-serving to defend one's own actions, I am not sure my British friends ever quite understood the strong efforts I had made to keep American oil companies from taking advantage of AIOC's difficulties, and that, with one minor company as an exception, to whom I had made clear our government's opposition, our companies had no desire to do so. A Briton could not have understood, either, since there were no independent oil producers in Britain, that I had never been associated with any of the "Seven Sisters"—the major oil companies—operating in the Middle East, but had spent my years of active oil exploration competing with them as an independent producer in South Louisiana.

I flew to London and consulted with our embassy officials before my meetings at the Foreign Office. With me for the meetings were Samuel Kopper from the Department and Joseph Palmer for our London Embassy. The British group, which was under the chairmanship of my old friend Michael Wright, included Geoffrey W. Furlongue of the Foreign Office and Sir Ernest Rowe-Dutton of Treasury. The British version of our meetings is available in the Public Records Office.[5]

Our discussions with the Foreign Office concentrated on ARAMCO's impending move, Razmara's Four Points, and AIOC's beginning installment royalty payments. Razmara had asked for increased Iranianization of the personnel of the company in Iran over a ten-year period. The Foreign Office advised me that AIOC had replied to the effect that the company was already 97 percent Iranian (largely the laborers) and that qualified Iranian professionals and executives were hard to find. Razmara had asked for Iranian rights to inspect the AIOC books, as a partner participating in profits. The reply was that Iran was not entitled to more information than any other shareholder, as the AIOC had many interests outside Iran. Razmara wanted an internal Iranian price equivalent to the lowest to any customer and related to the cost of production. AIOC thought they could yield on this, as well as on Razmara's insistence on knowing where Iranian oil was being shipped.

I told the group that in my judgment the situation required immediate action. I had before I left discussed Razmara's four points with representatives of the American companies operating in the Middle East, who felt that they could, under the circumstances, be met. Standard Oil of New Jersey had met demands for increased local personnel and inspection of the books in Venezuela. I told them that ARAMCO was on the verge of a negotiation with the Saudis that would result in a concession so large (I could not divulge the actual terms since ARAMCO had not yet decided on its fifty-fifty offer), that there would be no chance for Iranian ratification of the AIOC Supplemental Agreement.

At the insistence of Michael Wright, I later accompanied him to a meeting with the AIOC Board. I was very pleased at the opportunity to talk to the board but had been reluctant, as an American official, to suggest it. But Wright insisted. I reasoned that I would really be talking with the British government, who owned a majority interest in AIOC. I was to find that this was not the case. We had an elegant luncheon at Britannic House, a magnificent marble building on Finsbury Circus, the very symbol of wealth and power. To my great disappointment, Chairman Sir William Fraser was absent. Neville Gass, who had negotiated the Supplemental Agreement and was later to become chairman of AIOC, presided. I described my recent meetings with the ARAMCO officials and urged the AIOC to make concessions comparable to those being considered by ARAMCO before it was too late.

I said that since the British and Americans had helped put Razmara in office and counted on his help in getting a new AIOC agreement, we should support him by trying to meet his Four Points. I had discussed them with the American companies who had found them generally reasonable. Razmara opposed nationalization but must, if he was to remain in power, give evidence to his people that he was looking after their interests. I told the Board of the favorable comment the American oil company officials had made on AIOC's handling of its Iranian labor. The AIOC Board, in effect, told me that I should mind my own business. They knew more about Iran than we did. If you give the Iranians an inch they'll take a mile, they said. AIOC had better housing in Abadan than anywhere in the Middle East. I did not sense that I had made any impact on the Board.

The actual decision of ARAMCO to offer fifty-fifty profit sharing to Saudi Arabia was to come later. It was made in November 1950, after two meetings in my office with the company officials involved and other department representatives, fortunately including Ambassador Rives Childs who had returned from Saudi Arabia on a visit. During the first meeting held on November 6 with ARAMCO officials Fred Davies, J. T. Duce, W. Spurlock, and Col. William Eddy, they arrived at the common decision that increased benefits to Saudi Arabia were necessary and that ARAMCO could afford to pay them.[6] I offered department support for ARAMCO so as to prepare as favorable a basis for the negotiations as possible. ARAMCO representatives said they believed that Saudi Arabia preferred some sort of partnership arrangement.

The parents of ARAMCO were, however, not yet convinced that such a drastic concession was necessary. They thought that the ARAMCO officials were perhaps too close to the situation to resist Saudi demands that could be costly to the company. To help them better understand the situation I invited the parents to send representatives to another meeting on November 13.[7] Present were Orville Harden, Standard Oil Company (N.J.); Brewster Jennings, Socony-Vacuum Oil Company; and R. G. Follis, Standard Oil Company of California. At this meeting I, Ambassador Childs, and other Department officials, as well as ARAMCO representatives, described the situation in Saudi Arabia, including the strength of Saudi demands.

I advised the officials of the parent companies that, in view of the situation described, the Department was thoroughly convinced that ARAMCO must, if it did not want to endanger its concession, be willing to make substantial increased payments. We did not, however, wish to recommend a precise amount. I offered strong Department support in the negotiations, reading a note which we proposed to send to the Saudi government for this purpose which the parent representatives thought would be helpful. The necessity for increased payments was not questioned by the other representatives after Jennings conceded that there was little ARAMCO could do to resist Saudi demands. He thought there would have to be changes in the existing concession contract, for which there were many precedents.

Pending resolution of the U.S. income tax implications of a renegotiation, no final decision was made during the meeting on the profits split that would be offered. Davies, however, stated clearly that ARAMCO felt they were up against some sort of "share and share alike deal." The representatives of the parents did not dissent. They were convinced. The critical ARAMCO negotiations with Saudi Arabia started on November 28 and were concluded on December 30. Fifty-fifty had come to the Middle East to stay. The company officials involved in the decision had shown a high order of business statesmanship.

In retrospect, the AIOC failure to act at this time can only be seen as a great tragedy. If the company had moved quickly the crisis we both later faced could, I believe, have been avoided. Later the AIOC, in its anguish, accused ARAMCO of not having given them advance warning of the fifty-fifty agreement. Actually we had given the AIOC three months warning and it had come five months before the assassination of Razmara. After that it was too late. The fat was in the fire. There is evidence that the British had eventually told Razmara through a note verbal on February 24 that they were prepared to offer fifty-fifty profit sharing. He apparently did not consider himself in a strong enough position to advise the Oil Commission when he met with them on March 4, three days before his assassination.

All of this background was in my mind when I landed in Teheran at dusk on March 17. I was met by my old and dear friend Henry Grady, and his remarkable and vivacious wife Lucretia. Grady had been Chief of the Greek Aid Mission when I was Coordinator of Greek-Turkish Aid in Washington. I had seen much of him, both in Greece and Washington. It had been my idea to send him to Iran to succeed John Wiley. An outstanding economist with extensive government experience, he had been largely responsible for the Reciprocal Trade Agreements Act under Secretary Cordell Hull. The Department thought he was the ideal man to solve our perennial problem of aid to Iran. In Iran he had found himself in a very difficult situation with the British, who were fighting a rear-guard action for great stakes.

Immediately after my arrival I had a talk with the British Ambassador, Sir Francis Shepherd.[8] He gave me his interpretation of the situation as he saw it, and I made what he termed in his reporting telegram a "spirited attack" on the Anglo-Iranian Oil Company. I assured Shepherd that we hoped AIOC could avoid nationalization. I said that the company had, however, in our view, been too rigid and too slow to recognize that a new situation had been created in Iran which required a new approach. Despite the fact that the British government owned a controlling interest in AIOC, it had allowed Fraser to dictate its policy about oil in Iran. We provided more guidance to our companies even though they were privately owned.

I contested Shepherd's assertion that the new ARAMCO agreement had "thrown a wrench into [the] Persian oil machinery." I recalled to him that I had personally warned the AIOC board the previous September of the impending ARAMCO agreement, but that AIOC had been unwilling to cooperate with ARAMCO. I pointed out that the history of oil concessions did not encourage reliance on the sanctity of contracts and urged AIOC to fight a rear-guard action as gracefully as possible on the basis of their legal rights. In response to my question, Shepherd said that he did not consider some form of token nationalization inevitable, but that the "principle had evidently come to stay." The Foreign Office representative receiving Shepherd's telegram made the cryptic notation: "Mr. McGhee has previously made these views of his known to us."

Later I went to Grady's residence where, after a quiet dinner, I talked with the Ambassador and his staff late into the night. A meeting had been arranged for me on the following morning with Prime Minister Hussein Ala, who would later take me to the Shah. Ala was an old friend from the years he had spent as Iranian Ambassador in Washington. We had had many rounds together over aid to Iran, and he had only recently returned to be the Shah's Minister of Court. He was of retirement age but still feisty and full of energy. A short, slight man, he had been well liked in Washington by all of us who had dealt with him. However, he faced a very grave problem. Upon Razmara's death he had as an intimate of the Shah been appointed caretaker Prime Minister, but he could not get anyone to join his cabinet. Everyone eligible was afraid they would be shot: everyone, that is, except Ala.

After a thorough discussion with Ala of the current situation, including the role of National Front leader Mohammed Mossadeq, whom I was to see much of later in Washington, Ala took me to see the Shah. The resulting scene was one I will never forget. I had been with the Shah about a year and a half earlier during his much publicized official visit to Washington. He had then been a proud, erect young man, insistent that his requests be taken seriously. As I saw him in the darkened audience chamber in which he received me, lounging on a sofa, he was a dejected, almost a broken man. I sensed that he feared he, too, might be assassinated. I went over the issues as I had with Ala. We looked to him to make the best he could out of the present situation. We would support him in standing up to the National Front and their nationalization program. Both we and the British very much wanted to avoid nationalization of the AIOC concession. This would be bad both for AIOC and Iran. It would jeopardize oil concessions held by U.S., U.K., and other firms around the world. It would play into the hands of Iran's traditional enemies, the Soviets. Did he think with our support he could avert nationalization?

The Shah said he couldn't do it. He pleaded that we not ask him to do it. He couldn't even form a government. Everyone was afraid. There were unseen enemies everywhere. I then went over various alternative arrangements with the Shah that might do lip-service to nationalization, but cut it so thin that it would be workable for the AIOC and Iran and not upset concessionary arrangements elsewhere. The key was the fifty-fifty split that the British had now offered in behalf of AIOC. If the Iranian people were advised of the offer, maybe the National Front would accept it. Ownership was not as important as operating control and the split of the profits. (This, in essence, was the basis on which a consortium of Western oil companies, including AIOC, was to come back into Iran three years later, three disastrous years for Iran and the U.K.)

The Shah, however, was at this juncture still too much in shock from the assassination of his Prime Minister, and the rise to power of the National Front, to consider such a strategy. He looked lost, as if he thought the whole affair hopeless. I left him alone in his darkened room. I will always remember his sad, brooding face. I was greatly influenced in reaching my own conclusion, from the Shah's attitude, that neither he nor anyone else could persuade the Iranians not to nationalize the AIOC. It was not long after this that the Shah fled the country.

The Minister for Foreign Affairs, an able but innocuous man, Mohsen Ra'is, and Mrs. Ra'is, gave me a dinner on Sunday, March 18, at the Ministry of Foreign Affairs. The following evening Ambassador and Mrs. Grady included me as co-honoree with Princess Fatimah Pahlavi in a formal private showing in the U.S. Information Service auditorium of the new 20th Century–Fox film *The Mudlark*, starring Irene Dunne as Queen Victoria. It was an excellent film. I sat next to the Princess, who was young, attractive, and well groomed. I can't seem to remember, however, what we talked about. This was no time for entertainment. The specter of death and impending chaos hung gloomily over Teheran like a dark cloud. I was sad when I said good-bye to the Gradys the next morning and departed on the Embassy plane for England via Baghdad.

The British had, on March 20, suggested to the Department that on my return from Iran I stop off in London to discuss the Anglo-Iranian oil crisis with the British government. After leaving Teheran, I gave a great deal of thought to what I would say to the British about Iran when I arrived in London. On March 26, while I was visiting in Jordan, I attempted to put efforts to solve the AIOC problem in the context of an agreed U.S.-U.K. position on all Middle East oil. I sent a long telegram from Amman to the Department with copies to Teheran, Baghdad, Jidda, London, Damascus, and Beirut.[9] I suggested that the future of Middle East oil concessions could only be resolved through a more precise and comprehensive U.S.-U.K. policy, and closer coordination of actions.

I proposed that the oil income to Saudi Arabia, Iran, and Iraq should be put on a basis comparable to the fifty-fifty ARAMCO agreement, and that Kuwait, Bahrain, and Qatar, in light of their lesser needs, should be permitted to catch up gradually. Over a period of time, production rates in the different countries should be related to their productive capacities and each country's financial needs. The full benefit to the peoples of these countries should be assured by investing their oil receipts in sound development projects. Adequate refining capacity should be built for local consumption, with local price related to cost and not the existing U.S. Gulf Coast "basing point" system.

Finally, I proposed that the U.S. and U.K. should, after consultations with their oil companies, make a joint statement based on my proposals. The statement should affirm that the oil of the Middle East is the natural heritage of the people, who should receive the benefits from its exploitation. We would say that exploration and production of Middle East oil should be continued by the existing companies, who had the necessary expertise, capital, and access to markets. We would also make clear that this should be on the basis of a working partnership, between company and country, which would make the question of nationalization irrelevant.

Following visits to Baghdad, Beirut, Amman, and Cairo, which I will report later, I proceeded to London. The following describes my discussions on Iranian oil. Awaiting me was a telegram from the Department authorizing me to explore, on the basis of my telegram from Amman with a certain number of reservations, all possible action recommendations (including those in my Amman telegram) that might help the unstable Middle East oil situation.[10] Comments received at that time from other recipients of my telegram were in general favorable.[11]

After my arrival in London I met with the representatives of the Foreign Office, Treasury, and Ministry of Power and Fuel on both the morning and afternoon of April 2, and on the following morning. Later, U.S. Ambassador Walter Gifford, with whom I was staying, accompanied me to see Foreign Secretary Herbert Morrison. The situation in Iran was still confused. It was difficult to see how the nationalization threat would develop.

My conversation with Morrison is, I believe, of sufficient interest to give in full the record approved by Morrison himself, which he sent by telegram to Sir Oliver Franks, U.K. Ambassador in Washington. The message is available in the British archives.[12]

Mr. George McGhee, Under-Secretary of State for Eastern Affairs in the State Department, called on me today accompanied by the United States Ambassador. He told me that he was on his way home after making an extensive tour, in the course of which he had visited many of the Middle East capitals, as well as Karachi, New Delhi and Colombo.

2. I asked Mr. McGhee to give me his impressions of his tour. He told me he had found the whole area much unsettled. The old discipline imposed by British imperial power had been removed and had not been replaced by stable national Governments co-operating among themselves. The struggle between Russia and the Western Powers and the growing spirit of nationalism, provided further causes of unrest. In Mr. McGhee's view the principal problems in the area were Kashmir, the oil question in Persia, Arab-Israel hostility and the Anglo-Egyptian issue. All these problems prevented co-operation between the countries of the area and the Western Powers. The situation could be re-established when the United Kingdom and the United States had built up their strength. During the next eighteen months we should be facing a critical situation in the whole area, especially in Persia, and in Mr. McGhee's view we should do all we could to hold the position during that critical period. With these considerations in view, Mr. McGhee said, the United States Government had decided to adopt a new policy towards the Middle East. Hitherto, they had concentrated mainly on the countries on the periphery, Greece, Turkey and Persia. Now they

appreciated that the countries behind the outer line, though none of them of considerable individual strength, could nevertheless provide stability in depth. The United States Government proposed, therefore, to supply those countries with arms on a limited scale and to invite them to accept military missions. The object of this new policy would be to build up a more stable structure in the Middle East. This policy would be carried out in close co-ordination with the United Kingdom.

3. I asked Mr. McGhee if he had any criticisms of United Kingdom policy in the Middle East. He said that there had been periodical talks about the Middle East between the State Department and the Foreign Office, which had resulted in close co-operation. Only in Persia had this co-operation been absent. The State Department were very critical of the Anglo-Iranian Oil Company who, in their opinion, subordinated broader political considerations to purely commercial interests. The State Department felt, moreover, that His Majesty's Government had failed to exercise sufficient control over the company's policy.

4. In reply to my enquiry whether Mr. McGhee had anything to say about Egypt, he told me that during his visit to Cairo, the Egyptian Ministers had explained their position very forcibly to him. They made it clear that they feared that His Majesty's Government had receded somewhat from the position which had been adopted by Mr. Bevin. They told him that they must stand firm on a planned evacuation to be completed within a defined period and on the close association between the defence issue and the Sudan. Mr. McGhee said that he had done his utmost to defend the United Kingdom's position. He had warned the Egyptians that it was not in their interests to remove United Kingdom forces from Egypt at this critical moment. He had pointed out that there was no longer any element of Colonialism in British foreign policy, and that the Egyptians would do well to appreciate the formidable dangers of the new imperialism of Russia. To me Mr. McGhee expressed the hope that we should find it possible to reach an agreement with Egypt; that His Majesty's Ambassador at Cairo would be given enough latitude for the purpose, and that talks with the Egyptians would be resumed as quickly as possible. He also expressed the view that it would be unwise to link the question of Egyptian restrictions on the passage of oil through the Suez Canal with the defence issue.

5. Referring generally to the United Kingdom's present difficulties in Persia and Egypt, Mr. McGhee said that as long as they remained unresolved they would hinder the implementation of the United States' policy in the Middle East.

6. Commenting on Mr. McGhee's remarks, I recalled that we had a long experience of the Middle East and of the difficulties of dealing with the various countries in the area. The hostility between Israel and the Arab countries increased our difficulties considerably. We were traditionally friendly to the Arabs, but we also wanted to be friendly to Israel. The new States which had grown up in the Middle East were nominally democratic, but there were dangerous contrasts between rich and poor, and enmity between political parties prevented the establishment of strong Governments. The Nationalist Parties, particularly in Persia, were using "nationalisation" of oil not on its merits but as an instrument of foreign policy. The Anglo-Iranian Oil Company had put money, brains and skill into the development of the oil industry, which the Persians could not run themselves. The Company had a pretty good labour record in Persia. His Majesty's Government were very ready to talk to the Persian Government, and to deal with the present crisis, on imaginative lines, but they must take care to protect their essential oil supplies. As regards Egypt, I said that Mr. McGhee should appreciate the serious trouble which His Majesty's Government have recently had in Parliament. There was very strong feeling on both sides of the House of Commons, that we should not facilitate the supply of oil to Egypt as long as the Egyptians were preventing the passage of our tankers through the Canal. But in all this it was profoundly important that United States officials should not adumbrate policies in regard to the Middle East until we had had time to consult together. I hoped that the United States Government would take special care to ensure that there was no crossing of wires. We were always ready to confer with the United States about Middle East policy in relation to our joint interests.

7. Mr. McGhee repeated again that he felt there was no divergence of view between us on the Middle East, except as regards Persia.

8. I am sending copies of this despatch to His Majesty's Representatives at Cairo and Tehran.

I am, &c.

HERBERT MORRISON.

In my general discussions with Bowker and the other British officials on April 2,[13,14] I emphasized the need to combat rising neutralism in the Near East (Arab states and Israel), which appeared to result mainly from a feeling of insecurity. We must try to raise these countries' morale, which had been slipping since independence had been gained. We recognized British responsibility for the general defense of the area, except in Saudi Arabia, but, in order to back the British up, we proposed once we obtained congressional approval to initiate token arms shipments to selected Arab states and Israel. We were, of course, already supplying Greece, Turkey, and Iran on a large scale and were proposing Greece and Turkey for entry into the North Atlantic Pact. Anything we did would, of course, be closely coordinated with the U.K. Bowker welcomed the new U.S. interest in Middle East defense. He emphasized the importance of consulting in advance before we took any decisions on the basis of our new policy and the importance of creating a suitable command structure for the Middle East.

In my talks with the British officials I expressed full appreciation of the importance to Britain of their oil rights in Iran. From our point of view the most important objective was internal Iranian political stability and the preservation of Iran as an independent nation. The loss of Iran to the free world would be incalculable. In that eventuality the oil would, of course, be lost too. Any solution to the oil crisis must take into account the expressed desire of the Iranian people to nationalize their oil, which they considered a fait accompli, while retaining operating control for the AIOC. As I had proposed in my telegram to the Department from Amman, I suggested a U.S.-U.K. statement supporting a demonstrably fair profit-sharing arrangement, such as the fifty-fifty split, as the basis for oil concessions throughout the Middle East. This had been accepted by Venezuela and Saudi Arabia and would appeal to the ordinary people in other countries. The statement might also deal with the rationalization of rate of production and price in the various countries. I observed that the AIOC still seemed to be pursuing its own commercial policy in Iran, citing recent examples which had increased tension. We should support the Shah and urge him to back up Prime Minister Ala. I warned against attempts at financial or other pressures against Iran at this stage.

At the instigation of the Treasury Department, my proposal for a joint U.S.-U.K. statement was taken up on the day following at the Ministry of Fuel and Power. The report of the Foreign Office representative, my good friend P. E. Ramsbotham, concluded that the profit-sharing principle was "here to stay" and that none of the objections which had been raised against it by Treasury were insuperable, although certain practical difficulties must be overcome. Such a statement, Ramsbotham said, would provide AIOC a new basis for negotiations, on a simple formula which would appear fair and reasonable. It would help stabilize the Middle East on a common concessionary basis, which should help avoid future rivalries between the oil-producing states. Ramsbotham recommended joining the U.S. in a statement supporting "the principle of a profit-sharing arrangement" and covering some of my other proposals. Reluctance was expressed by other participants of the meeting to accepting the fifty-fifty formula as such publicly, but there was support for appointing Iranian directors to the AIOC board and breaking with the Gulf of Mexico basing-price system. The Foreign Office asked that the results of the meeting be included in the briefs for the upcoming Washington talks.

On April 4, I lunched with Sir William Fraser, later Lord Strathalmond, chairman of the board of the Anglo-Iranian Oil Company. We were guests at his club of my old friend and former neighbor in Washington, Sir Roger Makins, later Lord Sherfield, who was currently a high official in the Treasury Department and would later serve a very successful term as British Ambassador to the U.S. It was my first meeting with Fraser. He knew only too well of my criticism of him to British officials. There was a certain tenseness as we made sparring comments. At Fraser's request I went over in detail the issues we had raised over Anglo-Iranian's recent difficulties with Iran. After listening with apparent patience, Fraser said in his characteristically gruff Scottish voice, "The trouble with you, McGhee, is that you are operating on the basis of the wrong information." He thereupon went into a strong defense of the Anglo-Iranian record in Iran. He said, however, that all of this should be put aside and that we should find a way for the Anglo-Iranian and U.S. companies to cooperate in the Middle East. "Fifty-fifty is a fine slogan," said Fraser, "but it seems to me to be of dubious practicality." He had not yet learned.

The British archives reveal that on April 6 Foreign Secretary Morrison sent the following message of particular secrecy, not to be passed on, to Ambassador Franks in Washington.[15]

In his talks with us McGhee was so free with his criticisms of His Majesty's Government's and the Anglo-Iranian Oil Company policy in Persia and of His Majesty's Government's policy in Egypt that we were not altogether convinced by his assurances that he had "not given anything away" in his conversations with the Persians and the Egyptians.

While I do not want to appear to be going behind Mr. McGhee's back I should like you, if you see no objection to convey tactfully to the Secretary of State that Mr. McGhee's approach to some of our Middle East problems struck me as being a little light-hearted and that I thought it was well to tell him when he called on me that it was profoundly important that United States officials should not adumbrate policies in regard to the Middle East until we had had time to consult together and that I hoped that the United States Government would take special care to ensure that there was no crossing wires.

In his reply Franks said:[16]

I found opportunity to convey to Acheson, while talking to him yesterday about the Persian situation, the sense of paragraph 2 of your telegram under reference. Acheson listened to what I said, but made no comment.

Immediately upon my return to Washington I started preparation for my talks that the Department had scheduled with the British to attempt to develop a common policy toward Iran. The British side was under the chairmanship of Ambassador Sir Oliver Franks who, by chance, had been my moral tutor while I was a graduate student in Queen's College, Oxford, where he was a young dean. The British attached great importance to the Washington talks and made it a full-dress affair. There were, at the first meeting on April 9, in addition to their chairman, five other British representatives, including my friend Dennis Greenhill then stationed in Washington. Dennis, who was an outstanding diplomat, later became Permanent Under-Secretary of the Foreign Office which led to a peerage. After retirement he became a member of the board of British Petroleum, successor to the AIOC.

There were also two Foreign Office representatives from London and one each from the Treasury and the Ministry of Fuel and Power. There were thirteen on the American side, of which I was chairman, including Harold Linder, Assistant Secretary for Economic Affairs, and William Rountree, head of Greek-Turkish-Iranian affairs. It was an exciting experience for me. I felt that the eyes of the world were on our talks—in which I was negotiating with my former tutor. We were to have four full meetings, the final one on April 18.

The discussions engendered by the meetings revealed a large area of agreement between the two governments on the Iranian situation: the importance of Iranian oil and refining capacity generally; the importance of AIOC as an asset and source of oil and foreign exchange to the U.K.; and the importance of the precedent that would be set by the U.S.-U.K. response to Iranian nationalization. The British representatives presented in forceful terms the significance they attached to the AIOC concession. It provided 30 percent of Anglo-Dutch oil and £100 million annually to British balance of payments. They did not wish to give up, weaken, or shorten the life of their concession. They saw in nationalization only loss of control and profits.

We on the American side made it clear we found nationalization of oil concessions as distasteful as the British. We had been forced to accept it as a bitter pill in Mexico, where our companies had received only $14,000,000 for their vast oil reserves. As regards Iran, however, we had somewhat different priorities than the British. Our first priority was to prevent the loss of Iran to the free world, reasoning that if Iran was lost the AIOC concession would go also. (It was difficult to state this, however, without giving the British the impression we did not fully appreciate the importance of AIOC to them, which we did.) We also felt there was no hope of success unless the Iranian nationalization law, considered in Iran as a fait accompli, was accepted at least in principle, and negotiations conducted to assure continuing AIOC operational control and a suitable share of the profits. Because of its success in Venezuela and Saudi Arabia, we felt a fifty-fifty split, which had an aura of fairness understandable to the ordinary man, offered the best hope for success.

I pointed out that one advantage of accepting a façade of nationalization would be to eliminate from a practical standpoint the troublesome question of compensation. We opposed so-called strong measures with the Iranians. We made it clear that we would not interfere with British efforts to negotiate any agreement they wished, but that we could not give positive support to a proposal we thought had no prospects of success. Prime Minister Ala and the Shah had both told us they could not oppose nationalization. We wanted something the Iranian Prime Minister could present to the Majlis with some hope for success.

The meetings bridged part of the gap between us. The British agreed to go to fifty-fifty profit sharing on Iranian operations, and what they believed was some accommodation to nationalization. We know now that on April 12 Franks phoned Roger Makins of Treasury in London, pleading for as much imaginative latitude as possible in his instructions.[17] He did not feel that the Foreign Office representatives had made a sufficiently constructive case and felt it important that the U.K. make a bow in the direction of nationalization if this could be done without serious harm. Franks advised us that future oil negotiations with Iran would be carried on, not by the AIOC, but by a representative of the British government. A mission would go out shortly.

In the end, however, I was, with great regret, forced to advise Franks in our final meeting on April 18 that their proposals did not, in the case of accommodation to nationalization, meet the requirements we saw for success. I assured Franks that we would, as a minimum, give the impending British negotiations our benevolent backing, which we hoped could be strengthened if their discussions went well. Franks and I agreed to a bland communiqué which termed the talks "satisfactory" to both governments, while recognizing that the problem must be worked out elsewhere by the parties directly concerned. The Iranians had increasingly resented discussions of their problems without their presence. The U.S.-U.K. difference over the principle of nationalization was referred to by the press, not because of any leak as the British often felt, but because it had lain so long and obviously in the public domain.

The failure of these talks, although they represented only one stage in a continuing process, was a great personal disappointment. It was not just that we had failed to persuade our English friends, led in this case by a man I so greatly admired, but that our failure, I feared, greatly reduced hope for the resolution of a problem which I considered the greatest current threat to world peace, and in which I had become so heavily involved. In order to clarify our position on the Iranian nationalization, which was being widely misinterpreted, the Department on May 10 issued a press statement which our bureau had prepared and which said, in part:[18]

> The United States is deeply concerned by the [AIOC-Iranian] dispute and the terms of arrangements which might be worked out.
>
> In our talks with the British Government, we have expressed the opinion that arrangements should be worked out with the Iranians which give recognition to Iran's expressed desire for greater control over the benefits from the development of its petroleum resources. While the United States has not approved or disapproved the terms of any particular British proposal, it is pleased to note a sincere desire on the part of the British to negotiate with the Iranians on all outstanding issues.
>
> We fully recognize the sovereign rights of Iran and sympathize with Iran's desire that increased benefits accrue to that country from the development of its petroleum. In talks with the Iranian Govern-

ment, we have pointed out the serious effects of any unilateral cancel-lation of clear contractual relationships, which the United States strongly opposes. We have stressed the importance of the Iranians achieving their legitimate objectives through friendly negotiation with the other party, consistent with their international responsibilities. This would have the advantage of maintaining confidence in future com-mercial investments in Iran and, indeed, in the validity of contractual arrangements all over the world.

Iran has been urged, before it takes final action, to analyze careful-ly the practical aspects of this problem. In this connection, we have raised the question of whether or not the elimination of the established British oil company from Iran would in fact secure for Iran the great-est possible benefits. We have pointed out that the efficient production and refining of Iranian oil requires not only technical knowledge and capital but transport and marketing facilities such as those provided by the company. We have also pointed out that any uncertainty as to future availability of Iranian supplies would cause concern on the part of customers which might lead to shifts in their source of supply with a consequent decrease in revenue to Iran.

Those United States oil companies which would be best able to conduct operations such as the large-scale and complex industry in Iran have indicated to this Government that they would not in the face of unilateral action by Iran against the British company be willing to undertake operations in that country. Moreover, petroleum technicians of the number and competence required to replace those presently in Iran are not, due to extreme shortages of manpower in this specialized field, available in this country or in other countries.

The United States has repeatedly expressed its great interest in the continued independence and territorial integrity of Iran and has given and will continue to give concrete evidence of this interest.

I was during this period accused in the British press of having, during my visit to Teheran, encouraged the Iranians to nationalize the AIOC and suggested that U.S. companies might replace AIOC. Nothing, of course, could have been more disadvantageous to U.S. interests in Iran and Saudi Arabia and to our concessions around the world and nothing was further from my mind. The U.S. companies, as stated in our press release, had no desire to replace AIOC. The Majlis had, moreover, already made its decision to nationalize the AIOC before my arrival and I did not, for fear of arousing U.K. and Iranian government suspicions, meet with any members of the National Front. The Shah and Ala were both opposed to nationalization, and I had tried in my conversations with them to strengthen their opposition and support the AIOC, not criticize it.

I was, however, on June 21, attacked on the floor of the House of Commons on these same grounds by Labour member Richard Crossman, whose lectures I had attended at Oxford and whom I respected, and by other Labour members.[19] Crossman, condemning me in advance by the characterization of "millionaire oil tycoon" as well as a very high Department official, accused me of "shooting my mouth" in Teheran, presumably to the Iranians, to whom I thereby gave the impression that "if the British were kicked out they could rely on somebody else and they might do a little better." He reported that I had also said that "nationalization was a good idea." Crossman was joined in his attack by George Wigg, who had at least taken the trouble to find out that I had studied at Oxford as a Rhodes Scholar under Sir Oliver Franks.[20] Wigg said that no conclusions could be reached about me until the Foreign Office found out exactly what I had said to local officials in my many trips around British territory, although it appeared to him that I favored replacing British with American technicans and that I had said the Iranians could "go ahead with nationalization." I was mystified as to how Crossman and Wigg had gotten this impression. I had to wait thirty years to find out.

In the course of the same Commons debate Morrison had referred to "people, not of outstanding importance, who were associated or have been associated with the American oil industry who have said some foolish, unwise and perhaps dangerous things in the course of their travels through the Middle East."[21] Later in his remarks when Morrison expressed appreciation for the help and cooperation from the State Department, he said that he did not wish to pursue what had been said "about one gentleman." A friend of mine, a Conservative member of Parliament, wrote his regrets that he had not been present to defend me. If I had known the members involved, he said, I would realize what an honor it was for me to have been attacked by them. The *Chicago Daily News* of June 30, which reported these same criticisms, confirmed that the British government would say nothing on the subject, also that "British critics do not think that McGhee was really responsible for the Iranian crisis. They agreed that the whole affair was badly handled by the Anglo-Iranian Oil Company with the connivance, by default, of the Foreign Office."

Amidst criticisms by Morrison against me, I complained to the

British Minister in Washington about the Foreign Secretary's ambiguous—but what I considered damaging—reply during the debate in Commons. The Minister attempted to reassure me, and a couple of weeks later advised me that he had received a message from Morrison explaining that his reference to oil men had not meant me, but others.[22] That portion of his remarks expressing appreciation for the cooperation of the State Department had been intended to deal with the charges against me, although he had declined to name me personally.

Morrison had sent an instruction to Franks to raise my presumed indiscretions with Acheson. The Minister of the Washington Embassy had, in Franks's absence, written Bowker of the Foreign Office urging that this not be done.[23] He said that Acheson would probably not accept their viewpoint and that he and the Embassy would endanger their close, frank, and valuable association with me. He continued that I was not, as a successful oil man, in a vulnerable position in the Department, nor with the American public.

His predecessor in Washington, a good friend of mine then in the Treasury in London, also advised Morrison by a memorandum dated July 3, that I was "fundamentally well disposed to Britain." He said that my faults early in AIOC difficulties (this always cropped up) were due to inexperience and overconfidence and that I suffered from an Irish ancestry (wrong) and a Texas upbringing. "Mr. McGhee needs education and encouragement and not abuse."[24] It is interesting to be able to read Morrison's writing in his own hand on this document. "I certainly have my views abt. Mr. McG but I was not thinking of McGhee but the oil men. Let me see the Hansard. Anyway I'm not gunning for Mr. McGhee—just taking an interest in him." Although I now know that Morrison later spoke to Ambassador Gifford about me,[25] Acheson never raised the question with me except for one joking reference to my troubles with the British.

I had always wondered how the rumor started that I had, during my visit to Teheran, undercut the AIOC in discussions with Iranian officials. To the best of my knowledge I had not. I was to find in the British archives that it was first reported in London by an AIOC official. The relevant Foreign Office telegram dated March 21 is as follows:[26]

Anglo-Iranian Oil Company inform us in strict confidence that Persian Prime Minister, in conversation with Chisholm on March 19th, stated that while critical of the Company's past policy "he was not prepared to associate himself with the strong adverse criticisms of the Company, the Foreign Office, and Sir William Fraser which had been voiced by a prominent visiting American statesman."

While we are of course fully aware from your telegram No. 203 [of March 18th] and previous reports of McGhee's views, it seems particularly unfortunate, at this juncture that he should apparently have expressed them thus freely to Persians. Please telegraph your comments and any indications you may have of any such indiscretions on his part. Can you say whether he proposes to visit London and if so when?

Had I known of this telegram at the time, which was based on a telegram from an AIOC man named Chisholm who was visiting in Iran, I would, of course, have protested. I knew I had made no such criticisms to Ala in Teheran. The British Ambassador in Teheran replied on March 24 that he knew of no other indiscretions on my part.[27] He deplored the criticism of AIOC to Ala attributed to me by AIOC in London as giving Iranian minds the belief that there was a U.S.-U.K. rift over Iranian policy.

Fortunately for me, D. A. Logan of the Foreign Office was to discover that Chisholm, after his return to London, had quite a different story to tell.[28] Logan's reporting memorandum is as follows:

> Mr. Chisholm of the Anglo-Iranian Oil Company told me last night that nothing occurred during his conversation in Tehran with Husain Ala, the Prime Minister, to suggest that Mr. McGhee had spoken critically to Ala of the Foreign Office or Anglo-Iranian Oil Company.
>
> Mr. Chisholm had heard from Mr. Middleton of the critical attitude which Mr. McGhee adopted during his conversation with Sir Francis Shepherd. When talking to Ala on the day following his conversation with Mr. Middleton, Mr. Chisholm attempted to draw him on his attitude to Anglo-Iranian by saying that American officials, and Mr. McGhee in particular, were critical of the Company's attitude. To this Ala replied that two days earlier he had been at the U.S. Embassy at Teheran on St. Patrick's Day and had proposed the health of two Irish Americans Mr. Grady and Mr. McGhee [wrong again, Scotch]. He added "There are many Irishmen in the United States who are critical of Britain." Nothing more was said on this subject, but Mr. Chisholm formed the impression that Ala did not wish to associate himself with American criticisms, of which he was no doubt aware. It was this conclusion which he wished to report in his telegram to the Company's London office.
>
> Mr. Chisholm has no information about the activities of Mr. McGhee in Teheran nor of other U.S. officials.

Thus is history made. I had been accused in London, Teheran, and Washington of an indiscretion on the basis of Chisholm's own words to Ala, not mine. It was AIOC itself that had told Ala of my criticisms, which I had made great efforts to confine to British officials. There is unfortunately no record that the quite different story Logan reported was ever sent out as a telegram to correct the message of March 21, 1951. It was the early story implying I was practically responsible for AIOC's losing their concession that was to crop up again and again as my indiscretion in the beginning of the nationalization crisis. Lord Selwyn-Lloyd, in his book *Suez 1956: A Personal Account*, written in 1978 shortly before his death, repeats the same accusations without questioning them, characterizing me as anti-British. This was soon after I had concluded four years as Chairman of the English-Speaking Union of the United States.

For the next nine months following the Washington talks with Franks, I was to be deeply involved in attempting to bring Iran and the AIOC together, including some seventy-five hours of conversation with Prime Minister Mossadeq in New York and Washington and at my farm in Middleburg. With other Department officials I helped put together an offer to the British which I believed Mossadeq would accept, only to be turned down by the new Eden government.

The questioning of AIOC policy and Sir William Fraser's continuation as chairman was apparently raised forcefully within the British government for the first time in late August, 1951, by Sir Donald Ferguson of the Ministry of Fuel and Power, as revealed by British archives.[29] After a visit to Iran Ferguson concluded that although the AIOC was an efficient business organization, Fraser, who completely dominated the company, had no other thought than to exact the last possible pound from the 1933 agreement, and should cease to be chairman. He said that his view was shared by the Governor of the Bank of England and by the National Provincial Bank, AIOC's bankers.

At the same time, Walter Levy, leading U.S. oil consultant, in reporting to the Foreign Office his one-and-a-half-hour conversation with Fraser and other board members on August 28, had advised that he regretted to say that Fraser had learned absolutely nothing from past events, was completely out of touch with the situation, and should be replaced.[30] The same applied to the other directors and senior staff. Levy advised that Ambassador Averell Harriman shared this view. This was not the first time that Americans, apart from myself, had expressed criticism of AIOC and Fraser. During the U.S.

Chiefs of Mission meeting held in Istanbul February 14–15, 1951, as has been reported, a motion expressing appreciation for U.K. cooperation in the Middle East carried with it an exception in the case of Iran, because of the stiffness of the AIOC in meeting Iranian government claims for better treatment, for which Fraser was considered to be responsible.[31]

On March 6, Colonel Harold Hoskins, eminent U.S. Middle East specialist and chairman of the board of Beirut University, whom I had recently recruited to head up policy planning for the NEA Bureau, had during a visit to London expressed strongly to the Foreign Office the view that the AIOC was greatly to blame for allowing the situation in Iran to develop, and that he thought the British government had also contributed. He saw little hope in continuing to "plug" the legal aspects of the company's case. He was particularly critical of Fraser, who he alleged completely dominated the AIOC board. Foreign Office comment was that "Hoskins will obviously work well with his new master" (meaning me).[32]

The British archives, curiously enough, reveal that Earl Mountbatten of Burma, then Fourth Sea Lord, had joined in the criticism of AIOC policy. In a letter dated April 15 to Viscount Hall, First Sea Lord, Mountbatten expressed the view that the nationalization of Iranian oil had resulted from a deep-seated movement among the Iranians that could not be reversed and that any attempt to do this by force would be disastrous.[33] He urged the British government to exercise its control over AIOC by entrusting future negotiations with Iran over oil to a minister with adequate powers. Mountbatten urged that an attempt be made to persuade the Majlis Oil Commission to accept the concept of nationalization as adequate compensation for AIOC assets, and said that this would lead to cooperation between the two governments to extract the maximum value from the oil.

It is interesting that Mountbatten's suggestions, which were in my judgment well taken, included the concept I had put forward only a few days before in the second meeting of my negotiations with British Ambassador Sir Oliver Franks in Washington on April 10. I had proposed "nationalization without compensation," leading to a fifty-fifty profit-sharing agreement with AIOC in control. Although Foreign Office comments disparaged Mountbatten's experience with Iran, it was apparently his suggestion that led to the British decision, of which we were advised on April 18, that future negotiations with Iran would be conducted by representatives of the British government. So much, for the moment, for Iran and AIOC.

Continuing my trip home in 1950, I arrived in Baghdad from Teheran on March 20 for a brief visit, my first since my unsuccessful search for homes for Arab refugees in the spring of 1949. I was met by my old friend Ambassador Edward Crocker, a fine, experienced, old-line career officer, and his charming wife, Lispinard. Since we accepted British dominance in Iraq, I had never become deeply involved in internal Iraqi affairs. My visit was largely exploratory. I did not attempt to engage in discussions of policy with the Iraqi leaders.

Three months before, I had had a long discussion in Washington on U.S.-Iraqi relations with my old friend, Dr. Fadhil Jamali, chairman of the Iraqi delegation to the UN; the discussion provided a valuable background for my Baghdad visit.[34] On this occasion Jamali had stressed Iraqi need for assistance in agricultural development and for private industry, particularly in textiles, perhaps in partnership with the Iraqi government. He expressed disappointment with the small size of the loan the International Bank had extended Iraq, and with the lack of interest of outsiders in investing in Iraq.

Jamali further expressed the view that the British were trying to keep out possible U.S. and other outside investors. Acting under the cover of their treaty with Iraq the British, he said, preserved in power the government they had created in 1932 and sought to exploit Iraq rather than treat it as an equal partner, opposing reforms. Jamali said that he would like to see the British treaty replaced with a regional Arab-U.S.-Western treaty along the lines of the North Atlantic Pact. The Arab peoples of Iraq all reject the British treaty and have no fear of Communism, although some of their religious leaders preach anti-Communism. Jamali thought an active Iraqi government could, within three years, set to rest religious rivalries and defeat Communism on the theme of a Muslim religious revival. He said that Soviet propaganda continued to make headway, in part because of Palestine and the refugees. Prime Minister Nuri Said had in a recent letter to him said, "Can't the U.S. do something? If not our cause will continue to remain shaky."

Crocker assembled the key Iraqi leaders for a dinner in my honor.[35] In addition to Prime Minister Nuri Said, there were present Tawfig Suwoidi, Deputy Prime Minister and Acting Foreign Minister, and four former prime ministers. It was the first time I had met Nuri Said. A Sunni Arab, he had participated with King Faisal I and T. E. Lawrence in the Arab revolt during World War I. As a staunch supporter of the British, Nuri was easily the dominant political figure in Iraq whether in or out of office. He was Prime Minister many times. In 1955 Nuri would sign a mutual defense treaty with Turkey, to which the British would accede, thereby creating the Baghdad Pact. At the time of my visit there was, largely as a result of government corruption, limited opportunity for political expression by the Iraqi people. This stood in the way of close Iraqi ties with the West and caused increasing discontent in Iraq centering on Pan-Arab nationalism.

I found Nuri to be a picturesque, forceful man. Our discussion at dinner centered largely on his efforts to broaden the base of the Iraqi-U.K. treaty, which was his idea and currently his most important objective. However, he was later proved insensitive to the rising tide of nationalism in Iraq. He and the Regent for young Faisal II, Prince Abd-al-Illah, first cousin to Faisal II's father, King Ghazi, to whom Nuri had always been closely allied, were as a result to suffer a harsh fate. I did not see Faisal but called on the Regent. He offered me tea in his modest palace. A small, shy, and somewhat diffident man, the Prince gave no appearance of being the "strong man" he was reputed to be. The monarchy was overthrown in a military coup in 1958 led by Brigadier Abd-al-Karim Kassim, which was accompanied by a violent public uprising directed against the regime and foreign residents. Faisal II and the Regent were both executed, and Nuri was killed by a mob while attempting to escape disguised as a veiled woman. After the Arab Socialist Ba'ath party seized power in a coup in July 1968, Soviet influence reached a high point and waned. General Saddam Hussein, who succeeded to the presidency in July 1979, soon after plunged his country into a disastrous war with Iran. The troubled history of Iraq in recent years, which has prevented it from making use of its ample oil production for the betterment of its people, continues.

28

Syria and Lebanon in Transition

Visit to Damascus, President Khalid Azm Bey, Prime Minister
Dr. Nazim al-Qudsi, March 22–24, 1951. Visit to Beirut, Lebanon, President Bishara al-Khuri, March 24–25, 1951.

I arrived in Damascus from Baghdad for my second visit to Syria on
March 22. I was met by Minister Cavendish W. Cannon, a veteran
career member of the Foreign Service with a varied background of
European posts and other members of the legation staff, also by the
Syrian Chief of Protocol. Lily Cannon, who was of aristocratic Eastern European background, was a delightful hostess in their official
residence, which was to suffer as a result of my visit.

Syria has always been to me an enigma. Modern Syria is an artificial state carved out in the twentieth century from an area called
Syria by the ancient Greeks (later called Greater Syria), which comprised in the time of the ancient Greeks the whole settled area at the
Eastern end of the Mediterranean. Greater Syria has seldom governed itself. Its vulnerable crossroads position, the attraction of the
oasis of Damascus, and its rich coastal and Jazirah plains, had made it
a prize for conquest by Middle Eastern empires from all sides. Damascus, Aleppo, Byblos, Joffa, Homs, Gaza, Tyre, and Sidon, all cities
in Greater Syria, dating from the early second millennium B.C., are
among the oldest continuously inhabited settlements in the world.
The area was a center of Hellenistic civilization, and was later a part
of the Romano-Byzantine Empire.

Since Syria came under Muslim rule in 636, its history has been
dominated by the vicissitudes of the expansion of Islam, by Syria's
search for unity with the rest of the Arab world, and now by Syria's
antagonism to the state of Israel. Syria reached the peak of its influence in the early eighth century under the Umayyad Caliphs, whose
empire, based in Damascus, extended from Spain to the borders of

345

India, and beyond the Oxus into what is now the U.S.S.R. Successively occupied by the Seljuk Turks, the Crusaders, and the Saracens, Syria was conquered in 1516 by the Ottoman Turks, fellow Muslims, whose rule was terminated only after their defeat in World War I. Syria was mandated to France by the League of Nations in 1922.

Syria was, after years of struggle, recognized as an independent state in 1944 by the U.S. and later by others. Syria was beset from the beginning by divisive tendencies, various factions among its population being united only by their opposition to the creation of the new state of Israel—which Syria invaded in May 1948. In March 1949, General Husni Zaim staged the first of a series of military coups, which were succeeded in September 1950 by a weak civilian government under a new constitution drawn up by a constituent assembly. In a letter to Cannon of November 14, 1950, soon after his arrival, I had outlined our hopes as to what he could achieve in Syria in the general chaotic situation of assassination attempts, bribery, and unrest that then prevailed.[1] We placed our hopes on the success of the Second Syrian Republic under Dr. Nazim al-Qudsi, who appeared to have made a good start. He seemed inclined to ignore the Palestine question as an issue in Syrian politics and to place greatest emphasis on economic development. I urged Cannon to encourage him along these lines. Among other things we wanted to help Syria get a loan from the World Bank.

This was the situation when I arrived in March 1951.[2] I was later to characterize the Syrian government I found then as a "bunch of mush." Its role became increasingly ineffective until its overthrow by former dictator Colonel Adib al-Shishakli in November 1951. After establishing myself in the Legation residence I called at the Syrian presidency to sign the visitors' book. I was received by the Secretary General, with whom I spent about an hour in general conversation. Later I met with the officers of the Legation, who gave me a thorough briefing on the current situation in Syria. I talked with them about Department thinking on the Middle East generally, prospects for Arab-Israeli peace, the refugee situation, likelihood of U.S. assistance for Syria and other Middle Eastern countries, and U.S. strategy for countering the Soviet threat to the Middle East.

At 5 P.M., accompanied by Cannon, I called on the President of the Republic, Khalid Azm Bey, at his residence. The Secretary-General, Dr. Shatula, and Dr. Khani of the residency staff, who acted as interpreter, were also present. Our conversation soon passed beyond pleasantries to the substance of the position of Syria in the present world situation. The President, contrary to recent reports of detachment due to his advancing age, showed himself to be very well informed. He talked with alertness and, at times, with feeling. On the Palestine question his chief preoccupation was with the plight of the Arab refugees, and he expressed hope that the U.S. would increase its help to them. He did not object when I spoke of our expectation that Syria, with large areas of fertile undeveloped land, would be willing to absorb large numbers of these unfortunate people into the Syrian economy by resettlement. I did not press the point, having in mind my conversation with the Prime Minister to follow. I brought up the doctrine of neutralism, pointing out its dangers to a country like Syria.

The President spoke with appreciation of America's assistance to Syria in the past, which he considered had been on a disinterested basis. He expressed his confidence that our happy early relations, which had been interrupted by the Palestine problem, would be restored. He knew that at heart we were friends and that the Arab peoples would not lose through having closer ties with us. As for the Russians, he knew them of old, he said. He had been a Turkish official in his younger days, and mistrust of Russia was bred into him. Now that the Soviets had joined Communism with imperialism, the danger was doubled. Syria wanted peace in the world, he assured me, especially since the present unsettled conditions prevented Syria from achieving the progress it so badly needed. Soviet Communist domination was unthinkable for any sane Syrian.

In the evening I called on Prime Minister al-Qudsi. Our conversation ranged over the whole field of U.S.-Syrian relations. Perhaps because of the strain of the present political situation (Dr. al-Qudsi's government had resigned only a week earlier and various efforts to achieve a successor had failed), his conversation was not well organized. He devoted more time to a review of past events and policies than to present trends and plans for the future. The Palestinian question, to which he had been giving most of his attention in recent weeks, loomed large in everything he said. The Prime Minister told me that the major threat to Syria was Communism, and the main problem was Palestine. Relations with the U.S. must be conditioned by these two factors. He spoke of Syrian determination to resist Communist aggression, but only indicated rather than stating clearly a desire for a steady improvement in relations with the West. The principal deterrent, he said, was large-scale U.S. aid to Israel. In my reply I emphasized the impartiality of U.S. policy as between Israel and the Arab states and our very real interest in the economic development of Syria.

This led into a discussion of the refugee question, on which Dr. al-Qudsi was less specific then he had been in his recent talks with Ambassador John B. Blandford, U.S. representative on the refugee agency, and Minister Cannon, on which I had been briefed. The Prime Minister's remarks followed the general theme that Syria could make good use of refugees in resettlement, but that there must be prior formal assurance of continued help from international sources. He then spoke briefly of Syria's general economic development program. He brightened when I made reference to the undeveloped resources of the rich Jazirah Plain in northern Syria. I also touched on our Point Four Program, in which Dr. al-Qudsi showed genuine interest. We discussed briefly possible U.S. loans.

Dr. al-Qudsi seemed to pay particular attention to my remarks on the evils of neutralism. He stated that his government had no illusions about the Communist threat, but that he always had to reckon with certain dissident elements in the parliament and in Syrian public opinion, which he must be careful not to outdistance. Dr. al-Qudsi was obviously restrained in his remarks by his current difficulties in forming a government. (He announced a new cabinet the next day, which lasted only overnight.) He also knew that we would be talking again at the luncheon he was giving me that day, and at the Minister's dinner the next evening. Early that evening, Cavendish Cannon gave an informal reception at the Legation, where I received the American residents, including the heads of American educational, philanthropic, and commercial organizations in Syria. After dinner I had a long discussion of the internal Syrian political situation with the British Minister. I would naturally have had a similar discussion with the French Minister, in view of the importance the French still attached to their position in Syria, of which they were very jealous. However, he was away.

The day following I had a long discussion during the morning with Dr. Carlton, president of Aleppo College. Carlton was one of the great Arab and Middle Eastern scholars with a wealth of experience in the Middle East. I learned much from him, particularly about the attitude of the people of Aleppo, who are rivals of Damascus and quite different, being more business-oriented. One of my great disappointments is never to have had an opportunity to visit Aleppo. Later when I was Ambassador to Turkey I planned a trip to Aleppo, only to have it canceled by the Department because our ambassador in Syria thought it would be construed as having political significance and lead to misunderstanding in Syria. The Levantine mind is very complex. Nothing is forgotten from their long history of intrigue and maneuver. I was guest of the Prime Minister at lunch the following day at the Damascus Club. I enjoyed the Arab atmosphere and the food of the club even though the conversation was largely perfunctory. The Syrian officials were shy and noncommittal, reflecting the divisions and uncertainties among them. It was prudent in Syria to be cautious in what one said.

In prepared remarks to the Syrian press later in the day I said that I thought neutralism was losing ground in the Middle East and South Asia. "It is losing ground because more and more people realize that collective security offers them their only true safeguard against armed Communist aggression." I was later to be contradicted on this conclusion by the Syrian press. Considering subsequent Syrian history I believe I was right, but for the wrong reason. Syrians have often abandoned neutralism, but only for a more direct relationship with the U.S.S.R., not us.

In response to a question as to whether Syria was pro-Western or pro-Eastern, I replied that I was sure it was pro-democratic which meant pro-Western. I explained that I didn't mean that the West could take Syria for granted. The basic question was not whether Syria or other Arab countries were pro-U.S. or pro any specific Western country, but whether we all had the same goals. The U.S. did not consider itself a protagonist in a world struggle. We were engaged in defending certain principles over which we had no monopoly, and which I was convinced all free nations would elect to adhere to. I said that this was more important than the grievances the Syrians have clung to from the past.

In their comments on my press conference, several papers said that my conclusion that the Middle East was abandoning neutralism came from my contacts with governments, not the people. *Al-Kibah* said that my visit was a harbinger of good relations. However, it also quoted the "Conference of Syrian Workers," who denounced my visit and the Syrian authorities' "leniency" with me. The conference said I was engaged in a conspiracy against Syria to turn it into an imperialist battlefield. *Al Hadara* and *Al-Kibah* reported a similar charge by 250 Syrian university students. They said that they refused to yield to my "insolent" demands and "will not put their necks in the yoke of the Western camp."

Al-Insha published a memorandum urging neutrality, which had been issued by certain Iraqis after my visit to Baghdad. Given Syrian strategic importance, *Al-Insha* said, neutrality is impossible. Arab states should arm and either enter a regional neutrality pact or "bargain with those who wish to use our lands as a second line of defense for their fighting forces in Iran and Turkey." *Al Ba'ath*, organ of the extremist Arab Socialist Resurrection Party, saw in my statements an attempt to pressure Arabs into joining the Western camp. Its conclusion was: "Contrary to what McGhee said, Syrians have chosen neutrality for their own particular purposes. The statement that this conflict is a war between freedom-loving people and enemies of freedom is untrue because people in the former group deprive other people of their freedom and preach the doctrine of imperialism, and are not therefore fit to defend freedom. Such statements might fool Americans but they cannot fool Arabs. It is not a case of Arabs trying to be neutral freedom-loving people and enemies of freedom, but their trying to be neutral between two camps, both of which are oppressive."

On my last evening I presided over a dinner at the Legation for the Prime Minister, cabinet ministers, and important secretaries general. Although it was a pleasant occasion, the conversation was not very revealing. Those present were very cautious, speaking only in well-known, safe Arab expressions.

On the morning of March 24, I departed by car over the mountains for Beirut for an official visit to Lebanon. Cavendish had long planned a trip to a ceremony in Bethlehem, and I insisted he carry it out, so we left about the same time. The following morning I was advised in Beirut that the room I had been occupying at the Legation in Damascus had been dynamited during the evening. Fortunately, since neither I nor the Cannons were there no one was injured. My curiosity was such, however, that I insisted on being driven back to see the result. The room in which I would have been sleeping had I remained was shattered; the bed was a shambles; glass was everywhere. The Cannons' room was only slightly disturbed. Damage was later estimated at $50,000.

I concluded that I would not have been seriously injured, only shaken and sprayed with glass. I wanted to believe that the perpetrator knew I had gone and wanted only to register a protest. The Syrian government expressed regret. An Arab refugee was later arrested and charged; however, I never heard what happened to him. I didn't care. Poor fellow. But I will always remember the reaction I had to my dynamited room. It gave me an insight into the deep feeling of anger and desperation of the Arab people in the plight of the refugees and other consequences of the Arab-Israeli war.

The Syrian officials I saw during my visit there represented the old regime. Their attitudes were quite similar to those of the French and British, who had continued to dominate the Middle East after World War I. The officials who ruled for them feared Communism as a threat to their position and way of life. Those who overthrew them later became our enemies as well as theirs. After World War I Prince Faisal, the Hashemite Governor of Syria, had with Woodrow Wilson's support attempted to gain independence for Syria and was, for a brief period, successful. The suppression of Faisal's regime by the French on the basis of a mandate from the Supreme Allied Council caused deep resentment in Syria. It contributed to the eventual rise of the nationalist Ba'ath (Arab Socialist Resurrection Party), which in a coalition with Communists and other leftists came to power in 1957. The Ba'athists, themselves divided into factions, have ruled Syria ever since, from time to time in coalition with various outside allies.

The Ba'ath party, founded just prior to World War II by two Damascus schoolteachers, represented the intellectual revival of the 1920s and 1930s. Its aims were to adapt European socialism to the Arab world and make it the rallying point for the reformist intellectuals of the times. The party hoped to achieve a great renaissance among the Arabs. Alas, we did not have the foresight to see, in 1951, the course Syrian political life would take. Since we were dealing with leaders whose views were congenial to us, we had little interest in a change. In 1951 we knew little about the Ba'athists. Their goals as they had developed by 1957 were, first of all, anti-Western. They sought sweeping economic and political reforms to dislodge the ineffective leadership of Syria, which still represented feudal·and business interests subservient to the West. Their fundamental goal was Arab unity. The Ba'athists never considered Syria a genuine country, but only a part of the Arab world. They sought close cooperation with the Soviets in order to dislodge Western control of the Arab homeland. Although the party today professes neutrality, it remains anti-Western.

Following my visit to Damascus, I made a brief stop in Beirut on March 24. Lebanon, one of the loveliest countries in the world, has been called "the playground of the Near East," offering the snow-capped Lebanon Mountains with their celebrated cedars of Lebanon in close proximity to beautiful sand beaches. Lebanon at the time of my visit was still fulfilling its traditional function as the center for trade and intercourse between the Near East and Europe. Here were the ancient trading centers of Byblos, Sidon, and Tyre. It survived politically on the basis of the precarious fifty-fifty balance between Muslims and Christians. Once a part of the Ottoman Empire, Lebanon, along with Syria, was given as a mandate to the French by the League of Nations after World War I. It was proclaimed an independent republic by the French in 1941, ten years before my visit. Bishara al-Khuri, who received me, became its first President. At the time I was there, Lebanon faced grave difficulties as a result of the 120,000 Arab refugees it had received from the 1948 Arab-Israeli War.

Arriving by car from Damascus, I was received by Minister Lowell C. Pinkerton, a capable veteran career officer, who arranged for me to meet the Lebanese political leaders. It was my first official visit to Lebanon, my only purpose being to familiarize myself with the country and to show U.S. interest.[3] I first paid a call on the Prime Minister, Hussein Queini, in accordance with tradition a Sunni Muslim, who was also acting Foreign Minister. Later I met with President Bishara al-Khuri, a Christian. Pinkerton had as guests for luncheon in my honor the Prime Minister and two members of his cabinet. I held a press conference at 6 P.M. The dinner that evening included not only the Prime Minister again but also leaders of the various political parties. I have little of substance to report from my visit. My discussions with the officials were general in nature: prospects for an Arab-Israeli peace treaty, the problem of the Arab refugees in Lebanon, and our Point Four assistance. Although al-Khuri had been jailed by the French in 1943 for changing the constitution, he was firmly pro-Western. He was concerned about possible Communist and radical Palestinian influence among the refugees in Lebanon. A protégé of the French, who still had great influence in Lebanon, he represented the old regime and posed no problem to us. In retrospect, of course, we should have been concerned about the stability of the regime.

It could not be foreseen in 1951 that Lebanon would, in 1958, be literally torn asunder by communal warfare, to which we would respond by landing six thousand Marines to save the government; would become the center for the terrorist activities of the Palestine Liberation Organization (PLO); and would be partially occupied by Syrian forces. The invasion by Israel in June of 1982, which caused tens of thousands of casualties and massive destruction, resulted in the complete destruction of the military power of the PLO, and the removal of their leader Yasser Arafat with his surviving military cadres, to other Arab countries.

In my brief remarks to the press, I stressed U.S. interest in economic development in Lebanon, particularly in the completion of the Litani River irrigation project, as a benefit to the Lebanese people and as a means of alleviating the refugee problem. We felt that development would help achieve stability in Lebanon and in the Near East generally. Our Point Four Program had funds available to Lebanon. I refused to comment on internal Lebanese issues and, in response to questions, disclaimed any intent on our part to ask Lebanon to grant us base rights or abandon her traditional neutrality. Although we considered the repatriation of refugees desirable, they would undoubtedly find hostility to their return. Under the circumstances many might prefer to settle in the countries that had taken them in. Little did I realize that open warfare would develop between Israel and the PLO based in Lebanon. I left this lovely country with no premonition of the disaster that was to befall it.

Only recently, while perusing the Foreign Office records in the British Public Record Office, I found the most candid report of any encounter I ever had with a British official.[4] This was from an officer in the British Legation in Beirut, whose home I had visited briefly with Pinkerton on the evening of March 24. He took careful aim and fired at me in a letter back to James Bowker in the Foreign Office. Present by chance were his house guests, Air Marshal Sir John Baker and Captain Derick H. Hetherington, Chief of Staff to the Naval Commander-in-Chief's representative in Fayid. They represented the British Middle East military forces, who were using the rights held under their treaties to move freely from country to country and organize an area defense. This was their turf.

Referring to me as "that infant prodigy McGhee who is only 39," he characterized me as "pretty definite—indeed almost too definite" about my opinions arising out of my recent "hurry around" trip through the Middle East and South Asia. He reported that I was affable and friendly enough, and that Pinkerton had advised that on coming down from Oxford (getting my college wrong) I had amassed a fortune in a few years (giving an amount which was greatly exaggerated). He recommended solid British reflection before accepting any of my snap impressions, which were obviously based on a lack of experience. I am sure I fully deserved his rebuke. I must have been very full of myself.

29

The Hashemite Kingdom

Visit to Amman, Jordan.[1] King Abdullah Hussein,
March 25–27, 1951.

Jordan, or the Hashemite Kingdom of Jordan, was before the first
Arab-Israeli War an Arab Emirate under British mandate, called
Transjordan. In 1951 it had a population of only a little over a million
and a half, approximately one-third the indigenous population of
Jordan, one-third the inhabitants of the West Bank, and one-third
refugees to both. Jordan occupies a barren limestone plateau with an
elevation of three thousand feet, which terminates abruptly near the
western boundary of the country in a steep fault whose downthrown
western side extends below sea level, forming the Jordan River, the
Dead Sea, and the Wadi El Araba, which is a dry river extending to
the Gulf of Aqaba.

The seat of early kingdoms under the Amorites and Nabateans,
the area which is now Jordan was conquered by the Romans in A.D.
106 and enjoyed prosperity as a part of the Roman province of Arabia. Neglected after conquest by the Arabs in 636, it was taken by the
British after World War I and separated from the Palestine mandate.
Although there was little basis for making it a separate country, either from the standpoint of history or geography, the British in 1921,
as a reward for the services rendered by the Hashemites during the
war, put the area under the rule of Amir Abdullah, second son of
Hussein, the head of the family. In 1926 Hussein, despite his support
by the British, lost the Hejaz to Ibn Saud. The British helped Abdullah create the famous Arab Legion to defend Transjordan against
raids from Saudi territory, and made Amir Faisal, first son of Hussein, king of what is now Iraq.

Transjordan achieved complete independence in May 1946, and
Transjordan's national assembly proclaimed Amir Abdullah the coun-

try's first king. On May 8, 1948, the British surrendered their mandate over Palestine lying west of Transjordan, in part of which the Jews founded the new state of Israel as provided by the UN. The remainder was to be part of a proposed Arab state. On the same day the armies of Transjordan, Syria, Lebanon, Egypt, and Iraq entered Palestine to prevent the Israeli takeover. Mediation by the UN ended the fighting in a ceasefire on January 1949, with most of that part of Palestine set aside for the Arab state being occupied by Transjordan.

My first visit to Jordan had been in April 1949, the month the name had been changed from Transjordan. As Special Assistant to the Secretary of State in charge of U.S. efforts to solve the Arab refugee problem, I had met King Abdullah at that time. Since then there had been no progress in reaching a peace treaty or resettling any appreciable number of the Arab refugees who had been living before the war in what became Israel. The UN Relief and Welfare Agency offered a meager subsistence to the refugees living in Jordan, who refused to give up hope of return. I arrived in Jordan for my present visit as assistant secretary by car from Damascus late in the day on March 25, 1951. I had always wanted to see the ruins of the ancient city of Jarash, which was built, mainly by the Romans, in the second and third centuries A.D. I insisted that we make the necessary detour, which was over bad roads, even though it threatened to delay our arrival in Amman beyond the time set for the dinner in my honor. It was raining when, in failing light, I hastily examined the impressive ruins of Jarash: the Great Temple, the Forum, the two theaters, and the Great Street of Columns, all in a remarkable state of preservation. Even though my visit was brief, it made a lasting impression.

We arrived in Amman, the ancient capital of the Amorites, after dark. Our chargé in Amman, David Fritzlan, had arranged for me to stay in his residence. Fritzlan was a young and rather junior officer to be in charge of our legation (Amman had not yet been made an embassy). However, he and his wife managed the arrangements for my visit with skill in the face of great difficulties. For dinner, which was black tie at 8:30, they had assembled the Prime Minister, the Foreign Minister, the Minister of Development and Reconstruction, the British, French, and Turkish ministers, and the fabulous Major General John Bagot Glubb, commander of the Arab Legion, together with the other Legation officers. It was a most interesting evening. There was an air of excitement, as if almost anything could happen.

From the general atmosphere in Amman one got the impression of being in a war zone after a battle. King Abdullah was heavily involved in negotiations to make the necessary postwar adjustments. Jordan was overrun with refugees, who had virtually doubled the country's population. The limited facilities of the country were strained. The Jordanian officials present at dinner reflected an apprehension for the future. Would the refugees be permitted to go back? Would hostilities be renewed? Would the U.S. help them bear the burden of supporting their refugees? I felt very much on the spot.

My meeting with King Abdullah was set for the following morning at the palace. I had looked forward to it. Abdullah had been described as "the most ebullient, likable, resilient, and intelligent of Hussein's sons." He was nicknamed by the family "the hurried one." It was he who had fostered the Hashemite connection with the British. He had at first wanted to be made King of Iraq, which logically went instead to the senior and more dignified Faisal. After his feint at driving the French from Syria, the British gave Abdullah Transjordan. In 1921 it was an unimportant corner of Syria, with only 350,000 inhabitants. They hoped that he would relieve Britain of the enormous responsibility of governing it. Abdullah soon made himself master of the country and earned the loyalty of its people. He was to govern for thirty years until, on July 20, 1951, he was shot at point blank by an assassin as he entered the Haram esh-Sherif, the enclosure around the sacred Muslim shrine, the Dome of the Rock, to which he had gone to worship at the Mosque of Aksa within.

Once on the throne in Amman, Abdullah had built two modest palaces and governed as a Hashemite patriarch. Highly individual and unpredictable, he became a leader of Arab nationalism. In fact, the government was for the first twenty years of his reign run by the British, who supported the country with an annual subvention as a colonial protectorate linked to the Palestine mandate. The defense of Transjordan was entrusted to the Arab Legion, which in 1930 came under the command of a remarkable young Englishman, John Bagot Glubb. Glubb loved the Bedouin tribesmen and undertook as his mission to explain the West to the Arabs and bring the two together.

During the Second World War, Abdullah, Glubb, and their Arab Legion helped the British put down the pro-Nazi Rashid Ali regime in Baghdad, ending the Axis threat in that part of the Middle East. Following the 1948–1949 Arab-Israeli War and the ensuing armistice, Abdullah annexed about half of prewar Palestine, the so-called West Bank of the Jordan, which included the Holy Places of Jerusalem and the territory set aside for an Arab state. This created many problems for him. The assimilation of a million Palestinians, the most advanced of the Arabs, was difficult for the monarch of an impoverished state supported by an outside power. Other Arabs were jealous and critical of Abdullah's actions during the Arab-Israeli War. And finally, alone among the Arabs, he engaged for five months in secret negotiations with Israel. It was perhaps these unsuccessful negotiations that led to his assassination, reportedly by a kinsman of his enemy the former Mufti of Jerusalem.

The King received me in the throne room of his comfortable but unpretentious palace at 9 A.M. on the morning of March 26. He was a short, wiry man with a handsome face, smooth dark skin, and a mustache and goatee. He wore a light white wool shirt buttoned at the top and covered with an unbuttoned light wool jacket. His eyes shone. He talked quickly and with extravagant gestures. He offered me Turkish coffee. During my hour with him we talked about many things, but several stand out. He took a long view of the Palestinian problem, and was willing to be patient. After all, the hostilities had resulted in his acquiring an unexpected territorial and population windfall. He had never forgotten his family's loss of the Hejaz, the key to the Arabian Peninsula, to King Ibn Saud. Although he knew he could never recover it, he could still dream.

"If I had your power I would not be able to restrain myself," he said to me with a roguish smile. I sensed that he feared possible trouble from Ibn Saud, having in mind past Wahhabi raids from Saudi Arabia. I recalled that Saud, fearing not so much Abdullah as the imagined machinations of the British who supported him, had expressed a similar apprehension during my visit to Saudi Arabia in March 1950. It was in part to help relieve tension between Saud and Abdullah that I had helped launch the Tripartite Declaration of 1950. Also at my meeting with the King were Prime Minister Samir Pasha Rifai and Foreign Minister Ahmad Bey Tuquan. I expressed appreciation to Abdullah for receiving me and my pleasure to be back in Jordan. I congratulated him on the progress made in the development of the country. Our government appreciated the strong support the King had given the U.S. and the UN in connection with the war in Korea. My only regret was that since Jordan was not a member of the UN the Arab Legion was not able to participate in the defense against Communist aggression in Korea. The excellent organization of the Legion and the courage of its soldiers were widely recognized in the U.S.

The King appeared genuinely touched. He expressed regret that the Legion could not do more. However, he assured me that the U.S.

could count on his forces to do all within their power to repel Communist aggression in the Middle East. I expressed appreciation for the fine way in which the Jordanians had taken care of the Arab refugees. The King said he was convinced that large numbers of refugees, if not all, could be settled in Jordan if sufficient assistance was forthcoming and if there were changes in the UN administration of relief and settlement. I agreed that changes were indeed required, and that with the cooperation of Jordan and other Arab states large numbers of refugees could be resettled. I assured the King that we would continue assistance to countries receiving refugees, and continue to make large contributions to the relief and integration fund. Jordan could also count on economic assistance under the expanded Point Four Program.

The King then raised the question of the Middle East as a whole. The defenses of Greece, Turkey, and Iran must be strengthened, he said, particularly those of Iran because of its exposed position. The disunity, indecision, and political instability in most Arab states had prevented them from building effective defense against invasion. I assured the King that the U.S. recognized the great danger posed by the Soviets to the Middle East, and explained that we and Western Europe were engaged in a large-scale rearmament and mobilization program. If the Soviet attack could be delayed for at least eighteen months, the West would have overwhelming superiority in war materiel and manpower. This would remove any fear of Soviet attack against the countries on its borders. I gave the King the precise number of aircraft, tanks, and guns that we were presently producing. The King was surprised at the size of these figures. However, he said that lack of unity would prevent the Arabs from creating strong defenses even if weapons were available. He stressed that the unity of the Arab world must be encouraged, suggesting that if Syria and Jordan could be united under the Hashemites he could build up a strong Arab Legion which would contribute to stability and end the threat of a fifth column. Abdullah assured me that Turkey would welcome such a development. If the U.S. would just look the other way, he would be able to carry out this project.

I replied that we were not against the voluntary union of likeminded people, nor did we oppose decisions freely made to disunite. We could not, however, sanction a union imposed by force. This would threaten rather than increase security in the area, and we would have to oppose any unilateral move he might make against Syria. Abdullah assured me that he would take no action contrary to

U.S. policy, but would work to improve the security of the area as a whole. In the event of invasion, the U.S. could count on him to fight on its side.

I expressed appreciation to the King for his cooperation in helping solve the many problems outstanding between Jordan and Israel. Should there be violations of borders within the Middle East, our government would carry out our commitments made in the Tripartite Declaration. The King said he had no fear of Israel. He indicated resentment, however, that the Tripartite Declaration would stand in his way if he had to use force against Syria. Turning to Israel he advised of discussions he had conducted with the Israelis in recent weeks. He had found that they would make no concessions. Unless they could reach agreement with Prime Minister Rifai, who was friendly to Israel, they would never be able to make peace with anyone else. I congratulated the King on his keen grasp of world affairs and thanked him for his frankness in laying before me his innermost ambitions in the Arab world, even though we had points of disagreement.

At 10 A.M., I met separately with Prime Minister Rifai, Foreign Minister Tuqan, and other members of the Jordanian government. I had known the Prime Minister's brother, Abdel-Monem, during his service with the Jordanian mission in Washington. The Prime Minister and Foreign Minister apologized for the King's "greater Syria scheme." It was difficult for him to abandon his hope of taking Syria, which had been his ambition for thirty years. They did not agree with him and would see to it that no such action took place. They did, however, wish to make a contribution toward Arab unity. "Union of the Fertile Crescent is inevitable and it is the duty of all Arabs to work for it," the Prime Minister said. "How this would take place and under whose leadership must be worked out later on the basis of common agreement."

The Prime Minister stressed that Jordan was in dire need of substantial aid to take care of the refugees. I repeated assurances I had given the King that we would give economic assistance to Jordan, mentioning an expanded Point Four Program as a possible source of funds. Rifai emphasized his determination to implement fully the Jordan-Israeli armistice agreement, particularly Article 8 dealing with Mt. Scopus, assuming the Israelis would cooperate. Israel had not done so up to this point. Jordan had made every effort to provide the Israelis access to Mt. Scopus to carry on their normal educational work there. Assuming that UN relief to Jordan for the refugees continued, the Jewish institutions on Mt. Scopus would be treated in the same way as all other foreign institutions. He was surprised that Israel continued to claim the Mt. Scopus area and produced a copy of the armistice agreement showing that it belonged to Jordan.

I said that from the evidence he gave me he appeared to have a good case. However, the Israelis would probably try to make a case for their control. I hoped that both sides could avoid local quibbling, and reach agreement on how they could coexist on Mt. Scopus. The Prime Minister complained that the armistice commission was too ready to compromise, rather than stick with principles. Jordan had arranged for an international lawyer to come from England to advise them on their rights under the armistice agreement. I later called on the Foreign Minister and met with the Chiefs of Diplomatic Missions, who had been present at dinner the previous evening. At noon, I attended a luncheon in my honor given by the King at the palace. In addition to Jordanian officials, Glubb Pasha, as he was called, was again present. We agreed to meet that afternoon, since no formal appointment had been made. The luncheon had atmosphere: excellent Arab food was served in Arab style. The King was an amiable host. He jokingly poked fun at his colleagues.

In the afternoon I held a press conference at the Legation.[2] Before my arrival a telegram had arrived for me from Nablus signed by four Arabs. It said, "Good results will not be achieved by your endeavors to appease the rulers at the expense of the masses. The wish and will of the people will finally prevail. The net result of your activities would lead to winning the rulers and losing the people." As a starter for the press conference, I issued a statement expressing pleasure in being in Jordan again and in having been received by the King, who had been most cordial. Our conversation had touched on local and world-wide problems of common interest. The U.S. was interested in assisting the peoples of the Middle East to improve their economic conditions and build up their security as a deterrent to aggression from any quarter. I recalled the assistance we had given Jordan with her refugee problem and expressed appreciation for the helpful attitude Jordan had adopted toward the refugees. I praised King Abdullah's support for the UN action in Korea, particularly since Jordan was not a member of the UN. I pointed out that Jordan's entry into the UN had been vetoed by the Soviet Union on the grounds that it was still a British mandate.

On March 23, two days before my arrival, the local paper, *Al*

Urdon, describing me as a "moving force" behind American Middle East policies, called on Jordanian officials to "tell this man frankly and without leniency that we stand heart and soul on the side of democracy in this huge cold war and warm war in the future, but that the joining necessitates a price. This price is to recover our usurped rights, to recover our lost prestige and to find justice on our side, at least for once. The case of Palestine cannot remain unsolved, and the condition of the refugees must be improved. America is mainly responsible for what has taken place." The same paper, on March 25, questioned my statement reported from Damascus that the U.S. did not have the means to accomplish repatriation of the refugees. "The question is asked how the U.S. can aid an aggressor on one hand and yet refuse to exert the required pressure to force Israel to abide by the UN decision and accept the refugees who wish to return to their former homes."

The reporting of the conference was largely factual. The papers said that I had not been willing to brand Israeli refusal to receive refugees as aggression. I had expressed concern about the plight of the refugees and their effect on stability in the Middle East. The U.S. had, I pointed out, helped create the Clapp Mission to ameliorate the refugee problem, and we must all cooperate to this end. I said that those who were inclined to look favorably toward the U.S.S.R. should look and see what was occurring behind the Iron Curtain.

The press reported that I had made it clear that we favored voluntary cooperation in the Middle East toward collective security rather than the creation of blocs. The aim of the Tripartite Declaration was to assure inviolability of frontiers, not to encourage division as one journalist had suggested. U.S. interest in the Middle East was increasing because of cultural and economic ties and our appreciation of the strategic importance of the area. I believed the Middle Eastern countries would be inclined to join the West rather than the Soviet Union. Both the *New York Times* and *Washington Post* reported me as telling King Abdullah that the U.S. wanted to help the Middle East check aggression from any quarter. Fritzlan telegraphed that the opportunity given to local journalists to talk with an American official from Washington had led to their abandoning some of their bitterness toward the U.S. He did not know how long this would last.

After the press conference I had a good meeting with Glubb Pasha. He was quite different from what I had expected. He appeared quiet and reserved; his cherubic face showed where his jaw had been shot away, but he still maintained a soft, merry smile. Glubb was a romantic like Lawrence of Arabia, and had identified himself completely with the nomadic Bedouins. He was reputed to be withdrawn, self-sufficient, emotional, of strong and profound convictions, and devoted to helping achieve Middle Eastern peace. He was not in such a position that I could discuss major policy with him: my call was social and out of interest in the man. He told me of his deep affection for the Bedouin soldiers and for Jordan. He hoped the time would come when we could help strengthen the Arab Legion which, since the Arab-Israeli War, had suffered shortages of equipment and loss of morale. I said I would do what I could to help him.

Later I met the few American residents of Jordan at the consulate. They asked many questions, seeking some basis for hope in overcoming the Arab-Israeli impasse. I tried, but was not really able to help them. In the evening the Prime Minister gave a dinner in my honor in the Philadelphia Hotel. This was the hotel at which I had stayed in 1949; it was built during the British era and was still the center of social life in Amman. Ptolemy II of Egypt, who was called Philadelphus, had added his name to the city when it was rebuilt under his rule, and the hotel took its name from history. I observed that the old Roman amphitheater, which faced the hotel, had been cleared of its Arab refugee inhabitants since my last visit. Progress was being made.

The dinner given by the Prime Minister was a splendid one, attended by all of the ministers, former prime ministers, presidents of the two Houses of Parliament, officials of the court, and other high officials. Rifai, the Prime Minister, was a genial host. As a result the normal reserve of the Jordanians was let down during what turned out to be a most enjoyable evening. I kept in touch with Rifai for some years as he regularly went in and out of office. I left Jordan on the morning of March 27, entering Israel through the Mandelbaum Gate in Jerusalem. Abdullah met his fate four months later.

In my memorandum to the Secretary of State on July 20, 1951, advising him of the situation created in the Middle East by the assassination of King Abdullah, there was included in my own hand the statement, "Of all the Arab leaders Abdullah was most cooperative toward Israel." It was to me ironic that the French journal *Le Monde*, commenting on July 23 on Abdullah's assassination, said, "For years, through weakness or calculation, certain English elements have encouraged these [nationalist] passions [assassinations]. Can it be hoped that Americans of McGhee's tendency who seem to want to follow in these footsteps will understand in time how enormous [the] price is which has to be paid when fanaticism is encouraged, even in the name of anti-Communism." The assassin of Abdullah was not anti-Communist. Abdullah was.

The British Minister, whom I had met the first evening, was the respected Sir Alex Kirkbride, who had long been the British conduit to Abdullah. He reported my conversation with Abdullah as told him by Samir Pasha, the King's aid who had translated for me.[3] My meeting was, according to Kirkbride, not a great success. The King had lectured me on the rise of Arab nationalism and his claim to leadership of the Arab world. The masses must be "guided or driven." Abdullah was reportedly irritated by my "blunt" statement that we would oppose the use of force to bring about the union of Syria and Jordan. The King had reported through Samir that he had not mentioned the use of force and couldn't understand why I had. Samir had apparently not reported the King's side remarks to me, which I felt I had to respond to unless we wanted to give Abdullah a free hand in carrying out his Greater Syria scheme. Samir did not, of course, know about the Prime Minister's apology to me for and disavowal of the King's long-held imperial aspirations. The Foreign Office official who commented on Kirkbride's despatch said "I am afraid Mr. McGhee has done nothing to enhance his country's popularity in the M.E."

Abdullah's successor, his son Talal, brought Jordan into the Arab League's Collective Defense Pact, which the old King had rejected. Although popular with the people, Talal suffered from a progressive mental illness and was persuaded to abdicate in favor of his heir, Hussein, who was allowed to assume the throne in 1952 when he had reached the age of eighteen. Guided by the example of his grandfather, Hussein leaned for support on the Bedouin tribes. Two-thirds of his subjects, however, were Palestinians, many of whose spokesmen looked on Egypt's Nasser as their champion and demonstrated open hostility to the Hashemite monarchy.

The Jordanians for their part attempted to close the border with Israel against infiltration by Palestinian guerrillas, after Israel adopted a policy of massive retaliation against Jordanian territory in response to terrorist raids. The widespread rioting that followed Hussein's announcement early in 1956 of his intention to bring Jordan into the Baghdad Pact, persuaded him to back down on the plan and also led to Glubb's dismissal from the command of the Arab Legion.

The Suez invasion in November compelled Hussein to end Jordan's special relationship with Britain, although this did not prevent the Hashemite's former patrons from sending troops to prop up his regime during the unrest coinciding with the crisis in Lebanon and the fall of the Iraqi monarchy two years later. The U.S. soon replaced Britain as Jordan's principal source of assistance, supplemented in the late 1960s by grants from Saudi Arabia.

Drawn by Egypt into the June 1967 war with Israel, Jordan suffered heavily in the forty-eight hours of intense fighting that culminated in the total defeat of its army. Israel was left in possession of the West Bank, from which an additional 200,000 Palestinians fled as refugees to the Jordanian East Bank. A test of strength ensued between the Palestinians, who were backed by Syria and Iraq, and the Jordanian government, and in the late 1960s and early 1970s it broke into open warfare, bringing Jordan to the verge of civil war. Hussein and his army prevailed over the Palestinians, however, averting what some observers saw as a Palestinian attempt to seize control of Jordan. But the bad feeling continued even after the Jordanians and Palestinians, both based in Jordan but fighting under separate commands, joined in the 1973 Yom Kippur War against Israel.

Over Hussein's objections, the Arab summit at Rabat in October 1974 accepted the PLO claim to represent Arabs on the West Bank. Hussein's acquiescence to his defeat at Rabat amounted to a renunciation of Jordanian sovereignty west of the Jordan river. PLO-backed candidates won overwhelming victories in the 1977 mayoralty elections conducted on the West Bank, where there is scarcely any evidence of loyalty to the Hashemite monarchy. Hussein has continued to stress Jordan's self-sufficiency, but the concern has persisted that the East Bank—where Palestinians play a significant role, holding prominent positions in the armed forces and civil service—could become a "substitute Palestine" if there is no settlement on the occupied territories.

30

Britain and Egypt at the Brink

Visit to Cairo, Egypt, Nahas Pasha, Salaheddin,
February 22 and March 29–April 1, 1951.

Egypt: the legendary land of pharaohs, sphinxes, Cleopatra, and the Nile. Its ancient history, dating back to 5000 B.C., fills volumes; recent history brings to mind Egyptian seizure of the Suez Canal, war with Israel, the Camp David accords, and the 1981 assassination of President Anwar Sadat.

My visit to Egypt took place shortly before a watershed in the country's evolution. For centuries Egypt had been dominated by foreign powers. In turn the Persians, the Greeks, the Romans, the Arab Muslims, the Turks, the French, and finally the British had established colonial governments to run Egypt's affairs. From 525 B.C. until 1952, no native Egyptian was head of state of the country. When I was there in 1951, the Egyptians were in the final throes of ousting the British from military control. Eighteen months later, in July 1952, nationalist military officers overthrew the monarchy and established a modern, social-welfare-oriented state in Egypt.

Bordered to the west and south respectively by Libya and Sudan, Egypt faces northward toward the Mediterranean Sea and eastward, across the Red Sea, toward Saudi Arabia. To the northeast, Egypt shares a substantial border with Israel. Both the Sudanese and Israeli border areas have been the subject of dispute, and warfare, over the years. A vast portion of Egyptian territory is composed of inhospitable desert. As a result, much of the population, which was 20 million in 1951, is now 43 million, and is projected to rise to 80 million by 2000, is crowded into the narrow coastal areas and the cities. Cairo, the capital, is today the largest city on the African continent, and has a population density of close to 70,000 persons per square mile, which presents serious socio-economic problems. The great mass of

Egyptians, known as *fellahin*, live in poverty. Today, barely able to eke out a living on the land, they crowd into Cairo.

In 1951 the monarchy—represented by King Farouk—and Egypt's policymakers as a whole, were less concerned with the plight of the fellahin than with doing away with the final remnants of British colonial power, following Egypt's formal independence in 1922. World War I had focused attention on the strategic importance of Egypt and the Suez Canal (completed in 1869), which provided a lifeline to Britain through the Middle East to India. Since 1798, when Napoleonic France's army occupied Egypt, it had been progressively drawn into the European power struggle in the Middle East. British interests became increasingly important after 1801. Later in the nineteenth century, however, at the same time the British became the major shareholders in the Suez Canal Company, a nationalist movement began to emerge in Egypt, drawing on anti-British and pro-Muslim sentiments.

In 1882, following a series of nationalist outbreaks, Britain sent an expeditionary force to occupy and rule the country. Thus, despite the formal declaration of independence, Britian's influence in Egypt remained strong through the period of the Second World War, and Egyptian nationalism grew in response. In 1936, an Anglo-Egyptian Treaty provided for the end of British occupation in return for British rights to maintain troops at the Suez Canal, Cairo, and Alexandria for twenty years, and a pledge of mutual assistance in case of war. The treaty also included an agreement to respect the Egyptian-Sudanese border. Sudan was then still ruled by Britain, but had long been the object of Egyptian expansionist desires.

Nonetheless, following World War II, when Egypt had served as a major military base for the British, tension heightened over the extent of British involvement in Egyptian national life. The establishment of the state of Israel in 1948 provided a second major source of discontent for Egyptian nationalists, and war broke out between the two nations almost immediately. Following elections in 1950, the newly appointed Prime Minister, Mustafa Nahas, asked the Egyptian parliament to abrogate the Anglo-Egyptian Treaty and to proclaim King Farouk ruler of the Sudan. Military scuffles between Egyptians and the British ensued.

Thus, at the time of my arrival on March 29, the two countries were engaged in delicate negotiations over Britain's right to keep troops in the Suez Canal zone, and the tension was running high on both sides. Although the U.S. was hopeful for an agreement that would permit the British to stay, our policy was to maintain strict neutrality. Egyptian Foreign Minister Mohammed Salaheddin had gone to London for talks on the troop issue on November 28. British Foreign Minister Bevin was not, however, able to pin him down on practical details of an orderly transfer of power in the Canal Zone from Great Britain to Egypt. Salaheddin had argued that if Egypt was given military assistance comparable to that going to Greece, Turkey, and Iran, British forces could be replaced in one year. The British raised the difficult question of their right of re-entry, if required, after withdrawal.

Salaheddin for his part would give no assurances that the Egyptians would not denounce the 1936 treaty. On March 28, the day before my arrival in Egypt, Prime Minister Nahas Pasha was quoted as protesting against "this Cold War waged against us." He complained of British procrastination and warned that "We cannot be expected to remain patient indefinitely." The British reply, received on April 11, offered withdrawal starting within a year, to be completed in 1956. Egyptian troops supplied on a priority basis would have control of security on the Suez bases, but essential British civilian technicians would be introduced as British troops were withdrawn. The Egyptians rejected the British terms in toto.

My own experience in Egypt consisted of two prior visits, the first of which was only a brief stopover on March 26, 1950, en route to Washington from Saudi Arabia. At the time, the Egyptian press peppered me with questions about the series of regional conferences I had just presided over and raised questions about what was referred to as the "McGhee Plan" for economic assistance to Palestinian refugees. I laughingly replied that the McGhee Plan had been to get Clapp (Gordon Clapp of TVA) to produce the Clapp Plan. The second visit took place on February 22, 1951, when Cecilia and I stopped off in Cairo for a day en route to the South Asia regional conference in Ceylon.[1] There had been considerable Egyptian press interest in the Istanbul conference over which I presided February 14–21. Their chief concern, however, was the negotiations in progress over British base rights in Egypt, which were at a critical stage.

Le Progrès Egyptien of February 15, 1951, editorialized:

> It will not be the first time that Mr. George McGhee, Assistant Secretary for Near Eastern Affairs, expected in Cairo at the end of the month, will meet His Excellency Mohammed Salah-ud-Din Bey, Egyptian Minister of Foreign Affairs. In Washington, where we fol-

lowed very closely the steps of the Egyptian Foreign Minister, there was a cordial and frank exchange between the two eminent personalities. In Cairo, this exchange will assume a new importance by virtue of the study, at the Istanbul Conference, of the national aspirations of the Arabs and notably those of Egypt.

By her attitude, Egypt has clearly demonstrated what would be her position in case of a world war. Disillusioned repeatedly during the last sixty years, Cairo considers that her final alignment, integral and total, with the Western camp, depends on the realization of her national aspirations. It is true that, according to the Department of State, this attitude is inimical to Western democracy because it encourages pro-Soviet and pro-neutral sentiments, but in spite of the repeated attempts of the leaders and the experts of the Department of State, the Wafdish Cabinet has not modified its attitude. It remains firmly opposed to communism but puts a price on its alignment to the cause of the West.

Hence the importance of the visit of Mr. George McGhee to Egypt towards the end of the month. Mr. McGhee will try, in the light of the conversations held at Istanbul, to determine to what degree Egypt has decided to align herself with the Western powers. He must also see if the Egyptian authorities will openly declare themselves for the Western cause without laying themselves open to communist attack. Also, from these very important conversations, it must be determined in a large measure if Egypt will make use of her military, economic, and political resources in a system of regional defense. At any rate, the American experts consider that the taking of such a stand in Egypt would remove certain obstacles which today hinder London and Cairo from arriving at a satisfactory *modus vivendi*.

I thought this was a very accurate description of the situation. According to U.S. Ambassador Jefferson Caffery, the turnout of journalists to meet me was the largest to greet any American since he had been in Cairo. We were accompanied by Joseph Palmer from the London Embassy and a representative of the Arab League. It was the first time the Egyptian Under Secretary of State had gone to meet any arrival except for Indian Prime Minister Nehru. Later that afternoon I held a press conference.[2] After paying tribute to the "imaginative" Egyptian press, I summarized the results of the recent Istanbul conference. The ensuing questions largely concerned Egypt's role in Middle East defense. In response to a question as to whether I believed that Egypt and other Arab countries would be on the side of the West, I replied that, although this would be up to them, I felt instinctively that they would be. They expressed considerable interest in possible Point Four assistance for Egypt. In response to another query I told them that I saw no internal Communist threat to the Middle East. I refused to take sides in the current confrontation between Britain and Egypt over base rights.

The independent *Al Mokattam,* reversing a critical "Open Letter to McGhee" of the previous day that had complained about U.S. exploitation of the Middle East, expressed gratification with my claim that American public opinion had become more enlightened over the Middle East and noted that my statements were generally satisfactory and at least not hostile to the Arabs. The *Gazette* reported that my press conference was "probably the biggest since those given by Mr. Churchill in Cairo during the war—a mark of enormous interest taken by the Egyptians in prospective American help." The *New York Times* of February 22 quoted me as saying: "I feel distinctly the Arab world is on our side." It continued, saying that "Cairo newspapers speculated that Mr. McGhee might discuss the question of United States use of five air bases in the Suez Canal Zone, currently in British hands."

I had intended, during my meeting with the Foreign Minister, to report on the Istanbul conference.[3] However, I discovered that he was more interested in reciting Egyptian grievances generally, and in discussing the Anglo-Egyptian negotiations and the Palestine problem. Upon his return from his recent visit to London, he said, he had been optimistic about reaching an agreement with the British on military bases. However, the "technicians" had whittled so much away from the area of agreement reached he felt what was left would not be acceptable. If negotiations failed he would have a very difficult internal problem. I expressed confidence that a satisfactory agreement would be reached. The U.S. was determined not to take sides.

Later I signed the King's guest book and left my card for Prime Minister Mustafa al Nahas Pasha, whom I was scheduled to see during my upcoming, longer visit. In the evening we dined quietly at the Embassy with the Cafferys. Other guests were the independent Egyptian leader Hussein Sirry Pasha and the Belgian Ambassador. Since we were scheduled to depart at 4:30 the next morning, we retired early. My return to Cairo in March was intended to complete the discussions held during this brief stop. I wanted to tell the Egyptians more about the results of the Istanbul conference and our thinking on Middle East defense. I hoped to push the British-Egyptian negotiations, which had been stalled since November 1950. I also wanted to demonstrate our increased interest in Egypt as the potential leader of the Arab world.

I had, of course, had many discussions about Egypt with British officials. I later learned from the British archives that, in advising the British Ambassador in Cairo of my April 1951 visit,[4] the Foreign Office assured him that I was "friendly and helpful." They told the Ambassador that the Foreign Office had kept the U.S. fully informed of British problems in Egypt since 1947, and that we had, in turn, expressed ourselves as anxious to help. The U.S. Joint Chiefs of Staff had assured the British that we attached high importance to their maintaining their facilities in Egypt, also that we recognized the importance of the Egyptians' realizing that they could not play the Americans off against the British.

The Foreign Office suggested to the British Ambassador, Sir Ralph Stevenson, that he have a frank talk with me during my visit about Anglo-Egyptian relations, particularly the defense question.[5] If he considered it desirable he might arrange a meeting for me with the British Middle East Office or the commanders-in-chief or both. I might be sounded out as to whether the Department thought a word from us to the Egyptians now, or at a later stage, would be valuable, assuming we would agree to it. The Foreign Office suggested I might include in my talks with the Egyptians the strategic importance of the Middle East, the danger of a vacuum there, and forceful advice on concluding defense arrangements which met Anglo-American needs.

I arrived in Cairo for my planned visit via Jerusalem on the Cairo air attaché plane on March 31.[6] In addition to Ambassador Caffery and members of the Embassy staff, I was met by the Egyptian Chief of Protocol, Azzam Pasha, leader of the Arab League, and a large press representation. Security precautions were more elaborate in light of the bombing of our legation in Syria following my recent visit there. After signing the palace register, I accompanied Ambassador Caffery and Sirry Pasha's wife to an opening of an excellent exhibit of the paintings of Mohammed Said in the Grand Palais at the Exhibition Grounds at Gezira. That evening the British Minister, Chapman Andrews, and General Sir Brian Robertson, the celebrated British commander-in-chief of British Middle East Forces, called on me at the Caffery residence.[7] The British Ambassador was in London. They filled me in on the negotiations and urged our support for the British position. Continued free use of their bases in the Canal Zone was absolutely vital to their Middle East defense, they stressed. Robertson was skeptical of the ability of the Egyptians to organize their own defense. Cairo, he said, could be taken very easily. He did not say by whom, but the inference was that it might have to be done by British forces.

In discussions with the British about their troops and bases in Egypt one sensed their traditional condescension toward the Egyptians, with whom they have always appeared to me to have a love-hate relationship. The slur word "Gippies" slipped out frequently in their remarks. I went to great lengths to assure Robertson that, although we had to remain officially neutral in the negotiations, we hoped that the British would be able to retain adequate troop and base rights and that I would do what I could to nudge the Egyptians toward this end during my present visit.

It seemed to me, however, that despite our reassurances there was always a lingering suspicion on the part of the British that we were undercutting them in their troop negotiations. They had had a dominant position in Egypt for over one hundred and fifty years. They seemed to suspect that we wanted to control Egypt. Actually, we had every incentive to support the British, since we were interested in Egyptian defense and had no desire to relieve the British of their responsibility. On the other hand, we wanted to build strong ties with the Egyptians as a means of helping the British and to fill any gap which might be created in case of future difficulties in Anglo-Egyptian relations. We were also, of course, aware of the importance of Egypt as the leading country in the Arab world, which included an important role in any Arab-Israeli peace negotiations.

On April 6, a week after my visit to London which followed my Cairo visit, Major Harry Leffe-Bourke, a Conservative M.P., asked the government in the House of Commons what was discussed with me during my visit to London and what decisions had, as a result, been taken on the British troop question.[8] Kenneth Younger, Minister of State in the Labour Government, replied that no decisions had resulted from the talks nor was there any question of the American government being directly involved.

The highlight of my stay from a purely personal viewpoint was a visit to the rural social center at Burg-el-Arab in the Nile Delta. The establishment of a network of rural social centers was the pet scheme of Minister of Social Affairs, Dr. Ahmed Hussein, who accompanied me on the trip and made sure that a large group of journalists was also present to provide a maximum of publicity. Hussein's idea, first put into practice in 1941, was to coordinate all government services, such as those provided by the Ministries of Health, Agriculture, and Education, in the form of rural centers where an attempt would be made to uplift the standard of living through concerted action. By 1946, the program had proven so successful that a decision was made to put centers throughout the country, on a basis of one per 10,000 inhabitants.

In order to coordinate the efforts of the various ministries, one district with a population of 300,000 was selected as a headquarters for regional offices. The central unit provided local residents with a hospital, lecture hall, cinema, theater, and library, all of which were partially funded by the residents themselves. The work of the center was to combat illiteracy, improve health standards, improve agricultural techniques, and encourage the development of cottage industries and handicrafts production. While touring the maternity ward of the Burg-el-Arab "social city," as the centers were called, I was advised that the parents of a child born the previous evening had decided to name their baby McGhee in honor of my visit. I was, of course, delighted, and the press took ample photographs of me awkwardly holding young Mohammed McGhee. (Despite having six children of my own, I never learned how to hold one properly!) The Minister of Social Affairs beamed, but I never imagined the repercussions that would ensue.

After touring other facilities at the center, including a sewing room, a cheese factory, and a sports center, I asked to see the home of a *fellah*, a common man. Someone suggested that I visit the house of an *omdeh*, or local official, but Ahmed Hussein insisted I see how the "masses" really lived. So we entered the dwelling of Sheikh Fathallah, whose wife, after my apology for arriving unannounced, said simply, "With us, when a guest crosses the threshold, he becomes master of the house." The house, which was made of unplastered mud brick, contained two or three rooms bordering a small garden surrounded by a wall. The family, poultry, and animals shared it all. I found the Fathallah family to be friendly and hospitable people; my visit with them was spontaneous, and revealing of how such people really lived.

Egypt also boasted at that time a network of urban social centers, known as "settlements," that were part of the work of the Pioneer movement. This had been founded by university graduates (including Foreign Minister Salaheddin) in 1929. The graduates, the elite of Egyptian society, had begun meeting to discuss how Egypt, then fighting for its independence, could meet the problems it would face after liberation. They decided that two essential elements for social progress were raising the overall standard of living and accepting the idea that all educated Egyptians had an obligation to fulfill social duties that the state could not be expected to undertake. These duties would include volunteer social work, study of social forces, and promoting social legislation. His pride in the work of the Pioneer movement led the Foreign Minister to arrange for me to visit the Ahmed Hussein Pasha Settlement in the Teibi quarter of Cairo, which featured a library, games, classrooms, meeting rooms, playgrounds, handicrafts facilities, a medical clinic, and a social-assistance bureau. My two hours there, following my earlier visits that day, reinforced my growing feeling of hope for the future of Egypt.

That evening I was treated to a stag dinner by the Secretary-General of the Arab League, Azzam Pasha, whom I had come to know through his frequent visits to Washington. We sat on cushions and ate from small tables at the Club Mohammed Ali, which served up a delicious repast. Not only were all the delegates to the Arab League Council present, but I was pleased to discover that my companion on the right was none other than the legendary Amir Abd el-Krim, the Riff leader who in 1926 had leapt into the Suez Canal to avoid capture by the French, and who appears briefly in my chapter on Morocco.

The next day I spent with the Foreign Minister and Azzam Pasha. I had gotten to know Salaheddin earlier when he visited Washington. I had given a luncheon for him at our farm in Middleburg, Virginia, and had attempted to make up for what I considered to be a cool reception by Secretary of State Dean Acheson at the State Department. I am a great admirer of Dean Acheson, but unfortunately he did not always seem to attach significance to visiting foreign ministers from the developing world. He largely ignored my briefing memorandum and did not raise with Salaheddin any of the critical issues Egypt was facing that I had suggested.

During my present visit the Foreign Minister sought to repay my hospitality. After an hour's meeting with Caffery and me in his office, Salaheddin took us to visit the nearby Mohammed Ali dam. In company with Azzam Pasha and others we had a picnic at the government rest house. Later Caffery and I met with Salaheddin and Under Secretary Hakki Pasha for two and a half hours. My discussions that day, the most important of my visit, dealt, as reported by Caffery, solely with the Anglo-Egyptian base issue, with which Salaheddin had been preoccupied since his return from London.[9]

Salaheddin told us that the Egyptians were willing to agree to the re-entry of British forces in the event of aggression against the U.K., Egypt, or any country adjacent to Egypt, but that they could not stay there in time of peace except for one year after reaching an agreement. The Egyptians considered this adequate time for their armed forces to be built up to the strength allowed under the treaty. They would assure that the Fayad base was well taken care of. Although British Foreign Secretary Ernest Bevin had agreed in principle to withdrawal within a year, Herbert Morrison, who had succeeded him, was going back on Bevin's position. Bevin had insisted on separating the issue of a base agreement from that of British evacuation of Sudan within two years, at which time Sudan was to become an independent state. Salaheddin agreed to the two-year period but insisted on linking the two issues, and also specified that Sudan should come under the Egyptian crown.

I told Salaheddin that, although we were not willing to be a party to the talks, we recognized that Egypt had certain legitimate national aspirations which the Egyptian people felt deeply about. We recognized also that the British had certain rights under the treaty. We believed Britain had a genuine desire to make a contribution to solving the present impasse. We considered the defense of the Middle East to be so important, for the countries of the area as well as those outside with interests in the area, that we wanted Egypt to develop its full military potential. We did not believe, however, that the base issue should be linked to the evacuation of the Sudan.

Salaheddin said that the Middle East countries themselves should have control over their own defense. The Egyptians could operate the Suez base. The British forces could be joined by the forces of other Middle Eastern states once a war began. Salaheddin said he was personally willing to extend the deadline for British withdrawal from the Sudan to three years. He summed up to the effect that Egypt and the other Arab states were prepared to make their defense contribution toward preserving peace and unity among free nations. But, he added, they must have the first say in their own territory. Assistance by others was secondary. Egypt could not side with any bloc of nations that violated its rights.

I replied that I accepted what he had told me as being the Egyptian view, and assured him that we would take it seriously. I said that we entirely approved of the development of indigenous Egyptian and other Middle East military forces. It was our understanding that

Britain did too. It was one of the principal objectives of the Tripartite Declaration of 1950, in which the U.S. had taken the lead over considerable opposition, to establish a framework for us and others to supply arms to Egypt. In our recent Chiefs of Mission meeting in Istanbul, we had agreed that Middle Eastern forces should be developed to the maximum extent possible in order to fill in the existing defense gaps.

Continuing, I said that the West must strengthen itself if it hoped to deter a Soviet invasion of the Middle East. Our present weakness created an emergency comparable to a state of war. The Soviets represented, in our view, a much greater danger than any remaining colonialism. The British were withdrawing everywhere, having already given up most of their former colonies. We were, however, now caught in a desperate short-term situation in the Middle East that would be greatly exacerbated by a U.K-Egyptian impasse. I suggested to Salaheddin that, in such a situation, national leaders had a duty to lead, and not merely follow the mood of their people. The U.S. was not willing to see fuel added to the crisis situation created in Iran, by encouraging undue nationalist expectations elsewhere. I concluded by assuring Salaheddin that the U.S. would never permit the revival of colonialism. Any remaining vestiges of colonialism must be dealt with through an evolutionary process.

When Salaheddin asked me what we would do if a break occurred between Egypt and Britain, I replied that I could not possibly predict. At that time, of course, it seemed inconceivable to me that the U.S. would ever take a stand against Great Britain, the NATO ally closest to us with which we had maintained a long special relationship. But the course of history is full of surprises. Only five years later, when the British consorted with the French and Israelis in an attempt to seize the Suez Canal (which Nasser had nationalized), the U.S. did the "inconceivable," by siding with Egypt.

That evening Ambassador Caffery gave an elegant dinner in the charming old Cairo Embassy in honor of the Egyptian Prime Minister, Nahas Pasha. He arrived early so we could have an informal talk. Other guests were the Foreign Minister, the Turkish and Greek ambassadors, Azzam Pasha, Abboud Pasha, and other dignitaries and their wives. Nahas Pasha, who was at the time one of the top Middle Eastern leaders and personalities, was the star of the evening. His striking appearance, enhanced by his pronounced "cocked" eye and grand manner, made him the center of attention. My discussions with the Prime Minister were interesting but much more general than those I had had with the Foreign Minister, of which he had been advised and said he approved. I emphasized that neutralism was an unrealistic and unsound approach to the threat now posed by the Soviets to the Middle East.[10]

Neither I nor anyone else suggested I see King Farouk during my visit. He had degenerated by this time into his self-indulgent bad-boy period and seemingly took no interest in affairs beyond the intrigues of the palace. It is amusing that Caffery, who saw the King occasionally, was on one occasion criticized in the press for not taking a fatherly interest in reforming him. Those who knew Farouk then would have realized what an impossible undertaking this would have been. Even Jefferson Caffery, whom I consider one of the great American diplomats and who had held many more important posts including Paris, could not have been expected to do this.

Local press coverage of my visit was extensive. Editorial comment focused on the purpose of my visit, criticism of U.S. Middle Eastern policies, and evaluations of the results of the visit.[11] Speculation as to purpose centered around peace with Israel, mediation of the Anglo-Egyptian question, Middle East defense, Iranian oil, Communism, Point Four, and private investment. Criticism of U.S. policy included accusations that we sided with the British in the Anglo-Egyptian negotiations and assertions that we could expect no cooperation from Egypt until Arab aspirations regarding Israel were met. Improvement in economic and social conditions could only come after Arab sovereignty and freedom had been achieved. The opposition paper, *Arkbar el Yom*, at least wrote that the government was pleased with my praise of their rural social institutions, which augured well for future U.S. aid. Several papers attacked American "imperialism" in Korea and elsewhere.

Al Misri, in speculating on the results of my visit, gave me undeserved credit for having concluded during my Middle East tour four base agreements with Pakistan, Syria, Lebanon, and Israel. Others concluded that I would intervene during my forthcoming visit in London to "iron out Anglo-Egyptian difficulties," and that as a result of my report on my return, U.S. Middle Eastern policies would be entirely changed. I must credit the Egyptian press for its imagination. Before leaving Cairo I left with Jefferson Caffery a sum of money and asked him to look into the question of a suitable gift for Mohammed McGhee, one which would help give him a good start in life. Caffery wrote advising that I give a gemusa, or water buffalo. It was said to be the prize possession of a fellahin family, providing labor, milk, fuel, and security. Concern for a gemusa's safety was so great, in fact, that a family could not sleep at night unless the animal was sleeping close enough to be heard. Needless to say, the result was not very hygienic.

I concurred by telegram and Caffery, one of our senior and most dignified ambassadors, was sporting enough to deliver the water buffalo personally, holding it by a rope as pictures were taken for the morning press.[12] To my great disappointment, however, Caffery discovered during the presentation that Mohammed McGhee's parents had separated. The water buffalo had been given to the mother. Upon receiving this sad information I wrote back, saying that although I did not wish to intervene in the domestic affairs of Egypt, for Mohammed McGhee's sake would the Embassy please try for a reconciliation. The reply was that the Embassy's inquiry had revealed that the father had made an effort to return but the mother had refused since she was sure he only wanted her back because she was now a wealthy woman. This showed clearly how the best of intentions to help others in their domestic difficulties can go astray. The local press publicity on the affair of Mohammed McGhee rippled on for some time. I received a letter from an Egyptian civil servant who had a son named something very much like McGhee. Could I help him buy a house? I decided to draw the line.

I have already referred to the fact that, in response to a British request, the State Department had arranged that I stop off in London on my way home to give the Foreign Office my impressions of a number of current critical issues, including the situation in Cairo. I have already reported my discussions concerning the AIOC-Iranian oil crisis. The British were at the time also engrossed in their treaty difficulties with Egypt. On April 2 Jim Penfield and John Root of our Embassy accompanied me to a meeting with James Bowker, who had succeeded Michael Wright as Superintending Under Secretary; Ambassador to Egypt Sir Ralph Stevenson; and Roger Allen, head of the Foreign Office African Department.[13]

Bowker described the current British proposal to Egypt as involving: the phased withdrawal of all British troops and headquarters by 1956, the termination date of the treaty; the placing of British civilian staff remaining after 1956 under Anglo-Egyptian control; negotiation of an Air Defense Pact providing for retention of RAF squadrons and ground defense forces after 1956; the right of re-entry in the event of war; and recognition that Sudan must determine its own future. In the meantime the British would help the Egyptians develop their armed forces.

I assured Bowker that although we did not want to be a party to the negotiation we fully understood the importance of the Suez base and wanted to support its continued British use. I summarized the results of my two-and-a-half-hour meeting with Salaheddin. Egypt offered the British another year, perhaps eighteen months, under the treaty, with right of re-entry if any contiguous country were to go to war. They agreed that Sudan must decide its own future, but not while Britain was in control. They were confident that the Sudanese would elect to maintain a foreign affairs, defense, and financial link with Egypt. I said that I had made clear to the Egyptian Foreign Minister the importance we attached to a continuation of the British position in Egypt, not only from the standpoint of Egyptian defense but for defense of the Middle East as a whole. The world was practically in a state of war. Although local forces must be built up, British forces were still essential. I had pointed out to the Egyptians the adverse political impact of their confrontation with the British on the other Middle Eastern countries. I gave no specific encouragement that Egypt would receive U.S. arms, despite the Tripartite Declaration.

I told Bowker that I felt the U.K. should demonstrate the utmost flexibility. The next two and a half years, while the West was rearming, were critical. The Egyptians had it within their power by denying labor and supplies to neutralize the British base, and it would be difficult for the British to retaliate. Perhaps, I suggested, the UN or the U.S. could help by furnishing a deputy commander under General Robertson. I warned against carrying out rumors I had heard, that the British might under certain circumstances seize Cairo. (I did not refer to General Robertson's remarks to me in Cairo.) Ambassador Stevenson interjected that this would not occur as long as he was there, unless British lives were threatened, and Bowker agreed. None of us realized how close we were to the brink of a complete break in Anglo-Egyptian relations. As has been described in Chapter 3, this occurred on October 15, when the Egyptian parliament unilaterally abrogated the 1936 treaty with Britain and the Sudan Condominium Agreement of 1899. This act prompted skirmishes between the British and Egyptians, and the resultant chaos contributed to a growing dissatisfaction with King Farouk's rule. This culminated in July 1952, when a group of young military officers overthrew him in a bloodless coup that came to be known as the 1952 Revolution.

Among the officers, Gamal Abdel Nasser emerged as the strongest and most popular of the new power holders, and ruled Egypt until 1970. Under his leadership important social and economic reforms were instigated, and Egypt came to play a leading role both in the Arab world and among Third World countries in general. Nasser's political philosophy, based on egalitarian principles found in Muslim and socialist thinking, and the close relationship he developed with the Soviets and other bloc countries, in 1956 led Secretary of State Foster Dulles to refuse to help Egypt in financing Nasser's ambitious Aswan Dam project. In response, Nasser nationalized the Suez Canal, which in turn provoked retaliatory military measures by France, England, and Israel. Following these dramatic events, the Soviet Union came to play a greater role in Egypt, initially through financing a large part of the cost of the Aswan Dam.

Throughout the 1950s and 1960s, tension mounted between Israel and the bordering Arab states, especially after the latter recognized the Palestine Liberation Organization in early 1964. In June 1967 hostilities increased between Israel and Syria, and as a measure of solidarity with its fellow Arab state, Egypt closed off the entrance to the Gulf of Aqaba to Israeli ships. Israel, deeming this an act of war, launched a devastating attack on Arab airfields that quickly routed Egyptian troops from the Sinai Peninsula and the Gaza Strip and destroyed vast quantities of Arab military material. During this brief war Israel occupied some 23,000 square miles of Egyptian territory.

Much of the rest of Nasser's term and that of his successor, Anwar Sadat (who took office in 1970 when Nasser died unexpectedly of natural causes), were devoted to overcoming the national humiliation that permeated Egypt following this devastating war. When a high-level Egyptian delegation that had gone to the Soviet Union seeking military equipment returned empty-handed, Sadat ordered all Soviet military advisers and technicians out of the country immediately. In October 1973, Sadat launched a surprise offensive against Israel that resulted in a small but psychologically important victory for Egypt, and Egypt began once again to exert a leading role among the Arab states.

These moves, followed by the many meetings between Sadat and Secretary of State Henry Kissinger, when the latter utilized his "shuttle diplomacy" to help settle the 1973 war, eventually led to vastly improved relations with the U.S. Later came Sadat's visit to Jerusalem and his participation in the Camp David agreements sponsored by President Jimmy Carter, which were signed by Sadat and Israeli premier Menachem Begin in September 1978. However, Sadat's increasing identification with Israel and the U.S. provoked the ire of Egypt's Muslims, who were responsible for his assassination in 1981. The manner in which Sadat's successor, Hosni Mubarak, will handle the complicated problems of the Middle East is of intense interest to the entire world.

In 1950 and 1951, the extraordinary developments which were to take place in Egypt over the succeeding thirty years could not have been anticipated. Our role at that time was concentrated on assisting the British to withdraw from Egypt under conditions that would not create instability and make Egypt vulnerable to Communist penetration. We wanted to demonstrate our friendship and interest in Egypt's future as an independent state. The fact that England did not achieve its own plan of withdrawal led to a great deal of conflict, bad feeling, and losses to all concerned. Although our actions during this time were not of decisive influence on the outcome, I would like to feel that they earned us goodwill from the Egyptians and may have contributed to the fruitful years of collaboration we later developed with Anwar Sadat.

Since I am an acknowledged Anglophile, the occasions on which I found myself in disagreement with the responsible British officials were always disappointing to me. Britain was at this time in a difficult situation, particularly in Iran and Egypt. Although my basic desire was to support British policy, the U.S. had its own national goals and interests, and occasionally they diverged from those of the British. I naturally reserved our right, where necessary, to take an independent line. In the Middle East, which had for so long been their almost exclusive domain, this was somewhat hard for the British to take, particularly from a friend. They often found it difficult to grasp that I did not give to Iranian and Egyptian officials the frank appraisals and suggestions I would make to British officials, which were directed toward helping us both work out a common policy.

The British archives provide the reports sent by the British Embassy in Cairo, starting with my meeting with General Robertson the evening of my arrival.[14] It was reported that ". . . the Egyptian Minister for Foreign Affairs had already got to McGhee and won him over." Actually I had not yet seen the Minister. They reported the line I told them I would take with Salaheddin reasonably accurately. Their summary of the principal points I tried to make with them, which I explained would not necessarily be part of my talk with the Foreign Minister, were as follows:

(i) If a choice had to be made, Egyptian "friendship" was more important than the 1936 treaty.

(ii) Prospect of retaining both now seemed hopeless and Anglo-Egyptian relations "looked pretty bad."

(iii) Therefore the only solution was for Britain to evacuate after an agreed period. Nahas wanted this "within 12 months" but Salah el Din [or Salaheddin] thought he could make it 18 months.

(iv) Peacetime base facilities in Egypt were not militarily essential. Granted Egyptian "friendship" and agreement about facilities in war a rapid build up on the outbreak was perfectly feasible, as Americans had proved in the Pacific.

My pessimistic view of the British position was unfortunately true. The Egyptians abrogated the 1936 treaty seven and a half months later. The key point I tried to make with General Robertson, and later with the Foreign Office in London, was that without Egyptian cooperation they could not get the necessary labor, supplies, and facilities to use the base effectively. Although I did not say so, their only alternative was to retake military control of Egypt, which Eden tried to do, and failed to do, five years later. The Embassy message summed up as follows:

> Although our talk was most friendly in tone, Mr. McGhee seemed very sure of himself and to have an idea at the back of his mind that we British were making rather a mess of [the] Middle East, what with Egypt and Persia. He obviously stands for a forward American policy in the Middle East though admittedly in agreed friendly collaboration with us with the *possible* exception of Turkey, Persia and Saudi Arabia which countries he frequently mentioned and where he seems to think the Americans have already acquired a leading position. I think he may have a vision of dwindling British and increasing American power and influence which within 18 months will completely change the picture here and make all things safe. The temper of the House of Commons and the United Kingdom generally about concessions to Egypt and British difficulties over sterling oil, seem to mean little or nothing to him. In this respect he and the Minister for Foreign Affairs are a pair.

It was undoubtedly my remarks as quoted in this letter, which were probably too frank although they were reported rather baldly, that disturbed both the British Embassy and officials in London. The officer handling the matter in the Foreign Office noted, "Mr.

McGhee certainly seems to have swallowed every inch of the Egyptian line and the only things he forebore to reproach us for were the 1882 Bombardment and the 'Massacre of Dammanhour' (a town 38 miles SE of Alexandria). However, we shall see what he says tomorrow." Even in their most difficult times the British kept their sense of humor.

On April 3, the Minister of Defense in London, Emanuel Shinwell, M.P., in a memorandum to the Secretary of State for Foreign Affairs, Herbert S. Morrison, M.P., acknowledged receipt of the telegrams from Cairo I have referred to "reporting the conversations which Mr. McGhee, the United States under secretary of state, has been having with the Egyptian foreign minister."[15] It read:

> It seems to me quite intolerable that a comparatively junior American official should be permitted to inferfere in this way in our negotiations with the Egyptian Government: Those negotiations are already difficult and delicate enough without unhelpful interventions from third parties.
>
> It may be that you contemplate taking the matter up strongly with the United States Government: If not, I suggest that it ought to be brought before the Cabinet at the earliest opportunity.
>
> Yours sincerely,
E. S.

Shinwell added in his own hand, "P.S. It would seem to me that he has contrived to weaken our position in the forthcoming negotiations. E. S." In reply Morrison said to Shinwell, "You should by now have seen a record of my conversation with the US ambassador and McGhee on April 3.[16] I am also proposing to ask Franks to take the matter up with Acheson." The British Embassy in Cairo reported that from my press conference there was "little doubt that I was converted" (to the Egyptians), but "that I was very impartial and gave the impression I wanted to help both sides."[17] At my suggestion Ambassador Caffery showed the British Embassy his reporting telegram of my meeting with the Foreign Minister. The Embassy sent a summary to London without comment.[18]

About a month after my return to Washington from London, I was asked to report to the Joint Chiefs of Staff on the Istanbul meeting and my impressions from my tour of the Middle East.[19] I first reaffirmed the need, which I had expressed to them on February 2, for a more positive U.S. security policy toward the Middle East basically on political grounds. The Iraqis, Syrians, Lebanese, and Israelis all wanted arms. Iraq had said that they could with more arms place two more divisions in the north. The Lebanese said they would give us bases in time of war if the French were not involved. The Israelis expressed disappointment that the Arabs insisted on limiting their role to their own territory. I also reported on the situation in Egypt, where the latest U.K. proposal on its treaty rights had been turned down. The Egyptians demanded British withdrawal in eighteen months. If the British did not accede, the Egyptians said they would attempt to force them out by withdrawing labor and cutting off water supplies. An impasse with Egypt would, I predicted, negate the value to the British of keeping troops in Egypt. Although the British do not consider it necessary to keep a striking force in Egypt, they attach great importance to maintaining their headquarters there.

I described to the Chiefs the rising tide of nationalism in the Middle East, which was increasingly being pitted against the British. This made it difficult for us to support British policy there. I was more convinced than before I left of the need for furnishing U.S. arms in small quantities to selected Arab countries and to Israel. In doing so, we should coordinate our efforts with the British. I pointed out, however, the necessity for the Chiefs to reach an understanding with their British opposite numbers on our relative responsibilities in the Middle East in peacetime, apart from Greece, Turkey, and Saudi Arabia, where we should maintain primacy. General Collins questioned whether the Middle East countries were really worked up over defense against Communism, or just about the problem of Israel. I assured him they were concerned and determined to resist Communism. Admiral Sherman was still worried about the dissipation of our limited military equipment. General Bradley commented that we could not equip everyone. The Chiefs all agreed that they must get an overall view of the Middle East situation, which Sherman thought would lead them to conclude that it was a very important area.

Although we had won approval of Greek-Turkish entry into NATO, military aid to the Middle East countries apart from Greece and Turkey had to await the passage in October of the Mutual Security Act of 1951, the first of its kind. The Middle East and Africa received $396 million in military aid and $160 million in economic aid. For the first time we had tools to work with in building Middle East security.

Morrison's conduct of foreign policy during the period March to October, 1951, that he served as Foreign Secretary, has recently been evaluated by Kenneth Harris in his excellent biography of Prime

Minister Clement Attlee.[20] Harris says that Morrison's "widely criticized conduct of foreign affairs reflected badly on Attlee." After the closure of the Abadan refinery on July 13, Attlee sent The Lord Privy Seal, Richard Stokes, to Iran, who on his return urged Attlee to negotiate with Mossadeq and deal generously. Morrison, on the other hand, still supported forceful action. Attlee is reported to have told Stokes "I am handling Persia. I have made it quite clear that troops will go in only to save lives." Under strong criticism from the conservatives on the Labour government's handling of both Iran and Egypt, Attlee dissolved Parliament on September 5 and called for new elections.

In perusing the British archives for 1951 which were released early in 1982, I was most interested to find an exchange of letters some three months after my London visit between the two British officials most intimately concerned with my Middle East activities. Both are close friends to this day, and men I greatly admire. It seems like taking advantage from reading their mail; however, the content of the exchange provides such a valuable insight into the evolution of British policy that I believe them worth quoting in their entirety. They are to me very gratifying. Franks's description of Britain's alternatives, as being reliant on her treaties with Egypt, Iraq, and Jordan, or attempting to create a partnership with these countries, was very astute. In a sense this would have meant that the British would have to get out of their treaty countries and come in again. The Egyptians denounced their treaty three months after Franks's letter. Iraq and Jordan renounced theirs seven years later.

Sir Oliver Franks, later Lord Franks, is one of the great statesmen of our times. A distinguished Oxford philosopher, he later became head of two Oxford colleges; chairman of the committee of European recipients that launched the Marshall Plan; following his retirement as Ambassador to the U.S., chairman of Lloyd's Bank; chairman of many commissions of inquiry, including that which investigated the Argentine invasion of the Falklands; and originator of the term "North-South relations" as an alternative to relations between the developed and developing nations. His analysis of our dinner conversation of July 1951 is eminently fair and objective. It reveals the type of thinking that results in re-evaluations of policy. Sir James Bowker, Superintending Under Secretary of State for Foreign Affairs, my opposite number in the Foreign Office at that time, had an outstanding career in the British service, his previous assignment having been Ambassador to Burma. He was a thorough gentleman, soft-spoken, fair, and friendly to Americans. He and his vivacious wife Elsa still entertain Cecilia and myself at dinner during our annual visits to London.[21]

British Embassy
Washington, D.C.
19th July, 1951

Dear Bowker,

I had George McGhee to dinner by himself the other night. I asked him deliberately when there was no immediate business to transact so that we could have a general talk. George, as usual, talked a good deal and left me with several pretty clear impressions which I think may be of sufficient interest to send on to you.

First of all, I have no doubt of George's own basic friendliness to Britain and support of our position in the Middle East. His support for our position springs in part from sentiment but more substantially from his belief that the United States in the foreseeable future can not and will not be ready to take over any position such as that we enjoy with the Middle East, even if on other grounds it were desirable that an attempt should be made. He is still firmly within the general lines established in the earlier conversations between Michael Wright and himself.

At the same time, George is clearly deeply impressed with the power and violence of the Nationalist movements which have grown up in the major Middle Eastern countries. He sees them as examples of a much wider movement in men's minds which affects virtually the whole of Asia apart from the Soviet-controlled countries. He believes this narrow, heady nationalism is something which has come to stay and which is very seriously to be reckoned with in any broad approach to policy in dealing with the Middle East. In this George is reflecting much more than his own personal view. I should judge that he speaks for the general opinion of the State Department.

At present George has no very clear ideas about how to deal with the countries of the Middle East, save in one respect. He believes that somehow or other we have got to get our relations with these countries on a basis of equality and do it in such a way that it is recognized by these countries that they are being treated as equals and partners. George would relate this view not merely to the rise of nationalism in the Middle East but also to the position we have all taken up in the United Nations which makes some more old-fashioned ways of dealing with these countries very difficult or impossible. Apart for [sic] this it is much more of a business to make the use of force effective. We have both been sending arms to these countries and an army with some modern guns and tanks is a much harder proposition to deal with. In all this I think George speaks for a wider body of opinion in the State Department than his own.

I think he is deeply worried about our own policies and methods of approach in the Middle East. He sees that we are much more deeply involved in the area than the Americans. He sees that what happens there matters far more to us than to them. He sees that we are in the lead and he wants to preserve that relation between the Americans and ourselves. But he thinks if we are to preserve our interests and our position we have got somehow to be able to put a convincing new look upon our relationships with Middle Eastern countries. At present they do not feel that we come to them as equals and partners however wise and helpful we may be as guides and advisers. Without a convincing new look he fears an explosion, and in this, of course, he worries particularly about Egypt.

In the particular case of Egypt I think members of the State Department have really begun to ask themselves whether there is not a limit to the extent to which they can go along with us. For the time being they see no alternative. They do not want to have to find an alternative. But they have a depressing fear that the present course of events may lead to a situation in which they have to choose between diverging from us and losing any influence they may have on Egypt when ours is gone.

I expect that these impressions, when written down in words, are rather sharper than the state of mind they are intended to reflect. But I do not doubt their existence nor their power, if left unmodified, in the long run to affect American policy. And they have not been made less lively, though possibly more confused, by recent history in Persia and our various exchanges about the Persian oil situation.

Yours sincerely,
OLIVER FRANKS.

Following is Bowker's reply.[22]

Foreign Office, S.W.1
1st August, 1951.

We have read with great interest your letter of the 19th July, recording your conversation with George McGhee and are particularly glad to note your conviction that he is basically friendly to us. As you know, we have frequently been exercised by his indiscretions and tactlessness, especially in regard to Persia, but we realise that when in addition he has seemed unhelpful this may well be due to his having been badly advised.

2. We should not wish to dissent altogether from his views on the danger of Nationalism in the Middle East countries, nor from his conclusion that the way to deal with it is to promote the conception of "partnership." It may well be that the virus of Nationalism will spread, in which event the problem it presents will be difficult indeed to solve.

3. At present, however, we think that he, like many Americans, tends, perhaps unconsciously, to overlook or discount the real volume of goodwill which we, more than the Americans or any other foreigners, retain in certain parts of the Middle East. Our vicissitudes in Persia and Egypt, and the abuse and criticism to which we are too often subjected in the press of other Arab countries and the conversation of individuals, are no doubt liable to obscure in his mind the fact that we retain extremely close and friendly relations, based on Treaties of Alliance, with Iraq and Jordan, are rapidly improving our relations with Israel, and have at least fairly satisfactory relations elsewhere.

4. The point is important, particularly in connexion with our plans for Middle East defence. The Americans, conscious that they have the arms and money required to buttress a defence organisation, and conscious also that that organisation must depend on the establishment of close cooperation with the countries of the area, sometimes seem to us to overlook that we can bring to it an asset which they lack, namely close cooperation with Iraq and Jordan, and the possibility, if we wish to avail ourselves of it, of similar cooperation with Israel.

5. Nevertheless we are very conscious of the fact that a greater effort on our part is required in the Middle East, and indeed increasingly expected from us by the Middle East countries themselves, and we are therefore pursuing certain proposals, which were discussed at a meeting you recently attended in William Strang's room. We hope these may enable us to make a new approach in regard to economic development, as a complement to what the Americans are proposing. We shall hope to be able to send you something about this before long.

R. J. Bowker.

31

Talks with Mossadeq

Prime Minister of Iran, Mohammed Mossadeq,
October 8–November 18, 1951.

Even for New York it was an event. Mohammed Mossadeq, the "crying" Prime Minister of Iran, arrived there on October 8 to represent
his country before the UN Security Council on the question of Iranian nationalization of the Anglo-Iranian oil concession. Mossadeq represented the National Front, a reformist party allied with traditional-
ist and religious elements with strong nationalist, even xenophobic
tendencies. The oil nationalization issue had been taken to the Security Council by the British government following failure to get action
from the International Court.

Mossadeq had with him a son; a daughter; Allahyar Saleh, President of the Iranian Joint Oil Commission; three other members of the
commission; Karen Sanjabi, Minister of Education; Javad Busheri,
Minister of Roads; three editors; two translators; and a photographer.
The Prime Minister, whose health was poor, was taken to New York
Hospital, where he was to remain for several days before moving to a
hotel. I had flown up from Washington during the afternoon and
called on Mossadeq in his hospital room at 8:36 P.M. With me were
Ambassador Ernest Gross, U.S. representative to the UN, and Lieutenant Colonel Vernon Walters, veteran translator. Mossadeq, who
attended school in France and had earned a degree in political science at the University of Neuchâtel in Switzerland, spoke French
fairly well.

Six months had now passed since my original involvement with
the Iranian nationalization of the AIOC concession. I had not met Dr.
Mossadeq during my visit to Teheran in March. In the meantime our
government had carried on continuous discussions with the British
and Iranians in efforts to bring about an agreement. These had in-

volved Secretary of State Dean Acheson and British Foreign Secretary Herbert Morrison, U.S. Ambassador to London Walter Gifford and British Ambassador to Washington Sir Oliver Franks. A U.S. mission headed by one of our government's most experienced negotiators, Ambassador Averell Harriman, later joined by Richard Stokes, who had been appointed by the Attlee government to head a British mission to Iran, had gone to Iran in July. These groups spent two months in Teheran in a valiant effort to educate Mossadeq sufficiently about the international oil business to make an agreement possible. Mossadeq was, however, unrelenting.

The International Court refused jurisdiction over the Iranian case on July 22, freeing the Security Council to consider the problem. Mossadeq's decision to represent Iran personally was a surprise and was influenced, we thought, by a mix-up in the communications section of our Embassy in Teheran. Although little publicized at the time, it is an amusing story and shows how small matters can have larger significance. It also created a rather tense experience for those of us in the Department concerned with Iran. The Department had, in the course of our efforts to bring about a settlement, sent a rather bland telegram from President Truman to the British Prime Minister urging flexibility in his negotiations with Mossadeq. The following morning the British Ambassador called to say that he would like to come in and discuss a report he had received from the British Embassy in Teheran, which indicated that we had presented a note to Prime Minister Mossadeq from President Truman which seemed somewhat similar to the one given to Attlee in London. As we sat trying to figure out what had happened Bill Rountree burst in bearing a telegram from Teheran fresh from the code room. "It starts out," said Bill with a straight face, " 'I regret to inform the Department that a regrettable mistake has been made today in this embassy.'"

There was suppressed amusement in our group as we tried to piece together the sequence of these events. The action telegram which had been sent to London merely addressed to the Prime Minister had correctly been delivered to Attlee. The copy of the telegram sent to Iran to inform the Embassy and so labeled appeared such a reasonable message for Mossadeq that he was erroneously taken to be the Prime Minister for whom it was intended, and it was given to him. We had on our hands the unusual situation of having delivered to Mossadeq a message from Truman intended only for Attlee. The British were concerned that the Iranians would discover that the message had been intended for Attlee and not Mossadeq, and be encouraged by the knowledge that we were pressing the British to make concessions. We could not bring ourselves to admit the error publicly, which we were sure would make us look ridiculous.

After several days of frantic exchanges between London, Teheran, and Washington, with our Embassy in Teheran urging that we bluff it through, we came up with a solution. It was, perhaps, a classic example of the "waffling" often attributed to the State Department. We would send a real predated message to Mossadeq, similar to that sent to Attlee, which would satisfy the British by creating a balance with what we had told Attlee. We would then leak the story that these almost identical messages, both to Prime Ministers, had mistakenly been switched. There were already sufficient rumors afloat that a mistake had been made in delivering a message to demand some explanation. We figured that having to admit an erroneous switch was easier to take than sending one Prime Minister's message to another. It worked pretty well. There was a slight snicker in *Time* magazine and the affair blew over. But we had the uneasy feeling that the personal message sent by Truman to Mossadeq had had the effect of elevating him, in his own mind, to a new world level— which meant he must personally represent Iran before the Security Council in New York.

Much has been written about Mossadeq, who was a most interesting character. Tall, gaunt, always half smiling, he had developed a reputation for emotional outbursts of crying in public, and for his preference for doing business in bed. He never cried in my presence, perhaps because our meetings were not in the public eye and not worth the effort. Almost all of my talks with Mossadeq took place with only Vernon Walters present, the two of us sitting on opposite sides of the foot of Mossadeq's bed. These conversations involved countless jokes and sallies on his part, often on ours, which would be followed by Mossadeq's convulsive laughter. One could not help but like him. He was, I considered, an intelligent man and essentially a sincere Iranian patriot, whose reasoning was influenced by his age (he was in 1951 about seventy) and warped by his extreme suspicion of everything British. There was no way I, an acknowledged Anglophile, could influence his attitude toward the British. He interpreted almost everything bad in terms of British machinations.

It is true, I believe, that his attitude probably doomed from the start our efforts to facilitate an agreement with the British. Despite great efforts I was unable to get him to understand the facts of life about the international oil business. In the end he would always smile and say, "I don't care about that," when I would talk with him about oil prices, discounts, or technicians. "You don't understand," he would say. "It is a political problem." I do not believe that Mossadeq "formed an alliance of his own with the Soviet Union" as my friend Kermit Roosevelt charges in his recent book, *Countercoup*.[1] The U.S.S.R. obviously tried to take advantage, through the Communist Tudeh party in Iran, of the disorder created by Mossadeq, and the National Front party was probably glad to accept the support of the Tudeh party when they found it useful. Mossadeq, however, was fully aware of the Soviet threat to Iran. He was the one member of the Majlis who had had the courage to force cancellation of the Soviet oil concession in the north of Iran in 1947. Mossadeq was in my view first and foremost a loyal Iranian. The Tudeh party, in 1951, consisted of only some 25,000 members and did not have enough strength to take advantage of its many opportunities. Later Mossadeq, unable to sell Iranian oil because of AIOC legal threats, and unable to obtain aid from us, undoubtedly felt beseiged by the British and was willing to accept help from wherever he could get it.

During our long talks together, aggregating perhaps some eighty hours in more than twenty meetings, I naturally got to know Mossadeq well. Vernon Walters describes our conversations in his excellent book, *Silent Missions*.[2] Walters was much more than an interpreter. Having accompanied Harriman to Teheran, he knew Mossadeq well and was a catalyst in any meeting he participated in. He was extremely helpful to me. On one occasion, after a meeting with Mossadeq, I told Walters that I was afraid that at one point I had gone a little too far. Without batting an eye Vernon replied, "I thought so too. I didn't translate it that way." Walters had developed the disarming gambit, which he has given me permission to reveal, of making a conspicuous show of tearing the notes he had presumably taken as an aid to his translation, and discarding them. Later he would piece them back together, which is why the *Foreign Relations of the United States* will have such an accurate record of our discussions.

Mossadeq spent the latter half of his visit to America in Washington, in a suite at the Shoreham Hotel. On one occasion he jokingly told me that he came to Washington so I wouldn't have to fly up to New York every day to see him. Upon his return to Iran he made several complimentary remarks about me in the Majlis, which did not help me with the British. While in Washington he came, along with Vernon Walters and Paul Nitze, to spend a day at our farm near

Middleburg. He and my farmer, a dignified, elderly man whom everyone respectfully called Mr. Lloyd, got along well. With Walters interpreting, they exchanged their experiences on crops and animals. Mossadeq's farm was reputedly a large one, which included six villages. Cecilia and I gave a small reception at our home for Mossadeq and his aides on October 24. Because of Mossadeq's health, we invited only a few key U.S. officials. There was, however, little real exchange with the Iranians. They appeared insecure and afraid to speak frankly. Mossadeq seemed to enjoy himself and stayed late. He greeted heartily our young son, Michael, who had slipped downstairs in pajamas to join the party.

Mossadeq had come to the U.S. uninvited and with little warning, but I wanted to take advantage of the opportunity to see whether some progress could be made in bridging the gap between Iran and the British over the nationalization issue. The British had concluded that there was no hope and were reconciled to waiting until a successor to Mossadeq would emerge who would be more amenable to negotiate with. Many Americans shared this view, which probably turned out to be right. Nevertheless, I thought we must try. There was a problem, in that we could expect no final British reaction to whatever compromise proposals we might turn up with, until after the British election on October 25. Our best hope was to keep Mossadeq in the U.S. until then so we could discuss with him any counterproposals made by the incoming government. To do this we had to provide a means of killing time. Mossadeq understood this and agreed to cooperate. This explains to some extent the large number of meetings held and the invitation by President Truman for Mossadeq to have a thorough medical examination at Walter Reed Hospital, where our discussions continued. Actually the doctors at Walter Reed could find nothing in particular wrong with Mossadeq apart from the natural debilities of his age, so the Prime Minister moved back to the Shoreham Hotel. He apparently just preferred operating from a bed.

The Harriman-Stokes talks had not been successful because of their inability to get agreement on practical arrangements for continuing the Anglo-Iranian oil operations in Iran. I tried to help Mossadeq understand the practical situation underlying the various issues on which agreement must be reached: compensation for the properties nationalized, price of oil, discounts in price, allocation of markets, role of the AIOC as intermediary in sales to third parties, overall control of the oil operation in Iran, and technical control of its various aspects. I tried to make it clear to Mossadeq that, although we wanted to help work out an agreement, it must be a fair one to both sides. Otherwise a dangerous precedent would be set which would endanger all oil concessions of U.S. and other oil companies around the world. The terms of the agreement as to price, operational control, and right to purchase oil could not be permitted to endanger the international oil industry. I told him that we were not prepared to pay, as a price to save Iran, the disruption of the delicate system that produced the world's vitally-needed oil supplies.

On October 5, a few days before Mossadeq's arrival in New York, I had, in a speech to an oil group in Oklahoma City, presented five points which would guide our government in assisting in the solution of Middle East oil disputes, by "orderly negotiation and arbitration through established machinery." These points were: the development of good relationships between the oil companies and Middle Eastern governments, with flexibility to adapt to changing circumstances so as to ensure stability for the oil operations; a fifty-fifty sharing of profits between companies and governments; the same terms for each Middle East country to prevent jealousy; the scrupulous observance of contracts, which must be fair and clearly stated and subject to orderly negotiation and arbitration of disputes; and, finally, the largest possible contribution by oil revenues to the welfare of the peoples and the states of the Middle East.

Our first meeting with Mossadeq in New York on October 8 had been arranged by Iranian Ambassador to the U.S. Nasrollah Entezam. He had explained to us that Mossadeq was eager to talk and wished a delay in the Security Council action. He introduced Gross, Walters, and me to the Prime Minister at the hospital and left. Either he had been told to, or he was wise enough to know that the Prime Minister would not speak freely in his presence. At any rate, that was to be the pattern throughout all of the ensuing discussions. Mossadeq apparently trusted no member of his group fully. I sensed that there lay in the back of his mind a strong fear that something he said might become public and could lead to his sharing the fate of his predecessor—assassination.

Mossadeq was, however, on this occasion in a good mood. He expressed appreciation for the invitation from President Truman and Secretary Acheson to come to Washington. When should he come? He preferred to delay the Security Council consideration of the Iranian nationalization question, since what he would be forced to say would end any hope of subsequent negotiations. He would like for the Security Council to call on the two parties to negotiate in an informal action. If it claimed jurisdiction he would be forced to make his diatribe against the British. Gross sought to reassure him with regard to the impending meeting. Nothing would happen that would necessitate a break.

Turning to the oil question, Mossadeq said he was prepared to accept an executive with adequate authority to run the Iranian oil operation, the issue which had caused a breakdown in his talks with Harriman and Stokes. He was also willing to accept an arrangement with an outside source to assure Iranian access to the necessary oil technology. He wanted to start talking about the nationalization question. He said he was agreeable to meeting with me the following morning. As I emerged from the hospital into the dark canyons of New York streets, I felt that the weight of the world had been transferred to my shoulders.

The following morning, with Walters translating, Mossadeq and I began the first of our many talks about Iranian oil. Mossadeq started by offering to provide compensation to AIOC for their properties on the basis of the aggregate market value of the company's shares before nationalization (later he indicated $27 million as his understanding of what this would be). Compensation could, alternatively, be either on the basis of the most favorable nationalization law in existence in any other country, or by direct amicable negotiation. When I asked him if he would accept the findings of a suitable international commission, he wouldn't say. He would prefer his first suggestion.

Mossadeq then volunteered that former purchasers of Iranian oil would be assured the same amounts for purchase for a fixed number of years. If they chose, AIOC could represent third parties as well as AIOC subsidiaries. The price could be that posted in the U.S. Gulf of Mexico, less freight, insurance, and other expenses. When I pointed out that much of Persian Gulf oil had to be sold at discount, Mossadeq offered 10 percent. I told him that discounts for long-term contracts went as high as 50 percent. There was an oversupply of oil in the world, which created a buyer's market. Mossadeq thought this discount too high. He volunteered that he would accept former AIOC employees as technicians in individual capacities, and that they could also serve as chiefs of various staff sections. The top technical director of the Iranian oil operation, however, who would have executive authority, must be of some other nationality than British— American or Dutch, whatever, but not British. He was adamant. The board of the nationalized company could consist of three Iranian nationals and four neutrals. We broke here for lunch.

After lunch Mossadeq began by insisting that the question of compensation must be resolved first. He had promised his parliament that he would let President Truman decide what a fair price should be. There was little time. He could not assure that the present situation in Iran would last longer than a month. Mossadeq indicated a willingness to give a discount to all purchasers. In response to my question he said he would consider giving a larger discount in lieu of compensation, if the duration of the discount could be settled. He agreed to combine the position of executive director with the channel by which the Iranian Company obtained access to technology (i.e., the director could be furnished by an oil company that had suitable technology).

Mossadeq would not, however, give an answer to my proposal that an existing international oil company or a consortium of companies, as in Iraq, operate the Iranian oil industry on a fee basis. I assured him that American companies were not seeking to take AIOC's place, since this would encourage "concession jumping" on their own properties. Our government would, in any event, ask them not to, in view of the disastrous effect this would have on U.S.-British relations. We would naturally have been accused of using our role as mediator for our own advantage. Mossadeq refused to sell for cash oil stored in Iran, which he estimated as constituting only an eight-month supply for Iranian needs. He emphasized that all of his suggestions were exploratory, not commitments. We should use our good offices, he said, to try to bridge the gap between Iran and Britain. He expressed confidence in my efforts. I went over the agreements that had been made by the international companies with other countries, including Venezuela and Saudi Arabia. Iran could not expect a better deal. We continued our meetings.

The climax of our discussions came late one evening in the Prime Minister's hotel room, with Walters the only other person present. I had pointed out the complications created by Iranian nationalization of the AIOC's Abadan refinery, the largest in the world. A refinery, I pointed out, was too complex to be operated by a government agency with hired technicians. The refineries of the world were run by companies with the full range of technical competence required. "But," said Mossadeq, "the refinery hasn't been nationalized." Dumbfounded, I stammered, "What do you mean? The world thinks the Abadan refinery was included in the nationalization package." "You can't quote me," said Mossadeq, "but you can take my word that it wasn't."

I told Mossadeq that if this was the case there was a real possibility for a breakthrough. This might make an agreement possible. I would protect his position but would he object to both of us initialing identical statements, one in French by him and another in English by me, that the refinery had not been nationalized? Walters prepared the two papers in longhand and Mossadeq and I both initialed. I could scarcely contain my excitement. Mossadeq had given back, via *me*, the largest refinery in the world. I could see a real chance for agreement. Later I treated Walters to the most elaborate available meal at the Chambord, one of the best restaurants in New York. He later told me he was worried at the cost. I assured him that nothing was further from my mind. My elation was complete. Mossadeq's slip was in my pocket.

The next day Mossadeq leaked to the press that Iran would not fail to nationalize the refinery. I took this to be his insurance against being shot by an Iranian nationalist. I was confident that he would try to live up to his commitment to me. I never referred to it publicly, only to the British confidentially and orally. The Department apparently took the security of the slip Mossadeq had initialed so seriously that it has never, to my knowledge, been found again. It is not referred to in the Department publications.

Mossadeq had his innings in the Security Council on October 15, when the British resolution against the Iranian oil nationalization was taken up. We had been consulted on the new draft which superseded the original resolution submitted September 29. The resolution asked the Security Council to intervene in the matter, citing the Iranian expulsion order of September 19 as being in violation of the July 5 order of the International Court of Justice. It called on both parties to take certain "provisional measures" to preserve "the rights which may subsequently be adjudged by the Court to belong either to the [United Kingdom] or [Iran]." In Mossadeq's address, he reviewed Iran's recent experience with the AIOC, denied the Council's competence to consider the issue, and offered to negotiate for the sale of oil and for compensation.

The discussion continued for five days. India and Yugoslavia presented an amendment, Revision 2, which we agreed with and which removed reference to the International Court of Justice. It was evident, however, that there were insufficient votes to pass the resolution, and the French moved that in this case the International Court could rule on its own competency in the case. On July 22, the court held that it had no jurisdiction to consider the application of the U.K.

of May 26, 1951, and that its order giving interim measures of protection consequently ceased to be operative. In New York, Mossadeq had told me, when I asked him when he wanted to come to Washington, "When I get out of jail (meaning the Security Council). Will you help me get out of jail?" At least he didn't actually have to go to jail then, as he did later.

In the meantime our daily talks continued. By October 15 Mossadeq was willing to state his offer as follows: Iran would allow the National Iranian Oil Company to sell to consumers on the basis of what they had taken over the preceding three years, through any intermediary (including AIOC) requested in writing. The Board of the National Iranian Oil Company (NIOC) would consist of three Iranians and four neutrals, but no British. To obtain technicians and access to technology the NIOC would enter into a contract with an outside company—a Dutch company (Shell, which is actually Anglo-Dutch) would be acceptable—on a fee basis, with technicians under contract to NIOC on an individual basis. He said that Iran would borrow the required capital from the World Bank. Oil procurement rights would continue for ten years. The price that Iran would receive for oil would be negotiated subject to a renegotiation each year to reflect changes in world prices. The NIOC would choose the technical director, the only requirement being that he be a neutral, not British. Payment for oil would preferably be in sterling; however, Swiss or Dutch currency would be satisfactory.

Every move Mossadeq made, including his many meetings with me, was highly publicized in the press. News reports came from New York, London, and Teheran. On October 22, en route to Washington, he stopped in Philadelphia and addressed two hundred people in Independence Square, linking Iran's nationalization of its oil to the idealism that inspired the U.S. to wrest freedom and liberty from Britain in 1776. He was met at Union Station in Washington by Secretary Acheson with a small official group. He was given an ovation by 150 Iranians.

The *New York Times* story of October 22 from Teheran reported Iranian leaders as believing the prestige of the U.S. in Iran was dependent on some action favorable to Iran. If Mossadeq obtained nothing for Iran he would be execrated by the nationalists as well as the Tudeh party. If abandoned by the U.S., Iran would have no choice but to turn to the Soviets. The Iranian Supreme Economic Council had that day approved a trade and barter agreement with Russia. There were expressions of disappointment that the U.S. had failed to live up to expectations for assistance given the Shah during his visit to Washington in 1949, and that now was the time to make good on past promises.

Mossadeq lunched with President Truman and Secretary Acheson at Blair House on October 23. Also present were the Iranian Ambassador, Secretary of Defense Robert Lovett, and several of us from the Department. Walters was also present as interpreter. In his remarks to Mossadeq, the President said that he didn't want to discuss the details of Iran's problems at lunch. He did, however, want to assure Mossadeq that, as a friend of both Iran and Britain, we had no public or private interest in Iranian oil and only wanted to help the two parties reach a fair settlement. Acheson observed that the fundamental point appeared to be that the British oil company's operations created the possibility of interference in internal Iranian affairs. He assured Mossadeq that he would be protected in anything he might say.

Mossadeq observed that the U.S., although it aided many nations, had given little aid to Iran. The President replied that American assistance to Iran up to this point would have considerable long-term significance. The U.S. was limited in the total aid it could give to others. We were aiding many countries. Mossadeq said that he must seek assistance apart from oil, otherwise the present situation in Iran could endanger the general security and threaten world peace.

President Truman likened the Soviets to a "sitting vulture on a fence waiting to pounce on the oil. It would then be in a position to wage a world war." Mossadeq said that Iran's budget deficit was 400 million tomans. Poverty and unrest were widespread. Iran's army of 100,000 could be increased only at the expense of agriculture. Truman, as a rejoinder, compared Iran's situation to America's 1933 depression. We then had 12 to 13 million people unemployed. The farmers were desperate and mortgages were being foreclosed, yet as a result of the New Deal and Fair Deal a floor was set for wages, prices were fixed, rents were controlled, and conditions eventually improved. If Iran could settle its differences with the British and take the necessary measures to utilize their enormous possibilities, we would be happy and willing to help. Acheson emphasized that the settlement with the British must be on a basis which would not destroy the whole fabric of oil agreements around the world, to which Mossadeq agreed.

Secretary Acheson continued his discussions with Mossadeq on the following day at Walter Reed Hospital, to which he had returned, even though the hospital's examination had found nothing wrong with him not explainable by his age. Paul Nitze, the Director of the Policy Planning Staff who had had valuable business experience, and I, were present as well as Vernon Walters. Acheson opened by expressing the hope that we could formulate a possible solution to the oil problem, which Acheson could discuss with the British in his forthcoming meetings in Paris. He went over Mossadeq's proposals submitted to me on October 15. Mossadeq interjected that there was only one change. He had decided that he could not accept British technicians. He said that this would look like a defeat. He would, however, make a unilateral statement, since he considered it an Iranian matter, that he would also not accept Russians as technicians. He reviewed his recent political activities, which had brought him into the leadership of the National Front government. He denounced the 1933 Anglo-Iranian Agreement as illegal because it resulted from duress. He felt that the situation in Iran was very grave.

Secretary Acheson then went over some of the other terms of the Iranian proposal. If, as Mossadeq had agreed with me, the refinery could be taken over by a non-British company which would compensate the AIOC and run it, the remaining claims and counterclaims on both sides might cancel out. Mossadeq volunteered that, if the AIOC would release Iran from further claims, he would not demand payment for back revenues due. At Acheson's urging, Mossadeq agreed to increase the length of the contract with AIOC's purchasing organization to fifteen years. No progress was made, however, on the question of price. Despite Acheson's efforts to convince him that there were two markets, wholesale and retail, and that to be competitive Iranian oil must sell at around $1.10 a barrel, Mossadeq insisted that he must get the Persian Gulf posted retail price of $1.75 a barrel. His people would never accept such a difference.

Acheson illustrated his point by citing the difference between the price of beef on the hoof in Maryland, where his farm was located, of 25 cents per pound, with the retail butchers' price of 90 cents. The Secretary urged Mossadeq to take credit for having raised Iran's oil income from $25 to $75 million a year, for eliminating British interference, and settling claims and counterclaims, and use the increased income to make social reforms. Mossadeq said he was willing to proceed to a solution of the other issues, and was willing for the Abadan refinery under certain conditions to use imported oil from Kuwait, but he remained obdurate on price. There was no way to shake him. His meeting with Acheson ended on this note.

In *Present at the Creation,* Acheson gives the following impressions of Mossadeq:[3]

> From the first moment I saw him a few months later Mossadeq became for me the character Lob in James Barrie's play *Dear Brutus.* He was small and frail with not a shred of hair on his billiard-ball head; a thin face protruded into a long beak of a nose flanked by two bright, shoe-button eyes. His whole manner and appearance was bird-like, marked by quick, nervous movements as he seemed to jump about on a perch. His pixie quality showed in instantaneous transformations. Waiting at Union Station in Washington, I watched a bent old man hobble down the platform supporting himself with a stick and an arm through his son's. Spotting me at the gate, he dropped the stick, broke away from his party, and came skipping along ahead of the others to greet us.

> He had, I discovered later, a delightfully childlike way of sitting in a chair with his legs tucked under him, making him more of a Lob character than ever, with many and changing moods. I remember him sitting with the President and me after lunch in Blair House, his legs under him, when he dropped a mood of gay animation and, suddenly looking old and pathetic, leaned toward the President.

> "Mr. President," he said, "I am speaking for a very poor country— a country all desert—just sand, a few camels, a few sheep . . ."

> "Yes," I interrupted, "and with your oil, rather like Texas!" He burst into a delighted laugh and the whole act broke up, finished. It was a gambit that had not worked.

Acheson's final summation was:

> Mossadeq's self-defeating quality was that he never paused to see that the passions he excited to support him restricted his freedom of choice and left only extreme solutions possible. We were, perhaps, slow in realizing that he was essentially a rich, reactionary, feudal-minded Persian inspired by a fanatical hatred of the British and a desire to expel them and all their works from the country regardless of the cost. He was a great actor and a great gambler. Speaking in the Majlis, he would rant, weep real tears; and fall in a faint at his climactic moment. He told us once that nationalization would cost Iran nothing, since any damages which Anglo-Iranian could prove would be exceeded by Iranian counterclaims. This unique character truly sowed the wind and reaped the whirlwind.

Although the terms which Mossadeq had agreed to in our meetings left much to be desired, they did, I felt, represent a distinct advance, particularly in light of Mossadeq's private assurances to me on the refinery. I was exhilarated. My hopes were high. The distinguished journalist Elmer Davis, commenting on my many visits with Mossadeq each of which was duly noted by the press, wrote that if I succeeded in reaching agreement I should get a Nobel Peace Prize. I felt that the fate of the world was in my hands. In order to educate Mossadeq further, Paul Nitze and I asked if we could meet with him and his advisers, who, up to that point, had been off limits to us—although not to the press. We met in Mossadeq's parlor in the Shoreham. Paul and I had prepared elaborate charts showing world supply, demand, price, markets, and other relevant factors. Each of us took a turn at explaining the situation Iran faced. When we finished we turned to the members of the Joint Iranian Oil Commission present for questions or comments. Quick as a flash Mossadeq beat them to the draw. He said, "You see? They agree with me." And the meeting was over before it began.

Despite our frustrations, however, we thought we had managed to make some headway. The final proposal for settlement which we had formulated as a result of all of our discussions with Mossadeq can be summarized briefly. With respect to management, the NIOC would be responsible for exploration, production, and transportation of crude oil. They would do this on an efficient basis. The Abadan refinery would be sold to a non-British firm which could, if it chose, use its own technicians, or others as agreed to by Iran. Iranians would be trained for employment in the refinery at all levels. The refinery would operate on the basis of cost plus a fixed profit or fee, to be agreed on by Iran with the AIOC purchasing organization. The Kermanshah refinery (a smaller one) would be owned and operated by the NIOC for the internal Iranian market.

As for marketing, the AIOC would establish a purchasing organization to buy, ship, and market Iranian oil for those requesting this in writing. The contract would last fifteen years for a minimum of 30 million tons a year, both for the Abadan refinery and for export, after meeting Iranian requirements. Iranians would be entitled to up to one million tons of oil a year at cost plus a reasonable profit. NIOC could market oil in excess of that required by the AIOC purchasing organization for old customers, at prices which would not prejudice the organization's long-term contracts.

The price of oil would be agreed to between the Iranian and British governments, assisted by the U.S. government, with an understanding regarding periodic adjustments with changing world prices. Payment would be in sterling, with the NIOC paying all costs of production and transportation. The NIOC would be responsible for decisions on amounts to be invested in maintaining production. Refined products could be turned over to the purchasing organization. All claims and counterclaims would be canceled. It was to be understood, even if not stated, that "non-British firm" meant Dutch, that refining costs would include housing for Iranian workers, and that the price paid by the purchasing organization for oil would not exceed $1.10 per barrel. This last concession by Mossadeq on price we considered a major breakthrough. It would provide AIOC with enough margin for a substantial trading profit, which could balance any deficiency in compensation. It should have produced a final result close to fifty/fifty profit-sharing.

We were, undoubtedly, overly optimistic about the prospects for gaining approval of our proposal by the new Churchill government. Neither Churchill nor his Foreign Secretary, Anthony Eden, was familiar with the details of the main issues. Since they had been critical of the Labour government's handling of Mossadeq, it was difficult for them politically to make concessions to him. They considered that it would, in any event, never be possible to make a suitable deal with Mossadeq and preferred to await his fall in the hope that his successor would be more tractable. If they negotiated with him unsuccessfully, they concluded, that they would only strengthen him.

Anthony Eden, when he came to office in October 1951, had had considerable experience with Iran going back to his period as Under-Secretary of the Foreign Office in 1933 when the Iranians had renounced the AIOC concession. In his memoirs Eden describes his trip to Iran in 1948 as a member of the opposition, following which he warned Chancellor of the Exchequer Sir Stafford Cripps of possible trouble because of decreased payments to Iran, resulting from reduced AIOC dividends forced on the company by the British government.[4]

When Eden came back in power, he says, he was determined to seek common ground with respect to Iran on which the two governments could stand, based on "fixed principles." Principles which he planned to propose to Acheson in their first meeting in Paris on November 4 included: fair compensation to be agreed upon between the parties or by arbitration; security for the payment of compensation, which Eden understood could only be paid in oil; denial to Iran of any more favorable terms than those accorded concessionary governments who respected their contracts; and refusal to negotiate on the basis of discrimination against U.K. nationals.

There were five discussions on Iran, in which Acheson urged Eden to accept the compromise agreement we had worked out with Mossadeq as a basis for negotiations, in order to prevent a further deterioration of the situation in Iran. Eden says that he "refused to accept the argument that the only alternative to Mossadeq was communist rule." He could not accept exclusion of British technicians from Iran and handing over a valuable asset on the basis of "confiscation without compensation." "In my view no agreement would be better than a bad one." Acheson declined to accept Eden's proposal for participation of American companies in Iran, Eden stood by his "principles," and both parties reluctantly agreed that Mossadeq should not be encouraged to stay longer in Washington. The U.S. and U.K., almost two years after I had my first encounter with AIOC, still had divergent views over the future of Iranian oil. Eden sent me a personal message thanking me for my efforts.

A group of us—Paul Nitze, I, and several others who had been closely involved in the negotiations—were waiting in the Department communications room when Acheson returned to our Paris Embassy from his fateful luncheon with Anthony Eden. Acheson said over the Paris line that Eden wouldn't buy it, that he thanked us for our efforts but that he couldn't accept our proposal and didn't want to negotiate any further. He asked us to tell Mossadeq that it's all off. There was silence as we grasped the fact that we had failed. To me it was almost the end of the world—I attached so much importance to an agreement and honestly thought we had provided the British a basis for one.

I asked for an appointment with Mossadeq, and when I entered his bedroom at the Shoreham he merely said, "You've come to send me home."

"Yes," I said. "I'm sorry to have to tell you that we can't bridge the gap between you and the British. It's a great disappointment to us as it must be to you."

It was a moment I will never forget. He accepted the result quietly, with no recriminations.

On November 13, the Department issued a statement admitting our failure. It said: "While progress has been made, no new basis has emerged on which a practicable solution could be reached." On the following day Mossadeq made a speech before the National Press Club announcing that he was asking the U.S. government for a loan to keep his country from being paralyzed for lack of funds in the ensuing twelve months. A Department spokesman said the U.S. would give the Prime Minister's request for a loan every consideration. Mossadeq left Washington on November 18 for Teheran. He stopped in Cairo during violent anti-British riots and was received in a frenzy of emotion. After several days of talks with Prime Minister Nahas Pasha, the two signed a pact of friendship and stated that "a united Iran and Egypt will together demolish British imperialism."

I never saw Mossadeq again. I had delayed my impending appointment as U.S. Ambassador to Turkey, a most welcome post, in the hopes of helping Iran and Britain reach an oil agreement. It was a great disappointment to have to acknowledge that it wasn't possible, and I left for Ankara a few weeks later. My successor as Assistant Secretary was also destined to leave his post before a solution was reached. The agreement which was to permit Iranian production to be resumed came only in late 1954, largely as a result of the efforts of Under Secretary of State Herbert Hoover, Jr., himself an oil man.

Only a miracle had, in the meantime, saved Iran from the disaster that had threatened the country since March 1950. Economic difficulties eroded Mossadeq's popular support, while his authoritarian tactics had alienated the Majlis from his government. In August 1953, the Shah attempted to replace him as Prime Minister, but Mossadeq responded by deposing the Shah and forcing him to leave the country. After several days of chaos in Iran, the army rallied to the Shah and arrested Mossadeq and his key supporters. After a trial, the former Prime Minister was convicted of treason and sentenced to prison, where he spent three years before being allowed to return and live quietly in banishment on his farm until his death, at the ripe old age of ninety.

Mossadeq, of course, failed. He succeeded in nationalizing Iranian oil but did not succeed in making nationalization work for the benefit of his country, which was almost ruined in the process. He could have made, three years earlier, the same deal that later started Iranian oil flowing. But Mossadeq must be accorded some credit, at least, for the effort he made, and for his success, even at a high price to his people, in eliminating from Iran the last vestiges of foreign control.

This is the Iranian story, which is in a sense the story of this book. Despite the tremendous sacrifice and effort that the countries of the Middle World had to make in achieving their final freedom, despite their many mistakes and self-inflicted wounds, they were at least finally their own masters. Future mistakes would be their own.

32

The Middle World Today: The Changing World Scene

Résumé of the Middle World, Conclusions and Lessons, 1951–1983.

Before I attempt to analyze what has happened in the Middle World over the thirty-two years that have ensued since the end of these memoirs, I would like to look at the major changes in the broader world framework. These have, of course, influenced, just as they have been influenced by, events in the Middle World. Although there have been many favorable developments in the world scene over this period, it is safe to say that they have not met the expectations of those who were, to quote Acheson, "present at the creation" of the post-World War II era. The industrialized nations have achieved unexpectedly high levels of gross national product and living standards, although often at the expense of mass unemployment, economic stagnation, and trade conflicts. Many countries have achieved affluence for the first time. Much of the developing world, however, particularly sub-Saharan Africa and South Asia in the Middle World, has failed to share in this progress.

A third world war has been avoided and now seems unlikely. However, despite the efforts of the UN, which was created largely to protect the nations of the world against aggression, wars between states continue. The Argentine aggression against the Falklands and the Israeli invasion of Lebanon are only the most recent examples. On the other hand, NATO, despite the loss of French forces in peacetime, Greek reservations, and constant disagreements over national military budgets, is hopeful of adding Spain as a new member and still retains sufficient forces and unanimity of action to constitute a significant deterrent to a Soviet attack against Western Europe.

An important development during this era has been the relative decline of the U.S., both as an economic and a military power. However, although we are no longer the superpower we were in 1951, we must not forget that we are still, looking at it broadly, the strongest nation in the world. The Soviet Union, it is true, has gained on us over the period 1951–1983. Although not successful in developing its economy, the U.S.S.R. has achieved at least rough parity with us militarily. There has, in addition, been a marked diffusion of power all around the world. Japan, in particular, has emerged as an economic giant because of its mastery of the production and marketing of high-technology products. There is a new concentration of economic power in a number of individual countries. In addition to the OPEC oil-producing states these include Korea; Malaysia; the Far Eastern states and dependencies populated by overseas Chinese: Taiwan, Singapore, and Hong Kong; and several other states with essentially European origins: Mexico, South Africa, Venezuela, and Brazil. A score of nations around the world have, or could attain, a nuclear weapons capability. Unparalleled levels of conventional arms sales are being made to the developing countries, according to official U.S. sources $36.3 billion dollars worth in 1980, including $14.9 billion from the U.S.S.R.

The Western European states continue to occupy a key role in the world's economy and power structure, although they have failed to unite politically and do not exert the world influence they are capable of. The European Community has survived over this period reasonably well, although it is beset by bickerings over agricultural prices and budget support. Among the European states the principal change has been the emergence of Germany as the leading economic power, and with increasing political strength which has been used successfully in forging links with the East. France has recovered economically and, because of its central position in Europe and its special link with Germany, wields considerable power within the Community.

Of particular significance to the Middle World in the last three decades has been the decline of the British position there. Having withdrawn from Africa, Egypt, and the Persian Gulf, Britain retains little influence in the vast Middle World area it once dominated, less than that of France in its former colonies, with which France still maintains close links. Although the U.S. still gives substantial assistance to developing countries, the European Community has a development program for the former colonial possessions of its members, and many other OECD and OPEC members have national development programs, the industrialized nations as a whole have never devised a joint policy toward assistance to the developing countries.

The Soviet Union has, during recent years, greatly enhanced its military strength through increased conventional and nuclear forces, and military-assistance programs to many nations involving equipment, advisers, weapon manning forces and Cuban surrogate troops. The Soviets have, through these means, acquired positions of influence in the Middle World in Angola, Ethiopia, South Yemen, and Syria. As a result of the split in the fifties between the Soviet Union and Communist China, there occurred a breakup of what was once called the Communist bloc. This has helped reduce what we considered in 1949–51 to be the dangerous world-wide threat of revolutionary Communism, which in fact never demonstrated great appeal to Middle World countries. There remains a Soviet and Eastern European Communist influence, and a separate and competing Communist power center in China.

The victory of UN forces in Korea, which were predominantly U.S. forces, gave hopes at the time for a peaceful Asia; however, those were to be short-lived. The long and bitter Vietnam War which followed not only failed to resolve the problem of succession to the French colonies in Southeast Asia in a way favorable to the West, but resulted in disillusionment on the part of the U.S. public in military solutions of such problems. Strong opposition developed to undertaking any more similar involvements. Disappointed also in both the economic and political results of the large-scale military and economic assistance given under the Mutual Security Program, the American people expressed their feelings by forcing drastic reductions in foreign aid. A withdrawal from political intervention in the developing areas occurred under the banner of the Nixon Doctrine. There has also been a withering away of U.S. efforts at building regional defensive arrangements, such as the Central Treaty Organization and the Southeast Asia Treaty Organization.

The years between 1951 and 1983 saw the final demise of the colonial system (except for that which continues internally within the Soviet Union) with which this book has been deeply involved. The end came with few regrets with the withdrawal of the Portuguese from Angola and Mozambique, some five hundred years after Portugal had founded the first European colony of the modern era. The final removal of the discipline once exerted over Middle World peoples by the colonial powers, and the protection once afforded against border warfare, contributed greatly to Middle World instability. Apart from the lingering influence of the former metropoles and ourselves, and the new positions of influence achieved by the U.S.S.R., the Middle World states became their own masters. They reflected this in their almost unanimous decision to join the non-aligned movement.

The period under review also saw the emergence of the Middle East as the most important oil producing area in the world, and the organization of the non-industrialized oil producing countries, mostly Middle World, into the OPEC cartel. OPEC has achieved a twenty-fold increase in the price of oil since 1971. This has had a devastating effect on the economies of the industrialized world, but even more on the hopes for progress in the non-oil producing countries of the developing world, which include most of the Middle World. Hard pressed to finance their development programs because the high cost of oil absorbs most of their meager earnings, these countries have experienced severe limitations to further increases in gross national product, despite greater lending by the World Bank and its subsidiaries and by the regional banks.

The high hopes in the postwar era for the development techniques on the drawing boards of global economic planners have not been realized. With little prospect for cheaper energy and, because of the world recession which started in 1981, reduction in markets for their new manufactures or traditional raw materials, hope for economic progress in the Middle World has waned. A recent phenomenon which may have a beneficial effect has been the mass influx of temporary outside workers: Egyptians, Koreans, Filipinos, Indians, Pakistanis, Algerians, and Turks, into Europe and the oil-producing Middle World countries.

And if the world has changed since 1951, so have I. My two years as Ambassador to Turkey gave me a deeper insight into this new successor state to a great empire, and also into the Middle World as a whole, in which Asia Minor has always played a central role. When I resigned in 1953 I returned to my original field of oil prospecting, while keeping alive my interests and contacts with our government and the Middle World. When John F. Kennedy was elected president in 1960, I was quick to accept Dean Rusk's invitation to rejoin the State Department. As chairman of the Policy Planning Council and later Under Secretary for Political Affairs, I had opportunities to renew my Middle World associations, including six months' management of the U.S. involvement in the Congo crisis of 1962 and 1963. I also had an opportunity to obtain a broader world perspective.

During my subsequent five years as Ambassador to Germany, I obtained a new insight into the key role Germany, and Western Europe, play in world affairs. I was also able to see the Middle World from the viewpoint of a country which, though thwarted as a late-aspiring colonial power, has been highly successful in developing a vast network of trade throughout the Middle World. In the end I had a brief tour of duty as a trouble-shooter as ambassador-at-large.

After retiring finally from government in 1968, I returned once more to business, including a second career as director of several large multinational corporations. Among other advantages, they offered the opportunity to learn more about world trade and investment and world oil. I have also served during my post-government period as a member of the board or chairman of a wide variety of educational, foreign affairs, and cultural institutions, which have been both interesting and broadening. But I have never lost touch with the Middle World. Each year Cecilia and I spend a month at our home, Turkish Delight, in the lovely unspoiled little town of Alanya on the Mediterranean coast of Turkey, equidistant from Istanbul, Jerusalem, and Cairo, all ancient centers of the Middle World.

Looking back now at what has happened to the Middle World over the last thirty-two years, in the light of U.S. hopes and policies over this period, I have tried to appraise the results of our efforts and see what lessons we might learn for the future. During the period 1949–1951, we faced a Middle World about which we knew little and in which we had few involvements. The peoples of the area were undergoing a traumatic change: creating fifty-four nations that emerged from colonialism to independence.

Looking at it broadly, U.S. objectives in 1949 were fairly clear-cut. We wanted to make friends with these new states, allay fears on their part as to our motives, and establish a basis for future political, cultural, and business ties with them. We wanted, as an "honest broker," to help the new states and their former metropoles accomplish the difficult task of colonial withdrawal. We wanted to encourage the metropoles to bear as much of the burden of launching the new states as possible. We did not want to undercut them, but to be ready where necessary to help fill any vacuum that might be created. At the same time, we sought to minimize the drain on our own limited resources.

And we sought, with our diplomacy, to help the new states get a fair start in the world and begin to solve their difficult, inherited problems.

We wanted, in particular, to help the new Middle World states cope with their internal economic problems, making use of the limited tools we had available at the time to offer them. We wanted to convince the new states of the dangers of Soviet Communism and help them develop internal security forces adequate to protect themselves from Communist subversion. We tried to persuade them that neutralism would weaken their defenses against Communism, and to encourage them to accept a generally pro-Western and democratic point of view. Greece, Turkey, and Iran, border states already under Soviet attack, were the only countries we thought could develop forces strong enough to deter Communist aggression against the Middle World.

These were our aims. Were they realistic? Were our efforts to carry them out helpful? Was our overriding concern in 1949–51 over the Communist threat to the Middle World in the aftermath of Korea justified in light of subsequent events? Did it lead us to push those states in the development of their security forces too fast and too far, harming their economies, endangering their leadership and eventually alienating them from us? Would they have been endangered by closer ties with the Soviets? Certainly India, which was never attracted to alignment with us, has gained from the close relationship it developed with the Soviets. At times, certainly during the height of the detente efforts of the 1970s, some might have concluded that we had exaggerated the Soviet threat to the Middle World, that we had misinterpreted longer-range Soviet goals. Recent events in Afghanistan have, I believe, reconfirmed our original interpretation of Soviet intentions, with the result that the Soviets and ourselves appear to be slipping back into the Cold War, with us pursuing a revived policy of containment, as originally defined by George Kennan—right where we started. The greatest challenge of our times is to reverse this trend.

Before the Second World War there were only eleven independent countries in the vast Middle World herein described: Iran, Iraq, Jordan, Afghanistan, Saudi Arabia, Egypt (although British troops remained there until 1956), Muscat (now Oman, then closely linked with Britain), Yemen, Nepal (dependent then on Britain and later on India), Ethiopia and Liberia (dependent on the U.S.). Syria and Lebanon could not at that time have been considered independent of France.

Today there are sixty-six independent countries in the Middle World and no remaining colonies apart from small enclaves. They comprise 1½ billion people, one third of the population of the world. The South Asian countries achieved independence from 1947 to 1949, just before I became Assistant Secretary. The remaining Arab states, except for Comoros and Djibouti, became independent by 1970 pretty much as anticipated in 1951. The colonial territories of Africa south of the Sahara became separate, fully sovereign states between 1957 and 1977, except Zimbabwe, which did not attain independence until 1980. Fifteen African states achieved statehood in the year 1960. Namibia is still not independent.

Although it was expected in 1951 that independence would eventually come to the African colonies, no one had a timetable in mind. The U.S. was not pushing for any particular schedule. In my discussions in London with British colonial officials, particularly with Andrew Cohen, the influential colonial office Assistant Under Secretary of State, I always made this very clear. We had no desire to see these new countries left to take care of themselves without adequate preparation. Nevertheless, the British officials involved always felt under pressure from U.S. public opinion, which they found difficult to disassociate from U.S. policy. I think it safe to say that nobody expected independence to come as fast as it did in the end, particularly the freeing of Zaire by Belgium within a year in 1960. Independence for Angola and Mozambique from Portugal, which came in 1975, seemed very remote indeed in 1951.

Of the sixty-six states of the Middle World, Afghanistan, which was occupied by the Soviet army in December 1979, is the only free country which has lost its freedom to an outside power. Lebanon has for many years been in a state of political anarchy, occupied by the military forces of Syria and the Palestine Liberation Organization before it was invaded by Israel. The Libyan occupation of Chad was a temporary internal African affair. But a few other countries have come under varying degrees of Communist influence or control. Guerrilla activity to achieve independence from Portugal was started in Angola in 1961 and in Mozambique in 1965. Both movements were assisted from the beginning by the Soviets and other Communist states.

The U.S., largely because Portugal was a member of NATO and because we hold our Azores base only at the pleasure of Portugal, did not become involved in Angola until 1974, through our unsuccessful support of the National Front Party. The Soviet-backed Popular Movement in Angola and the Front for the Liberation of Mozambique received massive Soviet aid, and established Marxist governments after the two colonies achieved independence.[1] In Angola, Soviet influence was strengthened by 25,000 Cuban forces plus East German and Soviet advisers, as well as the remaining Portuguese Communists. Most of these are still there. Mozambique negotiated a friendship treaty with the Soviets in 1977. Both Angola and Mozambique, however, trade with and are aided by the West, and Angola appears to be moving toward a more neutral stance between the Soviets and the West.

Among the other newly independent African countries, Guinea turned to the Soviet bloc, with a push from General de Gaulle, when it broke with France in 1958. It has, however, since strengthened its contacts with the West. In Ethiopia, the military regime that had overthrown the monarchy in 1974 switched dramatically from dependence on the U.S. for arms to total reliance on the Soviets, when the Carter administration halted deliveries in 1977.[2] The Soviets lost their Somali clients and signed a cooperation accord with the strategically more significant Ethiopia, which accepted as many as 20,000 Cuban combat troops and a large number of Soviet military advisers. Ethiopia also absorbed large quantities of Soviet military equipment, to turn back the Somalis in the contested Ogaden area. As a result, Somalia has been negotiating an arms aid and base agreement with the U.S. Both Somalia and Ethiopia accepted Soviet military aid because of their war with the other, just as Angola and Mozambique had in their wars for independence against Portugal.

Tribal wars, some of which required British military intervention, broke out in Aden, now known as South Yemen, in 1953. In 1964 the situation was aggravated when the British attempted to assert authority in an area in the interior where they had not done so before. After South Yemen achieved independence in 1967, the South Yemen National Liberation Front, which had been aided both by the U.S.S.R. and China, came under Communist influence. The war South Yemen provoked with North Yemen in 1979 was terminated, at least officially, by a unification agreement later in the year negotiated with an assist from the Arab states, but to date it has not been carried through. Soviet influence is still evident in South Yemen. North Yemen, which remains torn by civil war, also receives significant Soviet military and economic assistance, but more from Saudi Arabia and the Western states.

Of the other Middle World states, many have at various times accepted assistance from the U.S.S.R. and other Communist states and have come temporarily more or less under Communist influence. Egypt, particularly after American withdrawal of support from the Aswan Dam project in 1956, accepted large-scale economic and military assistance from the Soviet Union (which had actually started in 1955), including some 20,000 Soviet military personnel as advisers to Egyptian forces. This was terminated abruptly in 1972 by President Anwar Sadat. Soviet personnel were expelled and Soviet influence has not returned. In 1972, Iraq signed an aid pact with the Soviets, who furnished arms on a large scale, as well as several thousand advisers.[3] Since the execution of twenty-one Iraqi Communists by the government in 1978 and a shift of trade to the West, however, relations with the Soviets have been strained. Although General Saddam Hussein, who came to power in Iraq in July 1979, turned to the Soviets for arms for his war against Iran, there is no evidence of any overall shift back to the Soviet bloc.

Of all the Middle World states that have flirted with the Soviets, Syria has been the most consistent.[4] The Ba'ath party came to power in 1957 on a wave of anti-Western sentiment. Syria received large quantities of arms from the Soviets in 1972 (perhaps before) following fighting between Syrian-supported Palestine guerrillas and Jordan, and again in 1973 when Syria joined Egypt in an attack on Israel. Further large-scale shipments of Soviet arms to Syria occurred in 1974 and 1978. Syria still shares many of the Soviet aims in the Middle East. Soviet military assistance to Syria, including Soviet-manned anti-aircraft missiles, was stepped up after the Israeli invasion of Lebanon. It is difficult to tell whether Syria could extricate itself from the Soviets even if it desired to do so.

Most of the other Middle World countries that came under Soviet influence, however, are in the process of distancing themselves, largely as a result of the Soviet seizure of Afghanistan. India, although it accepts Soviet arms and maintains close relations with the Soviets partly as a counterpoise to close Pakistan-Chinese relations, has spoken out against the Soviet occupation of Afghanistan. The grouping of Islamic states has taken a strong position in demanding Soviet withdrawal from Afghanistan. Although this does not necessarily result in the Islamic states having closer relations with us and the West, Soviet occupation of Afghanistan was an important turning point, down, in Soviet relations with the Middle World.

Our warnings in 1949–51 of the Soviet threat to the new Middle World states seemed at the time to have had little effect. In particular, our attempts to persuade Nehru and other South Asian leaders to reverse their trend toward neutralism fell on deaf ears. Both they and the new states of Africa as they emerged in the 1950s and 1960s became strong supporters of the non-aligned movement, which was the response of these nations both to the Soviets and us. Nasser of Egypt, then leader of the Arab nations, was a co-founder of the non-aligned movement and Nehru, prime minister of the most influential South Asian country, was a strong non-aligned backer. This group now comprises two-thirds of the nations of the world, ninety-four in all, including almost all of the Middle World. The essence of non-aligned policy is to avoid association with either bloc and to work against political polarization and bloc rivalries.

Even though such a policy provides no basis for comfort to us, we must keep in mind that, if faithfully carried out, it also helps protect the Middle World against undue influence by the Soviets. Our early efforts with the Middle World states may at least have influenced them toward carrying out their non-aligned policy impartially. It is true that many Middle World countries, despite their non-alignment, have been willing to accept favors from the Soviet bloc, and some have undoubtedly profited thereby. Egypt got its Aswan Dam from the Soviets and Tanzania its railway to Zambia from China. But there appears to have emerged in the process little basis for lasting ties between the Soviets and the emerging nations of the Middle World.

Angola, Mozambique, Ethiopia, South Yemen, and Syria would have accepted arms aid from the devil himself to use against their mortal enemies. Arms were not at the time available elsewhere. But neither these nor other Middle World countries could be expected to develop any lasting affinity for the Russians as a people or Communism as an ideology. Russians tend as individuals to appear humorless and inflexible, scarcely with the same appeal that the British, for example, had for many of their subject peoples. The ideological base for Communism, as devised by the German Karl Marx while studying in England how to help the workers of the industrialized countries seize power from the bourgeoisie, is scarcely applicable to Ethiopia, an agricultural and pastoral society struggling to emerge as a modern state. Marxism has no monopoly over socialism.

Most of the Middle World peoples are deeply religious. Many, particularly the adherents of Islam, can be expected to have more tolerance for states with other religions than for a country which denies the basis for any religion. This was corroborated in many of my discussions with Middle World leaders, as I have reported. The Soviets have, moreover, established a reputation as loners in the world, without natural allies and not capable of generosity in their dealings with others. Realpolitik has brought the Soviets opportunistic alliances, such as that with India, and they have profited from the Arab-Israeli and Sunni-Shī'ite conflicts. In general, however, they have given more military than economic aid to other countries, and this only where there was a strategic advantage to them. The Soviets are under constant and relentless attack within international Communism by China and other enemies. And now Soviet conquest of Afghanistan seems to prove what many have said all along, that in a showdown Soviet imperial interests will always take precedence over other considerations. The Brezhnev doctrine of "once a Communist state always a Communist state" has been extended beyond Eastern Europe with a vengeance. Angola, Ethiopia, and South Yemen should draw the necessary conclusions—if it is not too late.

No, I do not think, in retrospect, that we were wrong in 1949–1951 in warning the Middle World about the dangers of Soviet Communism. Any doubts on this point have, in my view, been removed by recent events. Some of the states involved may have suffered because we pushed them too indiscriminately and too fast. I believe, however, that it is more likely that, as a result, they were better able to protect themselves from Communist dangers they later avoided. Viewed in perspective, the Russian Middle World "take"—four or five relatively unimportant countries out of sixty-six—is pretty thin. In 1949–1951, we feared the whole Middle World might be lost.

But we certainly must recognize how overly optimistic we were that we would be able to draw the Middle World into close cooperation with us, or that they would seek to emulate us. For this we never had a chance. To them we were as alien a society as they were to us. The residents of the Middle World have a low living standard, which they tend to blame on the rich Western nations, including us. They find it difficult to distinguish us from our wealthy European allies who were formerly their colonial rulers. Many unpopular Middle World rulers, like the Shah of Iran, have had close ties with us. The animosity that ordinary citizens of their countries feel toward them is often also directed at us.

An important influence on the Middle World and its relations with us will undoubtedly result from the large number of its students who have come to the U.S. for their higher education. Foreign students in the U.S. from all countries in 1981 aggregated 300,000, and the number is expected to double by 1990 and to decline only by the year 2000. Many, of course, elect to remain in the U.S. Many study engineering, science, or medicine, and are not particularly interested in politics. The majority, it is believed, will go back with a favorable impression of America. Many would like their country to accept much of our culture and copy our political institutions. Others, however, consider that they were not well treated here, that we consider people of color second-class citizens. Some will return with an unfavorable reaction to the U.S. and an attitude of defiance.

A disproportionate number of these students come from the oil-wealthy Middle World states. Indeed, Iran, as a holdover from the Shah's era, currently leads all others with 47,000. Although it is too early to judge the effect under the Khomeini regime of those who will return, the tens of thousands of returnees up to this point have not prevented Iran from becoming strongly anti-American. We have a great opportunity, however, in offering scholarships to students from the non-oil producing Middle World countries, and helping them have a rewarding experience here.

Our private enterprise market system is perceived by the average Middle World citizen as similar to the way business was done in colonial days. Exxon appears to many to be in the same tradition as the Anglo-Iranian Oil Company of the past. The impulse to free themselves from all aspects of colonialism, which was a part of the post-colonial syndrome, has led many new Middle World countries to want to change their way of doing business, and this required government intervention. In many cases there was no alternative. An economic vacuum had been created with independence that only the state could fill. This did not necessarily mean that the ordinary citizen wanted Communism, or even Socialism as an alternative. Even if he understood them, he tended to consider them just another alien ideology.

Whether they approached it from the left or right, however, the new Middle World states usually ended up with the economic initiative in the hands of the state. The systems created vary widely but most do not correspond to socialism as ordinarily perceived. Atatürk, when he rebuilt Turkey from its ruins after World War I, first sought foreign private capital, which was not forthcoming. Etatism, or state control, which in this case was imposed from the political right, was the only alternative available and Turkey has pursued it until quite recently. Yet Turkey has, over all these years, banned the Communist party. The same could be said for Reza Shah of Iran. Mobutu runs the economy of Zaire, but not as a state socialist economy; he runs it as an economy for Mobutu.

We must recognize that socialism, although often not well understood, is widely considered an appealing concept throughout the Middle World. It is, as I have said, associated with the desire for change. The Soviet Union has widely capitalized on its proclaimed support for socialism, and for revolution against imperialism, a term which includes not only the ex-colonial powers and us but our economic system. Actually the Soviets are not socialist on the basis developed by Karl Marx, nor as applied, for example, by the socialist British Labour Party. The U.S.S.R. is in essence an economic as well as a political dictatorship by the Communist Party.

If we reject states just because they appear to have adopted an economic system that looks to us like socialism, and assume that they have as a result been taken over by the Soviets, we acknowledge a loss we have not sustained and isolate ourselves from these countries unnecessarily. We also thereby give the Soviets more credit than they deserve and help push the new states into Soviet arms. This is true even in the case of an avowed socialist state which is not Communist, like Burma or Tanzania. We are capable of dealing with state-run economies, even Socialist or Communist ones. Our multinational companies operate throughout the Middle World. Gulf Oil has so far maintained its concessions in Angola. China is seeking help from the international oil companies to develop its offshore oil.

In traditional free market capitalist theory, the development of the economics of the Middle World countries should best be attained by the free interplay of international trade and investment under liberal GATT (General Agreement on Tariff and Trade) rules. This would have been, from our viewpoint, the most natural way. We were, however, far too optimistic in 1949–1951 about the beneficial results the newly emerging countries could expect from doing business our way: from the proliferation of locally-owned limited-liability companies; from foreign private trade and investment, including the multinationals; from technical assistance; from World Bank and Ex-Im Bank loans. These seeds fell largely on infertile ground. There have been no economic miracles in the Middle World like those of South Korea, Hong Kong, Singapore, or Brazil, although, despite not having oil, Jordan and Sri Lanka have done reasonably well.

Although U.S. firms trade with Middle World countries on a considerable scale, our private investment there, outside of oil and other extractive mineral industries, has not been great. U.S. private investments in South Asia have never been significant. Net private investment from all sources to the twenty-seven Middle World countries classified by the World Bank as low-income (GNP per capita under $410) was only $130 million in 1970 and $160 million in 1980. The same figure for the twenty-three middle-income countries (GNP per capita under $1,410) was $313 million in 1970, of which $205 million was to Nigeria for oil, and $2,015 million for 1980, of which $1,136 million were to Egypt and Nigeria, mostly for oil.[5]

U.S. government-to-government aid of all types to the Middle World has in recent years declined drastically except to Israel, Turkey, Egypt, and Pakistan, where it is sustained largely for strategic and political reasons.[6] Our government aid to African countries has always been small compared to what the Europeans have given their former African colonies and aid provided by the European Community. U.S. government assistance during fiscal year 1983 is scheduled for $2,516 million to the Middle East and South Asia as a whole. However, all except $704 million of this is for Israel and Egypt, to complement the massive military aid given both countries. The total to all other Middle World countries, except Israel and Egypt, is $1,220 million. This is not great, on a per capita basis, for a billion and a half people. Although helpful, it cannot be considered a decisive factor in their prospects for future progress.

Assistance of all kinds, including what is called Official Development Assistance, which comprises all payments by the World Bank and other multilateral institutions is, of course, being extended to the Middle World by the other OECD states and some of the OPEC countries.[7] Starting in 1960, when we extended in aid to the Middle World $2,702 million out of a total world assistance of $4,628 million, we gave well over half, a generous percentage from any viewpoint. The corresponding U.S. contribution for 1981, however, was $5,760 million out of $25,461 million, or a little over 20 percent. In 1981, with 0.20 percent, we ranked next to last among the nineteen donor countries in percentage of GNP given for Development Assistance, the average for all being .35 percent. The increased giving of other states is a welcome development. However, the total aid extended, not just by us but by all donors, must be judged inadequate. In constant 1978 prices the aggregate of Official Development Assistance for 1981 was $21,200 million. Although this was approximately 50 percent above 1960, the total has since 1978 remained at constant prices virtually level, in the face of increasing need.

The few important economic breakthroughs in the Middle World have been largely through isolated events, such as the discovery of major oilfields, the drastic increase in the price of OPEC oil, development of large copper projects, and the discovery of the new grains which have freed India from imports, at least temporarily. Because of OPEC, Iran, Iraq, Saudi Arabia, Kuwait, and a few other Arab states have become oil rich, and Egypt has benefited substantially. In 1980, for example, per capita GNP of the United Arab Emirates, with a population of about 1 million, was $26,850; that of Saudi Arabia, with 9 million population, was $11,260.[8] Some of these states help less favored countries. However, the Arabs mainly help other less fortunate Arabs. East of Iran the Middle World nations have not profited greatly from oil, and their prospects for the future are not good.

The ultimate benefits to be derived from these large oil incomes, moreover, are being brought increasingly into question. Public investment, increase in living standards, and improvements in social services have been attained, but often at the expense of inflation, unemployment, and economic and social dislocations, including disruption of agriculture and mass movement to the cities. There have also been adverse political consequences which threaten existing regimes, and little provision for something to take the place of the oil income when reserves are exhausted. But overall, the results of the world's development efforts, by both donors and recipients, has been disappointing by any standard. Of the 125 countries above 1,000,000 population listed in the 1982 World Bank World Development Report, thirty-three are called low-income.[9] Of these twenty-seven, the only important exception being China, are from the Middle World. Of the sixty-two middle-income countries, twenty-three are from the Middle World. The remaining four Middle World countries are the so-called high-income oil exporters as defined by this study.

South Asian per capita GNP ranged in 1980 from $80 in Bhutan to $300 in Pakistan. India, after all of its exertions, remained at $240 per capita that same year, its GNP increase of 1.3 percent giving the average Indian only an additional $3.12 per year. This is not much any way you look at it. It is not going to bridge any gaps. This increase is, moreover, not uniformly distributed, the more productive members of society getting more, some nothing. The sub-Saharan African states show a greater variation in income, at even lower levels. Nigeria's oil production lifted its per capita GNP to $1,010. Land-rich Ghana and the Ivory Coast stood at $402 and $1,150, respectively. However, Chad at $120 and Ethiopia at $140 remained among the poorest countries per capita in the world. The typical African gets only $150 to $400 a year in income.

There are also grave deficiencies in the quality of African life. Life expectancy for a citizen of Chad was 41 years in 1980, when he was receiving only 72 percent of his daily calorie supply requirement. Literacy in many states of black Africa is still only between 5 percent and 25 percent, although several, including Zimbabwe, Kenya, Somalia, Rwanda, Zaire, and Tanzania, claim to have attained levels of over 50 percent.[10] Average index of food production per capita in the twenty-seven low-income Middle World countries, from a 1969–71 base to that in 1978–80, has declined 5 percent, if India, which increased 1 percent, is considered separately. India's record in increasing food production per capita in the face of its large population increase is outstanding. A number of sub-Saharan countries have, however, registered decreased per capita food production in the order of 10–15 percent over this ten-year period.

The economic prospects for the Middle World for the future remain grim. The 1982 World Development Report found that the middle-income developing countries can be expected to achieve a per capita growth in GNP in the 1980s of at least 2 percent.[11] Those in the Middle East and North Africa, however, which are few, will change only between 0.0 percent and 0.9 percent and those in sub-Saharan Africa, which are fewer, between 0.0 percent and 0.3 percent. Low-income countries in sub-Saharan Africa are predicted to change in per capita GNP at −1.0 percent to 0.1 percent. With the exception of India and possibly Pakistan, GNP for remaining low-income Middle World countries will not increase during the 1980s; many will decline and will remain in a more desperate situation than they were a year ago. The prospects for economic development of the Middle World generally, therefore, remain poor. It cannot be improved without more investment than is now envisaged from all sources, in human resources, development institutions, and physical infrastructure.

The continuing low living standards of the Middle World result from many causes apart from high cost oil and world recession: limited and marginal land, primitive farming methods, lack of capital and experience in developing industry, too few technical specialists, confusion between modernization and industrialization, the absence of a suitable economic infrastructure, lack of educational opportunities, backward traditional social customs and institutions, and inefficient and often venal government.

A general problem, which almost forecloses the possibility of raising living standards in the countries concerned, is the continuing high birth rate. This averages 46 per 1,000 population in Africa and 40 per 1,000 in the Arab states, which results in some of the highest rates of overall population increase in the world.[12] During the period from 1951 to 1981, the population of the Middle World practically doubled to a total of a billion and a half people. This not only requires the sharing of limited resources with more people, but the creation of a larger base for later increases. India, although it had by 1981 reduced its birth rate to an estimated 36 per 1,000 population, imposes this increase on a population of almost 700 million, double that of 1951, resulting in 25 million new births a year. At the same time the death rate is 14 per 1,000 and steadily declining. This created an overall growth rate in 1981 of 2.2 percent, or about 15 million people. Except for sub-Saharan Africa, birth rates in the Middle World have, however, fallen below natural birth levels, which provides some hope for the future.

The Western world has for some time attempted to help the Middle World solve its population problem. Our efforts have, however, run counter to deep-rooted customs and religious beliefs, and have in general not been accepted. In the Middle World, children and their labor are usually considered assets in survival and insurance against bad times, particularly as agricultural land becomes scarce. The related crowding into already congested urban areas, which occurs at double the rate of overall population increase, creates new and almost insoluble problems, making it even more difficult to achieve higher living standards. No Middle World state has yet devised a way to keep its large cities, like Lagos, the capital of Nigeria, from being strangled by the invasion of its own people. The percentage of urban population in cities of over 500,000, in the low-income Middle World countries, has increased from 19 percent in 1960 to 40 percent in 1980.

Statistics do not tell the whole story of development. Many developing countries do not, because of their mild climate and relative self-sufficiency in basic foods and raw materials at low but tolerable living standards, place so much emphasis on rising economic indicators. On the other hand, one must not forget that the percentage increases in GNP per capita achieved by the developing countries, some of which compare favorably with those in the industrial market economies, are added to a very low base. As a consequence the possibility of closing the gap between the poor and wealthy nations of the world is virtually foreclosed. As cited, the average Indian received in 1980 an average increase in income of $3.12 a year. How could he ever hope at this rate to boost his $240 a year to the level of the lowest industrial market economy, Ireland, at $4,880 per capita GNP? Peoples in such a situation cannot, of course, attain European levels. Indeed, it is not necessary in order to live a tolerable life in India. Present levels do not, however, provide for subsistence on any scale compatible with twentieth-century standards, much less the minimum in education, health, entertainment, and other amenities that most peoples have now come to expect. Many countries, like India, appear to have been in a race between population increase and increase in per capita GNP, both of which cannot win. Up until now population increase has won, and time is running out.

And what about the American image in the Middle World over the last thirty-two years? How has it fared? Americans want to be liked by other peoples. We tend to believe that we should have earned the world's approbation. Collectively we are, I believe, widely respected as decent, well-meaning people. But we must, as a nation, expect to continue to be the target of the politicians, the journalists, and the coffee-house gossipers of the Middle World. The leaders of most of the new Middle World states cannot, even if they wanted to, accept too close a political association with us. It would hurt their standing in their own country and in world non-aligned circles. We must accept the fact that there is widespread anti-Americanism in the Middle World, and that it is not likely to go away. This is particularly true in Iran and in the Arab countries most hostile to Israel including Libya, South Yemen, and Iraq.

Although we were not in 1949–1951 so naïve as to believe that we could induce the countries of the Middle World to become parliamentary democracies on the European-American model, we nevertheless hoped they would progress from absolute monarchy and military dictatorship at least toward constitutional government. India had adopted its constitution only a month before my first visit there in December 1949. Both India and Pakistan were initially dominated by their parties of liberation. The Congress Party in India continued to submit its maintenance in power to elections. Pakistan, however, did not have its first election (of two) until 1970. Sri Lanka started with democratic government, and although some considered it to have been set back with the introduction of the presidential system in 1978, democracy was reconfirmed in the 1982 elections. An effort is being made to bring democracy to Lebanon. Few serious efforts at democracy, however, have been made in other Middle World countries.

The leaders of the Middle World have, of course, changed over the years. To quote a phrase from Rudyard Kipling, "The captains and the kings depart." None of the Middle World leaders of the period 1949–1951 have survived in power until today. Liaquat of Pakistan, Abdullah of Jordan, Nuri Said of Iraq, Zaim of Syria and Haile Selassie of Ethiopia met violent deaths, as did a later outstanding leader, Sadat of Egypt. Today monarchs still rule in Morocco, Jordan, Saudi Arabia, Kuwait, Bahrain, Qatar, Oman, the United Arab Emirates, and in Nepal. Most of the other Middle World countries—although some go through the motions of accepting a constitution and holding elections—are essentially run by strongmen.

Typically these are military leaders, Colonel Muammar-al-Qadhaafi, dictator of Libya, being one of the worst examples, along with General Idi Amin, erstwhile dictator of Uganda, who was violent and irrational. Some of the Middle World strongmen rulers have been intelligent and well-intentioned, some even indispensable. Many have not. Kwame Nkrumah, as has been discussed, although apparently well suited and trained for leadership, threw away Ghana's excellent prospects soon after it achieved statehood, through his vanities and ambitions. Anwar Sadat of Egypt, on the other hand, although he ruled as a strongman, showed remarkable statesmanship.

In October 1958, General Mohammed Ayub Khan took over power in Pakistan following a coup. I happened to be in Pakistan with Admiral Arthur Radford, the two of us constituting the Middle East sub-committee of President Eisenhower's Committee to Study the Military Assistance Program (the so-called Draper Committee). Ayub Khan, with whom Radford had had a close association, invited us to join a dinner which turned out to be the first meeting of his new cabinet. Also present was Ali Khan, son of the Aga Khan, who was at the time the Pakistan UN representative. As we sat down to dinner one of the younger cabinet members remarked jokingly, "Look at us. There are those who say we are dictators. How could anyone possibly believe that who knows us?" Pakistan has, however, never really had a democratic government since.

India, among the major countries of the Middle World, has perhaps come closer than any other to achieving a democracy as we in the West know it. Many had doubted that India was really democratic. In 1977, however, after governing India as leader of the Congress Party and its successor, the New Congress Party, since 1966, Indira Gandhi, after a disastrous defeat in a free election, stepped down and was succeeded by Morarji R. Desai, leader of the victorious Janata Coalition. She came back as prime minister for the second time in an equally free election in 1980. India had met an important test of a democracy: its defeated government had retired without resistance. In both elections the Indians also displayed strong democratic abilities, and a capacity to respond to changing situations. On the other hand, the permanence of democracy in India cannot be taken for granted as long as 64 percent of India's populace remain illiterate, and extreme poverty and "untouchability" continue on such a scale.

The lack of experience in self-government, the absence of a democratic tradition, poverty, and illiteracy, unfortunately continue to prevent the evolution of democracy throughout most of Africa. Beginnings have been made in Gambia, where a republic was created within the Commonwealth in 1970, which survived an unsuccessful coup in 1981. There have been recent trends toward democracy in Senegal and Cameroon. Nigeria, sub-Saharan Africa's most populous and potentially its wealthiest country, made an orderly return to democratic civilian government in 1974 after a long period of military rule. The bloody overthrow of the government of President Tolbert of Liberia in April 1980, by the Army Redemption Council of enlisted men, is, however, indicative of what has been happening in other African states. Democracy as we know it remains a very distant possibility in most of Africa. In many countries it is not even an accepted goal.

In certain Islamic countries there has occurred in recent years a move toward the union of political and spiritual authority, as originally practiced under Islam. Pakistan has been an avowed Islamic state since 1949. In November 1979, Ayatollah Khomeini, who had forced the Shah into exile in January, put in power a government committed to the establishment of an Islamic republic. Whether the union of religion and state in Islamic countries will continue, and whether it will be accompanied by the adaptation of economic life to closer conformity with Islamic concepts, as many Muslims desire, remains to be seen.

There are important lessons we can draw from our experiences over the last thirty years in the Middle World. We have discovered that we ourselves are not omnipotent or infallible, even in our dealings with new and weak states. We have over the years sustained many failures in the Middle World: our failure to gain allies, our inability to help the new states develop their economies, our inability to help solve the Arab refugee problem, the twenty-fold increase in oil prices by OPEC with its devastating world-wide effects, the nationalization of Western oil concessions, the fall of the Western-oriented Shah of Iran, the development of strong Soviet influence in Mozambique, Angola, Ethiopia, and the Yemen, and now the Soviet conquest of Afghanistan.

We have also had demonstrated to us the great importance attached by the Middle World to old conflicts, overriding all other considerations. The smoldering ancient rivalries of the Middle World continue, occasionally bursting into flame. Tensions between India and Bangladesh, and India and Pakistan with the centerpiece still the Kashmir dispute, remain unresolved. The Pushtu issue between Pakistan and Afghanistan has not been settled, only overshadowed by the Soviet invasion of Afghanistan. Iran and Iraq are at war. Israel has occupied Lebanon. The hope for progress in an overall Palestine settlement seems more remote than ever. The Arab Gulf states prepare to defend themselves against Iran. Libya and Sudan remain hostile, also Libya and Egypt. Morocco and Algeria continue their indirect war for control of the former Spanish holdings in Western Sahara.

We have had little success with political initiatives we have taken to help resolve these ancient rivalries. Progress in our relations with Pakistan has usually been at the expense of our relations with India, and vice versa. We have, unfortunately, found that our policy toward Israel has cast a pall over our relations with the Arabs, and many non-Arab Muslim states. The differences of the Arab states with Israel transcend any fear they might have of Communism. Over 600 million of today's 800 million Muslims live in the Middle World. Although there is little basis for cooperation among the Muslim countries, their ties have been strengthened by their common sympathy for the Arab refugees. Their resentment against Israel is also directed against us as Israel's principal supporter. The Islamic Conference, with twenty-two members, even though it has not been very effective, provides a forum for joint action on this and other issues.

Despite our failures and the criticism we reap, we must not forget, however, that sixty-five of the sixty-six Middle World nations remain independent, and at least sixty-one are their own masters. By and large they trade, cooperate, and visit with us and the free world much more readily than with the Soviets. The Middle World nations cannot help but be aware of the fact that the U.S. remains the greatest industrial power in the world. Our economy is over twice as large as that of the Soviets, who are faltering on many economic fronts. We have friends, allies, base rights, and profitable investments all around the world, while the Russians remain relatively isolated in their vast landlocked citadel, with no real allies except those they have forced or bribed to their will. Moreover, many in the Middle World are more impressed with the economic opportunities in the U.S., our Declaration of Independence, our Bill of Rights, and our free press, than with our power. Although the struggle for the Middle World goes on, I for one do not believe it is likely to be lost to the Soviets.

The fate of the Middle World is, I believe, beyond our ability to control. We can, at best, exert only a marginal influence. The danger is that the Middle World countries, each in its own way, will continue to drift, unable to establish representative or effective governments or improve the lot of their peoples. Within a few decades even the invigorating income from oil will largely be gone, except in Saudi Arabia. Will the Middle World, denied the prosperity which much of the rest of the world has attained, its peoples' energies sapped by internal struggles for power and conflicts with their neighbors, become increasingly introverted, brooding over past injustices. The three million Arab refugees from Palestine spread across the Middle World will not likely become reconciled to the loss of their homeland. Already the people of Iran have effectively isolated Iran from the U.S. and other Western countries. The same thing can happen in India and elsewhere, with or without encouragement by their governments.

Undoubtedly we have been far too optimistic about our ability to understand the peoples of the Middle World and what we had to offer them. Indeed, the question arises as to whether we have, even now, penetrated the superficial façade that separates us from these complex, ancient peoples. Is the regime of the Ayatollah Khomeini finally representative of the Iranian people, or is there some other underlying layer of reality in Iran yet to be uncovered? Beyond Nehru and his daughter, will we be dealing with leaders representative of a different India? Did Sadat really speak for the fellahin of the Nile Delta? Will some new Ethiopia emerge from the ruins of Haile Selassie's empire?

And, even though we learn to understand these countries better, what can we do to help them? Since the Soviet seizure of Afghanistan there has, I believe, been a drastic increase in U.S. public interest in the Middle East. Alerted to the possible loss of Middle East oil, we have stepped up expenditures for U.S. forces to defend the area. We have attempted, even though with little response, to organize a new "consensus" among the Middle East states for defense against a possible Soviet attack. There is no question that we must continue these efforts. However, we must also seek some other approach which will provide better hope for making common cause with the Middle World, some more positive basis for a continuing cooperation which can keep us from drifting further apart.

We must do this not just because of the threat posed by the Soviet Union, which continues undiminished. We are also threatened by the spectre of a possible break between the West and a hostile other world, whether you call it the Third World, the Developing World, the Non-Aligned World, or the South of the North-South axis of the world. And no matter what you call it, it comprises mainly what has been herein described as the Middle World. Recent events demonstrate how easily angry people can disrupt the fragile fabric of modern international society. This can be accomplished through political assassination, aircraft hijacking, anti-foreign demonstrations, boycotts of goods, seizure and destruction of property, denial of landing rights and berthing of ships, denial of visas, closing of embassies, jamming of the radio, censoring of the press, and in an infinite variety of other ways. Recent events have shown how easily desperate Mexicans in search for work can penetrate our borders with impunity. Escapees from an overpopulated India could easily attempt unarmed seaborne penetrations of less populous countries.

But how can such catastrophes and the anarchy they could create be averted? How can there be a revival of hope and progress in the Middle World? We have learned from experience that economic improvement in the low-income countries cannot be assured just as a consequence of normal international trade and investment, nor by Official Development Assistance. Although these can act as catalysts, they are not enough to bring about the necessary restructuring of the economies and societies of these largely new and untried nations. And yet, something must be done to break the present stalemate. More leadership and resources must be supplied. There must also be a revival in spirit.

If these efforts are to succeed they must, first of all, be based on goals chosen by the Middle World states themselves. They must be allowed to set their own priorities and decide how to go about accomplishing them. There is no blueprint for such an effort. It must be developed painfully over many years, after discussions in many private and public groupings, as agreed at the heads of state Cancun Summit meeting in Mexico in 1981. The Brandt Commission Report provides a useful beginning, but only a beginning. Projects for which assistance is required will vary with different countries: education, cultural revival, energy development, improved agriculture, better transportation, reforestation, private loans, reduction in tariffs against their products, and many more.

The essence of such an effort is to provide the people concerned with a tangible basis for hope that they can share in world progress, that cooperation with other free world countries pays off. In such an effort the U.S. must play a leading role. The American people must see the necessity for our providing assistance on a scale comparable to our rank among the industrialized nations. We must understand that this will not just be an act of altruism on our part. It is necessary to support our economy, which is heavily dependent on imported oil and other materials, and on our foreign trade and investment. But more importantly, the whole future security of our nation is at stake.

There is, moreover, also the vital question of the kind of world there will be in the future for us to live in, that we are all now creating. It is clear that neither we nor the Soviet Union will be able to impose our views as to the world of the future. All nations, with due consideration for their relative contributions, must be involved. Indeed, there is already a groping for some new world order going beyond the East-West and North-South struggles.

The goal we must seek is to join with other independent nations in creating a Free World Community, within which relations between nations will increasingly be governed by mutual respect and accommodation with each other. No matter what illusions we may have held in the past, the lesson of the last thirty years should be clear—that all who inhabit this limited, overcrowded, interdependent planet Earth, share it together, and must work out our future here together. The creation of world community will be a slow and painful process. Nations with wealth and power, such as ours, must be willing to restrain themselves. We must be willing to assist those less favored. But they, in turn, must be willing to exercise patience in the long struggle they face in improving their lot. They must understand that their grave problems are their heritage from the past, and cannot be overcome easily. In the final analysis, they themselves must assume responsibility for their future, and be willing to make the necessary effort.

The Middle World has throughout history been the seat of great nations and civilizations. The states of the Middle World have, after centuries of domination by the West, won their freedom to develop their future in their own way. The response of the gifted peoples of the ancient Middle World to the challenge of the modern age will determine whether their future will reflect the greatness of their past.

Source Material

This volume is based largely on my personal notes and recollections, which have in most cases been reinforced and added to by the official State Department documents available covering the period under review. These include memoranda of conversations, telegrams, letters, and miscellaneous reports, some drafted by myself and some by others. Most of the State Department documents referred to have been declassified and published in *Foreign Relations of the United States,* Volume VI, Near East, South Asia and Africa, for 1949, and Volume V for 1950 and 1951. Material has also been obtained from unpublished documents in the State Department archives which have at my request been declassified and released for publication. In addition much declassified material from the British Foreign Office for the years 1949, 1950, and 1951 obtained from the Public Records Office, Kew, London, has been used either in verbatim or summary form.

2. The State Department and the World Scene, 1949–1951.

1. Dean Acheson, *Present at the Creation: My Years in the State Department.* New York: W. W. Norton and Company, 1969, pp. 257–258. (Hereafter referred to as Acheson, *Creation.*)
2. Ibid., pp. 258–259.
3. Ibid., pp. 260–263.
4. Ibid., pp. 592–593.

3. Middle East Defense, 1949–1951.

1. U.S. Department of State, *Foreign Relations of the United States,* 1947, Vol. V, p. 575. (Hereafter referred to as DOS, *For. Rel.*)
2. DOS, *For. Rel.,* 1949, Vol. VI, pp. 45–47.
3. Ibid., pp. 50–90.
4. Ibid., pp. 165–179.
5. DOS, *For. Rel.,* 1950, Vol. V, p. 122.
6. Ibid., p. 123.
7. U.S. Congress, House, H.R. 7797, *Report of the Committee on Foreign Affairs,* Report No. 1802, Part 3 on Foreign Economic Assistance, Supplementary Report of the Committee on Foreign Affairs, Statement by Mr. McGhee, March 1950.
8. Great Britain, Foreign Office, FO 371/81907, E1023/8G, Top secret letter from B. A. B. Burrows to M. R. Wright, March 23, 1950. (Hereafter GB, FO.)

9. GB, FO, FO 371/81467, E 1195/3, Top secret letter from B.A.B. Burrows to M.R. Wright, September 14, 1950.
10. DOS, *For. Rel.*, 1950, Vol. V, pp. 147–150.
11. Ibid., pp. 188–192.
12. Ibid., pp. 193–196.
13. Ibid., pp. 217–221.
14. Ibid., pp. 233–238.
15. Acheson, *Creation*, pp. 562–563.
16. Ibid., pp. 563–564.
17. DOS, *For. Rel.*, 1951, Vol. V, pp. 212–226.

4. Early Days of the Arab Refugee Problem.

1. DOS, *For. Rel.*, 1949, Vol. VI, pp. 688–689.
2. Ibid., p. 788.
3. Ibid., p. 818.
4. Ibid., pp. 827–842.
5. Ibid., pp. 857–859.
6. DOS, Dispatch No. 128, American Embassy, Baghdad, Iraq, April 25, 1949, Confidential, now declassified, Archives, No. 867 N. 48/4–2549.
7. DOS, *For. Rel.*, 1949, Vol. VI, p. 963.
8. Ibid., pp. 1319–1320.
9. Ibid., p. 1085.
10. Ibid., pp. 965–966.
11. Ibid., p. 1014.
12. Ibid., p. 1110.
13. Ibid., pp. 906–910.
14. Ibid., p. 918.
15. Ibid., pp. 934–943.
16. C. L. Sulzburger, *A Long Row of Candles: Memories and Diaries*, 1934–54. New York: The Macmillan Company, 1969, p. 447.
17. Ibid., p. 173.
18. United Nations, United Nations Conciliation Commission for Palestine. *Final Report of the United Nations Economic Survey Mission for the Middle East*, Part I, Lake Success, N.Y., 1949.
19. Ibid., pp. 983–984.
20. Ibid., pp. 1048–1049.
21. Palestinian Council of North America, Washington, D.C.

5. Nehru's First Visit to Washington.

1. DOS, *For. Rel.*, 1949, Vol. VI, pp. 1750–1752.
2. Acheson, *Creation*, pp. 334–336.
3. Vijaya Lakshmi Pandit, *The Scope of Happiness: A Personal Memoir*. New York: Crown Publishers, Inc., 1979, pp. 251–254.

6. British-American Middle East Relations.

1. DOS, *For. Rel.*, 1949, Vol. VI, p. 55.
2. Ibid., pp. 54–55.
3. Ibid., pp. 60–90.

7. The Shah's First Official Visit to Washington.

1. DOS, *For. Rel.*, 1949, Vol. VI, pp. 569–572.
2. Ibid., pp. 572–574.
3. Ibid., pp. 574–579.
4. Ibid., pp. 581–582.
5. Ibid., pp. 583–585.
6. Ibid., p. 588.
7. Ibid., pp. 592–593.
8. Acheson, *Creation*, pp. 501–502.
9. DOS, *For. Rel.*, 1949, Vol. VI, pp. 545–555.
10. Kermit Roosevelt, *Countercoup*. New York: McGraw-Hill Book Company, 1979, p. 2.

8. Middle East Chiefs of Mission Conference.

1. DOS, *For. Rel.*, 1949, Vol. VI, pp. 165–167.
2. Ibid., pp. 60–90.
3. Ibid., pp. 165–179. Additional material in complete report of conference in Department archives, Conference of Near Eastern Chiefs of Mission held at Istanbul, November 26–29, 1949.

9. Invitation to Liaquat.

1. DOS, Archives, Secret memorandum, air pouch, American Embassy, Karachi, No. 628, pp. 1–5, declassified.
2. DOS, Archives, Dispatch No. 1351, unclassified, air pouch, American Embassy, Karachi, to Department, March 24, 1951.

10. Encounter with Nehru.

1. DOS, Archives, Restricted dispatch, No. 128, air pouch, American Embassy, New Delhi, January 12, 1950, No. 110.15 Mc/1–1250, now declassified, p. 1.
2. Ibid., Enclosure No. 1, p.1.
3. Ibid., p. 3.
4. Ibid., p. 2.
5. DOS, *For. Rel.*, 1949, Vol. VI, pp. 29–31.
6. DOS, Confidential dispatch, American Embassy, Rangoon, No. 479, December 31, 1949, p. 1.
7. Ibid., p. 2
8. GB/PRO, FO 371/81636, confidential letter, December 29, 1949, from James Bowker to the Right Honorable H. McNeil, M. P., Foreign Office.

11. Developing an African Policy.

1. DOS, *For. Rel.*, 1950, Vol. V, pp. 1503–1512.
2. Ibid., p. 1514; also DOS, Archives Secret Report, East-West African Conference of U.S. Diplomatic and Consular Officers, Lourenço Marques, February 27 to March 2, 1950, now declassified.
3. DOS *Bulletin*, June 19, 1950, pp. 999–1003.
4. DOS Unclassified dispatch, air pouch, American Consulate, Johannesburg, South Africa, No. 197, June 5, 1950.
5. Ibid., No. 195, June 5, 1950, pp. 1–2.
6. DOS, Unclassified dispatch, air pouch, American Consulate, Nairobi, Kenya, N0. 177, May 17, 1950.
7. DOS, Confidential telegram, American Embassy, Paris, No. 2305, May 19, 1950.
8. DOS, Restricted dispatch, American Consulate, Leopoldville, Congo, No. 90, June 2, 1950.
9. DOS, Archives, Confidential letter, American Consul, Salisbury, S. Rhodesia, October 6, 1950, now declassified.
10. DOS, from the dossier of Nkrumah visit to Washington, June 7–8, included in McGhee files: Lot 53–D 468: File Africa, pp. 1643–1645.

12. Our Next Friend, Liberia.

1. DOS, Archives, Confidential Departmental Memorandum, 110.15-McG/2-1650, Mr. Berry, ANE, to Mr. McGhee, NEA, Feb. 16, 1950, now declassified, pp. 1–3.
2. Ibid., Confidential Departmental Memorandum 110.15 McG/4-2450, Mr. McGhee, NEA, to the Secretary, April 24, 1950, now declassified.
3. DOS, *For. Rel.*, 1950, Vol. V, p. 1711.
4. Ibid., p. 148, p. 1716.

13. Introduction to Apartheid.

1. DOS, *For. Rel.*, 1950, Vol. 1, pp. 187–190.
2. DOS, Secret Dispatch 54, American Embassy, Capetown, March 21, 1951, now declassified, 110.15 Mc/3-2150, Department Archives, Confidential Enclosure No. 9.
3. Ibid., Enclosure No. 2. See also *For. Rel.*, 1950, Vol. V, pp. 1815–1817.
4. DOS, Secret Dispatch 54, American Embassy, Capetown, March 21, 1951, now declassified 110.15 Mc/3-2150. Department archives, Confidential Enclosure No. 3.
5. Ibid., Confidential Enclosure No. 4.
6. Ibid., Confidential Enclosure No. 10.
7. Ibid., Confidential Enclosure No. 7. See also *For. Rel.*, 1950, Vol. V, pp. 1818–1823.

14. Other African Visits.

1. DOS, Archives, East-West African Conference of U.S. Diplomatic and Consular Officers, Lourenço Marques, February 27 to March 2, 1950, now declassified, Country Summaries, pp. 78–81.
2. Ibid., pp. 63–68.

15. Into the Lion's Den.

1. DOS, *For. Rel.*, 1950, Vol. V, p. 1691.
2. Ibid., pp. 1692–1698.
3. Ibid., pp. 1703–1705.

16. Negotiations with the King of Oil.

1. DOS, *For. Rel.*, 1950, Vol. V, p. 1112. Report of the joint U.S. Survey Group to Saudi Arabia, undated.
2. Slocum, William, *Reilly of the White House*. New York: Simon & Schuster, 1947.
3. DOS, *For. Rel.*, 1950, Vol. V, p. 106.
4. Ibid., pp. 1131–1145.
5. Ibid., p. 1127.
6. Ibid., p. 1145.
7. Ibid., p. 1146.
8. Ibid., pp. 1146–1147.
9. Ibid., p. 1136.
10. Ibid., pp. 1147–1148.
11. Ibid., pp. 1149–1151.
12. Ibid., pp. 1151–1152.
13. Ibid., p. 1152.
14. Ibid., pp. 1152–1153.
15. Ibid., p. 1153.
16. DOS, Unpublished restricted dispatch Dhahran No. 50, April 10, 1950, Visit of Assistant Secretary McGhee, p. 1.
17. DOS, Secret now declassified, not published, Jidda No. 153 to Department, April 3, 1950, air pouch, Visit to Saudi Arabia of Assistant Secretary the Honorable George C. McGhee, p. 4.
18. DOS, Unpublished secret memorandum, now declassified, covering discussion with Senator Connally of my conversation with King Ibn Saud of Saudi Arabia, May 8, 1950.
19. Personal communication.

17. Tripartite Declaration.

1. DOS, *For. Rel.*, 1950, Vol. V, pp. 125–130.
2. Ibid., p. 135.
3. Ibid., p. 135.
4. Ibid., pp. 135–138.
5. Ibid., pp. 138–141.

6. Ibid., pp. 163–167.
7. Ibid., pp. 167–168.
8. GB/PRO, FO 371/81911, Memorandum "Reception of the Tripartite Statement on the Middle East" No. 1023/104 of June 3, 1950.

18. Beginnings of Aid Programs to the Middle East and South Asia.

1. DOS, *For. Rel.*, 1950, Vol. V, pp. 169–171.
2. Ibid., pp. 173–174.
3. Ibid., pp. 174–176.
4. Ibid., pp. 178–180.
5. Ibid., pp. 180–181.
6. Ibid., pp. 181–184.
7. Ibid., pp. 185–186.
8. Department of State, International Security and Economic Cooperation Program FY 1983, March 1982 Special Report No. 99.

19. Meeting with the French Foreign Ministry.

1. DOS, *For. Rel.*, 1950, Vol. V, pp. 1558–1568.

20. The End of an Era in Tunisia and Libya.

1. DOS, *For Rel.*, 1950, Vol. V, pp. 1782–1785.
2. Ibid., pp. 1786–1788.
3. Ibid., p. 1788.
4. Ibid., pp. 1788–1790.
5. Ibid., p. 1790.
6. Philip Jessup, *The Birth of Nations*. New York: Columbia University Press, 1976, p. 126 (hereafter referred to as Jessup, *Birth*).
7. Ibid., p. 237–238.
8. DOS, *For. Rel.*, 1950, pp. 1629–1631.

21. The Embattled Sultan.

1. DOS, Air Pouch, Rabat 117, October 2, 1950, Declassified, Restricted, Department Archives, No. 110.5 McG/10-250, pp. 1–2.
2. DOS, *For. Rel.*, 1950, Vol. V, pp. 1747–1751.
3. DOS, Unclassified Dispatch No. 439, Tangier, March 21, 1950, Department Archives No. 110.15 McG/3-215.
4. DOS, *For. Rel.*, 1950, Vol. V, p. 1751.
5. Ibid., p. 1751.
6. Jessup, *Birth*, p. 126.
7. DOS, *For. Rel.*, 1951, Vol. V, p. 1371.
8. Ibid., pp. 1371–1373.
9. Acheson, *Creation*, p. 561.

22. Conference on North Africa.

1. DOS, *For. Rel.*, 1950, Vol. V, pp. 1569–1573. Additional material in complete report of conference in Department archives, Secret Report North African Regional Conference of U.S. Diplomatic and Consular Officers, Tangier, Morocco, October 2–7, 1950, now declassified.

23. Greek-Turkish Entry to NATO.

1. DOS, *For. Rel.*, 1951, Vol. V, pp. 27–42.
2. Ibid., pp. 50–76.
3. Ibid., pp. 78–79.

24. South Asia Evaluated.

1. DOS, *For. Rel.*, 1951, Vol. VI, Part 2, pp. 1664–1688; also DOS Secret Report, South Asia Regional Conference of United States Diplomatic and Consular Officers, Nuwara Eliya, Ceylon, February 26–March 3, 1951, now declassified.
2. DOS, Archives, No. 110.15, McG/3-851, Colombo, Dispatch No. 654, March 8, 1951, Confidential, now declassified.
3. Ibid., McG/3-3051, Colombo, Dispatch No. 739, Confidential, now declassified.

25. Nehru Revisited.

1. DOS, Archives, No. 110.15 McG/14–351; New Delhi, No. 2384, April 3, 1951, Restricted.
2. DOS, *For. Rel.*, 1951, Vol. VI, Part 2, pp. 2120–2127.
3. Ibid., pp. 2127–2130.
4. DOS, Archives, No. 110.15, McG/14–351; New Delhi, No. 2384, April 3, 1951, Restricted.
5. DOS, *For. Rel.*, 1951, Vol. VI, Part 2, p. 2132.
6. Personal communication, McGhee's files.

26. The Pushtunistan Issue.

1. DOS, Archives, No. Kabul 291, March 23, 1951, Confidential, now declassified.
2. DOS, *For. Rel.*, 1951, Vol VI, Part 2, pp. 1948–1951.
3. DOS, Archives, No. 110.15 McG/3-2051, Karachi Dispatch 1330, Restricted, March 20, 1951, now declassified.
4. Ibid., McG/3-2251, Karachi Dispatch 1351, Restricted, March 22, 1951.
5. DOS, For. Rel., 1951, Vol. VI, Part 2, p. 1952.
6. Ibid., pp. 1964–1965.

27. Anglo-Iranian Oil Company Nationalized.

1. DOS, *For. Rel.*, 1950, Vol. V, pp. 13–15.
2. Ibid., pp. 75–76.
3. Ibid., p. 76, also U.S. Senate, Foreign Relations Committee, Hearings before the Subcommittee on Multinational Corporations and U.S. Foreign Policy, 93rd Congress, 2nd Session on Multinational Petroleum Companies and Foreign Policy, Part 8, Appendix III, p. 341.
4. GB/PRO, FO 371, 81922 15445, Private and Confidential letter, August 22, 1950, from Foreign Office to B. A. B. Burrows, British Embassy, Washington.
5. DOS, *For. Rel.*, 1950, Vol. V, pp. 595–598. Memorandum of Informal U.S./ U.K. Discussion in connection with the visit to London of the Honorable George C. McGhee, September 21, 1950, AIOC and IPC.
6. DOS, *For. Rel.*, 1951, Vol. V, pp. 106–109.
7. Ibid., p. 76; also U.S. Senate, Foreign Relations Committee, Hearings before the Subcommittee on Multinational Corporations and United States Foreign Policy, 93rd Congress, 2nd Session on Multinational Petroleum Companies and Foreign Policy, Part 8, Appendix III, p. 341.
8. GB/PRO, FO 371/91524, Confidential EP 1531/116, from Teheran to Foreign Office, No. 203, March 18, 1951.
9. DOS, *For. Rel.*, 1951, Vol. V, pp. 289–291.
10. Ibid., pp. 291–292.
11. Ibid., pp. 292–296.
12. GB/PRO, FO 371/91184, 33268, Foreign Office No. 395 to Sir O. Franks (Washington), Secret April 3, 1951, a conversation between the Secretary of State and Mr. George McGhee, Situation in the Middle East.
13. Ibid., FO 371/91470, X6/AO53710, Record of a meeting held in the Foreign Office on April 2, 1951, Anglo-U.S. Cooperation in Middle East Defense, Persia.
14. GB/PRO, FO 371/91244, E 1531/11, Mr. McGhee's Proposals on Middle East Oil.
15. GB/PRO, FO 371/91470, XC/A033710 No. 1354, from Foreign Office to Washington, April 6, 1951, Secret.
16. Ibid., EP1023/10, No. 1303, from Washington to Foreign Office, April 28, 1951.
17. Ibid., FO 371/91471, AO 33710, EP 1023/32.
18. DOS Bulletin, May 10, 1951, Memorandum: Anglo-American Talks on Persian Oil, April 12, 1951.
19. GB, Parliament. Parliamentary Debates (House of Commons), June 21, 1951, columns 775–778.
20. Ibid., columns 796–802.
21. Ibid., columns 830–833.
22. GB/PRO, FO 371/91562, No. 2903 to Washington, July 7, 1951.
23. GB/PRO, FO 371/91531, EP1531/291, Personal letter, April 30, 1951.
24. GB/PRO, FO 371/91562, unnumbered memorandum, July 5, 1951.
25. GB/PRO, FO 371/91553, No. 2698, from Foreign Office to Washington, Confidential, June 27, 1951.
26. GB/PRO, FO 371/91524, No. 148, EP 1531/116, from Foreign Office to Teheran, Secret, March 21, 1951.

27. Ibid., No. 246, EP 1531/127, from Teheran to Foreign Office, Secret, March 24, 1951.

28. GB/PRO, FO 371/91526, EP 1531/171, Foreign Office Minute, D. A. Logan, May 4, 1951.

29. GB/PRO, FO 371/91621, XC AO 33710, EP 153 G10, AIOC Management, August 28, 1951.

30. GB/PRO, FO 371.

31. DOS, *For. Rel.*, 1951, Vol. V, p. 71.

32. GB/PRO, FO 371.

33. GB/PRO, FO 371/91621, XC AO 33710, Letter from Mountbatten of Burma to First Sea Lord, April 5, 1951.

34. DOS, Secret Memorandum, 12/19/50, Iraq.

35. U.S. Embassy, Baghdad, Confidential Memorandum, Frank Allen to Ambassador, March 21, 1951.

28. Syria and Lebanon in Transition.

1. DOS, *For. Rel.*, 1950, Vol. V, p. 1221–1222.

2. DOS, Restricted air pouch, 4/9/51, Damascus 426 to Department, Archive No. 110.15 McG/4-951.

3. DOS, Confidential Dispatch from American legation Beirut, No. 489, 3/28/51, Archive No. 110.15, McG/3-2851.

4. GB/PRO, FO 371/91184, 33268, Personal and Secret letter from officer in Beirut Legation, to R. J. Bowker, E 1024/15, March 29, 1951.

29. The Hashemite Kingdom.

1. DOS, *For. Rel.*, 1951., Vol. V, pp. 977–981.

2. DOS, Unclassified Dispatch, No. 230, air pouch, April 2, 1951, Archive No. 110.15-McG/4-251.

3. GB/PRO, FO 371/91795, XC AO 33710, 3/28/51, Confidential letter from Kirkbride, British Legation, Amman, to G. W. Furlonge, Foreign Office, ET 10345/2.

30. Britain and Egypt at the Brink.

1. DOS, *For. Rel.*, 1951, Vol. V, pp. 347–348, DOS, Archives, No. 110.15 McG/2-2651, Feb. 26, 1951, Restricted, now declassified, pp. 1–2.

2. Ibid., p. 348 DOS, Archives, No. 110.15 McG/4-351, Cairo 2356 to Dept. unclassified, pp. 1–5.

3. Ibid., p. 348.

4. GB/PRO, FO 371/80218, 15445, J. 1903/11, Secret Memorandum, 4th March, 1950 from M. L. Wright.

5. GB/PRO, FO Secret 382 to Cairo for Ambassador, 6th March, 1950, FO 371/80218 15445.

6. DOS, Archives 110.15 McG/4-451, Cairo 2381 April 4, 1951 to Dept., Restricted, declassified.

7. DOS, Archives, Cairo No. 1003, April 1, to Sec. State, declassified.

8. GB/PRO, FO 371/91182, 002590, Draft reply to Parliamentary Question No. 104.
9. DOS, Archives, Cairo, No. 1001, April 1, 1950 to Dept., Top Secret, declassified.
10. DOS, Archives, Cairo No. 1005 to Sec. State. April 1, 1951, declassified.
11. DOS, Archives, 110.15 McG/4-751, Cairo 2414, April 7, 1951, to Dept. Restricted, now declassified.
12. DOS, Archives 110.15 McG/5-1151, Dept. to Cairo 1115, May 11, 1981, Plain.
13. DOS, *For. Rel.*, 1951, Vol. V, pp. 356–361.
14. GB/PRO, FO 371/90130, JE 1051/44 Cairo to Foreign Office No. 244, 2nd April, 1951, Secret.
15. GB/PRO, FO 371/9031, FE 1051/63, Secret, Letter Shinwell to Morrison, 3rd April, 1951.
16. GB/PRO, FO 371/90131, JE 1051/63, Unsigned memorandum, Morrison, 5 April, 1951.
17. GB/PRO, FO 371/90130, JE 1051/47, Cairo No. 248, 2nd April, 1951, to Foreign Office.
18. Ibid., 90131, JE 1051/83 Letter from Head of Chancery to Department, No. 1077/3/51, 9th April, 1951.
19. DOS, *For. Rel.*, Vol. V, pp. 113–120.
20. Kenneth Harris, *Attlee*. London: Weidenfeld & Nicolson, 1982, pp. 482–483.
21. Ibid., 91182, Secret Letter, 19th July, 1951, Sir Oliver Franks, British Embassy, Washington, to R. J. Bowker, Foreign Office.
22. Ibid., 91182, Secret Letter to Sir Oliver Franks from R. J. Bowker, August 1, 1951, Foreign Office.

31. Talks with Mossadeq.

1. Kermit Roosevelt, *Countercoup*. New York: McGraw-Hill Book Company, 1979, p. 2.
2. Vernon Walters, *Silent Mission*. New York: Doubleday and Company, Inc., 1978, pp. 259–263.
3. Acheson, *Creation*, pp. 503–504.
4. Sir Anthony Eden, *The Memoirs of Sir Anthony Eden, Full Circle*. London: Cassell & Company Ltd., 1960, pp. 200–202.

32. The Middle World Today: The Changing World Scene.

1. See Foreign Area Studies, *Angola: A Country Study*. Washington, D.C.: GPO, 1979, c. 3.
2. See Foreign Area Studies, *Ethiopia: A Country Study*, 1981, c. 4–5, and *Somalia: A Country Study*, 1982, c. 1, 4, and 5.
3. See Foreign Area Studies, *Iraq: A Country Study*, 1979, c. 4–5.
4. See Foreign Area Studies, *Syria: A Country Study*, 1978, c. 4–5.
5. The World Bank, *World Development Report, 1982*. New York: Oxford University Press, 1982, pp. 11 and 163; hereafter referred to as World Bank.

6. DOS, Mutual Security Program 1953.

7. World Bank, pp. 140–141.

8. Ibid., pp. 110–111.

9. Ibid., pp. 110–111.

10. World Bank, p. 144, and Bureau of the Census, U.S. Department of Commerce, *Demographic Estimates for Countries with a Population of 10 Million or More: 1981*, Washington, D.C.: GPO, 1981, p. 64.

11. World Bank, pp. 142–143.

12. Ibid., pp. 142–143.

Bibliography

Acheson, Dean, *Present at the Creation: My Years in the State Department*. New York: W. W. Norton and Company Inc., 1969.

American University, Washington, D.C., Foreign Area Studies, *Algeria: A Country Study*. Washington, D.C.: Government Printing Office, 1978. *Angola* (1978). *Ethiopia* (1978). *Iran* (1978). *Iraq* (1979). *Jordan* (1980). *Libya* (1979). *Morocco* (1978). *Nigeria* (1981). *Somalia* (1981). *South Africa* (1980). *Syria* (1979). *Tanzania* (1978). *Tunisia* (1978). *Turkey* (1979). *Zaire* (1978). *Zambia* (1979).

Barnds, William J., *India, Pakistan, and the Great Powers*. New York: Praeger Publishers, 1972.

Campbell, John C., *Defense of the Middle East*. New York: Harper & Brothers, 1958.

Dayan, Moshe, *Story of My Life, An Autobiography*. New York: William Morrow and Company Inc., 1976.

Eden, Sir Anthony, *The Memoirs of Sir Anthony Eden: Full Circle*. London: Cassell & Company Ltd., 1960.

Engler, Robert, *The Politics of Oil*. Chicago: The University of Chicago Press, 1961.

Fisher, Sydney Nettleton, *The Middle East: A History*. New York: Alfred A. Knopf, 1959.

Ford, Alan W., *The Anglo-Iranian Oil Dispute of 1951–1952*. Berkeley: University of California Press, 1954.

Hamilton, Charles W., *Americans and Oil in the Middle East*. Houston: Gulf Publishing Company, 1952.

Hance, William A., *African Economic Development*. New York: Harper & Brothers, 1958.

Harris, Kenneth, *Attlee*. London: Weidenfeld & Nicolson Ltd., 1982.

Hitti, Philip K., *Lebanon in History*. London: Macmillan and Co., Ltd., 1957.

Jessup, Philip C., *The Birth of Nations: U.S.A.* New York: Columbia University Press, 1976.

Landau, Rom, *The Sultan of Morocco*. London: Robert Hale Ltd., 1951.

—— *The Moroccan Drama: 1900–1955*. London: Robert Hale Ltd., 1956.

Lefever, Ernest W., *Spear and Scepter: Army, Police, and Politics in Tropical Africa*, Washington, D.C.: The Brookings Institution, 1970.

Longhurst, Henry, *Adventures in Oil*. London: Sidgwick and Jackson, 1959.

Longrigg, Stephen Hemsley, *Oil in the Middle East: Its Discovery and Develop-

ment. London: Oxford University Press, 1954.

Macmillan, Harold, *Tides of Fortune: 1945-55.* New York: Harper & Row, 1969.

Morris, James, *The Hashemite Kings.* New York: Pantheon Books, Inc., 1959.

Pandit, Vijaya Lakshmi, *The Scope of Happiness: A Personal Memoir.* New York: Crown Publishers, 1979.

Ramazani, Rouhollah K., *Iran's Foreign Policy 1941-1973, A Study of Foreign Policy in Modernizing Nations.* Charlottesville: University Press of Virginia, 1975.

Roosevelt, Kermit, *Arabs, Oil and History.* New York: Harper & Brothers, 1947.

———*Countercoup: The Struggle for the Control of Iran.* New York: McGraw-Hill Book Company, 1979.

Royal Institute of International Affairs, *The Middle East: A Political and Economic Survey.* London, 1954.

Sanger, Richard, *The Arabian Peninsula.* Ithaca: Cornell University Press, 1954.

Selwyn Lloyd, *Suez 1956: A Personal Account.* New York: Mayflower Books, 1978.

Slocum, William. *Reilly at the White House.* New York: Simon & Schuster, 1947.

Smuts, J. C., *Jan Christian Smuts.* London: Cassell and Company Ltd., 1952.

Sulzberger, C. L., *A Long Row of Candles: Memories and Diaries, 1934-54.* New York: The Macmillan Company, 1969.

Talbot, Phillips, and Poplai, S. L., *India and America.* New York: Harper & Brothers, 1958.

Thayer, Philip W., *Tensions in the Middle East.* Baltimore: The Johns Hopkins Press, 1958.

United Nations, *Final Report of the United Nations Economic Survey Mission for the Middle East.* Lake Success, New York, 1949.

U.S. Department of State, *Foreign Relations of the United States, 1947,* Volume V (1972); *Foreign Relations of the United States, 1949,* Volume VI (1977); *Foreign Relations of the United States, 1950,* Volume V (1978); *Foreign Relations of the United States, 1951,* Volume V (1982).

Walters, Vernon A., *Silent Missions.* New York: Doubleday and Company, Inc., 1978.

Index

About the Author

Ambassador McGhee was born in Waco, Texas, on March 10, 1912. He attended Southern Methodist University and later the University of Oklahoma, receiving his B.Sc. degree in geology in 1933. As a Rhodes Scholar he attended Oxford, earning a Doctor of Philosophy degree in 1937. He has been awarded honorary doctorates by five universities. He is a member of Phi Beta Kappa and Sigma Xi.

During the early 1930s he was employed as a geologist by various petroleum companies. He established his own oil producing firm in 1940. Mr. McGhee entered government service before the war in 1941 with the War Production Board, and served as Deputy Executive Secretary of the U.S.-U.K. Combined Raw Materials Board. He was later a lieutenant in the U.S. Navy, and was awarded the Legion of Merit and three battle stars for his service with General Curtis LeMay in the 21st Bomber Command in Guam.

He joined the Department of State in 1946 as Special Assistant to William Clayton, Under Secretary for Economic Affairs. He served as Coordinator for the Greek-Turkish Aid Program and was appointed Assistant Secretary of State for Near Eastern, South Asian, and African Affairs in 1949. In December 1951, he was named by President Truman as Ambassador to Turkey, from which post he resigned in 1953. In 1958 he was appointed by President Eisenhower as a member of the President's Committee to study the Military Assistance Program. He was named in the same year Consultant to the National Security Council. In 1961 he returned to government service as Counselor of the Department of State and Chairman of the Policy Planning Council. He was appointed Under Secretary for Political Affairs in December 1961. He served as a member of the Board of the Panama Canal Co.

He was named by President Kennedy as Ambassador to West Germany in May, 1963. He returned as Ambassador-at-Large in May 1968, and retired from government in 1969. He has been a director of twelve corporations, including several major multinational companies, and was Chairman of the Board of *Saturday Review* magazine. He has served as trustee of a number of civic, charitable and educational organizations including four universities.

He is married to the former Cecilia Jeanne DeGolyer. They have six children. They live in Washington, D.C. and Middleburg, Virginia.

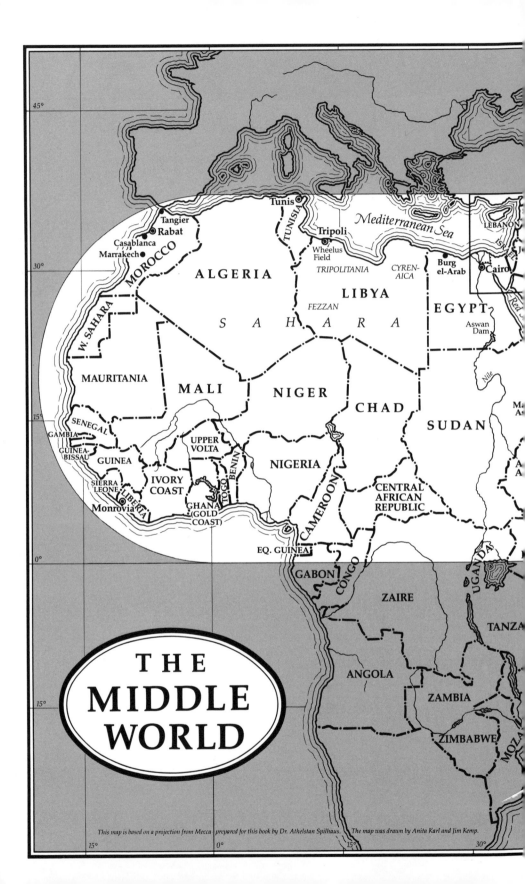

THE
MIDDLE
WORLD

This map is based on a projection from Mecca prepared for this book by Dr. Athelstan Spilhaus. The map was drawn by Anita Karl and Jim Kemp.